AMERICA'S CONTINUING REVOLUTION

America's Continuing Revolution

Irving Kristol • Martin Diamond
Paul G. Kauper • Robert A. Nisbet
Gordon S. Wood • Caroline Robbins
Peter L. Berger • Daniel J. Boorstin
G. Warren Nutter • Vermont Royster
Edward C. Banfield • Leo Marx
Ronald S. Berman • Kenneth B. Clark
Forrest Carlisle Pogue • Seymour Martin Lipset
Charles Burton Marshall • Dean Rusk

WITH AN INTRODUCTION BY STEPHEN J. TONSOR

ANCHOR BOOKS
Anchor Press / Doubleday, Garden City, New York
1976

America's Continuing Revolution was originally published by the American Institute for Public Policy Research, Washington, D.C. It contains the lectures sponsored by the American Enterprise Institute in celebration of the Bicentennial of the United States. They were delivered in the academic year 1973–1974 at historic sites across the nation. This edition is published by arrangement with the American Enterprise Institute for Public Policy Research.

Anchor Books edition: 1976

ISBN 0-385-09943-6

CONTENTS

FOREWORD

The scholars who participated in AEI's Distinguished Lecture Series on the Bicentennial of the United States have neither a common political view nor a common approach to their topics—except that all of them see our present situation through the lens of America's revolutionary heritage. Also, for some of them the revolutionary experience is paramount, for others the present situation is paramount, but all are looking at both past and present.

This is as it should be. The American Enterprise Institute is not a historical society and it is not an action group. Its mission is to study major public policy issues and their impact on American institutions and purposes. These lectures are a part of that study—a part devoted to the base of public policy research, the nature of the American system. Our contributors come at this subject from the perspectives of history, politics, economics, law, sociology, religion, culture and the arts—from the practical concerns of human welfare and our cities to the challenges of technology and America's role in the world. Notwithstanding this diversity, the question their answers all imply is, "What are the implications, for today and for the future, of the continuing revolution that flows from this nation's commitment to the idea of ordered liberty?"

The American Enterprise Institute conceived this series in an attempt to provide, through the bicentennial theme, a stimulus to sober discussion of America's successes and failures as a nation and, at the same time, an opportunity for the kind of forward thinking essential to building a better future. We are fortunate to have been able to persuade so many highly distinguished American scholars to participate in this effort. It is our hope that their thoughtful lectures will, in some measure, provide the summing up—the reflection about basic goals and aspirations—that is necessary before questions of public policy can be intelligently debated.

To bring these messages to a wide national audience, the lectures were held at historic sites across the country and were videotaped by the National Public Affairs Center for Television of the Greater Washington Educational Telecommunications Association, Inc., for nationwide showing by Public Broadcasting Service affiliates. We are grateful to Jim Karayn of NPACT and Donald Taverner of GWETA and their associates for their skilled assistance. We are also grateful to the National Endowment for the Humanities, which provided partial support for the television production.

The contribution of Dr. Stephen J. Tonsor, professor of history at the University of Michigan, in conceiving and guiding the project was a crucial factor in its success. Mention should also be made of two AEI staff members, Anne Brunsdale, the editor of this handsome volume and of the individual lecture pamphlets, and Earl H. Voss, the coordinator of the series from its inception to its completion.

Of course the views expressed in this volume, as in all AEI publications, are those of the lecturers and do not necessarily reflect the views of the staff, advisory panels, officers or trustees of AEI.

December 1974

WILLIAM J. BAROODY
President
American Enterprise Institute
for Public Policy Research

INTRODUCTION

In 1776 the American Revolution was already centuries old. Indeed the War of the Revolution was waged in the name of a conservative appeal to rights won and cherished—rights the American colonists believed to have been usurped and violated. At the distance of two hundred years it is easy enough to say that the claims of the colonists were simply skillful revolutionary rhetoric and that the cause of American independence had little or nothing to do with the traditional rights of Englishmen. No doubt the American Revolution was the first major break with the pattern of rule by monarchs and hereditary nobles according to principles derived from divine right, reason of state, and traditional and customary usage—substituting in their stead republicanism and a rational politics based upon the self-interest of the citizenry. However, it is difficult to believe that those articulate spokesmen of the American cause were insincere when they appealed not to revolution, but to political conservation and the hard-won but immemorial rights of free men.

It was precisely this conservative devotion to liberty which made and still makes the American Revolution the most radical political movement of the modern era. By putting liberty at the center of the American political order, the American revolutionaries served notice that they would not be distracted or deflected from its pursuit by other political, social, and economic objectives. Whatever the merits of equality or social justice, ethnicity or nationality, established religion or even public order, community or the evolution of a common high culture—if those objectives interfered with liberty, or deflected the citizenry from the pursuit of liberty, they were eventually rejected.

In the past two centuries, the world has witnessed the way in which liberty has permeated and revolutionized every aspect of American society. From the way in which we greet strangers to the way in which we pray, the most common and ordinary activities of our daily lives have been transformed by an ever greater participation by free men and an appeal to the sanction of their opinion. The very idea of the state has been moderated and changed. Under the impetus of the idea of liberty, the state, ideally conceived, stood aside and abandoned its domain to the action of individual men, voluntary associations, and corporate groups. At least in theory most Americans have believed that what the state necessarily does poorly individuals and voluntary associations can do better and that the supreme achievement of revolutionary liberty will be "the withering away of the state." When Americans have invoked the power of the state, they have (at least until recently) done so as a temporary expedient and with guilt and reluctance—for having made one revolution in the name of liberty, they do not relish the prospect of voluntary servitude. Even when the power of the state has been harnessed to personal or corporate advantage, this misappropriation has usually been defended as an enlargement or enhancement of liberty.

It is a characteristic of modernity that distances are foreshortened and time conflated. However, not only has space been overcome and ante- and post-meridional time shortened, but also our distance from the past, especially our revolutionary past, has, in recent decades, been steadily reduced. The spiritual, intellectual and political problems of modernity reduce rather than increase our distance from 1776. We know in an acute way the meaning of liberty—a way in which a more secure age and a more stable society could not know. But it is not simply the problems and the challenges of modernity which have made us contemporaries in spirit with the Founding Fathers. Lincoln began his Gettysburg address with a reference to the Revolution, and

Lincoln's contemporaries, because of the challenge of slavery to liberty, felt especially close to their revolutionary forebears. So too present day Americans—challenged by tyranny, tempted to sacrifice liberty in return for material and social well-being, spied upon and manipulated, threatened by bureaucracy and giant government, their ideals demeaned by the use of political power to circumvent the constitution—so too these Americans feel especially close to the cause of liberty and recognize the necessity of carrying forward the work of revolution and the confirmation of freedom.

This then must be the spirit of the bicentennial. It is not a time either for easy self-congratulations or for mere nostalgia. It must be a time, as the memorial service at Gettysburg was for Lincoln, of rededication and stock-taking. Where are we? By what route have we come? What are the unfinished tasks? To what ought we aspire?

The tree of liberty perennially puts out new foliage. That is because its roots drive so deep into the human heart and the total experience of mankind. After the winter of self-doubt, external challenge and internal distraction, it is time once more to think of the turn of the season and to renew our compact with a glorious past.

December 1974   STEPHEN J. TONSOR
The University of Michigan

AMERICA'S CONTINUING REVOLUTION

IRVING KRISTOL

The American Revolution as a Successful Revolution

Delivered in St. John's Church on Lafayette Square,

Washington, D.C. on October 12, 1973

As we approach the bicentennial of the American Revolution, we find ourselves in a paradoxical and embarrassing situation. A celebration of some kind certainly seems to be in order, but the urge to celebrate is not exactly overwhelming. Though many will doubtless ascribe this mood to various dispiriting events of the recent past or to an acute public consciousness of present problems, I think this would be a superficial judgment. The truth is that, for several decades now, there has been a noticeable loss of popular interest in the Revolution, both as a historical event and as a political symbol. The idea and very word, "revolution," are in good repute today; the American Revolution is not. We are willing enough, on occasion, to pick up an isolated phrase from the Declaration of Independence, or a fine declamation from a Founding Father—Jefferson, usually—and use these to point up the shortcomings of American society as it now exists. Which is to say, we seem to be prompt to declare that the Revolution was a success only when it permits us to assert glibly that we have subsequently failed it. But this easy exercise in self-indictment, though useful in some respects, is on the whole a callow affair. It does not tell us, for instance, whether there is an important connection between that successful Revolution and our subsequent delinquencies. It merely uses the Revolution for rhetorical-political purposes, making no serious effort at either understanding it or understanding ourselves. One even gets the impression that many of us regard ourselves as too sophisticated to take the Revolution seriously—that we see it as one of those naïve events of our distant childhood which we have since long outgrown but which we are dutifully reminded of, at certain moments of commemoration, by insistent relatives who are less liberated from the past than we are.

I think I can make this point most emphatically by asking the simple question: what ever happened to George Washington? He used to be a Very Important Person—indeed, *the* most important person in our history. Our history books used to describe him, quite simply, as the "Father of his Country" and in the popular mind he was a larger-than-life figure to whom piety and reverence were naturally due. In the past fifty years, however, this figure has been radically diminished in size and virtually emptied of substance. In part, one supposes, this is because piety is a sentiment we seem less and less capable of, most especially piety toward fathers. We are arrogant and condescending toward all ancestors because we are so convinced we understand them better than they understood themselves—whereas piety assumes that they still understand us better than we understand ourselves. Reverence, too, is a sentiment which we, in our presumption, find somewhat unnatural. Woodrow Wilson, like most Progressives of his time, complained about the "blind worship" of the Constitution by the American people. No such complaint is likely to be heard today. We debate whether or not we should obey the laws of the land, whereas for George Washington—and Lincoln too, who in his lifetime reasserted this point most eloquently—obedience to law was not enough: they thought that Americans, as citizens of a self-governing polity, ought to have *reverence* for their laws. Behind this belief, of course, was the premise that the collective wisdom incarnated in our laws, and especially in the fundamental law of the Constitution, understood us better than any one of us could ever hope to understand it. Having separated ourselves from our historic traditions and no longer recognizing the power inherent in tradition itself, we find this traditional point of view close to incomprehensible.

Equally incomprehensible to us is the idea that George Washington was the central figure in a real, honest-to-God revolution—the first significant revolution of the modern era and one which can lay claim to being the only truly successful revolution, on a large scale, in the past two centuries. In his own lifetime, no one doubted that he was the central figure of that revolution. Subsequent generations did not dispute the fact and our textbooks, until about a quarter of a century ago, took it for granted, albeit in an ever-more routine and unconvincing way. We today, in contrast, find it hard to take George Washington seriously as a successful revolutionary. He just does not fit our conception of what a revolutionary leader is supposed to be like. It is a conception that easily encompasses Robespierre, Lenin, Mao Tse-tung, or Fidel Castro—but can one stretch it to include a gentleman (and a gentleman he most certainly was) like George Washington? And so we tend to escape from that dilemma by deciding that what we call the American Revolution was not an authentic revolution at all, but rather some kind of pseudo-revolution, which is why it could be led by so unrevolutionary a character as George Washington.

Hannah Arendt, in her very profound book *On Revolution*, to which I am much indebted, has written:

> Revolutionary political thought in the nineteenth and twentieth centuries has proceeded as though there never had occurred a revolution in the New World and as though there never had been any American notions and experiences in the realm of politics and government worth thinking about.

It is certainly indisputable that the world, when it contemplates the events of 1776 and after, is inclined to see the American Revolution as a French Revolution that never quite came off, whereas the Founding Fathers thought they had cause to regard the French Revolution as an American Revolution that had failed. Indeed, the differing estimates of

these two revolutions are definitive of one's political philosophy in the modern world: there are two conflicting conceptions of politics, in relation to the human condition, which
are symbolized by these two revolutions. There is no question
that the French Revolution is, in some crucial sense, the
more "modern" of the two. There is a question, however, as
to whether this is a good or bad thing.

It is noteworthy that, up until about fifteen years ago, most
American historians of this century tended to look at the
American Revolution through non-American eyes. They saw
it as essentially an abortive and incomplete revolution, in
comparison with the French model. But more recently, historians have become much more respectful toward the American Revolution, and the work of Bernard Bailyn, Edmund S.
Morgan, Caroline Robbins, Gordon S. Wood, and others is
revealing to us once again what the Founding Fathers had, in
their day, insisted was the case: that the American Revolution was an extremely *interesting* event, rich in implication
for any serious student of politics. These historians have
rediscovered for us the intellectual dimensions of the American Revolution, and it is fair to say that we are now in a position to appreciate just how extraordinarily self-conscious and
reflective a revolution it was.

All revolutions unleash tides of passion, and the American
Revolution was no exception. But it *was* exceptional in the
degree to which it was able to subordinate these passions to
serious and nuanced thinking about fundamental problems of
political philosophy. The pamphlets, sermons, and newspaper
essays of the revolutionary period—only now being reprinted
and carefully studied—were extraordinarily "academic," in
the best sense of that term. Which is to say, they were
learned and thoughtful and generally sober in tone. This was
a revolution infused by *mind* to a degree never approximated
since, and perhaps never approximated before. By mind, not
by dogma. The most fascinating aspect of the American
Revolution is the severe way it kept questioning itself about
the meaning of what it was doing. Enthusiasm there certainly
was—a revolution is impossible without enthusiasm—but
this enthusiasm was tempered by doubt, introspection, anxi-

ety, skepticism. This may strike us as a very strange state of mind in which to make a revolution; and yet it is evidently the right state of mind for making a successful revolution. That we should have any difficulty in seeing this tells us something about the immaturity of our own political imagination, an immaturity, not at all incompatible with what we take to be sophistication.

Just a few weeks ago, one of our most prominent statesmen remarked to an informal group of political scientists that he had been reading *The Federalist* papers and he was astonished to see how candidly our Founding Fathers could talk about the frailties of human nature and the necessity for a political system to take such frailties into account. It was not possible, he went on to observe, for anyone active in American politics today to speak publicly in this way: he would be accused of an imperfect democratic faith in the common man. Well, the Founding Fathers for the most part, and most of the time, subscribed to such an "imperfect" faith. They understood that republican self-government could not exist if humanity did not possess—at some moments, and to a fair degree—the traditional "republican virtues" of self-control, self-reliance, and a disinterested concern for the public good. They also understood that these virtues did not exist everywhere, at all times, and that there was no guarantee of their "natural" preponderance. James Madison put it this way:

> As there is a degree of depravity in mankind which requires a certain degree of circumspection and distrust; so there are other qualities in human nature which justify a certain portion of esteem and confidence. Republican government presupposes the existence of these qualities in a higher degree than any other form.

Despite the fact that Christian traditions are still strong in this country, it is hard to imagine any public figure casually admitting, as Madison did in his matter-of-fact way, that "there is a degree of depravity in mankind" which statesmen must take into account. We have become unaccustomed to such candid and unflattering talk about ourselves—which is,

I suppose, only another way of saying that we now think democratic demagoguery to be the only proper rhetorical mode of address as between government and people in a republic. The idea, so familiar to the Puritans and still very much alive during our revolutionary era, that a community of individual sinners could, under certain special conditions, constitute a good community—just as a congregation of individual sinners could constitute a good church—is no longer entirely comprehensible to us. We are therefore negligent about the complicated ways in which this transformation takes place and uncomprehending as to the constant, rigorous attentiveness necessary for it to take place at all.

The Founders thought that self-government was a chancy and demanding enterprise and that successful government in a republic was a most difficult business. We, in contrast, believe that republican self-government is an easy affair, that it need only be instituted for it to work on its own, and that when such government falters it must be as a consequence of personal incompetence or malfeasance by elected officials. Perhaps nothing reveals better than these different perspectives the intellectual distance we have traveled from the era of the Revolution. We like to think we have "progressed" along this distance. The approaching bicentennial is an appropriate occasion for us to contemplate the possibility that such "progress," should it continue, might yet be fatal to the American polity.

II

In what sense can the American Revolution be called a successful revolution? And if we agree that it was successful, why was it successful? These questions cannot be disentangled, the "that" and the "why" comprising together one's basic (if implicit) explanation of the term, "successful revolution." These questions are also anything but academic. Indeed I believe that, as one explores them, one finds oneself constrained to challenge a great many preconceptions, not only about the nature of revolution but about the nature of politics itself, which most of us today take for granted.

To begin at the beginning: the American Revolution was successful in that those who led it were able, in later years, to look back in tranquillity at what they had wrought and to say that it was good. This was a revolution which, unlike all subsequent revolutions, did not devour its children: the men who made the revolution were the men who went on to create the new political order, who then held the highest elected positions in this order, and who all died in bed. Not very romantic, perhaps. Indeed positively prosaic. But it is this very prosaic quality of the American Revolution that testifies to its success. It is the pathos and poignancy of unsuccessful revolutions which excite the poetic temperament; statesmanship which successfully accomplishes its business is a subject more fit for prose. Alone among the revolutions of modernity, the American Revolution did not give rise to the pathetic and poignant myth of "the revolution betrayed." It spawned no literature of disillusionment; it left behind no grand hopes frustrated, no grand expectations unsatisfied, no grand illusions shattered. Indeed, in one important respect the American Revolution was so successful as to be almost self-defeating: it turned the attention of thinking men away from politics, which now seemed utterly unproblematic, so that political theory lost its vigor, and even the political thought of the Founding Fathers was not seriously studied. This intellectual sloth, engendered by success, rendered us incompetent to explain this successful revolution to the world, and even to ourselves. The American political tradition became an inarticulate tradition: it worked so well we did not bother to inquire why it worked, and we are therefore intellectually disarmed before those moments when it suddenly seems not to be working so well after all.

The American Revolution was also successful in another important respect: it was a mild and relatively bloodless revolution. A war was fought, to be sure, and soldiers died in that war. But the rules of civilized warfare, as then established, were for the most part quite scrupulously observed by both sides: there was none of the butchery which we have come to accept as a natural concomitant of revolutionary warfare. More important, there was practically none of the off-battlefield savagery which we now assume to be inevitable in revolutions. There were no revolutionary tribunals dispensing "revolutionary justice"; there was no reign of terror; there were no bloodthirsty proclamations by the Continental Congress. Tories were dispossessed of their property, to be sure, and many were rudely hustled off into exile; but so far as I have been able to determine, not a single Tory was executed for harboring counterrevolutionary opinions. Nor, in the years after the Revolution, were Tories persecuted to any significant degree (at least by today's standards) or their children discriminated against at all. As Tocqueville later remarked, with only a little exaggeration, the Revolution "contracted no alliance with the turbulent passions of anarchy, but its course was marked, on the contrary, by a love of order and law."

A law-and-order revolution? What kind of revolution is that, we ask ourselves? To which many will reply that it could not have been much of a revolution after all—at best a shadow of the real thing, which is always turbulent and bloody and shattering of body and soul. Well, the American Revolution was not that kind of revolution at all, and the possibility we have to consider is that it was successful precisely because it was not that kind of revolution—that it is we rather than the American revolutionaries who have an erroneous conception of what a revolution is.

Dr. Arendt makes an important distinction between "rebellion" and "revolution." By her criteria the French and Russian revolutions should more properly be called "rebellions," whereas only the American Revolution is worthy of the name. A rebellion, in her terms, is a meta-political event, emerging out of a radical dissatisfaction with the human condition as experienced by the mass of the people, demanding instant "liberation" from this condition, an immediate transformation of all social and economic circumstance, a prompt achievement of an altogether "better life" in an altogether "better world." The spirit of rebellion is a spirit of desperation—a desperate rejection of whatever exists, a desperate aspiration toward some kind of utopia. A rebellion is more a sociological event than a political action. It is governed by a blind momentum which sweeps everything before it, and its so-called leaders are in fact its captives, and ultimately its victims. The modern world knows many such rebellions, and all end up as one version or another of "a revolution betrayed." The so-called "betrayal" is, in fact, nothing but the necessary conclusion of a rebellion. Since its impossible intentions are unrealizable and since its intense desperation will not be satisfied with anything less than impossible intentions, the end result is always a regime which pretends to embody these intentions and which enforces such false pretentions by terror.

A revolution, in contrast, is a political phenomenon. It aims to revise and reorder the political arrangements of a society, and is therefore the work of the political ego rather than of the political id. A revolution is a practical exercise in political philosophy, not an existential spasm of the social organism. It requires an attentive prudence, a careful calculation of means and ends, a spirit of sobriety—the kind of spirit exemplified by that calm, legalistic document, the Declaration of Independence. All this is but another way of saying that a successful revolution cannot be governed by the spirit of the mob. Mobs and mob actions there will always be in a revolution, but if this revolution is not to degenerate into a rebellion, mob actions must be marginal to the central political drama. It may sound paradoxical but it nevertheless seems to be the case that only a self-disciplined people can dare undertake so radical a political enterprise as a revolution. This is almost like saying that a successful revolution must be accomplished by a people who want it but do not desperately need it—which was, indeed, the American condition in 1776. One may even put the case more strongly: a successful revolution is best accomplished by a people who do not really want it at all, but find themselves reluctantly making it. The American Revolution was exactly such a reluctant revolution.

The present-day student of revolutions will look in vain for any familiar kind of "revolutionary situation" in the American colonies prior to '76. The American people at that moment were the most prosperous in the world and lived under the freest institutions to be found anywhere in the world. They knew this well enough and boasted of it often enough. Their quarrel with the British crown was, in its origins, merely over the scope of colonial self-government, and hardly anyone saw any good reason why this quarrel should erupt into a war of independence. It was only after the war got under way that the American people decided that this was a good opportunity to make a revolution as well—that is, to establish a republican form of government.

Republican and quasi-republican traditions had always been powerful in the colonies, which were populated to such a large degree by religious dissenters who were sympathetic to the ideas incorporated in Cromwell's Commonwealth. Moreover, American political institutions from the very beginning were close to republican in fact, especially those of the Puritan communities of New England. Still, it is instructive to note that the word "republic" does not appear in the Declaration of Independence. Not that there was any real thought of reinstituting a monarchy in the New World: no one took such a prospect seriously. It was simply that, reluctant and cautious revolutionaries as they were, the Founding Fathers saw no need to press matters further than they had to, at that particular moment. To put it bluntly: they did not want events to get out of hand and saw no good reason to provoke more popular turbulence than was absolutely necessary.

One does not want to make the American Revolution an even more prosaic affair than it was. This was a revolution—a real one—and it was infused with a spirit of excitement and innovation. After all, what the American Revolution, once it got under way, was trying to do was no small thing. It was nothing less than the establishment, for the first time since ancient Rome, of a large republican nation, and the idea of reestablishing under modern conditions the glory that had been Rome's could hardly fail to be intoxicating. This Revolution did indeed have grand, even millennial, expectations as to the future role of this new nation in both the political imagination and political history of the human race. But certain things have to be said about these large expectations, if we are to see them in proper perspective.

The main thing to be said is that the millenarian tradition in America long antedates the Revolution and is not intertwined with the idea of revolution itself. It was the Pilgrim Fathers, not the Founding Fathers, who first announced that this was God's country, that the American people had a divine mission to accomplish, that this people had been "chosen" to create some kind of model community for the rest of mankind. This belief was already so firmly established by the time of the Revolution that it was part and parcel of our political orthodoxy, serving to legitimate an existing "American way of life" and most of the institutions associated with that way of life. It was a radical belief, in the sense of being bold and challenging and because this new "way of life" was so strikingly different from the lives that common people were then living in Europe. It was *not* a revolutionary belief. Crèvecoeur's famous paean of praise to "this new man, the American," was written well before the Revolution; and Crèvecoeur, in fact, opposed the American Revolution as foolish and unnecessary.

To this traditional millenarianism, the Revolution added the hope that the establishment of republican institutions would inaugurate a new and happier political era for all mankind. This hope was frequently expressed enthusiastically, in a kind of messianic rhetoric, but the men of the Revolution—most of them, most of the time—did not permit themselves to become bewitched by that rhetoric. Thus, though they certainly saw republicans as "the wave of the future," both Jefferson and Adams in the 1780s agreed that the French people were still too "depraved," as they so elegantly put it, to undertake an experiment in self-government. Self-government, as they understood it, presupposed a certain "way of life," and this in turn presupposed certain qualities on the part of the citizenry—qualities then designated as "republican virtues"—that would make self-government possible.

Similarly, though one can find a great many publicists during the Revolution who insisted that, with the severance of ties from Britain, the colonies had reverted to a Lockean "state of nature" and were now free to make a new beginning for all mankind and to create a new political order that would mark a new stage in human history—though such assertions were popular enough, it would be a mistake to take them too seriously. The fact is that Americans had encountered their "state of nature" generations earlier and had made their "social compact" at that time. The primordial American "social contract" was signed and sealed on the *Mayflower* —literally signed and sealed. The subsequent presence of all those signatures appended to the Declaration of Independence, beginning with John Hancock's, are but an echo of the original covenant.

To perceive the true purposes of the American Revolution, it is wise to ignore some of the more grandiloquent declamations of the moment—Tom Paine, an English radical who never really understood America, is especially worth ignoring —and to look at the kinds of political activity the Revolution unleashed. This activity took the form of constitution-making, above all. In the months and years immediately following the Declaration of Independence, all of our states drew up constitutions. These constitutions are terribly interesting in three respects. First, they involved relatively few basic changes in existing political institutions and almost no change at all in legal, social, or economic institutions; they were, for the most part, merely revisions of the preexisting charters. Secondly, most of the changes that were instituted had the evident aim of weakening the power of government, especially of the executive; it was these changes—and especially the strict separation of powers—that dismayed Turgot, Condorcet, and the other French *philosophes*, who understood revolution as an expression of the people's will-to-power rather than as an attempt to circumscribe political authority. Thirdly, in no case did any of these state constitutions tamper with the traditional system of local self-government. Indeed they could not, since it was this traditional system of local self-government which created and legitimized the constitutional conventions themselves.

In short, the Revolution reshaped our political institutions in such a way as to make them more responsive to popular opinion and less capable of encroaching upon the personal liberties of the citizen—liberties which long antedated the new constitutions and which in no way could be regarded as the creation or consequence of revolution. Which is to say that the purpose of this Revolution was to bring our political institutions into a more perfect correspondence with an actual "American way of life" which no one even dreamed of challenging. This "restructuring," as we would now call it— because it put the possibility of republican self-government once again on the political agenda of Western civilization— was terribly exciting to Europeans as well as Americans. But for the Americans involved in this historic task, it was also terribly frightening. It is fair to say that no other revolution in modern history made such relatively modest innovations with such an acute sense of anxiety. The Founding Fathers were well aware that if republicanism over the centuries had become such a rare form of government, there must be good reasons for it. Republican government, they realized, must be an exceedingly difficult regime to maintain—that is, it must have grave inherent problems. And so they were constantly scurrying to their libraries, ransacking classical and contemporary political authors, trying to discover why republics fail, and endeavoring to construct a "new political science" relevant to American conditions which would give this new republic a fair chance of succeeding. That "new political science" was eventually to be embodied in *The Federalist*— the only original work of political theory ever produced by a revolution and composed by successful revolutionaries. And the fact that very few of us have ever felt the need seriously to study *The Federalist* and that Europeans—or in our own day, Asians and Africans—have barely heard of it tells us how inadequately we understand the American Revolution, and how distant the real American Revolution has become from the idea of revolution by which we moderns are now possessed.

This idea of revolution, as the world understands it today, is what Dr. Arendt calls "rebellion." It involves a passionate

rejection of the status quo—its institutions and the way of
life associated with these institutions. It rejects everything
that exists because it wishes to create everything anew—a
new social order, a new set of economic arrangements, a new
political entity, a new kind of human being. It aims to solve
not merely the political problem of the particular political
community, at that particular moment, but every other
problem that vexes humanity. Its spirit is the spirit of
undiluted, enthusiastic, free-floating messianism: it will be
satisfied with nothing less than a radical transformation of
the human condition. It is an idea and a movement which is
both meta-political and sub-political—above and below politics—because it finds the political realm itself too confining
for its ambitions. Meta-politically, it is essentially a religious
phenomenon, seized with the perennial promise of redemption. Sub-politically, it is an expression of the modern technological mentality, confident of its power to control and
direct all human processes as we have learned to control and
direct the processes of nature. Inevitably, its swollen pride
and fanatical temper lead to tragic failure. But precisely
because of this pride and this fanaticism, failure leads only to
partial and temporary disillusionment. When this kind of
revolution gets "betrayed"—which is to say, when the
consequences of revolution lose all congruence with its original purpose—the true revolutionary believer will still look
forward to a second coming of the authentic and unbetraya-
ble revolution.

The French Revolution was the kind of modern revolution
I have been describing; the American Revolution was not. It
is because of this, one supposes, that the French Revolution
has captured the imagination of other peoples—has become
indeed the model of "real" revolution—in a way that the
American Revolution has not been able to do. The French
Revolution promised not only a reformation of France's political institutions, but far more than that. It promised, for
instance—as practically all revolutions have promised since—
the abolition of poverty. The American Revolution promised
no such thing, in part because poverty was not such a trou-
blesome issue in this country, but also—one is certain—

because the leaders of this revolution understood what their contemporary, Adam Smith, understood and what we today have some difficulty in understanding: namely, that poverty is abolished by economic growth, not by economic redistribution—there is never enough to distribute—and that rebellions, by creating instability and uncertainty, have mischievous consequences for economic growth. Similarly, the French Revolution promised a condition of "happiness" to its citizens under the new regime, whereas the American Revolution promised merely to permit the individual to engage in the "pursuit of happiness."

It should not be surprising, therefore, that in the war of ideologies which has engulfed the twentieth century, the United States is at a disadvantage. This disadvantage does not flow from any weakness on our part. It is not, as some say, because we have forgotten our revolutionary heritage and therefore have nothing to say to a discontented and turbulent world. We have, indeed, much to say, only it is not what our contemporaries want to hear. It is not even what we ourselves want to hear, and in *that* sense it may be correct to claim we have forgotten our revolutionary heritage. Our revolutionary message—which is a message not of the Revolution itself but of the American political tradition from the *Mayflower* to the Declaration of Independence to the Constitution—is that a self-disciplined people *can* create a political community in which an ordered liberty will promote both economic prosperity and political participation. To the teeming masses of other nations, the American political tradition says: to enjoy the fruits of self-government, you must first cease being "masses" and become a "people," attached to a common way of life, sharing common values, and existing in a condition of mutual trust and sympathy as between individuals and even social classes. It is a distinctly odd kind of "revolutionary" message, by twentieth century criteria—so odd that it seems not revolutionary at all, and yet so revolutionary that it seems utterly utopian. What the twentieth century wants to hear is the grand things that a new government will do for the people who put their trust in it. What the American political tradition says is that the major function of government is, in Professor Oakeshott's phrase, to "tend to the arrangements of society," and that free people do not make a covenant or social contract with their government, or with the leaders of any "movement," but among themselves.

In the end, what informs the American political tradition is a proposition and a premise. The proposition is that the best national government is, to use a phrase the Founding Fathers were fond of, "mild government." The premise is that you can only achieve "mild government" if you have a solid bedrock of local self-government, so that the responsibilities of national government are limited in scope. And a corollary of this premise is that such a bedrock of local self-government can only be achieved by a people who—through the shaping influence of religion, education, and their own daily experience—are capable of governing themselves in those small and petty matters which are the stuff of local politics.

Does this conception of politics have any relevance to the conditions in which people live today in large areas of the world—the so-called underdeveloped areas, especially? We are inclined, I think, to answer instinctively in the negative, but that answer may itself be a modern ideological prejudice. We take it for granted that if a people live in comparative poverty, they are necessarily incapable of the kind of self-discipline and sobriety that makes for effective self-government in their particular communities. Mind you, I am not talking about starving people, who are in a pre-political condition and whose problem is to get a strong and effective government of almost any kind. I am talking about *comparatively* poor people. And our current low estimate of the political capabilities of such people is an ideological assumption, not an objective fact. Many of our frontier communities, at the time of the Revolution and for decades afterwards, were poor by any standards. Yet this poverty was not, for the most part, inconsistent with active self-government. There have been communities in Europe, too, which were very poor—not actually starving, of course, but simply very poor—yet were authentic political communities. The popular musical, *Fiddler on the Roof*, gave us a picture of such a community. It is always better not to be so poor, but poverty need not be a pathological condition, and political pathology is not an inevitable consequence of poverty, just as political pathology is not inevitably abolished by prosperity. Poor people can cope with their poverty in many different ways. They are people, not sociological creatures and in the end they will cope as their moral and political convictions tell them to cope. These convictions, in turn, will be formed by the expectations that their community addresses to them—expectations which they freely convert into obligations.

In *The Brothers Karamazov*, Dostoevsky says that the spirit of the Antichrist, in its modern incarnation, will flaunt the banner, "First feed people, and *then* ask of them virtue." This has, in an amended form, indeed become the cardinal and utterly conventional thesis of modern politics. The amended form reads: "First make people prosperous, and then ask of them virtue." Whatever reservations one might have about Dostoevsky's original thesis, this revised version is, in the perspective of the Judaeo-Christian tradition, unquestionably a blasphemy. It is also, in the perspective of the American political tradition, a malicious and inherently self-defeating doctrine—self-defeating because those who proclaim it obviously have lost all sense of what virtue, religious or political, means. Nevertheless, practically all of us today find it an inherently plausible doctrine, a staple of our political discourse. This being the case, it is only natural that we ourselves should have such difficulty understanding the American political tradition, and that when we expend it to the world, we distort it in all sorts of ways which will make it more palatable to the prejudices of the modern political mentality.

III

It would not be fair to conclude that the American political tradition is flawless, and that it is only we, its heirs, who are to blame for the many problems our society is grappling with —and so ineptly. The American Revolution was a successful revolution, but there is no such thing, either in one's personal life or in a nation's history, as unambiguous success. The legacy of the American Revolution and of the entire political tradition associated with it is problematic in all sorts of ways. Strangely enough, we have such an imperfect understanding of this tradition that, even as we vulgarize it or question it or disregard it, we rarely address ourselves to its problematic quality.

The major problematic aspect of this tradition has to do with the relationship of the "citizen" to the "common man." And the difficulties we have in defining this relationship are best illustrated by the fact that, though we have been a representative democracy for two centuries now, we have never developed an adequate theory of representation. More precisely we have developed *two* contradictory theories of representation, both of which can claim legitimacy within the American political tradition and both of which were enunciated, often by the same people, during the Revolution. The one sees the public official as a "common man" who has a mandate to reflect the opinions of the majority; the other sees the public official as a somewhat uncommon man—a more-than-common man, if you will—who, because of his talents and character, is able to take a larger view of the "public interest" than the voters who elected him or the voters who failed to defeat him. One might say that the first is a "democratic" view of the legislator, the second a "republican" view. The American political tradition has always had a kind of double vision on this whole problem, which in turn makes for a bewildering moral confusion. Half the time we regard our politicians as, in the nature of things, probably corrupt and certainly untrustworthy; the other half of the time, we denounce them for failing to be models of integrity and rectitude. Indeed, we have a profession—journalism—which seems committed to both of these contradictory propositions. But politicians are pretty much like the rest of us and tend to become the kinds of people they are expected to be. The absence of clear and distinct expectations has meant that public morality in this country has never been, and is not, anything we can be proud of.

In a way, the ambiguity in our theory of representation points to a much deeper ambiguity in that system of self-government which emerged from the Revolution and the Constitutional Convention. That system has been perceptively titled, by Professor Martin Diamond, "a democratic republic." Now, we tend to think of these terms as near-synonyms, but in fact they differ significantly in their political connotations. Just how significant the difference is becomes clear if we realize that the America which emerged from the Revolution and the Constitutional Convention was the first democratic republic in history. The political philosophers of that time could study the history of republics and they could study the history of democracies, but there was no opportunity for them to study both together. When the Founding Fathers declared that they had devised a new kind of political entity based on "a new science of politics," they were not vainly boasting or deceiving themselves. It is we, their political descendants, who tend to be unaware of the novelty of the American political enterprise, and of the risks and ambiguities inherent in that novelty. We simplify and vulgarize and distort, because we have lost the sense of how bold and innovative the Founding Fathers were, and of how problematic—necessarily problematic—is the system of government, and the society, which they established. Witness the fact that, incredibly enough, at our major universities it is almost impossible to find a course, graduate or undergraduate, devoted to *The Federalist*.

What is the difference between a "democracy" and a "republic"? In a democracy, the will of the people is supreme. In a republic, it is not the will of the people but the rational consensus of the people—a rational consensus which is implicit in the term "consent"—which governs the people. That is to say, in a democracy, popular passion may rule—*may*, though it need not—but in a republic, popular passion is regarded as unfit to rule, and precautions are taken to see that it is subdued rather than sovereign. In a democracy all politicians are, to some degree, demagogues: they appeal to people's prejudices and passions, they incite their expectations by making reckless promises, they endeavor to ingratiate themselves with the electorate in every possible way. In a republic, there are not supposed to be such politicians, only statesmen—sober, unglamorous, thoughtful men who are engaged in a kind of perpetual conversation with the citizenry. In a republic, a fair degree of equality and prosperity are important goals, but it is liberty that is given priority as the proper end of government. In a democracy, these priorities are reversed: the status of men and women as consumers of economic goods is taken to be more significant than their status as participants in the creation of political goods. A republic is what we would call "moralistic" in its approach to both public and private affairs; a democracy is more easygoing, more "permissive" as we now say, even more cynical.

The Founding Fathers perceived that their new nation was too large, too heterogeneous, too dynamic, too mobile for it to govern itself successfully along strict republican principles. And they had no desire at all to see it governed along strict democratic principles, since they did not have that much faith in the kinds of "common men" likely to be produced by such a nation. So they created a new form of "popular government," to use one of their favorite terms, that incorporated both republican and democratic principles, in a complicated and ingenious way. This system has lasted for two centuries, which means it has worked very well indeed. But in the course of that time, we have progressively forgotten what kind of system it is and *why* it works as well as it does. Every now and then, for instance, we furiously debate the question of whether or not the Supreme Court is meeting its obligations as a democratic institution. The question reveals a startling ignorance of our political tradition. The Supreme Court is not—and was never supposed to be—a democratic institution; it is a republican institution which counterbalances the activities of our various democratic institutions. Yet I have discovered that when you say this to college students, they do not understand the distinction and even have difficulty thinking about it.

So it would seem that today, two hundred years after the American Revolution, we are in a sense victims of its success.

The political tradition out of which it issued and the political order it helped to create are imperfectly comprehended by us. What is worse, we are not fully aware of this imperfect comprehension and are frequently smug in our convenient misunderstandings. The American Revolution certainly merits celebration. But it would be reassuring if a part of that celebration were to consist, not merely of pious clichés, but of a serious and sustained effort to achieve a deeper and more widespread understanding of just what it is we are celebrating.

MARTIN DIAMOND
The Revolution of Sober Expectations

Delivered in Congress Hall, Independence Square,

Philadelphia on October 24, 1973

"I am filled with deep emotion at finding myself standing here in the place where were collected together the wisdom, the patriotism, the devotion to principle, from which sprang the institutions under which we live."[1] Those lovely words, I am sorry to say, are not my own. They were uttered by Abraham Lincoln in February 1861, only days before he assumed the terrible burdens of his presidency. But I cannot possibly find words better to express my own deep emotion at having the opportunity to share with you, in this hallowed place, my reflections as these are occasioned by the impending bicentennial of our national birth.

Because of the struggle then tormenting and dividing the Union, Lincoln was obliged to look back upon the origins of the American republic to find the wisdom, patriotism, and devotion to principle that might save the Union and reinspirit its republican institutions. We are under no such compelling necessity tonight. Our occasion is only inspired by the happy imminence of our bicentennial. And yet, for us too the backward glance remains a necessity. Lincoln was obliged to look back to the men who met in Independence Hall in 1776 because it was their thoughts and words expressed im-

[1] Roy P. Basler, ed., *Collected Works of Abraham Lincoln* (New Brunswick, N.J.: Rutgers University Press, 1953), vol. 4, p. 240.

mortally in the Declaration of Independence "from which sprang the institutions under which we live." We live still to an amazing extent under those same institutions. And like Lincoln, if we wish to understand those institutions, then we too must return to the thoughts of the Founding Fathers. We too must look to the architects for the plan of the house in which we still reside. No task could be more agreeable to me here, the child of immigrant grandparents whose grateful patriotism instructed my youth.

There is a fascinating ambiguity in those words of Lincoln which I have quoted. We must remember that there were two great happenings here at Independence Square, the first in 1776 when independence was proclaimed in the Declaration, and the second eleven years later when the Federal Convention met for four long months and drafted the Constitution. When we look back to our origins we look to the same place, here in Philadelphia, but to two different times and events—to 1776 and 1787, to the Declaration and the Constitution. They are the two springs of our existence. To understand their relationship is to understand the political core of our being, and hence to understand what it is that we are soon to celebrate the bicentennial of. It is to this never-to-be-severed relationship of the Declaration and the Constitution that I address my remarks. In doing so I simply follow the lead of Lincoln. Let me repeat his words.

> I am filled with deep emotion at finding myself standing here in the place where were collected together the wisdom, the patriotism, the devotion to principle, from which sprang the institutions under which we live.

Notice how neatly Lincoln blends in this single sentence both 1776 and 1787, both Declaration and Constitution. By the "institutions under which we live," he refers of course to the institutions devised by the framers of the Constitution. But these institutions, Lincoln reminds us in the same breath, sprang from a "devotion to principle," to the principle of the Declaration. Only in the unity of the Declaration's principle and the Constitution's institutions does the American Republic achieve its complete being, and Lincoln never

ceased from the effort to sustain or restore that unity. We
must do no less.

I

What wants understanding is precisely how our institutions
of government sprang from the principle of the Declaration
of Independence. How and to what extent were they generated by the Declaration of Independence? And what more
had to be added actually to frame those institutions? We
find a clue further on in Lincoln's speech—his "wholly un-
prepared speech," it is humbling and yet inspiring to note.

> All the political *sentiments* I entertain have been drawn,
> *so far as I have been able to draw them,* from the *sen-
> timents* which originated, and were given to the world
> from this hall in which we stand. I have never had a *feel-
> ing* politically that did not spring from the *sentiments*
> embodied in the Declaration of Independence.[2]

Now this sentiment that Lincoln drew from the Declaration
was that document's passionate devotion to the principle of
liberty.

> . . . something in that Declaration giving liberty, not
> alone to the people of this country, but hope to the
> world for all future time. It was that which gave promise
> that in due time the weights should be lifted from the
> shoulders of all men, and that all should have an equal
> chance. This is the sentiment embodied in that Declara-
> tion of Independence.

We must take careful heed of Lincoln's remarkable stress,
throughout this speech from which we are quoting, on the
words feeling and sentiment. He carefully limits his indebt-
edness to the Declaration only to certain sentiments and feelings, that is, to the spirit of liberty within which he conceives
American government and its institutions. Indeed, he could
not have done otherwise, for there is nothing in the Declaration which goes beyond that sentiment of liberty. As we shall

[2] Emphasis supplied.

see, noble document that the Declaration is, indispensable source of the feelings and sentiments of Americans and of the spirit of liberty in which their institutions were conceived, the Declaration is devoid of guidance as to what those institutions should be.

In addition to inferring this from Lincoln's speech, we have also the highest possible authority for this conclusion: namely, the testimony of the "Father of the Constitution," James Madison, and the acceptance of that testimony by the author of the Declaration, Thomas Jefferson. In 1825 the two patriarchs of the American founding engaged in a correspondence regarding a possible required reading list for students at the Law School of the University of Virginia. They took for granted, as Madison said, that the students should be required to read books that would inculcate "the true doctrines of liberty" which are "exemplified in our political system."[3] But it is not easy, Madison wrote, to find books that will be both "guides and guards" for the purpose. The work of John Locke, for example, Madison went on, was "admirably calculated to impress on young minds the right of nations to establish their own governments and to inspire a love of free ones." (This "love" would seem to be exactly what Lincoln meant by the "sentiment" of the Declaration.) But Locke could not teach those future lawyers how to protect "our Republican charters," that is, how to protect the American federal and state constitutions from being corrupted by false interpretations, because Locke gave insufficient guidance regarding the nature of our republican institutions.

Now to put these words in a letter to Jefferson, who, as the author of the Declaration, had clearly drawn inspiration from John Locke, would seem to be cutting pretty close to the bone. But Madison had no reason to hesitate in thus writing to his old friend because he could count on Jefferson's calmly agreeing with his view. Indeed, he proceeded to make his point even more explicitly. "The Declaration of Independence," Madison continued, "though rich in fundamental

[3] James Madison to Thomas Jefferson, February 8, 1825, in *The Writings of James Madison*, ed. Gaillard Hunt (New York: G. P. Putnam's Sons, 1900), vol. 9, pp. 218-19.

principles, and saying everything that could be said in the same number of words"—it never hurts to be gentle with an author's pride no matter how close a friend he is—"falls nearly under a like observation." What his careful eighteenth century language is saying is plainly this: The principles of Locke and of Jefferson's Declaration are infinitely valuable for inspiring in young minds a proper love of free government; but that is all that those principles reach to. The Declaration, Madison is saying and Jefferson cheerfully agrees, offers no guidance for the construction of free government and hence offers no aid in protecting the American form of free government under the Constitution. For that purpose, Madison does not scruple to add, one must turn to *The Federalist* "as the most authentic exposition of the text of the federal Constitution." In short, the patriarchs Jefferson and Madison agree with Lincoln, as I have interpreted him, in their understanding of the noble but limited work of the Declaration. The American founding, as we shall see, is only begun by the Declaration. It reaches its completion with the Constitution.

But civilly pious as we ought to be tonight, we need not let the argument I am making rest with the splendid authority of Lincoln, Madison, and Jefferson. We may sustain their judgment by our independent reading of the text of the Declaration. The relevant passage is the one usually printed as the second paragraph, the passage dealing with the truths the Declaration holds to be self-evident. Now this does not, by the way, mean evident to everyone, as it has come to be thought in these disbelieving relativistic days. The mockers say—Those truths aren't evident to me; I'm into a different bag, and since they aren't evident to me they cannot truly be truths. The author of the Declaration knew that these truths would not be self-evident to kings and nobles, not to predetermined adversaries, nor to anyone of insufficient or defective vision. Indeed Jefferson knew that those truths had not hitherto been held as evident by the vast majority of mankind. But, by self-evidence, the Declaration does not refer to the selves to whom the truths are evident, but rather means that the evidentness of the truths is contained within the truths themselves. That is, these truths are not to be reached at the end of a chain of reasoning; they are not the fruit of supporting evidence, inference, and argument; but rather, carrying the evidence of their truthfulness within themselves, their truth is to be grasped by a kind of direct seeing or perception. And, we may add, their truthfulness was to be vindicated by the excellence of their consequences. It would be by means of triumphant freedom that others would be led in time also to see and then to hold those truths to be self-evident. It was up to the American Revolution and the future American regime to vindicate them.

The Declaration holds certain truths to be self-evident: that all men are created equal, that they are endowed by their Creator with certain unalienable rights among which are life, liberty, and the pursuit of happiness, that governments, whose proper end is to secure these rights, may only be instituted by the consent of the governed, and that, when government becomes destructive of those rights, the people have the further right to alter or abolish it and reinstitute another in its place. Now these truths do not rise by inference one from the other, but are each equally and independently self-evident; and each is indispensably a part of a whole that forms the "sentiment" of the Declaration. Yet for our purpose tonight, and perhaps even intrinsically, we may single out as the most important political truth the comprehensive one regarding the institution of government, namely, that government exists to secure unalienable rights and must be instituted by popular consent. Intrinsically, this truth may be the most important because the other truths become political only in relation to it, or are ancillary to it. Thus men are created equal but only with respect to the equal possession of certain unalienable rights. Those rights give the content to and hence define our equality: what we are equally is equally free. But this equal freedom becomes, of course, political freedom, and hence politically interesting only under government. And, the final self-evident truth, that is, the right to overthrow despotic government and reinstitute a new one, is obviously ancillary to the truth that deals with what legitimate government is and must do.

What is especially interesting to us tonight is the way this political truth of the Declaration has been transformed as it formed and then was absorbed into the historical American credo of government. We must read the Declaration closely to free ourselves from two centuries of obscuring usage. We have transformed the Declaration in our minds by reading the phrase "consent of the governed" as meaning rule by majorities, that is, democratic government. Indeed we think of the Declaration as our great democratic document, as the clarion call to and the guide to our democratic nature. But the Declaration does *not* say that consent is the means by which government is to operate. Rather, it says that consent is necessary only to institute the government, that is, to establish it.

The people need not, then, *establish* a government which *operates* by means of their consent. In fact, the Declaration says that they may organize government on "such principles" as they choose, and they may choose "any form of government" they deem appropriate to secure their rights. That is, the Declaration was not prescribing any particular form of government at all, but rather was following John Locke's contract theory, which taught the right of the people, in seeking to secure their liberties, to establish *any* form of government. And by any form of government the Declaration emphatically includes—as any literate eighteenth century reader would have understood—not only the democratic form of government but also aristocratic and monarchical government as well. That is why, for example, the Declaration has to submit facts to a "candid world" to prove the British king guilty of a "long train of abuses." Tom Paine, by way of contrast, could dispose of King George more simply. Paine deemed George III unfit to rule simply because he was a *king* and kingly rule was illegitimate as such. The fact that George was a "Royal Brute" was only frosting on the cake; for Paine his being royal was sufficient warrant for deposing him. But the Declaration, on the contrary, is obliged to prove that George was indeed a brute. That is, the Declaration holds George III "unfit to be the ruler of a free people" not because he was a king, but because he was a *tyrannical* king. Had the British monarchy continued to secure to the colonists their rights, as it had prior to the long train of abuses, the colonists would not have been entitled to rebel. It was only the fact, according to the Declaration, that George had become a tyrannical king that supplied the warrant for revolution.

Thus the Declaration, strictly speaking, is neutral on the question of forms of government: *any* form is legitimate provided it secures equal freedom and is instituted by popular consent. But from this it follows that the Declaration, while richly nurturing in humanity a love of free government and thus supplying Lincoln with all his political sentiments, can offer no guidance whatsoever, as Madison said, for the American democratic institutions which sprang from that love of freedom. That guidance is to be found in the thought which shaped the Constitution and is to be found in the Constitution itself which framed the institutions under which we live. It is to the Constitution that we must ultimately turn as the completion of the American Revolution. As to those democratic institutions, the Declaration says no more than this: If you choose the democratic form of government, rather than the aristocratic or monarchic or any mixture thereof, it must be a democratic government which secures to all people their unalienable rights. But how to do that? The Declaration is silent.

II

Indeed this silence is the splendid distinction of the American Revolution. And it is the first evidence of the sobriety to which I allude in the title of this lecture, "The Revolution of Sober Expectations." The Revolution was, so to speak, only half a revolution. It *did* overthrow a government, albeit a distant one; it did in a revolutionary way abolish an existing government—and that is at least half a revolution—but it did not in the same breath commit itself to the shape of the new government to be instituted.

The makers of the American Revolution did not think themselves in possession of the simple and complete political truth, capable of instant application as a panacea for government. They claimed possession of only half the truth, namely, the self-evident truth that equal freedom must be the foundation of all political society. And in the name of that equal freedom they made half a revolution. But, soberly and moderately, they left open the question of institutions of government. These they knew would have to be forged from old materials, perhaps worked and reworked, and with a cool awareness that the new American institutions would be subject still to perennial human frailty and folly. The Declaration, then, limited the dangerous passions of revolution only to the unmaking of a tyrannical government. It gave no license to new rulers to carry those revolutionary passions directly into the making of new government. That making of new government would have to find its way through still uncharted paths to be trod soberly and prudently.

But what have I left, it may be asked, of our once glorious Declaration? I have argued, as emphatically as I can, that the Declaration soberly left open the question of forms of government and its institutions. And in so doing I have perhaps reduced its claims and its reach, *as these are now understood*. But after the French and Russian revolutions we have a utopianly grandiloquent idea of revolution, a different idea of revolution from that of the American revolutionaries. I do not believe that Jefferson and his colleagues, or that Madison or Lincoln, would have understood the Declaration otherwise than I have stated it; nor would they think me to have diminished it. From our perspective it may look like only half a revolution, but they understood that that was nonetheless revolution indeed and revolution enough. What was truly revolutionary in the American Revolution and its Declaration of Independence was that liberty, civil liberty—the doctrine of certain unalienable rights—was made the end of government. Not, as had been the case for millennia, whatever end power haphazardly imposed upon government; nor any longer the familiar variety of ends—not virtue, not piety, not privilege or wealth, not merely protection, and not empire and dominion; but now deliberately the principle of liberty. It was this that led Lincoln to offer "All honor to Jefferson—to

the man who, in the concrete pressure of a struggle for national independence by a single people, had the coolness,
forecast, and capacity to introduce into a merely revolutionary document, an abstract truth, applicable to all men
and all times."[4] A "merely revolutionary document" would
have demanded a mere revolving—such was the traditional
meaning of the word revolution—of power from one set of
hands to another, from the few to the many or the many to
the few; but the Declaration instead pledged the American
Revolution to an abstract principle, to the "definitions and
axioms of free society." For the same reason as Lincoln and
in the same spirit, Madison likewise praised the "leaders of
the Revolution" for accomplishing a "revolution which has
no parallel in the annals of human society."[5]

The events that culminated in revolution began modestly
in 1763 when, in response to new British imperial measures,
the colonists sought to assert the traditional English liberties
they had enjoyed during a century and a half of "salutary neglect." In this they were little different from Englishmen
before them who had fought their battles in the name of ancient privileges and feudal immunities and time-honored customs. But gradually the issue subtly changed, and the abstract idea of liberty came to overlay the appeal to traditional
and concrete English liberties. In the course of the intensifying struggle, the Americans gradually came to see those traditional English liberties, not as a growth merely peculiar to
English soil and custom, but as having happily embodied the
abstract principle of civil liberty as this had been stated, for
example, by Locke and Montesquieu. What Montesquieu
did as a deliberate work of political theory, the Americans
enacted in the course of a political struggle: Each transformed concrete English liberties into the universal principle
of liberty. And, finally, rejecting English rule as now
hopelessly despotic, America launched its Revolution simply
and expressly upon the principle of liberty. Thus Lord Acton

[4] Letter of April 6, 1859, in *Collected Works of Abraham Lincoln*, vol. 3, p. 376.
[5] *The Federalist*, Number 14, ed. Clinton Rossiter (New York:
Mentor Books, 1961), p. 104.

dramatically, but not implausibly, concluded that "In the strictest sense the history of liberty dated from 1776 'for never till then had men sought liberty knowing what they sought.'"[6]

This was the heady stuff of the American Revolution. But still in its very dedication to the abstract principle of liberty, which made the American Revolution authentically revolutionary, was contained also the second element of that sobriety which made it a "revolution of sober expectations." While modern followers of Edmund Burke may warn of the dangers of devotion to abstract principles, they cannot blink aside the revolutionary American devotion to precisely such an abstract principle. The American truth was undeniably as abstract as, say, Robespierre's tyrannizing truth or Lenin's tyrannizing truth. And yet there is indeed something moderate and nonutopian in the American devotion to liberty which warrants Burkean celebration. Whence then the difference? Wherein was the American Revolution one of sober expectations while the Jacobin and Leninist were revolutions of unbridled expectations? The answer lies not in degrees of devotion to abstractness, but in the substantive nature of the principle each was abstractly devoted to. It is one thing to be abstractly devoted to the Reign of Virtue or to unlimited equality in all respects or to mass fraternity or to classless society or to the transformation of the human condition itself, and quite another to be devoted to the abstract principle of civil liberty. Civil liberty as a goal constrains its followers to moderation, legality, and rootedness in regular institutions. Moreover, moderate civil liberty does not require terror and tyranny for its fulfillment. Liberty is an abstract principle capable of achievement; Jacobin or Leninist equality or mass fraternity are not. Moderate civil liberty is a possible dream, utopian equality and fraternity are impossible dreams. And the recent popular song to the contrary notwithstanding, the political pursuit of impossible dreams leads to terror and tyranny in the vain effort to actualize what cannot be.

[6] Gertrude Himmelfarb, *Lord Acton* (London: Routledge & Kegan Paul, 1952), p. 141.

The revolution in America, Tocqueville said, "was caused by a mature and thoughtful taste for freedom, not by some vague, undefined instinct for independence [that is, for absence of order and constraint]. No disorderly passions drove it on; on the contrary, it proceeded hand in hand with a love of order and legality."[7]

Not a revolution in the utopian expectation of the emancipation of humans from all constraint upon passion and desire, but only the sober and moderate expectation of certain unalienable rights under free government—freedom under law. That the goal of the American Revolution was moderate civil freedom made the struggle revolutionary indeed, but at the same time it is the second cause of that sobriety which distinguishes the American Revolution from the disastrous revolutions of our age and which is our theme tonight.

But what of democracy we must now ask? Perhaps, as I have claimed, the Declaration is neutral regarding democracy, but does the American Revolution not somehow have something to do with the establishment of democracy in this country? It does indeed, and the revolutionary establishment of democratic government in America is at once perhaps the most revolutionary element of the American Revolution, and its most sober aspect.

Americans, Tocqueville observed, were born equal. This was so because of historical reasons too familiar and also too complicated to dwell upon here. The Englishmen who came to this country were from the middling walks of life and the institutions they developed here were far more democratic than those of their contemporaries and kinsmen in England. America, as Marx observed in the same spirit as Tocqueville, did not have a "feudal alp" pressing down upon the brow of the living. During one hundred and seventy years of colonial life the *stuff* of American life was thus quietly being prepared in the direction of democracy. But democratizing as the American colonial experience had been, colonial *thought* on the eve of the Revolution remained essentially pre-demo-

[7] *Democracy in America*, translated by G. Lawrence (New York: Harper & Row, 1966), p. 64.

cratic. Colonial thought was in unanimous accord with the dominant English and Continental belief in the doctrine of the mixed regime, or, as Englishmen called it, the balanced constitution. This idea, more powerful than ever in eighteenth century England, derived from a two-thousand year tradition stemming from Aristotle. The traditional idea rested upon the premise that the pure forms of government —monarchy, aristocracy, and democracy—all tended to their own corruption; any unchecked ruler, be he the one, the few, or the many, would become tyrannical. Hence, the idea of the mixed or balanced regime—that is, a combination of the three kinds of government in one to prevent that otherwise inevitable degeneration or corruption. For example, in England this meant the balance of Crown, Lords, and Commons. There was nearly unanimous American agreement on this political prescription, especially on that part of the teaching which emphasized that pure democracy was peculiarly untenable. So great a leader of the American Revolution as John Adams subscribed to the idea of the mixed regime until the Revolution (and in fact never quite rid himself of it). For example, the English constitution, he said, is "the most perfect combination . . . which finite wisdom has yet contrived . . . for the preservation of liberty and the production of happiness."[8] It cannot be stated too emphatically how strong a hold this mixed regime concept had on all colonial thought up to the eve of the Revolution.

But the American Revolution changed all this and therein lay its profoundly revolutionary character. As Tocqueville said, when the American Revolution broke out, "the dogma of the sovereignty of the people came out from the township and took possession of the government."[9] The essentially popular character of American life was quickened by all the forces of the Revolution. The logic of the struggle against royal and aristocratic England tilted the Americans more wholly toward democracy. The flight of propertied Tories had

[8] Quoted in Bernard Bailyn, *The Ideological Origins of the American Revolution* (Cambridge: Harvard University Press, 1967), p. 67.

[9] *Democracy in America*, p. 52.

the same effect. The old colonial institutions of government, always predominantly popular, became still more so with the removal of royal governors and councils. Democracy became the dominant fact of the new American confederation of states. The Americans found themselves becoming democratic without having intended to become so, an apparently healthy way to ease gently into democracy.

Once independence was declared, each of the colonies was obliged to flesh out its existing institutions and assume full responsibility for its own governance. Each of these new state governments was more fully democratic than its colonial predecessor. But in almost all of them there were also significant vestiges, and perhaps more than vestiges, of the powerful old mixed regime idea. Thus wealth, for example, was given a privileged standing in many of the state governments. Suffrage qualifications differed for the different state offices, like the popular house, upper house, and governor; more property was required for the right of voting for the higher offices. And even more dramatically there were steep property requirements for office holding, the higher the office, the steeper the requirement.

These oligarchic elements in the state governments testified powerfully to the force of the old idea of England's balanced constitution. Thus, democratic as had been the pace of events during the Revolution, there still was the possibility that in time the democratic tide would recede, that property and privilege would reassert their perennial claims, especially perhaps in the South. Or perhaps, say, in Massachusetts in the aftermath of a struggle like the Shays' Rebellion. Whatever might have been the course of events, however differently things might have developed in each state and region, the massive and dramatic fact is that the issue of democracy was settled in this country by the drafting and ratification of the Constitution.

For example, with one single and little remarked clause of the Constitution, those vestiges of oligarchic privilege in the states, those live remnants of the mixed regime idea, were forever barred and the idea of democracy rendered legally complete in the American system. I refer to Article I, Section 2, which establishes the then broadest possible democratic franchise as the basis for the federal election. There was no practical possibility thereafter, under the Constitution, for the gradual reintroduction of aristocracy, wealth, or privilege into the federal suffrage—and if not in the federal suffrage, then inevitably, in time, also not in the state suffrages. To this may be added the total absence of any property qualifications, contrary to existing state practices, for any federal office, and also the clause barring the introduction of any titles of nobility. Finally, we may note the provision for the payment of salaries to federal officeholders, thereby insuring that men of relatively humble means could afford to serve the government.

These quiet and usually unremarked clauses of the Constitution are part of the means by which the Constitution completed the most dramatic aspect of the American Revolution—namely, the firm establishment of the democratic form of government. With the Constitution the Americans completed the half-revolution begun in 1776 and became the first modern people fully to confront the issue of democracy. But, again, the American Revolution precisely in its revolutionary thrust was simultaneously distinctively sober. The way the Constitution confronted democracy is the third and most important element in the "revolution of sober expectations" that we have been discussing.

The sobriety lies in the Founding Fathers' coolheaded and cautious acceptance of democracy. Perhaps not a single American voice was raised in unqualified, doctrinaire praise of democracy. On the contrary, there was universal recognition of the problematic character of democracy, a concern for its weaknesses and a fear of its dangers. The debate in American life during the founding decade gradually became a debate over how to create a decent democratic regime. Contrary to our too complacent modern perspective regarding democracy, which assumes that a government cannot be decent unless democratic, our Founding Fathers more skeptically, sensibly, and soberly, were concerned how to make this new government *decent even though democratic*. All the American revolutionaries, whether they were partisans of the theory that democratic republics had to be small or agrarian or only loosely confederated in order to remain free, or whether they

retained the traditional idea that democracy had to be coun-
terbalanced by nobility or wealth, or whether they subscribed
to the large-republic theory implicit in the new Constitution
—all the American revolutionaries knew that democracy was
a problem in need of constant solution, in constant need of
moderation, in constant need of institutions and measures to
mitigate its defects and guard against its dangers.

It was in this sober spirit that the American Revolution
cheerfully and cannily worked its way out of the eighteenth
century into the era of modern democracy. The half-revolution begun in 1776 reached its completion only when the
peculiar American posture toward democracy received its
definitive form in the framing and ratification of the Constitution a decade later. Nothing, then, is more instructive for
modern Americans who wish to understand the genesis and
the genius of the institutions under which they live than the
debates of the Federal Convention of 1787—that second
event which hallowed this hall. And in contemplating that
convention we would find the answer to our earlier question:
how did our institutions spring from the Declaration and
what had to be added to bring those institutions into being?
They sprang on the one hand from the love of free government inspired by the noble *sentiments* of Jefferson's Declaration, and on the other hand from the theoretic *wisdom* of
James Madison whose sober clarity regarding democracy gave
the shape and thrust to our unique democratic form of government and way of life.

The way was opened for the quiet and mild genius of
Madison to gain its ascendancy by a stroke of fortune that
could lead one almost to attribute the success of the Constitutional Convention to the direct intervention of Divine
Providence—namely, that during the summer of the convention John Adams happened to be in London and Thomas
Jefferson in Paris serving their country as ambassadors. Had
these two formidable figures—the one a lingering partisan of
the mixed regime, the other too easily given to a mere libertarianism that would have vitiated the effectiveness of government—had Adams and Jefferson been in Philadelphia in
1787, I do not believe that the single clear vision of Madison
would have been able to prevail. And had not Madison and

his great colleagues, Washington, Hamilton, Wilson, Morris and the others, prevailed, had not the Constitution prevailed, the half-revolution so brightly begun in 1776 would have had a far less successful outcome, indeed, perhaps a variety of disastrous outcomes.

Tocqueville who understood us so well understood that what distinguished the American Revolution was its successful ascent to the Constitution.

> If ever there was a short moment when America did rise to that climax of glory where the proud imagination of her inhabitants would constantly like us to see her, it was at that supreme crisis when the national authority had in some sort abdicated its dominion.

At precisely that moment of crisis when other revolutions turn turbulent, begin to devour their own, and dash all the initial hopes, at precisely that moment ripe for disaster, the American Revolution achieved its glory by a unique moment of stillness and sobriety.

> That which is new in the history of societies is to see a great people, warned by its lawgivers that the wheels of government are stopping, turn its attention on itself without haste or fear, sound the depth of the ill, and then wait for two years to find the remedy at leisure, and then finally, when the remedy has been indicated, submit to it voluntarily without its costing humanity a single tear or drop of blood.[10]

Only a "revolution of sober expectations" could have brought itself to successful completion in such a moment of stillness. And we have been celebrating tonight the causes of the sobriety that made that moment and that completion possible.

III

On this approaching bicentennium of the Revolution, I have tried to turn our attention to the two founding documents of our national being—the Declaration of Independence and

[10] Ibid., p. 102.

the Constitution—and I have tried to make it impossible for
us to think of the one without simultaneously thinking of the
other. In this I have followed but also reversed the magiste-
rial effort of Lincoln. He devoted himself to drawing the
Americans of his generation back from the Constitution to
the Declaration. He did so because Americans then were
emptying the Constitution of its inspiriting love of equal
freedom for all. In the interests of slavery or of compromising
with slavery, Americans of his generation were reducing and
corrupting the Constitution to a mere legalistic compact
emptied of the abstract truth which it had once embodied,
and which had made it a promise and a model to all men.
When the men of his day spoke of the Constitution, he
wished them always to think also of the Declaration and
hence of the liberty in which the nation had been conceived
and of the proposition regarding equality to which it had
been dedicated.

Today our needs are otherwise. Our two documents must
as always be seen as indissolubly linked. But now we need to
train ourselves, when hearing the Declaration's heady rhetoric
of revolution and freedom or when it is foolishly cited as authority for populistic passions, always soberly to see the Constitution as the necessary forming, constraining, and sustaining system of government that made our revolution a blessing
to mankind and not a curse. In an age of rising expectations,
unbridled, utopian expectations, nothing could be more
useful than to look back to the sources of the sobriety that
spared us in our birth the disasters of revolution which have
befallen so many others.

I have not spoken tonight to any of the grave contemporary issues that tear at us and surfeit us with apparently
endless crisis. But whatever we each think must be done to
solve this or that problem, I call on you here to take your
guidance and bearing from that double star of undiminished
magnitude—the Declaration and the Constitution—which in
two great exertions of political sentiment and intellect burst
forth from this place.

PAUL G. KAUPER

The Higher Law and the Rights of Man in a Revolutionary Society

Delievered in Old North Church, Boston, Massachusetts

on November 7, 1973

The American Revolution was both radical and conservative. It asserted the right of people to revolt against established authority. It declared that government derives its authority from popular consent. Its central document proclaimed the radical idea that all men are created equal.

But the Revolution had its conservative overtones. It found its intellectual justification in ideas and principles with long established historical foundations. It had its roots in English legal and political institutions and in a body of thought—theological, moral and philosophic—which had universal dimensions. Old and essentially conservative ideas and traditions were harnessed to the cause of revolution. In turn they laid the foundation for a new constitutionalism which has survived because it has a capacity for change and yet remains loyal to the ancient truths that have given continuity to the system.

It was no accident that men trained in law played prominent roles in the revolutionary struggle and the subsequent transfomation from a confederation to a federal union. Constitutional thinking was a key support in the intellectual structure which undergirded the American Revolution. Central to this thinking was the concept of the "higher law," to which ultimate recourse could be made in judging the validity of ordinary enactments. Two principal components merged to shape this concept. One was the idea of natural law and the corollary idea of natural rights. The other was the tradition of the English common law as embodying a system of justice founded on right and reason. Natural law and natural right on the one hand, and the view of the common law as basic and fundamental law on the other, were twin notions that fitted together naturally to produce the idea of "higher law" that emerged as a powerful force not only in supporting the claim of the colonists but in laying the foundation of the American constitutional system.[1]

I

The idea of a natural law that is transcendent, that has divine sanction, that epitomizes wisdom, truth and morality, and to which positive law is subject had its origins in classical antiquity. During the Middle Ages natural law found its classical theological exposition in the _Summa_ of St. Thomas Aquinas, which was the basis of the Church's juridical and political thinking and which came to be identified with large claims of ecclesiastical authority. Later came the writings of

[1] On this point, see Edward S. Corwin, _The "Higher Law" Background of American Constitutional Law_ (Ithaca, N.Y.: Cornell University Press, 1955).

For a survey of the lineage of natural law and natural rights thinking, see John C. H. Wu, _Fountain of Justice: A Study in the Natural Law_ (New York: Sheed and Ward, 1955). For concise treatments, see Corwin, _The "Higher Law" Background of American Constitutional Law_, and M. Cappelletti, _Judicial Review in the Contemporary World_ (Indianapolis: Bobbs-Merrill Co., 1971), pp. 25-43.

On natural rights generally, see C. J. Antieau, _Rights of Our Fathers_ (Coiner, Virginia: Vienna Publications, 1968), and "Natural Rights and the Founding Fathers—The Virginians," _Washington and Lee Law Review_, vol. 17 (1960), p. 43; J. Maritain, _The Rights of Man and Natural Law_ (London: The Centenary Press, 1944); J. C. Murray, _The Problem of Religious Freedom_ (Westminster, Maryland: The Newman Press, 1965).

Puffendorf, Grotius, Vattel and others which upheld the law of nature in laying the foundation for the law of nations. The Enlightenment gave new impetus to natural law thinking in the Western world and particularly in England from where in turn it influenced the American colonies. The natural law of the Enlightenment, while essentially humanistic and not to be identified with the natural law of the Church, which rests on revelation, nevertheless carried the imprimatur of deistic thinking. But it was John Locke, in his *Second Treatise on Civil Government*, who perhaps more than any other single person articulated the ideas of natural law that were influential in shaping American constitutional thinking.

Equally influential was the coupling of natural law with the idea of natural rights. The view that man is a creature of God, reflects the divine wisdom, enjoys the liberty to use his natural faculties and may assert a freedom against the arbitrary exercise of authority was a natural corollary of a transcendent law of reason that emphasized truth and morality. These rights were not created by law but were recognized and sanctioned by it: they were antecedent to positive law, and the law's function was to preserve and protect them.

This idea of natural rights was a basic ingredient in the thinking of the American colonists. Speaking for the Supreme Court in 1963, Mr. Justice Clark said: "the fact that the Founding Fathers believed devotedly that there was a God and that the unalienable rights of man were rooted in Him is clearly evidenced in their writings, from the Mayflower Compact to the Constitution itself."[2] The writings and speeches of the Founding Fathers abounded in expressions of the idea that men enjoyed basic freedoms which were the gift of God and were therefore immutable and unalienable. James Otis, defending the rights of the colonists, said that if the charter privileges of the colonists were disregarded or revoked, there still remained "the natural, inherent, and inseparable rights of men and citizens."[3] John

[2] School District of Abington Township v. Schempp, 374 U.S. 203 at 213 (1963).
[3] J. Otis, *The Rights of the British Colonies Asserted and Proved* (pamphlet privately printed in Boston, 1764), quoted in Adams,

Adams spoke of "rights antecedent to all earthly government, rights that cannot be repealed or restrained by human laws—rights derived from the great Legislator of the universe."[4] In a writing which preceded the Declaration of Independence, Jefferson asserted that "The God who gave life gave us liberty at the same time."[5] He also said that "our right to life, liberty, the use of our faculties, the pursuit of happiness is not left to the feeble and sophistical investigations of reason, but is impressed on the sense of every man. We do not claim these under the charter of kings or legislators, but under the King of kings."[6] George Mason identified natural rights as "the sacred rights of human nature."[7] Writing in 1774, Alexander Hamilton declared: "the sacred rights of mankind . . . are written, as with a sunbeam, in the whole volume of human nature, by the hand of the divinity itself, and can never be erased or obscured by mortal power."[8] Indeed, it is fair to say that, for the Founding Fathers, it was the idea of natural rights rather than rights developed at the common law which furnished the undergirding for the revolutionary movement.[9] King and Parliament had violated these rights and therefore the colonists were morally justified in asserting their independence.

These ideas found their classical expression at Jefferson's hands in the great language of the Declaration of Independence:

> When in the course of human events, it becomes necessary for one people to dissolve the political bands which have connected them with another, and to assume

---

Life and Works (Boston: Little, Brown and Company 1850–56), vol. 10, p. 293.

[4] John Adams, *Life and Works*, vol. 3, pp. 448–464.

[5] Thomas Jefferson, "Summary View," in *Papers*, ed. J. P. Boyd (Princeton: Princeton University Press, 1950), vol. 1, p. 135.

[6] Thomas Jefferson, *Works*, ed. Ford (New York and London: G. P. Putnam's Sons, 1904–05), p. 66.

[7] Helen Hill, *George Mason, Constitutionalist* (Cambridge, Mass.: Harvard University Press, 1938), p. 249.

[8] Alexander Hamilton, *Works*, ed. Henry C. Lodge (New York and London: G. P. Putnam's Sons, 1885–86), vol. 1, p. 108.

[9] Antieau, *Rights of Our Fathers*, pp. 191–192.

among the powers of the earth, the separate and equal station to which the laws of nature and of nature's God entitle them, a decent respect to the opinions of mankind requires that they should declare the causes which impel them to the separation.

We hold these truths to be self-evident, that all men are created equal, that they are endowed by their Creator with certain unalienable rights, that among these are life, liberty and the pursuit of happiness. . . .

The document speaks of "the law of nature and of nature's God," says that "all men are created equal" and are endowed by their Creator with "unalienable rights." Jefferson's preference for the phrase "the law of nature and of nature's God," rather than for "natural law," is a characteristic expression of deistic thinking. It is significant that he invokes an ultimate divine source of moral law and of natural rights. The appeal is to the divine law that governs men and their institutions and that is the source of the equality of men and of the rights which belong to them as creatures of God. This was the foundation for the Declaration's reasoned discourse on the grievances of the colonists and on their right to declare their independence of English rule. Resting its case on natural law and natural rights, the Declaration remains an abiding affirmation of the higher law to which men and their governments are subject.

A further line of natural law thought entering into the main stream of American constitutionalism is found in the theological and political contributions that stemmed from the Protestant Reformation and were given their most effective expression by the Puritans and Presbyterians. The idea of the two kingdoms (both under God), the necessity for law as a restraint on evil and on the abuse of power, the idea of civic righteousness, the combination of individualism and social conscience, the emphasis on the charter as basic law, the notion of limited power, and the commitment to democracy and majority rule helped shape not only the concept but also the substance of the higher law. They provided justification for revolt against established authority, and furnished an important strand of thought for the fabric of American constitutionalism.[10]

The contribution of common law tradition to the idea of higher law was equally impressive. The intellectual leaders of the colonies well understood the rights of Englishmen as they had been hammered out on the anvil of experience. Lawyers had been nurtured in Blackstone. They were well versed in John Locke. James Otis, in denouncing the infamous writs of assistance, demonstrated his intimacy with the English precedents that supported the freedom from unreasonable search and seizure. More important, however, than the specific contents of the common law and the rights that grew within its protection was the process and authority it claimed. A system hammered out on the anvil of pragmatic experience, embodying the rule of reason, relying on precedent for its development, and fortified by documents (beginning with Magna Carta) that resulted from constitutional crises and attested the rights of Englishmen, it acquired at the hand of lawyers and judges a concreteness and toughness which inspired respect, commanded authority, and gave direction to English constitutional development. Most important, in elevating the role of reason and emphasizing the central role of the judges, it became a symbol of a fundamental law that achieved justice, articulated and protected the rights of Englishmen, and served as a limitation against abuse of power. For Englishmen it epitomized the rule of law. Rulers were subject to it. Bracton had said that the king was "under God and under the law."[11] Sir Edward Coke, the preeminent prophet of the common law who had led the fight against the Crown, who went back to Magna Carta for his inspiration, and who was a champion of English right, found "common right and reason" to be the genius of English law and liberties. Indeed,

[10] See P. Miller, *Errand Into the Wilderness* (Cambridge, Mass: The Belknap Press of Harvard University, 1956), pp. 142–150; also Corwin, *The "Higher Law" Background of American Constitutional Law*, pp. 61–77.

[11] Henry Bracton, *Bracton on the Laws and Customs of England*, Samuel Thorne and George Woodbine, eds. (Cambridge, Mass.: The Belknap Press of Harvard University, 1968), vol. 2, p. 33; original title: *De Legibus et Consuetudinibus Angliae*.

Coke declared that "when an Act of Parliament is against common right or reason . . . the common law will control it and adjudge such Act to be void."[12] Thus common law became identified with a higher law, and a powerful tool was forged for asserting the supremacy of the law and the role of the judges in interpreting and applying it.

Great documents produced in time of crisis have added strength to the common law tradition. Out of Magna Carta, wrested by the barons from King John, had come the idea that men could not be deprived of life, liberty, or property except in accordance with the law of the land—an idea which later found expression in the notion of due process of law, an enduring English contribution to constitutional thinking. The Petition of Right (1628) and the Bill of Rights (1689) affirmed the basic rights of Englishmen. The written document, a symbol and a beacon to which men could appeal in later generations, assumed its place in the higher law tradition. Following in this great tradition, the colonists also looked to a written document wherein they publicly proclaimed their rights and gave a reasoned statement in support of the decision to assert their right to self-government.

Acceptance of natural law and natural rights, coupled with reverence for the common law as itself embodying the law of reason and for historic documents declaring right, combined powerfully to establish the "higher law" thinking which permeated the Revolution and laid the foundation for a remarkable constitutional development. Indeed, American constitutional history, the crises it has witnessed, and the development which has ensued can be viewed as an explication of the higher law.

The constitutions adopted by the individual states incorporated ideas that were a distillate of the experience and reasoning implicit in the natural law and its processes: the people as the source of power, the right of self-determination, the right of the people to vote and to participate in the government through their elected representatives, the rule of law,

[12] Dr. Bonham's Case, 8 Coke 118a (1610).

the charter as a limitation on power, the separation of powers
as a means of checking abuse of authority, the inherent rights
of the citizen, and the role of the independent judiciary in
protecting the citizens and asserting the supremacy of the
law.[13] Underlying it all was the central notion that government derived its authority from the people and was subject
therefore to limitations imposed and liberties reserved. The
new state constitutions contained "declarations of right."
The use of the word "declarations" warrants emphasis. The
constitutions did not create these rights; rather they declared
rights that were derived from what was stated in the Declaration of Independence to be the self-evident truth—that all
men are endowed by their Creator with certain unalienable
rights including the right to life, liberty, and the pursuit of
happiness.

The adoption of state constitutions preceded the adoption
and ratification of the federal Constitution drafted at
Philadelphia in 1787. Unlike the Declaration, which was a
political document, the Constitution was a carefully drafted
legal document. Resting on the authority of the people and
premised on republican principles of government, the Constitution defined and allocated authority. Its carefully devised system of checks and balances, implementing the separation of powers, was premised on the assumption, as
Madison noted, that men are not angels, that the grant of
power invites abuse, and that restraints are necessary to curb
its exercise.[14] Those limitations on power epitomized the
rule of law. When faithfully enforced by an independent
judiciary, they constitute the bulwark for protection of the
liberties of the citizen.

Noticeably absent in the Constitution, however, was a
declaration of rights. We need not rehearse all of the historical factors leading to this omission except to note that those

[13] For texts of the early state constitutions, see R. L. Perry and
J. C. Cooper, *Sources of Our Liberties* (Chicago: American Bar
Foundation, 1959).

[14] *The Federalist*, number 51 (Everman's Library Edition, 1911),
p. 264. Charles Beard ascribed this paper to Madison; see Charles
A. Beard, *The Enduring Federalist* (Garden City: Doubleday &
Co., 1948), p. 210.

who played a leading role in the drafting thought a bill of rights unnecessary because they did not find it conceivable that the scope of the federal powers would permit an intrusion into the rights reserved to the people or to the states. This view, however, did not go unchallenged. To meet the challenge, the first ten articles of amendment, commonly known as the Bill of Rights, were adopted shortly after the Constitution itself went into effect. Specific rights are guaranteed in the first eight amendments. The great freedoms are there—beginning with freedom of religion, speech, press and assembly, and petition for the redress of grievances. But significantly the Ninth Amendment declared that the enumeration of these privileges and rights should not be construed to deny or disparage others retained by the people. This was a clear expression that the rights set forth in the Bill of Rights were not created by the Bill of Rights but were simply declared there. The Ninth Amendment implicitly embodies natural rights philosophy.

Thus the stage was set for the great American experiment in government under a written charter. Two great principles of that government received their classic exposition by John Marshall in his opinion in *Marbury* v. *Madison*: the Constitution is the fundamental law of the land, and it is distinctively the function of the judiciary to give this law its authoritative interpretation. These two principles of paramount law and the judicial function in interpreting this law are unique aspects of American constitutional development. Their relationship to the theory of natural law and natural right is readily apparent. Once the people have reduced their thinking on the fundamental structure of government and on their reserved rights into a written document, the ideas of natural law and natural rights tend to merge into this document. The document then becomes the symbol of the higher law of the land. The veneration popularly accorded the Constitution amply demonstrates this tendency in the popular mind. The higher law acquires concreteness through a process whereby an independent judicial tribunal interprets the law in a final and authoritative way so that natural law and natural rights are happily absorbed into positive law through the process of empiric adjudication. Indeed, for some, the Constitution thereby acquires even a divine sanction.

Care must be taken, however, in identifying the Constitution with a transcendent natural law and the Bill of Rights with natural rights. Basic principles expressed in a constitution can certainly be identified with a body of universal and enduring ideas that reflect reasoned conclusions on human nature, the function of government, and the institutions designed to channel and limit power. But the particular institutional arrangements worked out at the Philadelphia convention, as a response to immediate historical experience and in a number of instances as a compromise of opposing ideas, should not be viewed as the ultimate expression of these principles. Indeed, the framers, while hoping to establish "a constitution intended to endure for ages to come and consequently to be adapted to the various crises of human affairs,"[15] recognized that specific institutional arrangements might be transient when they provided a mechanism for amending the Constitution.

An even more important consideration is that natural law, however conceived and whatever its authority, must necessarily remain outside the Constitution and not be confused with it. Ultimate values, goals to be achieved, principles relevant to new movements in national life, ideas of freedom, right, justice, and morality have their inception in theological, philosophical, moral, and social thinking which transcends the Constitution. The validity of any constitution may be judged by recourse to the higher law.

One constitutional scholar has observed that the natural rights on which there was the largest measure of agreement among the Virginians were freedom of conscience, freedom of communication, the right to be free from arbitrary laws, the rights of assembly and petition, the property right, and the right of self-government.[16] To these may be added equality in the enjoyment of right. These were rights inherent in

[15] John Marshall, in McCulloch v. Maryland, 17 U.S. (4 Wheat.) 316, at 415 (1819).
[16] Antieau, "Natural Rights and the Founding Fathers—The Virginians," pp. 45–46.

the idea of man as a moral and rational creature entitled to the full enjoyment of his faculties. Not all of these rights were expressly captured in the Bill of Rights. On the other hand, some rights receiving positive recognition, such as the right to trial by jury, can hardly be called natural rights. They are ancillary rights that help to protect natural rights.[17]

That there was still a natural law outside the Constitution was made manifest in the great struggle over the slavery issue. Jefferson had boldly declared in the Declaration of Independence that all men are created equal and that this is self-evident, as are those unalienable rights with which all men are endowed. It became painfully evident that this grand assertion could not be reconciled with an institution whereby one race held another in subjection for forced labor.[18] In the sharp and bitter struggles over the question of extending the institution of slavery to new territories and over the abolitionists' demands that all slavery be abolished, slavery emerged as the nation's great moral issue.

The abolitionists could point to the Declaration of Independence as stating a self-evident natural right on the part of all men to freedom and to equal treatment. The Constitution itself had made a nodding concession to the slavery problem in permitting the termination of the slave trade after 1808 and in fixing the formula for apportioning seats in Congress; but it also imposed a duty to return runaway slaves to owners. Morever, in the celebrated Dred Scott decision of 1857, the Supreme Court went so far as to say that the slave-owner had a constitutionally protected property interest in his slaves, so that for the law to deprive him of that interest when he took a slave into free territory was itself a deprivation of property without due process of law. But a judicial decision that rested on considerations incompatible with basic moral concepts could not in the end command respect. Abraham Lincoln said that the Dred Scott decision was morally wrong and should be changed. William Seward, in his

[17] Antieau, *Rights of Our Fathers*, pp. 103–104.
[18] See M. D. Howe, "Federalism and Civil Rights," in Cox, Howe and Wiggins, *Civil Rights, the Constitution and the Courts* (Cambridge, Mass.: Harvard University Press, 1967), pp. 30–55.

sharp criticism of the Court, declared that there is a higher law than the Constitution. In fact, the issue of slavery, unsolvable by judicial or political means, required four years of bloody conflict for its resolution.

II

Out of the Civil War came a radically revised constitutional order and an extraordinary increase in those rights accorded federal protection. The Thirteenth, Fourteenth, and Fifteenth Amendments were designed to give constitutional status and protection to the former black slaves and rested on the idea of human equality that the Declaration had declared to be a natural right. Viewed from the perspective of general constitutional theory, the Fourteenth Amendment had the widest and most pervasive significance. The provision that no state should deprive any person of life, liberty or property without due process of law or deny to any person the equal protection of the laws defined ideas of rights which were readily identifiable with natural rights. The Fourteenth Amendment marked a revolution in the protection of rights and led to what we may call the nationalization of right. In the hands of the judiciary, it became a tool for implementing the grand assertion of the Declaration of Independence that all men should have equal opportunities to enjoy life, liberty, and the pursuit of happiness.

Notwithstanding a very modest beginning in its interpretation of the Fourteenth Amendment, the Supreme Court eventually embarked upon a use of the due process clause which made it into an extraordinary tool for reviewing state laws that might impair what the Court came to call fundamental rights protected under the rubrics of life, liberty and property. In the process the Court formulated the "fundamental rights" interpretation of due process.[19] Although it

---

[19] For a brief review of this development, see Kauper, "Penumbras, Peripheries, Emanations, Things Fundamental and Things Forgotten: The Griswold Case," *Michigan Law Review*, vol. 64 (1965), p. 235.

never succeeded in arriving at a particularly illuminating definition of fundamental rights, it did try in various ways to define them. They were the rights that "are of the very essence of a scheme of ordered liberty,"[20] that are founded in "those fundamental principles of liberty and justice which lie at the base of all our civil and political institutions,"[21] that are "rooted in the traditions and conscience of our people,"[22] that are "essential to the orderly pursuit of happiness by free men."[23] Simply to repeat these phrases is to make clear that the judicial conception of fundamental rights draws its inspiration from natural rights tradition.[24]

For a period of about fifty years the Court employed the due process clause chiefly as a vehicle for invalidating legislation found to infringe arbitrarily upon economic rights such as the freedom of contract and the use of property. But the experience in this period, despite the perversion of natural rights thinking to serve ends inimical to legitimate public interests, had an enduring value because of the Court's identification of the due process clause with fundamental rights and because of its insistence that arbitrary or unreasonable restrictions on these rights resulted in a deprivation without due process of law.[25] During the New Deal the

[20] Palko v. Connecticut, 302 U.S. 319 at 325 (1937).
[21] Hebert v. Louisiana, 277 U.S. 312 at 312 (1926).
[22] Snyder v. Massachusetts, 291 U.S. 97 at 105 (1934).
[23] Meyer v. Nebraska, 262 U.S. 390 at 399 (1923).
[24] In his dissenting opinion in the Slaughterhouse Cases, 83 U.S. (16 Wallace) 36 at 105 (1873), Justice Field declared that the Fourteenth Amendment was intended "to give practical effect to the declaration of 1776 of inalienable rights, rights which are the gift of the Creator, which the law does not confer but only recognizes."
[25] It is worth noting that during this same period, the Court invalidated state laws which prohibited the teaching in public schools in any language other than the English language, Meyer v. Nebraska, 262 U.S. 390 (1922); which required parents to send their children to public schools, Pierce v. Society of Sisters, 268 U.S. 510 (1925); which unduly restricted freedom of the press, Near v. Minnesota 283 U.S. 697 (1931); and which violated freedom of assembly, De Jonge v. Oregon, 299 U.S. 353 (1937). It also laid the foundation for the fairness doctrine in applying the due process clause to protect the accused. See Moore v. Dempsey, 261 U.S. 86 (1923).

Court abandoned this emphasis upon economic liberty as a fundamental right and turned its attention toward the protection of the individual against arbitrary procedures and the protection of personal and societal freedoms, including the freedom of speech, press, assembly and religion.[26]

A great controversy within the Court has turned on the question of whether the due process clause should be interpreted to incorporate within its protection, as a limitation on the power of the states, the specific guarantees of the first eight amendments originally designated as restrictions on the federal government only. Some members of the Court held that fundamental rights were not necessarily those identified in the Bill of Rights but only those of a very basic character, more akin to natural rights.[27] Other justices, Mr. Justice Black among them, argued that the Bill of Rights set forth the ultimate wisdom of the Declaration of Rights and that any recognition of fundamental rights must at least begin with the first eight amendments, and perhaps even be limited to them. In a notable dissenting opinion, Mr. Justice Black attacked the fundamental rights interpretation of the due process clause as it had evolved historically in the Court's decisions. First, he said that the Fourteenth Amendment's original purpose was to make the Bill of Rights apply to the states. Second, he contended that the Court's use of the fundamental rights theory was premised upon an application of the idea of natural law, an idea which he characterized as "an incongruous excrescence on our Constitution."[28]

This latter observation is worth particular attention. It is evident that Justice Black was a positivist in his jurisprudential thinking and that his remark reflected the general decline of natural law and natural rights thinking in America. This decline can be traced to the rise of science and secular

[26] For a review, see Kauper, *Frontiers of Constitutional Liberty* (Ann Arbor, Mich.: University of Michigan Law School, 1956), p. 21 et seq.

[27] For a review, see Justice Cardozo's opinion in Palko v. Connecticut, 302 U.S. 319 (1937), and Justice Frankfurter's concurring opinion in Adamson v. California, 332 U.S. 46 at 59 (1947).

[28] See Justice Black's dissent in Adamson v. California, 332 U.S. 46 at 68 et seq. (1947).

humanism in the latter part of the nineteenth century. The idea of a transcendent natural or moral law then fell into disrepute. With this began the era of positivism in American jurisprudence, well epitomized in the writing and opinions of Mr. Justice Holmes. In the eyes of the positivist, law is viewed in historical and humanistic terms. To put it in constitutional terms, rights are significant only as they find concrete expression in the historic document. There are no rights outside the Constitution, and the business of the law is simply to develop concrete solutions to concrete problems based on the application of the text as informed by history and reason.

Justice Black's picture of natural law in his dissent in the *Adamson* case was particularly unfortunate because it disregarded the honored place that natural law thinking had had in the early days of the republic and had long enjoyed in the American legal tradition. To label natural law "an excrescence on our Constitution" was to be particularly insensitive to a significant part of American constitutional development.

Justice Black led a movement within the Court to divorce the Court's interpretation of due process from the idea that there were fundamental rights not identified in the Bill of Rights. For the most part he was successful—at least in his insistence that the express guarantees of the first eight amendments should be recognized as fundamental rights. But it is illusory to suppose that, even so, the Court has abandoned natural rights thinking. An examination of its opinions shows that the result is rarely dictated by the explicit language of the text. Rather it stems from a reasoned interpretation illuminated but not controlled by history and inspired by an understanding of ultimate values which are at most implicit in the constitutional order.

Examination of the Court's decisions in recent years makes it clear that the values of a democratic society have emerged as most important—religious liberty and freedom of conscience, the basic freedoms of expression, the rights attached to self-government and the citizen's participation in it, the protection of the individual against arbitrary restraint, his freedom to pursue his own way and cultivate his faculties, and the protection of minorities against invidious discrimination. These are readily equated with natural right categories. The emphasis on these aspects of liberty represents a choice of values by the Supreme Court, values which turn on the worth and dignity of the person and on the institutions and procedures that are unique to a democratic society. We come back, then, to what perhaps is the most fundamental aspect of natural right thinking: that man as a creature of God is entitled to be treated with dignity and respect, that he has unalienable rights, and that government is instituted to secure these rights.

III

Today we are in the midst of a great social revolution. Old ideas, conventions, institutions, and restraints are challenged. A fierce new individualism with large claims to personal liberty is being asserted. The old morality seems to have been discredited, and a new permissiveness is dominant. A parallel and related development is a new egalitarianism, manifesting itself in the movement to end all discrimination based on race, color, religion, national ancestry, sex, age, and economic status. We are so close to these movements that we are likely to be blinded to their revolutionary and even radical character. A striking aspect is the legitimizing of these movements by constitutional interpretation. Constitutional thinking has been accommodated to the great movements of our day and in turn has contributed to them.

Despite the efforts of some justices to discredit the natural rights doctrine, it has recently reasserted itself in an interesting and dramatic way. In its significant 1965 decision in *Griswold* v. *Connecticut,* the Supreme Court reaffirmed a fundamental rights interpretation of due process of law by finding implicit in the concept of liberty a notion of personal privacy that includes the privacy of marriage and of the family relationship. Here the Court held invalid a Connecticut statute which forbade the use of contraceptives by married couples. The case presented some illuminating insights into the thinking of the justices.[29]

Mr. Justice Douglas—who shares with Justice Black an abhorrence of natural rights thinking because he associates it with the laissez-faire philosophy of earlier years—tried valiantly but not very persuasively to link the right of privacy, nowhere mentioned expressly in the Constitution, with the rights expressly stated in the Bill of Rights. Mr. Justice Goldberg dealt with the matter in a more forthright way. He recognized the rights pertaining to the marital estate, to home, and to family as fundamental in character and held that the Ninth Amendment to the Constitution permitted the courts to recognize and protect other rights besides those mentioned in the Bill of Rights—a proposition which of course has support in the long history of the fundamental rights interpretation of the Constitution. Justices Harlan and White similarly rested their case on the idea that the privacy of married life was a fundamental right which cannot be invaded except to serve a substantial public interest. Clearly a majority of the Court was reaching toward the idea of rights existing outside the Constitution.

Notwithstanding the dissent and Justice Douglas's protestations, *Griswold* v. *Connecticut* marked a significant revival of natural rights thinking, whatever the formal argument employed by the majority. It has been followed by recent cases—specifically, *Roe* v. *Wade* and *Doe* v. *Bolton*—where the Court has found that the liberty secured by the Fourteenth Amendment protects the right of a female to abort a foetus within the first six months of pregnancy. Our interest in this case here centers on the Court's use of a concept of right not explicit or even implicit in the Constitution in order to strike down a state statute. Building on the right of privacy developed in *Griswold* v. *Connecticut*, the Court said that it was immaterial whether the right of privacy was derived from the fundamental rights interpretation of the due process clause or from the Ninth Amendment or from some peripheral aspect of a Bill of Rights guarantee. This

[29] See Kauper, "Penumbras, Peripheries, Emanations."

decision strikingly affirms the classic notion that the liberty secured under the due process clause protects the so-called fundamental rights which the Court articulates by natural rights reasoning. These decisions have gone far to provide constitutional legitimacy for the current claims that a person has a constitutional freedom to the pursuit of happiness subject only to restrictions designed to protect compelling public interests. This is the Declaration of Independence all over again.

The vitality and persistence of fundamental rights thinking in the interpretation of the higher law is strikingly demonstrated in the interpretation of the equal protection clause. Despite early intimations that only the newly emancipated blacks would come within the protection of this clause, its special use to protect the black was virtually forgotten after the 1896 decision in *Plessy* v. *Ferguson* upholding the "separate but equal" doctrine. The great revitalization of equal protection came in 1954 in *Brown* v. *Board of Education* when the Court held that compulsory racial segregation in public schools resulted in unlawful discrimination against black children. Chief Justice Warren's opinion on the effect of segregation upon the life of the black child makes clear that legally imposed segregation could not be reconciled with the moral imperative underlying the equal protection idea. The Court was giving constitutional flesh and blood to the premise of the Declaration of Independence. But *Brown* v. *Board of Education* was only the beginning of a new chapter on equality.

Starting with the 1964 one-man one-vote decision of *Reynolds* v. *Sims*, the Court branched out in all directions in revitalizing the equal protection guarantee. In branching out, the Court has employed a new method of analysis. Classification must be subject to careful scrutiny by the Court if it rests on so-called suspect criteria or if the effect is to impair the enjoyment of a fundamental personal right. Discrimination falling into either of these two categories can be tolerated only if required by some compelling public interest. Thus discrimination based not only on race, color and religion, but on national ancestry, alien status, economic status, and illegitimacy of birth has been judicially condemned. The Supreme Court is now engaged in the process of accommodating the equal protection idea to the movement for liberation of the female sex from discrimination long sanctioned in law and practice.[30]

The movement in favor of equality is instructive for two reasons. First, it gives further constitutional sanction to that democratization of American life so well portrayed by Boorstin in his recent volume.[31] It also reflects an increasing awareness of the ethnic, racial, and religious diversity of America's pluralistic society. The new insistence on equality, which lays open to inquiry distinctions long tolerated in the law, and the new liberty, with its assertion of personal identity and freedom of expression, are responses to strong social currents of our day. Second, the revival in judicial opinions of the idea of fundamental right is a tribute to the persistence and vitality of natural rights thinking.

The intellectual process central to natural law thinking has a vitality of its own. It is indigenous to the judicial process under a written constitution. When the Court says that there must be a compelling public interest to warrant the restriction of a fundamental right or to justify discrimination resting on a suspect basis or impinging on a fundamental right, the Court is employing its own reasoning process to identify the right, to weigh the public interest, and to arrive at some accommodation. The higher law of the Constitution is thus embodied in the overriding judicial reasoning to which legislation is subject.

Why do some justices of the Court still feel obliged to file

[30] For specific cases, see: national ancestry—Takahashi v. Fish & Game Commission, 334 U.S. 410 (1948); alien status—Graham v. Richardson, 403 U.S. 365 (1971); economic status—Douglas v. California, 372 U.S. 353 (1963), Harper v. Virginia Board of Elections, 383 U.S. 663 (1966), and Tate v. Short, 401 U.S. 395 (1971); illegitimacy—Levy v. Louisiana, 391 U.S. 68 (1968), and Weber v. Aetna Casualty & Surety Co., 406 U.S. 164 (1972); and women's rights—Reed v. Reed, 404 U.S. 71 (1971); Frontiero v. Richardson, 411 U.S. 677 (1973).

[31] Daniel J. Boorstin, *The Americans: The Democratic Experience* (New York: Random House, Inc., 1973).

formal disclaimers against natural right thinking in the exposition of the Constitution? It is understandable that the
general revulsion against ecclesiastical authority and the natural law associated with it, along with the decline in religious
thinking that accompanied the new secularism in the last
century, may have made the idea of natural right unpalatable
to some. It is equally understandable that the idea of natural
right became suspect when harnessed to support a laissez-
faire philosophy. Yet it is true also that the whole doctrine of
natural right, whether supported by religious or secular considerations, has had a long history in the thinking of the
Western world. Rooted in antiquity, it was widely accepted
at the time of the American Revolution, and the essential
processes behind it have continued to be vital forces in constitutional interpretation. Indeed it is by constant recourse to
these fundamental rights, however portrayed, that the Constitution has been accommodated to new strains of thought and
new developments in our national life.

It is sometimes believed that natural right thinking is necessarily identified with a fixed body of dogma that defines
natural rights so as to foreclose progressive application. This,
of course, is not the case. Natural right thinking is dynamic,
creative, and adaptable to new situations. As the late John
Courtney Murray pointed out, the old idea of religious liberty limited to tolerance had its source in a different day and
the new idea of religious liberty is a response to the new individual and social consciousness of our day.[32] It is also—one
should add—a response to the pluralistic character of our society.

The argument is made, as Justice Black has made it, that
unless the Court limits itself to the text of the Constitution
it will become lost in subjective speculation. This, too, is a
misconception. Natural right is not what any justice happens
at the time to believe it ought to be. It is rather the result of
rational discourse and dialogue based on the experience of
the race and on fundamental philosophic and moral consideration regarding the nature of man and his relation to society. One need only look at the Universal Declaration of

[32] J. C. Murray, *The Problem of Religious Freedom.*

Human Rights adopted by the United Nations in 1948[33] or at the preamble to the European Convention on Human Rights and Fundamental Freedoms of 1950[34] to see that appeals to rights inhering in the dignity of the person and to the freedoms essential for a democratic society are still very much the mode and that the consensus reflected in these documents establishes an objective basis for the formulations of basic rights.

IV

We have a strong constitutional system. It has adapted itself to the extraordinary transformations in American political, economic, and social life, has both inspired and weathered

[33] The U.N. declaration reads in part:

Whereas recognition of the inherent dignity and of the equal and inalienable rights of all members of the human family is the foundation of freedom, justice and peace in the world. [Preamble]

All human beings are born free and equal in dignity and rights. They are endowed with reason and conscience and should act towards one another in a spirit of brotherhood. [Article I]

For the text, see *Human Right: A Compilation of International Instruments of the United Nations* (New York: United Nations, 1967), p. 1.

[34] The preamble to the convention reads in part:

Considering the Universal Declaration of Human Rights proclaimed by the General Assembly of the United Nations on 10th December 1948; . . .

Reaffirming their profound belief in those Fundamental Freedoms which are the foundation of Justice and peace in the world and are best maintained on the one hand by an effective political democracy and on the other by a common understanding and observance of the Human Rights upon which they depend;

Being resolved, as the governments of European countries which are likeminded and have a common heritage of political traditions, ideals, freedom and the rule of law to take the first steps for the collective enforcement of certain of the Rights stated in the Universal Declaration; . . .

For the text, see 213 United Nations Treaty Series 221 (1955).

silent and peaceable revolutions, and has created the condition of a free, open, and pluralistic society. The Founding Fathers built better than they knew. Asserting the right of revolution, they laid the foundation for a society that provides peaceful means for growth and change. We have a system of judicial review which safeguards the integrity of our constitutional system and protects basic rights against abuse and the tyranny of the majority. Probably in no other democratic country are the freedoms for which the colonists were willing to sacrifice and die more fully protected. But, having grown accustomed to the constitutional protection of natural rights and having become self-indulgent in their enjoyment, we too easily forget that belief in natural rights helped spark the revolutionary movement. It is indeed good that we use the Bicentennial to refresh our appreciation of our freedoms and to capture again the excitement, daring, and devotion of the patriots who challenged authority when they threw the tea into Boston harbor, who responded to Paul Revere's midnight ride with the confrontations at Lexington and Concord.

This is not to say that all is well with the system. I suggested earlier that the idea of right is not static and that part of our current problem is to address the idea of right to our current needs. In this day of sophisticated electronic surveillance and data storage and retrieval, the newly formulated right of privacy requires recognition and implementation. At a time of proliferating regulation in a complex urban society, the liberty of the individual to maintain some degree of identity and to pursue a path of self-respect requires us to be skeptical of a paternalism whereby Big Brother peeks over the citizen's shoulder to tell him what is good for him. The unrestrained exploitation of our resources and the debasement of the environment require a recognition that all citizens together have a natural right to enjoy their common resources and environment, a right more compelling than the freedom once claimed in the name of laissez-faire to plunder resources, pollute the air, and impair the amenities of living. The rights of all citizens regardless of race or color to equal opportunity for achievement, free from the blight of discrimination, are still only imperfectly realized. Equally important is the realization that the classic idea of natural right as restraint on government, so well captured in our system, is no longer adequate to the needs of a society where substantial pockets of poverty, hunger, disadvantage and want persist, notwithstanding the general state of affluence. Indeed, for those trapped in the web of our system, the responsibility of society to meet basic economic and social needs may be more significant than the traditional restraints designed to protect liberty against the abuse of power.

Equally important in this day of heightened international concern, a day marked by the tide of rising expectations of the have-not peoples, is a recognition that their rights and freedoms are inextricably entwined with ours. We can no longer indulge in a parochial view of our rights and interests, ignoring the responsibility for sharing our resources with others and for supporting their aspirations to the freedoms and satisfactions we claim for ourselves. The Declaration of Human Rights adopted by the United Nations, a declaration to which the United States is a party, is a ringing affirmation of the great words that *"all* men are created equal and endowed by their creator with certain unalienable rights."[35]

More troubling are symptoms of an uneasiness in American thought and life as we approach the nation's bicentennial and contemplate the nation's future. Pessimism and cynicism are widespread. Power has been shamefully abused by men who have wielded it free from a sense of moral or political responsibility. Illegal tactics directed to winning elections are an ugly blow at the integrity of the political process. The trustworthiness and credibility of the people's servants have been deeply eroded, with a resulting loss of faith in the whole political process. Extravagant campaign expenditures, financed by large contributions from those who have special interests to protect, undermine the freedom of elected representatives to serve the public interest. Freedom of the press too often becomes an excuse for distortion and manipulation of news, invasion of privacy, and intrusions into those judicial

[35] Emphasis supplied.

processes designed to maintain the conditions of a fair hearing for those charged with wrongdoing. Private groups—business, labor, interests of all kinds—are bastions of power which sometimes rival the government in the authority they exercise. The new freedom characterized by the sloughing off of old moral restraints finds expression in license and permissiveness. The new egalitarianism risks cheapening American life and culture and eroding the sense of excellence. The pursuit of materialistic gratifications, also claimed in the name of liberty, has dulled the conscience and impaired our vision of the enduring spiritual values that make a people great.

And so it appears to many that the spark ignited by the American Revolution, the vitality and lively expectations which guided the Founding Fathers, have been dimmed and corroded by selfishness, corruption, and anomie.

But we need not despair. Indeed, a healthful pessimism underlies the idea of a government of limited powers and the rule of law—the recognition of the evil in man and the need for restraints to check his abuse of power. Power does corrupt. This in itself is a basic premise of natural law and one which underlies our system. The basic checks and balances of our system are even more essential to the maintenance of freedom than the rights formally declared in the Constitution. The very fact that flagrant abuse of power has been uncovered and that the Congress is now reasserting its authority against extravagant claims of executive authority is itself evidence of the strength and resiliency of our system.

We have the means of curbing large concentrations of power, whether in the public or private sectors, if only we have the understanding and determination to do so. But, even more important, we have the resources of mind and spirit needed to cleanse our society of its grossness, its preoccupation with material ends—to recapture the dedication and fire which inspired the Revolution in order to inspire the revitalization of today's society.

The pessimism that is an important ingredient of our constitutional thinking is balanced by an optimism—a faith that men can work together to achieve common goals in a society held together by a sense of civil righteousness. This is the faith we must again cultivate. But later generations cannot endlessly harvest fruit from the trees others have planted and cultivated. There must be in our day a restoration of faith in the basic institutions that have served us so well and that constitute what Walter Lippmann has called the public philosophy. There must be continued vigilance in the nurture of ideas and institutions which are our higher law heritage. There must be renewed appreciation of our heritage of rights and freedoms and renewed insistence on the premises underlying the conception of natural right. There must be a restoration of integrity in the affairs of government, decency in public life, and civility and reasoned discourse in the great debate on issues of public concern. There must be sensitivity, compassion, and generosity in response to human needs. There must be self-restraint and responsibility in the exercise of freedom, lest freedom degenerate into licentiousness and anarchy. There must be an affirmation of the moral values which undergird the public order. There must be an assessment of our rights and liberties as more than negative restraints, as positive means for self-development and service to others. Freedom without purpose, discipline, and regard for the common good is self-destroying.

I have suggested that, in the end, the institutions we deem important and the significance of the rights we assert must rest upon some consensus in the public mind about the values we hold—upon the content of the contemporary natural law. I have further suggested that this consensus depends upon shared moral perceptions and understanding. Whether a nation can long survive without substantial consensus on overriding values is a question which invites serious discussion. There was a time when it could be said that we were a Christian nation, guided in regard to national values by the Christian ethic. That time is past. In our pluralistic society with its diverse religious elements no single religion can claim for itself a favored position in the law, and the law in turn may not reflect the views of a single religious community.

Where, if at all, can a basis be found for the moral consensus which is the heart of natural law? Historical tradition is important. The accepted views of nations are relevant. To others it may appear that the Constitution and the values it embodies constitute our moral consensus and that the Supreme Court serves the function of moulding and interpreting our higher law. But as I have stressed before, dangers lurk in the view that ultimate ideas of wisdom, justice and morality are embodied in a written legal instrument. The ultimate ideas and the transcendent values must, in their very nature, lie outside the Constitution, just as basic rights have their source outside the Constitution. It is a form of idol worship to see the Constitution as the expression of ultimate values in our nation's life.

Moreover, it is dangerous to rely on an institution—more particularly a tribunal of nine men—for the ultimate exposition of our national values. It is sometimes said that the Supreme Court is the conscience of the nation. This is specious. The Court cannot impose its notion of conscience without regard to the accepted moral values of the community. It can lead, but within limits. In the end its decision on ultimate values must be sustained by some higher law rooted in the common consciousness and understanding.

The current revolution, centering on the new freedoms and making extraordinary claims in the name of personal liberty, raises questions about the limits of this liberty and the organ responsible for determining these limits. While natural law supports a theory of natural rights, it also asserts man's social obligations so that one man's rights are limited by the rights of others and by important social interests, including those moral values which are rooted in the conscience and traditions of the people. Moreover, the legislative branch too has a voice in expressing the people's moral concern, and its expression of that concern should not be lightly disregarded by the courts. The abortion cases reflect the danger of having the Supreme Court assume the role, at the expense of the Congress, as the nation's conscience in determining important questions of public policy.

The conscience of the nation lies outside the Constitution and supports it. The beliefs rooted in common understanding are the stuff of a nation's aspiration and moral vision. Our hope of giving contemporary meaning to the higher law and the natural rights of man lies in the shaping of a common ethic which draws its inspiration from religious, moral, and philosophical sources, which is illuminated by history, fortified by the ringing affirmation of the great Declaration, and given concrete application through the reasoned discourse which is the hallmark of a great society.

ROBERT A. NISBET
The Social Impact of the Revolution

Delivered in Gaston Hall, Georgetown University,

Washington, D.C. on December 13, 1973

Was there in fact an American Revolution at the end of the
eighteenth century? I mean a revolution involving sudden,
decisive, and irreversible changes in social institutions,
groups, and traditions, in addition to the war of liberation
from England that we are more likely to celebrate.

Clearly, this is a question that generates much controversy.
There are scholars whose answer to the question is strongly
negative, and others whose affirmative answer is equally
strong. Indeed, ever since Edmund Burke's time there have
been students to declare that revolution in any precise sense
of the word did not take place—that in substance the American Revolution was no more than a group of Englishmen
fighting on distant shores for traditionally English political
rights against a government that had sought to exploit and
tyrannize. The essence, in other words, was a war of restitu-
tion and liberation, not revolution; the outcome, one set of
political governors replaced by another. This view is widespread in our time and is found as often among ideological
conservatives as among liberals and radicals.

At the opposite extreme is the view that a full-blown revolution did indeed take place. This is clearly what John Adams
believed: "The Revolution was in the minds and hearts of
people; a change in their religious sentiments, of their duties
and obligations. . . . This radical change in the principles,

opinions, sentiments, and affects of the people was the real American Revolution." And Samuel Adams, more radical in ideology and hence more demanding in defining a revolution, asked rhetorically, "Was there ever a revolution brought about, especially one so important as this, without great internal tumults and violent convulsions?"

If there was a genuine revolution in America we shall find it not in the sphere of ideological tractarianism—which, history demonstrates, may or may not yield actual revolution—but rather in the social sphere. The comparative study of revolution makes clear, I think, that the heart of each of the great modern revolutions is to be seen in the complex of authorities, functions, bonds, and allegiances which we define as social. More specifically, I refer to property, kinship, religion, and social class. I shall refer to this area, following the practice of many French historians of the modern area, as intermediate—that is, intermediate between individual and state.

Without exception, the major revolutions of modern history have had immense and sometimes devastating effects upon this intermediate area. Whether we follow Tocqueville and Taine in seeing centralization and collectivization of political power as the principal consequence of revolution, or more radical historians in seeing individual liberty and welfare as the chief consequence, it is invariably the ties rising from land, kindred, class, estate, and servitude of one kind or another that are at the heart of the matter. If there was indeed a revolution as well as a war of liberation in America at the end of the eighteenth century, we should find its evidences in this intermediate social sphere.

It is always useful to turn to comparative aspects of one's subject. Consider the French Revolution. Scholars may differ among themselves as to whether, in the final analysis, it was the individual with his rights and liberties or the political state with its centralized power and national solidarity that had the greater triumph. But what obviously is not subject to debate, what is unmistakably clear, is that the whole complex of social authorities, allegiances, and functions which are intermediate to individual and state, so largely the heritage of the medieval period, was vitally changed during the French Revolution. The real essence of this Revolution was not its reign of terror, formidable as that was, but the legislation enacted by successive revolutionary governments—legislation that profoundly affected the nobility, the traditional family, the corporate nature of property, the laws of primogeniture and entail, the place of religion in society, the guilds, and other elements of traditional society.

Allowing only for inevitable differences of detail and intensity, such changes in intermediate society are to be seen vividly in other modern revolutions—in some degree in the Puritan Revolution of seventeenth century England, in far greater degree in the Bolshevik Revolution in Russia, and in our own time in some of the New Nations in the non-Western world. Whether in Europe or in other places, modern patterns of social individualism and political unification, even collectivism, take their rise in revolutionary circumstances, in the impact of political power, upon this intermediate social sphere.

Now, it is worth stressing that this sphere is commonly feudal in nature when we find it being assaulted by the hammer blows of revolution, using the word "feudal" in its broadest sense. More than any other type of social organization, feudalism seems not only to invite but to succumb to revolution. I am inclined to think that it invites revolution because it virtually consecrates inequality—the prime cause of revolution everywhere, as Tocqueville pointed out—and that it succumbs rather easily because of its seeming inability to command wide loyalties and because it is unable, by its nature, to mobilize the necessary military power quickly and effectively. Its characteristic diffusion and decentralization of power results in an inability to draw upon power in crises. Marxists have told us much about how capitalism and its associated political structures are subject to revolution. But, in all truth, all the revolutions of modern history have been those launched against systems more nearly feudal than capitalist. It may well be true, as a long line of scholars beginning with Tocqueville has emphasized, that the overriding effect of modernity in both its economic and political manifestations is to sterilize the revolutionary impulse.

I

In light of these observations, let us now consider our main subject, the American Revolution. Was there in the colonies a social order that can reasonably be called feudal? Can conflicts originating in inequality, in social class, property, and religion be discerned, in whatever degree, analogous to the conflicts leading up to the English, French, and Russian revolutions? Finally, can substantial changes, effected politically, within revolutionary circumstances, be found taking place in the social structure of America during the two decades following the outbreak of war with England?

If answers to these questions are affirmative, as I think they are, then I believe we are obliged to accept the view that revolution in the true sense of this word did indeed take place at the end of the eighteenth century in America, and that a good deal more than mere war of liberation from England was at work. That nothing resembling the zeal, ferocity, and terror of the other revolutions is to be found in the American experience need not be stressed here. That fact is obvious. But, as I have suggested, the essence of any genuine revolution is not the terror that may or may not be associated with it, nor even the kind of millennialist passion that is so often to be observed in modern revolutions. The essence lies in the social changes involved: changes in such institutions as property, family, religion, and social class. These changes, as I want to show, were very much a part of the American experience at the end of the eighteenth century.

The first point to make clear is that there was indeed a solid substructure of feudalism in the American colonies. Since a "feudal stage" has so often been denied to the Americans, has so often been effaced by historians in their stress on the homogeneous middle-class character of American colonial history, we must be emphatic on this point. Needless to say, in referring to feudalism, I do not mean the tidy thing Sir Henry Spelman had in mind when he coined the word in the seventeenth century, much less the ideal feudalism planned for Jerusalem by the medieval Crusaders. (It would indeed have been hard to find that feudalism even in Europe by the eighteenth century. And it is chastening to bear in mind that more than a few continental scholars have denied England its feudalism on the ground that the oath exacted by William I of all freemen in England in 1086 instantaneously removed the possibility of the true hierarchy of power, the stress upon intermediate institutions, and the decentralization which define feudalism.)

From the point of view of the comparative historian and sociologist, feudalism has less to do with political and military structures, with knights, castles, and dukedoms, than with what Marc Bloch calls "the ties of dependence" uniting individuals of all classes into a society. When we find a people in a large area for whom there is little sense of collective political solidarity, little centralization of administration, but great consciousness of localism, regionalism, and of the whole realm of intermediate association that begins with kinship, parish, and local community—a people strong in social classes and the obligations they embody, tending to make little distinction between the authority of property and the authority of law, depending heavily upon custom and tradition rather than prescriptive law, and closely associated with the land generation after generation in family lines—when we find these elements we can properly refer to a feudal society, at least in the social and economic sense of the word.

I am inclined to think that a feudal system necessarily emerges whenever a relatively small number of persons seek to live in a new territory with great expanses of land to be had by the well-off or energetic, where ties with a central authority are weak or absent, where localism is enforced by topography as well as custom, and where landed property tends to create the fundamental rights and privileges in society. Certainly by the middle of the eighteenth century the American colonies met these and other distinctively feudal criteria, no matter how loath we may be to apply these criteria to

Pilgrims and others of established historical fancy who, as we are prone to believe, left not only Europe but all European history behind them when they came to the New World.

In the colonies land counted for a very great deal. What Sir Lewis Namier has written with England in mind applies no less to the American colonies:

> The relations of groups of men to plots of land, or organized communities to units of territory, form the basic content of political history . . . ; social stratifications and convulsions, primarily arising from relationship of men to land, make the greater, not always conscious, part of the domestic history of nations—and even under urban and industrial conditions ownership of land counts for more than is usually supposed.[1]

From Maine to Georgia American life was rooted in the land, and this was just as true of New England—its fisheries and manufactures, so often exaggerated in their importance, notwithstanding—as it was in other parts of America. And where a social system is rooted in the land, land-hunger is the common and abiding accompaniment, and it directs itself particularly to the large manorial estates. These were much in evidence, New England excepted, in the colonies. We are told that nearly three million acres in New York alone were occupied by large, essentially manorial estates. The Van Rensselaer manor up the Hudson alone measured some twenty-four by twenty miles. The Fairfax estate in Virginia had, at the height of its prosperity, some six million acres. There were very large estates in the Carolinas, and in most of the other colonies as well—New England alone, as I say, forming the exception. How could there not have been a substantial admixture of feudalism in those parts of the colonies where such land holdings existed, assuming, as we have every right to assume, the grafting onto these of customs, conventions, and authorities brought to the New World from the Old?

There were indeed small independent farms in America.

[1] Lewis Namier, *England in the Age of the American Revolution* (New York: Mentor Books, 1964), p. 17.

But so were there in England long before the Puritan Revolution, and in France just prior to the Revolution there. We have Georges Lefebvre's word for it in his valuable study of the French Revolution that the majority of the French peasants had been free for generations and were in possession of some 30 percent of all French land at the time of the outbreak of that Revolution. These facts in no way minimize the hatred in both England and France for the large manors and their withholding of land from possible purchase and for the inequalities which were bound to seem intolerable once an opportunity for ending them arose. I would not for a moment suppose these hatreds were ever as great in the colonies as they were in France where class ties were much older and more deeply set. But to suppose they were altogether absent in the colonies is to suppose nonsense.

From these great manorial holdings in America sprang a class system that was a vivid, if today often minimized, feature of colonial life. Feudal in essence, it had the large landowners at the top. In wealth, power, breeding, and culture, this upper class was a fit analogue to anything in England. As Richard B. Morris has emphasized, families such as the Livingstons, De Lanceys, and Schuylers had a place in social class and in politics not a bit different from what was enjoyed in England at that time by such members of the nobility as the Duke of Bedford, the Marquess of Rockingham, and Lord Shelburne.[2] Below the landed class fell tenant farmers, artisans, mechanics, small freeholders, laborers, indentured servants and, not to be forgotten, the very large class of Negro slaves. There was little rhetoric in colonial times about homogeneity and equality when it came to classes as distinct in their powers and privileges as some of these were. Jackson Turner Main, in his *The Social Structure of Revolutionary America*, has concluded indeed that the long-term tendency was "toward greater inequality, with marked class distinc-

[2] Richard B. Morris, *The American Revolution Reconsidered* (New York: Harper & Row, 1967), pp. 57–58. In this splendid book Professor Morris builds admirably and also comparatively upon the seminal insights of J. Franklin Jameson and Allan Nevins a generation ago.

tions." Such distinctions, it may be safely inferred, were cultural and social, even psychological, as well as economic and political. Nor were class lines absent from the cities. Carl Bridenbaugh's studies of urban colonial America have made us vividly aware of the highly developed sense of solidarity—on a national, not simply local, basis—within the upper class that could be found in each of America's five important cities. A great deal of the inbreeding and the close social and political solidarity Sir Lewis Namier has found in eighteenth century England existed, and was surely increasing in intensity, in prerevolutionary America.

An established religion is another aspect of life that is feudal in root and connotation. In most of the colonies religious establishment existed in one degree or other. Congregationalism reigned in Massachusetts, New Hampshire and Connecticut, and the Church of England in a number of other colonies. In none, so far as I can ascertain, did a majority of the people actually profess the established faith. Is it difficult to suppose widespread resentment on the part of this majority at the thought of paying taxes to support a church they did not belong to and may even have detested? Even where, as was sometimes the case, taxes were light and only randomly collected, the symbolic aspect was important. It always is in these matters. Can one imagine, other than that the large numbers of Presbyterians, Lutherans, Baptists, and Methodists in Virginia, say, deeply resented paying taxes in support of the Church of England and a clergy notoriously given to sloth and drink?

Where feudalism exists in any degree, so do the customs of primogeniture and entail, the first granting inheritance of fixed property only to the oldest son, the second fixing land firmly to family line. These customs were to be found all over Europe, and it would have been extraordinary if the European settlers had not brought them to America. In fact, all the colonies knew both customs down until just before the time of the Revolution. When the Revolution broke out, only two colonies had abolished primogeniture, only one entail. And, as I shall indicate in a moment, among all the changes effected in the states after the war with England had ended, few could have been more popular, judging from the speed with which they took place, than those which terminated these ancient feudal restrictions on the inheritance of property.

I am aware that some historians of the American Revolution belittle the seriousness for the colonists of the laws of primogeniture and entail and of religious establishment, because contemporary research into the records of that time finds evidence of only infrequent legal recourse or attempted recourse. But the comparative study of revolutions makes plain enough that there is little correlation between the symbolic importance of issues involved in revolutions and measurable hardship. After all, is it likely that the issue of busing in our time, which we know to be of very high importance indeed with the American public, will loom that important a century hence when there are only legal records to examine?

The same can be said of the significance of the undoubted economic prosperity the colonies had experienced for decades before the war with England. Given this prosperity, it is sometimes argued, social tensions could not have been severe. Again, however, we learn from the study of revolutions that there is nothing so calculated to focus attention upon social resentments as a period of relative economic prosperity, one that raises popular expectations and demands.

II

I have suggested that there was a distinct feudal character to American colonial society, that inequalities existed which could only have generated tensions akin to (if not necessarily as intense as) those in Europe where the inequalities were necessarily much older, and that in matters of social class, religion, and property a real ferment can be found—the kind of ferment comparative history teaches us so often results in revolution. But would there have been a revolution in these social areas if the war with England had not broken out? Would internal social tensions themselves have led to revolution? The answer lies not simply in an intensive study of the

American experience but in a comparative study of all modern Western revolutions.

My own guess, and it can only be that, is that no such revolution would have occurred without a precipitating war in which ideological values were strong. Quite probably the social changes we see in the American Revolution would have occurred more slowly, under the spur of rising pressures during the next century, as such changes occurred in Canada. But who can be sure in these matters? The nature and consequences of a revolution are better known than the residual causes. So large is the myth that revolutions are invariably caused by volcanic pressures from below that we still find it difficult to fix attention upon factors other than these pressures. But such factors, although widely regarded as only extraneous or coincidental, may prove to have far more to do with causing revolutions than the explanations we so commonly draw from the familiar myth.

If war was the necessary precipitating factor in the American social revolution, let it be remembered that war has accompanied each of the other major Western revolutions of modern times. The link between war and revolution is both existentially and historically close, especially when war is either intense or prolonged. Both destroy traditional authorities, classes, and types of wealth; both create new kinds of power, rank, and wealth. With much reason, conservatives have been as suspicious of war as of revolution. It was, after all, in the wake of war that revolutionary changes occurred in ancient Athens at the end of the fifth century B.C. and in the Rome of Augustus. Nor should it be overlooked that almost all the intensity of the French Revolution burst upon the French people in war and under the justification of war emergency. Much the same is true of the development of communism in Russia, starting with the period of "war communism" and continuing through the subsequent hostile relationship with the West. Finally, we need only be reminded of the number of elements in modern welfare states whose actual historical origins lie not in socialist ideology, least of all in socialist governments, but rather in periods of war. Consider the United States and such matters as civil rights, minimum wage laws, management-worker councils, guarantees of union organization, improvements in working conditions, and so on.

Now let us again consider the American Revolution, this time looking at the changes which took place so suddenly in traditional social institutions and values, changes fully meriting the label "revolutionary."

There is first the relation between land and the family. As I have noted, although discontent with the laws of primogeniture and entail had certainly existed for a long time, only Pennsylvania and Maryland had abolished the former and only South Carolina the latter. Yet within a single decade of the signing of the Declaration of Independence, all but two states abolished entail, and in these two entail had become relatively insignificant in any case. Within another five years, all the states made primogeniture illegal and established some form of partible inheritance. In an astonishingly short time considering the number of separate state actions required, *partage forcé*, as the French revolutionaries were to call it, became the law of the land in America.

We may not be inclined today to regard abolition of primogeniture and entail as a revolutionary change in social structure. It is well to be advised in the matter by two nineteenth century authorities, Frederick Le Play and Alexis de Tocqueville. Le Play, without question the foremost comparative sociologist before Max Weber, considered the abolition of primogeniture and entail the most revolutionary changes effected during the French Revolution. Conservative and traditionalist in spirit as well as scientific in thrust, he thought that the reestablishment of both laws would do more for stability in the France of his day than any other single reform. His notable recommendation of what he called *la famille souche* (the "stem family") was based upon such a reestablishment.

So did Tocqueville regard the forced division of property inheritance as a revolutionary change, whether in its French or American form. Looking back a half-century into American history, on the occasion of his notable visit to America, he spoke of society being "shaken to its center" by the adoption of legislation leading to the abolition of primogeniture and entail. Tocqueville was already steeped in the comparative aspects of the study of revolution, if only by virtue of the obsessive influence of the French Revolution on his young and aristocratic mind, and he knew very well indeed that strong family systems everywhere are rooted in corporateness and continuity of family property. He also knew that the best possible prescription for the individualization and in time, the economic rootlessness of a population is to separate kinship from its foundation, the continuity of landed property. Not only does the law of partible inheritance make it difficult for families to preserve their ancestral domains, Tocqueville pointed out, but it soon deprives them of the desire to attempt the preservation. No one familiar with the social character of the France of his day, he added, would wish to question the influence of partible inheritance.

Tocqueville, after interviewing responsible Americans in order to discover the effects of the abolition of primogeniture and entail, was convinced that the effects were substantial. Historians of our own day such as Jameson, Nevins, and Morris only echo his conviction (though with far greater documentation). One need reflect but a moment on the incentives—to land speculators, not to mention to the heirs—that would have been aroused by this abolition. Only two states, North Carolina and New Jersey, failed to include daughters as well as sons in the new laws of inheritance. Elsewhere full equality was the rule.

As we think about it, the uniformity of action in the thirteen states is little short of astonishing. By comparison, how simple it was for France to effect such changes two decades later. After all, there only a single act by a single body of lawmakers was required, such was the centralization that had been wrought by monarchs and then confirmed by the revolutionary assembly. The same can be said of analogous Russian changes following the triumph of the Bolsheviks. How remarkable, then, that in America one of the most telling acts of equalization known in social history was effected virtually in unison by thirteen different legislatures. To say, as many American students of the Revolution have said, that laws of primogeniture and entail mattered little in the colonies—that they were at best hardly more than vestigial memories—scarcely fits the swift and uniform eradication of these laws by the state legislatures.

Nor, in this connection, should we overlook the revolutionary impact of the confiscations of large estates owned by Tories, with shares of these holdings going to American patriots. The exact number of acres involved is less significant than the fact of confiscation and distribution. For an appropriate parallel in our own day we should have to imagine government confiscation of a substantial number of large "disloyal" business corporations, with ownership of shares given over to loyal citizens of our nation. The popular sense of revolutionary acquisition in that day of overwhelmingly landed wealth should not be underestimated.

If it is said that these confiscations of Tory estates were measures of war—that is, acts of retribution against those who refused to disavow their ties with England—the same must be said of the later expropriations of the noble estates in France during the Revolution there. It was not originally out of passion for the abstract ideal of equality that the Jacobins took over the estates of certain aristocrats: if this had been the case, all of the land holdings of the French nobility would have been seized. But this was not what happened. French expropriations, like those earlier in America, were levelled at estate holders who had joined the enemy when war broke out. Again the lesson is taught: war is often as much the confiscator and equalizer as is revolution itself and it is not always easy to tell their effects apart.

Inevitably the shocks of the war with England were to produce revolutionary consequences in the religious as well as the civil realm. Agitation for release from the exactions of religious establishment could hardly help but become part of the very act of war against England in those colonies where the Church of England was established. And this agitation was bound to have reverberations in those colonies where the Congregational Church was established. True, the laws on religion were not everywhere overthrown in a single spasm. In parts of New England disestablishment did not occur until the nineteenth century. Nor was there by any means firm agreement among the leaders of the revolutionary war as to its desirability. John Adams and others had serious misgivings on the matter, and those Baptists and Quakers who had begun to work for religious freedom before the Revolution found considerable opposition to their labors.

It was the Revolution that changed this situation substantially. Granted that "disestablishment was neither an original goal nor completely a product of the Revolution," as Professor Bailyn has properly noted, it remains nevertheless true, also in Bailyn's words, that everything already existing along this line was "touched by the magic of Revolutionary thought, and . . . transformed."[3] It may be true that even had there been no Revolution, no war with England, disestablishment would still have taken place in due time. But the length of time actually required in parts of New England, and the fierce debate on the matter in Virginia where the Declaration of Rights was promulgated in 1776, should make us chary of assuming the certainty and especially the rapidity of change in this area.

How important religious liberty became to Americans as a result of the Revolution is evidenced by one response to the Constitution when this document was given to the states for ratification.

> The lack of any safeguards for liberty of faith at once struck critics in all sections. The Virginia Convention proposed an amendment guaranteeing freedom of conscience. North Carolina's Convention seconded the proposal, adopting the same language. . . . In the first Congress attention was directed to the oversight by James Madison, and the required guarantee was made the first constitutional amendment proposed to the nation.[4]

It is hardly necessary to stress here that, of all the consequences of the American Revolution, the most heralded in other parts of the world was the firm creation of religious

[3] Bernard Bailyn, *The Ideological Origins of the American Revolution* (Cambridge: Harvard University Press, 1967), p. 271.

[4] Allan Nevins, *The American States During and After the Revolution, 1775–1798* (Clifton, N.J.: Augustus M. Kelley, 1924), p. 440.

freedom. Tocqueville was but one of many who thought this creation the most remarkable of American achievements.

There remains the profound and deeply troubling question of the Negro slaves in America at the time of the Revolution. It would be splendid indeed if we could say that under the principles of liberty and equality proclaimed by the American founders these slaves had been given their freedom. Obviously we cannot. But from this it by no means follows that the position of the Negroes in America was insulated from revolutionary thought and action—not by any means. There were at the time of the Revolution—there had been for years in America—leading men who found the thought of slavery repugnant. It would have been strange if the agitation of the 1770s and 1780s, touching as it did so many vital areas, had not also touched the problem of slavery.

At the time the Revolution broke out, there were about a half million slaves in the thirteen colonies—most of them in the South, but a fair number, perhaps 55,000, in the North. The first anti-slavery society in the United States, or anywhere else for that matter, was founded in April 1775, largely by Philadelphia Quakers. Other societies soon followed. The Continental Congress in 1774 had decreed an "American Association" (that is, a non-importation agreement), and the prohibition on slave trading seems to have held up throughout the war. Legislatures began to act. In July 1774, Rhode Island enacted a law that thenceforth all slaves brought into the colony should be free. The law's preamble, which begins as follows, is instructive:

> Whereas the inhabitants of America are generally engaged in the preservation of their own rights and liberties, among which that of personal freedom must be considered as the greatest, and as those who are desirous of enjoying all the advantages of liberty themselves should be willing to extend personal liberty to others. . . .[5]

Delaware prohibited importation in 1776, Virginia in 1778, and Maryland in 1783 (for a term of years), with

[5] Quoted in J. Franklin Jameson, *The American Revolution Considered as a Social Movement* (Princeton, N.J.: Princeton University Press, 1926), p. 36.

North Carolina imposing an increased duty on each Negro imported. Even more to the point, the states where there were few slaves proceeded under the stimulus of the Revolution to effect the immediate or gradual abolition of slavery itself. In short, the seeds of abolitionism were first planted as one of the major acts of the American Revolution. True, there is a conflicting element in this that it would be disingenuous not to mention. A great many blacks saw, and had every reason to see, more hope of freedom with the British than with American plantation owners. Nor were the British timid about using the bait of freedom for the blacks as a weapon against the Americans. Moreover, there can be no doubt that the eagerness with which a good many southern plantation owners entered the war sprang from fear that an English victory would bring emancipation for the slaves. In other words, a case could be made that war with England only hardened the determination of many southerners to maintain the institution of slavery.[6]

Even so, we cannot miss the strong tide of abolitionism that rose at the time of the Revolution. The minds of the men who led that Revolution and its war were sensitive and humane. The contrast between the principles of freedom and equality on the one hand and the presence of a half million black slaves on the other no more escaped men like Jefferson and Adams than it did Edmund Burke and other Whigs in England. It is precisely awareness of this contrast that marks the real beginning of the long and tragic story of black liberation in America, a story that would have its next great episode in the Civil War and that would still be going on during the black civil rights revolution of the 1960s.

We must concede that the American Revolution failed the Negro. Nevertheless, as Bernard Bailyn has written, "as long as the institution of slavery lasted, the burden of proof would lie with its advocates to show why the statement that 'all men are created equal' did not mean precisely what it said: *all* men, 'white or black.'"[7] And Benjamin Quarles, whose

---

[6] Morris, *The American Revolution Reconsidered*, p. 74.
[7] Bailyn, *The Ideological Origins of the American Revolution*, p. 246.

study of the Negro in the American Revolution is the most detailed investigation of the subject yet made, has written:

> The American Revolution touches all classes in society, even Negroes. On the eve of the conflict, the same religious and political idealism that stirred the resistance to Britain deepened the sentiment against slavery. . . . Ultimately the colored people of America benefited from the irreversible commitment of the new nation to the principles of liberty and equality.[8]

III

Now I want to turn to a very different aspect of my subject: the justly celebrated moderateness of spirit of the American Revolution, the absence of the kind of passion, zeal, and millennialist conviction that in other countries produced terror and left a heritage of bitterness lasting to the present day. I have suggested that a revolution did indeed occur in America, one involving social structures and values, the same ones indeed which form the substance of the European revolutions. Why, then, did no Terror, no Thermidor, no military dictatorship make its appearance? We cannot doubt that egalitarianism was buoyant in America; we need look only at the many pamphlets written and circulated before and during the revolutionary war. Nor can we doubt that significant sections of the American people were bound to have felt the impact of laws directed at slavery, against religious establishment and traditional inheritance of property, not to emphasize the expropriation of estates. It is absurd to pretend we are dealing with issues which are not explosive, which do not ordinarily arouse the deepest passions. How do we account for the fact of the widespread spirit of acceptance of the Revolution in America, a spirit that included conservatives, liberals, and radicals, a spirit properly characterized as one of consensus and continuity?

[8] Benjamin Quarles, *The Negro in the American Revolution* (Chapel Hill, N.C.: University of North Carolina Press, 1967), p. 197.

Clearly these questions are difficult ones, and the efforts of some of our best historians have gone into their answer. There are those who explain the spirit of moderation by simply denying that a revolution worthy of the name occurred at all. This answer I have already rejected. There is no question in my mind that a real social revolution took place. Other historians speak of a *spirit* of moderation and pragmatism in the American experience that contrasts with the ideological passions of Europe. This does not, however, carry us very far, for such an explanation only restates, albeit in causative terms, what requires explanation: that is, the spirit of moderateness. In any event, looking at the subsequent history of America, from the War of 1812 through the Civil War down to World War I and II, and bearing in mind some of the fierce ideological passions that have flared often enough in our history, it would be risky to appeal to any such embedded spirit. Finally, there are many writers who refer to the temper of the leadership that the American Revolution was fortunate in having. We cannot fail to see the restraint, responsibility, and wisdom of such men as John Adams, Jefferson, Madison, Dickinson, Franklin, Hamilton, and others, and I would not for a moment dismiss the importance of this factor. It is crucial. It does leave the question, however, of how such restrained and moderate leadership survived throughout. After all, the English and French revolutions began in moderation, and something of the same can be said of the Russian if we are willing to consider the Kerensky government the first phase of that Revolution.

In sum, there were men of good judgment, temperateness, and moderation at one time or other in command of the European revolutions, as well as the American. Why, then, we must ask, did revolutions succumb to ever more radical and zealous leaders in Europe but not in America where individuals of this stripe assuredly existed? Any answer to so complex a question must be offered in the spirit of hypothesis. And it is in that spirit alone that I present the following possible explanations:

First, the American Revolution was, by virtue of the nature of colonial America, a *dispersed* revolution. This dispersion flowed from the demographic character of American colonial life—a character evidenced in the lack of social and political channels through which strong collective passions might easily have flowed. Nothing comparable to a London, Paris or Moscow existed in America, no large city steeped in historical traditions of turbulence and occasional revolt. Our five cities were small and uncongested by European standards, lacking moreover the kinds of visible evidences of extreme wealth or extreme poverty that could only be inflammatory in the European cities where revolutions broke out. Tensions rooted in social and economic conditions certainly existed in New York and Boston, and possibly in our other cities; but there was not, there could not have been, the cumulative disorder or the air of incipient revolt we know to have existed in the great European cities, if only by virtue of their size and long histories.

Nor was there anything in America, either before or after the Revolution, approximating the centralization of political power and administration that England, France, and Russia knew so well before the outbreaks of their revolutions. The concentrated nature of the French and Russian revolutions especially must be seen against a background of long developing centralization. Each of the European revolutions was a *focused* revolution, which made it easy for the sudden passions of ideologues or the crowd to be translated into acts which could affect the entire country.

In America, we must look to the thirteen separate colonies or states to find the vital elements of the social revolution. Communication among the colonies and states there certainly was; but it was communication among separate, independent, and proud political societies, and, as we know only too well, acts taken by the Constitutional Convention and then by the new federal government were watched carefully, often jealously, by the states. Dispersion and decentralization of power thus moderated passion and inclination so far as the nation as a whole was concerned. The vital principle of countervailing power—of intermediate au-

thority, of division of rule—operated to reduce, at least for a
long time, the national impact of intellectual and social
movements arising in any one part of the nation.

Second, religion remained a strong force in American society. I mean independent religion, one that was plural in
manifestation, closely connected with locality and region, and
not easy to mix with political passions. Admittedly religion as
a cultural force seems to have declined somewhat during the
eighteenth century, but once the symbols of establishment
were removed, evangelical religions began to transform the
religious landscape. We could not explain the immense burst
of religiosity in the 1820s and later—carrying with it the
birth of many new faiths and lasting through the century—if
seeds of it had not been present earlier.

This seizure of so much of the American mind by incon-
testably religious values and aspirations consumed psychic
energy that might otherwise have gone into political ideology
and political movement. As students of the French Revolution from Edmund Burke down to Hannah Arendt have observed, it was with religious passion translated into political
action that the Jacobins dealt with government and society.
In the English Revolution, by the time it was well under way
and the New Model Army had become a revolutionary as
well as a military force, the line between religion and political
evangelism was very thin indeed. In the twentieth century,
Marxism has become the substitute for established religion in
Russia and everywhere else that it has taken command. But
how very different was the American experience. No one saw
more clearly than Tocqueville, when he visited America during the Age of Jackson, how vital to democratic government
is the existence of a strong, separate, autonomous religion—a
religion that can prevent man's religious nature, his desire for
the sacred, from seeking fulfillment through government or
political ideology. In America, as was not the case in France
or Russia, revolution never had a chance to become God.

Third, and closely related to the first two factors, is the
idea of voluntary association. Even before Tocqueville mar-
velled at the fact, the American profusion of voluntary associations was well known in Europe and (as a matter of na-

tional pride) in America. Our reputation for being a nation of joiners was made early, and neither the fact nor the reputation could have been possible had it not been for an American attitude toward these associations vitally different from any attitude easily discovered in most European countries at the time. The hatred of internal associations by the French revolutionaries, a hatred manifest not only in the destruction of the guilds, monasteries, and other bodies deriving from the past, but also in explicit prohibition of almost all new associations, never existed in the United States. No specific constitutional provision guaranteed freedom of association but, given the guarantees of freedom of assembly and petition along with the strong social and cultural roots of the phenomenon, voluntary associations thrived. Granted there were occasional popular outbursts against the association that might seem an antidemocratic or secret society—for example, the Society of Cincinnati. But animus against voluntary associations for mutual aid or for eleemosynary, religious, journalistic, intellectual, and other purposes was not often found either at the grass roots or in government.

Few things are so calculated to divert human inclinations from focusing on the capture of political power and on a consuming ideology as the necessary avenue to secular salvation as is the proliferation of intermediate, voluntary, and autonomous associations. The American Revolution did not choke off voluntary association, as did the French and the Russian. Voluntary associations in America could become not merely a functional refuge of the individual but also a buffer against the invasions of political centralization. It is safe to say that a great deal of American passion that would otherwise surely have gone into political movements went instead into the innumerable intermediate associations which, along with local, regional, and religious loyalties, made the American social landscape so different from the French in the nineteenth century.

Fourth, post-revolutionary America had few if any of the politically important class divisions that we find in Europe. As I have stressed, the colonies did indeed have social classes, very distinct ones, and these were almost certainly becoming much sharper before the Revolution. It was in fact the war with England that significantly changed the pattern of social class in America, both moderating the thrust of pre-revolutionary class factors and, more important, preventing any class from becoming forever identified with a political position rising from the Revolution. Although it is true that most wealthy, educated, and socially influential Americans sided with Britain, in one degree or another, and that most members of the lower classes chose the side of the Continental Congress, there were altogether too many exceptions in each instance to make any generalization easy—to give, that is, a distinct character of class conflict to the war.

I do not think I exaggerate my point here. All serious students of social class, including Karl Marx, have noted the vital importance of conflict—conflict that is political in character, ideological in thrust—in shaping and hardening classes. Had the upper class in America solidly opposed the war instead of supplying most of that war's leaders, and had the lower class alone supported the war, the outcome (assuming war would have taken place at all) would almost certainly have been a class structure like that of Western Europe, with ideological conflict to match. That such a class structure did not materialize in America—much to the dismay of Marxists later—is, it would seem, the result of the "accident" of the war against England. For, with tenant farmers, indentured servants, and even Negroes frequently to be found on the Tory side, along with members of the upper class, and with the same kinds of individuals to be found on the patriot side, along with their leaders who were of the upper classes of New England and the South, only the slightest "class-angling" of the revolutionary war was possible.

Fifth, and by no means least in importance, I would adduce the absence of an intellectual class in America at the time of the Revolution as one of the prime reasons for the lack of ideological zeal and political ferocity both during and after the Revolution. That there were individuals of superb education, well grounded in philosophy, including the philosophy of natural rights, is not to be disputed. Thomas Jefferson, John Adams, John Dickinson and a good many others did not have to defer to the brightest of intellectual lights in the salons of Europe. And, as we know, the passion for freedom, equality, and national fraternity was strong in their hearts. As well as being philosophers, they were activists in every sense of the word.

Even so, they did not constitute the kind of intellectual class Europe has been noted for at least since the Renaissance. I am referring, of course, to the class of political intellectuals of which the Philosophes in France were such iridescent examples, a class that (as both Burke and Tocqueville stressed) had so much to do not only with setting the intellectual background of the Revolution in France but also with giving that Revolution the special ideological ferocity it came to have by 1791. This class may be said to have begun with the politically minded humanists of the Italian Renaissance, and it grew steadily in size during the succeeding centuries. We properly include in it not only the humanists and their successors, the Philosophes, but also, later, the *revolutionistes* of 1848 (to be found in just about all coffee houses on the continent), Saint-Simonians, Fourierists, Positivists and, eventually anarchists, socialists, and communists. Its dominant characteristics are and have been, from the time of the humanists' rootlessness in society, an adversary position toward polity, and a fascination with power and its uses. The capacity of this class for ideological fanaticism, for sacrifice of life and institution alike in the name of principle, and even for outright blood-lust and terror is well known to comparative students of modern revolutions.

This class was, however, almost totally lacking in America before and during the Revolution. Our principal intellectual leaders were, without exception, deeply rooted in the social order. For Jefferson or Adams or Dickinson, learning, even great learning in philosophy and the arts, could go with membership in society. It did not invite alienation or revolt. The intellectual leaders of the American Revolution were overwhelmingly landowners: they had a stake in society. That either a Jefferson or a Hamilton could have renounced what Burke called the wisdom of expediency in the interest of pursuing an abstract principle is inconceivable. No more could any of the American leaders have contemplated with delight mass executions or imprisonments, as did the millennialist intellectuals of 1649, 1793, and 1917. At no point in the American Revolution or in its aftermath do we find any New Model Army Council of Agitators, any Committee of Public Safety after the French fashion, any Council of the People's Commissars, any Lilburnes, Robespierres, or Lenins. I am inclined to think that nothing so completely gave the American Revolution its distinctive character as the absence in it of the European species of political intellectual. It is only in the present century that we have seen this species coming into prominence in America.

In conclusion, I would argue that there was indeed an American Revolution in the full sense of the word—a social, moral, and institutional revolution that effected major changes in the character of American society—as well as a war of liberation from England that was political in nature. And those who have seen it as a revolution of "great internal tumults and violent convulsions," as Sam Adams saw it, are on the whole better guides to its nature than those who have chosen to see it as only a war that changed one set of political governors for another. We err, it seems to me, in making the special fanaticism and ideological terror of the French and Russian revolutions the touchstone of revolution. To deny the status of revolution because of the absence of these qualities is like denying the status of war because of the absence of atrocities.

Furthermore, to see the American Revolution as a merely "local" affair fails utterly to account for the excitement it created in other parts of the world. Thomas Jefferson's words to John Adams reflect the universalism so many of the leaders of the Revolution saw in the events and changes beginning in 1775: "The flames kindled on the fourth of July, 1776, have spread over too much of the globe to be extinguished by the feeble engines of despotism." And as Richard B. Morris has made evident, it is sheer travesty to see and to proclaim the American Revolution as a central experience in our national life "and to ignore the libertarian currents that the event set off throughout the world." Certainly the view does gross injury to the sensibilities and perceptions of those who led the Revolution.

The line from the social revolution of the 1770s to the civil rights revolution of the 1960s is a direct one. It is a line that passes through the Civil War—itself certainly not without revolutionary implication—and through a host of changes in the status of Americans of all races, beliefs, and classes. The United States has indeed undergone a process of almost permanent revolution. I can think of no greater injustice to ourselves, as well as to the makers of revolution in Philadelphia, than to deny that fact and to allow the honored word *revolution* to be preempted today by spokesmen for societies which, through their congealed despotisms, have made revolution all but impossible.

GORDON S. WOOD

Revolution and the Political Integration of the Enslaved and Disenfranchised

Delivered in Kentucky's House of Representatives' chamber,

Frankfort, Kentucky on January 9, 1974

The radical character of the American Revolution is a subject of some historical controversy. Yet in one important respect there can be no denying its radicalism. The Revolution transformed the American colonies into republics, which meant that ordinary people were no longer to be considered "subjects" to be ruled as they were under a monarchy. They were thereafter to be citizens—participants themselves in the ruling process. This is what democracy has come to mean for us.

The profoundest revolution of the past 200 years has been this introduction of ordinary people into the political process. For America and the rest of the Western world, this Revolution was most dramatically expressed at the end of the eighteenth century—"the age of the democratic revolution," as it has been called.[1] This bringing of the people into politics extended through the next fifty years in the United States, while in Western Europe it took much longer, requiring at least the greater part of the nineteenth century. And of course for the rest of the world the process is still going on.

[1] R. R. Palmer, *The Age of the Democratic Revolution: A Political History of Europe and America,* 1760–1800, 2 vols. (Princeton: Princeton University Press, 1959, 1964).

In fact since 1945 with the emergence of new nations and the Third World, we have been witnessing what has been called a "participation explosion,"[2] the rapid incorporation into the political process of peoples who had hitherto been outside of politics, in a hurried, even a desperate, effort by underdeveloped nations to catch up with the modern democratic states.

More than anything else this incorporation of common ordinary people into politics is what sets the modern world apart from what went on before. Americans were in the vanguard of this development. Our assumption of the leadership of the democratic nations is not simply based on our preponderance of power since 1945. Ever since the American Revolution we have claimed the leadership of the Free World, even when we were an underdeveloped nation ourselves and our claims were treated with bemused contempt by Europe. Our assertions of leadership were based on our priority in time: we were the first modern nation to have a democratic revolution and to establish a republic in which citizenship and political participation belong to the whole community. The French Revolution and all the other European revolutions of the nineteenth century were in our eyes merely examples or species of the revolutionary genus that we had created. Part of the explanation for the intensity of the ideological confrontation between the United States and the Soviet Union since the Communist Revolution of 1917 comes from the Soviet Union's claim that it has created a new revolutionary tradition, a new revolutionary genus, one which threatens to usurp our position in the vanguard of history.

We Americans have never been able to figure out why the rest of the world has had such a hard time catching up with us. Because the process of creating a republican citizenry seemed so simple for us, we have believed it ought to be simple for others. It seems to us to be merely a matter of allowing the people to vote. Because voting is the most obvious means by which the people participate in politics, we have

---

[2] Gabriel A. Almond and Sidney Verba, *The Civic Culture: Political Attitudes and Democracy in Five Nations* (Boston: Little, Brown & Co., Inc., 1965), p. 2.

tended to emphasize the right to vote as the necessary and sufficient criterion of democratic politics. But this is a mistake. The suffrage is clearly a prerequisite for democratic politics, but it is hardly all there is to it. It is important for us in our bicentennial celebrations to examine our Revolution and its heritage and to seek to understand the sources of our political practice and values. Only with knowledge of the conditions that underlie the principle of consent in our polity can we confront the world and the future. Voting is in fact only the exposed tip of an incredibly complicated political and social process. How this process came about and how the people became involved in politics are questions that lie at the heart of the American Revolution.

I

The American Revolution was both a consequence and a cause of democracy. It came to mark a decisive change in the way political activity was carried on in America. It gave new legitimacy to the involvement of common people in politics. It was not, however, simply a matter of enfranchising new voters. Although the franchise in colonial America was confined by property qualifications as it was in eighteenth century England, property owning was so widespread that the colonists enjoyed the broadest suffrage of any people in the world: perhaps 80 percent of white adult males could vote. Yet the fact remains that most of those enfranchised did not exercise the right. The social structure and social values were such that colonial politics, at least when compared to politics in post-revolutionary America, were remarkably stable, and the percentage of the people actually voting and participating in politics remained small—much smaller even than today. In the eighteenth century the legal exclusion of the propertyless from the franchise was based not on the fear that the poor might confiscate the wealth of the aristocratic few, but on the opposite fear: that the aristocratic few might manipulate and corrupt the poor for their own ends. Established social leaders expected deference from those below them, and

generally got it and were habitually reelected to political
office. There were no organized political parties and no professional politicians in today's sense of those words. Established merchants, wealthy lawyers, and large planters held
the major offices and ran political affairs as part of the responsibility of their elevated social positions. It was rare for a
tavern keeper or small farmer to gain a political office of any
consequence. Men were granted political authority in accord
not with their seniority or experience in politics but with
their established economic and social superiority. Thus
Thomas Hutchinson, son of a distinguished Boston mercan-
tile family, was elected to the Massachusetts House of Representatives at the age of twenty-six and almost immediately
became its speaker. Social and political authority was indivis-
ible and men moved horizontally into politics from the society, rather than (as is common today) moving up vertically
through an exclusively political hierarchy.

Yet politics in eighteenth-century colonial America was un-
stable enough in many areas that members of the elite
struggled for political power and precedence among themselves. The social hierarchy was sufficiently confused at the
top that it was never entirely clear who was destined to hold
political office and govern. It was obvious that well-to-do lawyers or merchants were superior to, say, blacksmiths, but
among several well-to-do lawyers or merchants superiority was
not so visible and incontestable. These were the conditions
that led to the formation of political factions—the shifting
conglomerations of competing elites that characterized much
of eighteenth-century colonial politics. While some members
of the elite sought the leverage of the Crown in gaining and
wielding political power, others turned to the only alternative
source of political authority recognized in eighteenth century
Anglo-American political theory—the people.

In the half century before the Revolution these competing
elites found themselves, as a tactical device, invoking "the
people" to offset the power of the Crown and to gain political office. In the process they steadily mobilized elements of
the population that had not been involved in politics earlier.
This popularization of politics during the decades before the

Revolution can be traced in various ways—in the rise in voter participation, the increase in contested elections, the resort to caucuses, tickets and other forms of political organization, and the growth of campaign propaganda and professional pamphleteering. This is how democracy began to develop. It was not the result of the people arousing themselves spontaneously and clamoring from below for a share in political authority. Rather democracy was created from above: the people were cajoled, persuaded, even frightened into getting involved. Each competing faction tried to outdo its opponents in posing as a friend of the people, defending popular rights and advancing popular interests. Yet over time what began as a pose eventually assumed a reality that had not been anticipated. The people having been invoked could not easily be laid to rest. By the middle decades of the eighteenth century, American politics was on the verge of a radical transformation—a radical transformation that was both expressed and amplified by the Revolution.

The Revolution made the people sovereign. The practices of mobilizing the people into politics that had begun before the Revolution now increased dramatically, as political leaders competed with each other for the power and endorsement that being a friend of the people brought. First the authority of the English government was challenged for its inability to represent not only the American people but its own people as well. Then in America all authority was challenged by what eventually seemed to be ceaseless appeals to the people. For no institution seemed capable of embodying their will. The Revolution so intensified the people's dominance in politics that there could never thereafter be any escaping from them. In America's new republican consciousness there could be nothing else in politics—no orders, no estates, no lords, no court, no monarch, not even rulers in the traditional sense—only the people. How they expressed themselves, how they participated in government, how they gave their consent, how they were represented were questions that preoccupied Americans in the Revolution and ever after.

During the Revolution Americans put together an idea of popular representation in government that we have never lost. The controversy and debate with England in the 1760s exposed a basic Anglo-American difference of experience and viewpoint concerning representation—a difference that only widened with the Revolution. For their part the English clung to what they called "virtual representation." England's eighteenth-century electorate comprised only a small proportion of its population and bore little relation to shifts in that population. The electoral districts were a hodgepodge left over from centuries of history. Thus ancient rotten boroughs like Old Sarum, completely depopulated by the eighteenth century, continued to send members to the House of Commons while newer large cities like Manchester and Birmingham sent none. Such apparent anomalies were justified on the not unreasonable grounds that each member of Parliament should represent not any particular locality but the whole community. Parliament, as Edmund Burke said, was not "a *congress* of ambassadors from different and hostile interests . . . but . . . a *deliberative* assembly of *one* nation, with *one* interest, that of the whole."[3] To the English what made a member of Parliament representative was not voting or the electoral process, which were considered incidental, but the mutuality of interests that presumably existed between the representative and the people. This mutuality of interests tied the people to the representative even without the exercise of the franchise. Hence the English thought of the members of Parliament as virtually representing all those who did not vote for them—including the colonists.

To the Americans, however, whose experience in politics had developed differently from that of the mother country, representation possessed an actual and local character. Their electoral districts were not the consequence of history going back to time immemorial but were recent and regular creations that bore a distinct relation to changes in their population. When a new county or a town was created by the colonists, it was usually granted immediate representation in the legislature. Thus Americans came to think of their legisla-

---

[3] Edmund Burke, "Speech to the Electors of Bristol" (1774), *The Works of the Right Honorable Edmund Burke*, rev. ed. (Boston: Little, Brown & Co., Inc., 1865–66), vol. 2, p. 96.

tures as precisely what Burke denied they should be—as congresses of ambassadors from different and contending localities and interests, of all whose consent had to be real and explicit. Hence they could not accept the British contention that they were virtually represented, like the people of Manchester, in the English Parliament and therefore capable of being taxed by it. In the course of a century and a half the American colonists had developed such a keen awareness of the individuality of their interests that they could not understand how anyone could speak for them in whose election they had no voice. Such a sense of particularity put a premium on voting as the sole measure of representation and on ensuring that all participated equally in the process of consent.

The ramifications of these ideas about representation were immense and we are still feeling their effects today. During the Revolution and in the years following, they led, first, to heightened demands for an expansion of the suffrage and, second, to the growing notion of "one man, one vote," a notion which has resulted in continual attempts to relate representation to demographic changes. Finally the belief that voting itself was the sole criterion of representation has in time transformed all elected officials, including governors and members of upper houses, into other kinds of representatives of the people, standing in a sometimes awkward relationship to the original houses of representatives.

This extreme localism and the demand for actuality of representation had more than constitutional importance. It had social implications of even greater significance for the character of our politics. Even before the revolutionary turmoil had settled, some Americans were arguing that mere voting by ordinary men was not a sufficient protection of ordinary men's interests, if only members of the elite were being elected. It was coming to be thought that in a society of diverse and particular interests men from one class or group, however educated and respectable, could not be acquainted with the needs of another class or group. Wealthy college-educated lawyers or merchants could not know the concerns of poor farmers or small tradesmen. The logic of the actuality of representation expressed in the Revolution required that ordinary men be represented by ordinary men. It was not enough for elected officials to be simply *for* the people; they now had to be *of* the people as well.

Such an idea constituted an extraordinary transformation in the way people looked at the relation between government and society; it lay at the heart of the radicalism of the American Revolution. It was strengthened by a powerful ideological force—equality—the most important and corrosive doctrine in American culture. At the outset of the Revolution, equality to most American leaders had meant an equality of legal rights and the opportunity to rise by merit through clearly discernible ranks. But in the hands of competing politicians seeking to diminish the stature of their opponents and win votes, the idea of equality was expanded in ways that few of its supporters had originally anticipated to mean in time that one man was as good as another. This meaning of equality soon dissolved the traditional identity between social and political leadership and helped to give political power to the kinds of men who had hitherto never held it. Politics became egalitarian after the Revolution in ways it never had been before, and the political upstarts—obscure men with obscure backgrounds—launched vigorous attacks on the former attributes of social superiority—names, titles, social origins, family connections—and bragged that their own positions were based not on relatives or friends but only on what their money had made for them.

We have a particularly illuminating example of the new attitudes in the case of a William Thompson, an unknown tavern keeper of Charleston, South Carolina, of the early 1780s. John Rutledge, a distinguished social and political leader in South Carolina, had sent a female servant to Thompson's tavern to watch a fireworks display from the roof. Thompson denied the servant admittance and sent her back to Rutledge, who was furious and requested that Thompson come to his house and apologize. Thompson refused and, believing his honor affronted by Rutledge's arrogant request, challenged Rutledge to a duel. Now the social likes of Rutledge did not accept challenges from tavern keepers, so Rutledge went to the South Carolina House of Representatives, of which he was a member, and demanded that it pass a bill banishing Thompson from the state for insulting a member of its government. Thompson took to the press for his defense and in 1784 made what can only be described as a classic expression of American egalitarian resentment against social superiority —a resentment voiced, as Thompson said, not on behalf of himself but on behalf of the people, or "those more especially, who go at this day, under the opprobrious appellation of, the *Lower Orders of Men.*"

Thompson was not merely attacking the few aristocratic "Nabobs" who had humiliated him; he was actually assaulting the entire idea of a social hierarchy ruled by a gentlemanly elite. In fact he turned prevailing eighteenth century opinion upside down and argued that the social aristocracy was peculiarly *unqualified* to rule politically. Rather than preparing men for political leadership in a free government, said Thompson, "signal opulence and influence," especially when united "by intermarriage or otherwise," were really "calculated to subvert *Republicanism.*" The "persons and conduct" of the South Carolina "Nabobs" like Rutledge "in *private* life, may be unexceptionable, and even amiable, but their pride, influence, ambition, connections, wealth, and political principles," Thompson argued, "ought in *public* life, ever to exclude them from *public confidence.*" All that was needed in republican leadership, said Thompson, was "being *good, able, useful,* and *friends to social equality,*" for in a republican government "consequence is from the *public opinion,* and not from *private fancy.*" In the press Thompson sardonically recounted how he, a tavern keeper, "a *wretch* of no higher rank in the Commonwealth than that of Common-Citizen," had been debased by what he called "those *self-exalted* characters, who affect to compose the *grand hierarchy* of the State, . . . for having dared to dispute with a John Rutledge, or any of the NABOB *tribe.*" The experience had been degrading enough to Thompson as a man but as a former militia officer it had been, he said, "insupportable"— indicating how revolutionary military service affected social mobility and social expectations. Undoubtedly, said Thompson, Rutledge had "conceived me his inferior." But like many others in these years—tavern keepers, farmers, petty merchants, small-time lawyers, former militia officers—Thompson could no longer "comprehend the *inferiority*."[4]

Many new politicians in the decades following, likewise not being able to comprehend their inferiority, used the popular and egalitarian ideals of the Revolution to upset the older social hierarchy and bring ordinary people like themselves into politics. This was not always easy, for, as some politicians complained, "the poorer commonality," even when they possessed the legal right to vote, seemed apathetic to appeals and too accepting of traditional authority. Their ideas of government had too long been "rather aristocratical than popular." "The rich," said one polemicist, "having been used to govern, seem to think it is their right," while the common people, "having hitherto had little or no hand in government, seem to think it does not belong to them to have any."[5] To convince the people that they rightfully had a share in government became the task of egalitarian politicians in the decades after the Revolution, giving birth in the process to modern democratic politics. This democratization of politics involved not only the legal widening of the electorate, but also the extension of practices begun before the Revolution in activating those who legally could but often did not vote.

More and more offices, including judgeships, were made directly elective and everyone, it seemed, was now "running"—not, as earlier, simply "standing"—for election. New acts of persuasion using cheap newspapers and mass meetings were developed, and politics assumed carnival-like characteristics that led during the nineteenth century to participation by higher percentages of the electorate than ever again was achieved in American politics. In such an atmosphere of stump-speaking and "running" for office the members of the

[4] Gordon S. Wood, *The Creation of the American Republic, 1776–1787* (Chapel Hill: University of North Carolina Press, 1969), pp. 482–483.
[5] Philadelphia, *Pennsylvania Evening Post*, July 30, 1776, quoted in David Hawke, *In the Midst of a Revolution* (Philadelphia: University of Pennsylvania Press, 1961), p. 187.

older gentry were frequently at a considerable disadvantage. In fact by the early nineteenth century being a gentleman or professing the characteristics of a gentleman became a liability in elections in some parts of the country, and a member of the gentry campaigning for votes was forced to take off his white gloves if he wanted to beat the tavern keeper who was calling him an aristocratic dandy.

One of the most graphic examples of this kind of change in American politics occurred in the 1868 election campaign for the fifth congressional district of Massachusetts—Essex County, the former center of Massachusetts Brahminism but by the mid-nineteenth century increasingly filled by Irish immigrants. The campaign was essentially between Richard Henry Dana, Jr., a well-to-do and Harvard-educated descendant of a distinguished Massachusetts family and author of *Two Years Before the Mast*, and Benjamin Butler, son of a boardinghouse keeper who had never been to college and one of the most flamboyant demagogues American politics has ever produced. (One gets some idea of Butler's standing with the Massachusetts elite by realizing that he was the first governor of Massachusetts in over two centuries not invited to a Harvard College commencement.) In the congressional campaign Butler showed Dana what nineteenth century electoral politics was all about. While Dana was talking to tea groups about bond payments, Butler was haranguing the Irish shoe workers of Lynn, organizing parades, turning out the fire and police departments, hiring brass bands, distributing hundreds of pamphlets and torches, and charging his opponent with being a Beau Brummel in white gloves. Dana was simply no match for him. When Dana was finally forced to confront audiences of workingmen, he gave up talking about bonds and even doffed his white gloves, trying desperately to assure his audiences that he too worked hard. All the while Butler was making fun of his efforts to make common cause with the people. During one speech Dana told the Irish shoe workers that when he spent two years before the mast as a young sailor he too was a laborer who didn't wear any white gloves: "I was as dirty as any of you," he exclaimed. With such statements it is not surprising that Dana ended up with

less than 10 percent of the vote in a humiliating loss to Butler.[6]

The rise of egalitarian politics, evident in Butler's campaigning, was the result not only of an expanded electorate
but also of the final collapse of the older social hierarchy and
the traditional belief in elite rule. It was this kind of change
in the first half of the nineteenth century that made the rise
of political parties both necessary and possible. Indeed, the
United States was the first nation to develop modern political
parties. The broadened electorate and the end of any sort of
automatic assumption of political leadership by the social
elite required new instruments for the mobilization of voters
and the recruitment of leaders. Individuals, cut loose from
traditional ties to the social hierarchy, were now forced to
combine in new groups for political ends. Political office no
longer was set by social ascription but rather was won by political achievement within the organization of a party and
through the winning of votes. By vying for political leadership and competing for votes, new men—not necessarily as
flamboyant as Butler but having the same social obscurity
and doomed in any other kind of society to remain in obscurity—were fed into the political process and rose not
because they became gentry but because they knew how to
appeal to the people.

It was the American Revolution that helped to make possible and to accelerate these changes in our politics. As a result
of this republican Revolution, Americans could not easily
legitimize any status other than that of citizen. The people
were all there was in politics and all of the people were equal.
Any sort of unequal restrictions on the rights of citizenship—
on the right to run for office or to vote, for example—were
anomalies, relics of an older society, that now had to be done
away with. In the early decades of the nineteenth century the
permissive ideas of representation, citizenship, and equality
encouraged competing political parties to search out groups
of people hitherto uninvolved in the political process and

---

[6] Samuel Shapiro, "'Aristocracy, Mud, and Vituperation': The
Butler-Dana Campaign," *New England Quarterly*, vol. 31 (1958),
pp. 340–360.

bring them in—renters denied the suffrage because they were not freeholders, poor men who lacked the necessary property qualifications, or newly arrived immigrants, anyone who might become a voter and supporter of the party, or even one of its leaders. If they could not yet legally vote, the vote could be given them. If they could legally vote but did not, then they could be convinced they ought to. In these ways American politicians in the decades following the Revolution worked to establish universal manhood suffrage and democratic politics.

We take these developments for granted and easily forget how far ahead of the rest of the world the United States was in the early nineteenth century. Tavern keepers and weavers were sitting in our legislatures while Europeans were still trying to disentangle voting and representation from an incredible variety of estate and corporate statuses. In 1792 Kentucky entered the union with a constitution allowing universal manhood suffrage. A generation later the English were still debating whether voting was a privilege confined to a few; in fact England had to wait until 1867 before workingmen got the vote and became, in Gladstone's words, "our fellow subjects." Indeed, in many parts of the world today the people are still waiting to become citizens, full participants in the political process.

II

Yet, as we all too well know, America's record in integrating the people into politics has not been entirely a success story. The great anomaly amidst all the revolutionary talk of equality, voting, and representation was slavery. Indeed, it was the Revolution itself, not only with its appeal to liberty but with its idea of citizenship of equal individuals, that made slavery in 1776 suddenly seem anomalous to large numbers of Americans. What had often been taken for granted earlier in the eighteenth century as part of the brutality of life—regarded as merely the most base and degraded status in a society of infinite degrees and multiple ranks of freedom and un-

freedom—now seemed conspicuous and peculiar. In a republic, as was not the case in a monarchy, there could be
no place for degrees of freedom or dependency. In the North,
where slavery was considerable but not deeply rooted, the exposure of the anomaly worked to abolish it: by 1830 in the
northern states there were less than 3,000 black slaves out of
a northern black population of over 125,000.[7] In the South
the suddenly exposed anomaly of slavery threw southern
whites, who had been in the vanguard of the revolutionary
movement and among the most fervent spokesmen for its
libertarianism, onto the defensive and gradually separated
them from the mainstream of America's egalitarian developments.

Yet the very egalitarianism of America's republican
ideology—the egalitarianism that undercut the rationale of
slavery—worked at the same time to inhibit integrating the
free black man into the political nation. Since republican citizenship implied equality for all citizens, a person once admitted as a citizen into the political process was put on a level
with all other citizens and regarded as being as good as the
next man. With the spread of these republican assumptions
northern whites began to view black voters with increasing
apprehension, unwilling to accept the equality that suffrage
and citizenship dictated. In 1800 in many states of the North
free Negroes possessed the right to vote (often as a result of
the general extension of the franchise that took place during
the Revolution), and they exercised it in some areas with particular effectiveness. But in subsequent years, as the electorate continued to expand through changes in the law and the
mobilization of new voters, the blacks found themselves
being squeezed out. There is perhaps no greater irony in the
democratization of American politics in the first half of the
nineteenth century than the fact that as the white man
gained the vote the black man lost it. During the heyday of
Jacksonian democracy white populist majorities in state after
state in the North moved to eliminate the remaining prop-

---

[7] Arthur Zilversmit, *The First Emancipation: The Abolition of
Slavery in the North* (Chicago: University of Chicago Press, 1967),
p. 222.

erty restrictions on white voters while at the same time con-
cocting new restrictions to take away the franchise from
Negro voters who had in some cases exercised it for decades.
No state admitted to the union after 1819 allowed blacks to
vote. By 1840, 93 percent of northern free Negroes lived in
states which completely or practically excluded them from
the suffrage and hence from participation in politics.[8]

This exclusion of blacks from politics was largely a
consequence of white fears of the equality that republican
citizenship demanded. But it was also a product of competitive democratic politics. In some states, like Pennsylvania,
Negro exclusion was the price paid for lower-class whites'
gaining the right to vote—universal manhood suffrage having
been opposed on the grounds it would add too many blacks
to the electorate. In other states, like New York, exclusion of
the Negro from the franchise was an effective way for Democratic party majorities to eliminate once and for all blocs of
Negro voters who had tended to vote first for Federalist and
then for Whig candidates. Since the Democratic party, as the
spokesman for the popular cause against elitism, was in the
forefront of the move to expand the suffrage, it seemed to be
good politics for the party not only to attract new voters to
its ranks but to take away voters who supported its opponents. It was this kind of political pressure that led to the
peculiar situation in some states where immigrant aliens were
granted the right to vote before they became citizens whereas
Negroes born and bred in the United States had theirs
abolished—a development often based on a shrewd assessment by politicians of what particular parties the new immigrants and the blacks would support.

For a republican society it was an impossible situation and
Americans wrestled with it for over a half century. Federal
officials in the first half of the nineteenth century could never
decide the precise status of free Negroes, sometimes arguing
that blacks were not citizens in having the right to vote but
were citizens in having the right to secure passports. Others

[8] Leon F. Litwack, *North of Slavery: The Negro in the Free
States, 1790–1860* (Chicago: University of Chicago Press, 1961), p.
75.

tried to discover some sort of intermediate legal position for free blacks as denizens standing between aliens and citizens. But the logic of republican equality would not allow these distinctions, and sooner or later many sought escape from the dilemma posed by Negro disfranchisement by denying citizenship outright to all blacks, whether slave or free, the position Chief Justice Taney tried to establish in the Dred Scott decision of 1857. The suffrage had become sufficiently equated with representation in America so that if a person was not granted the right to vote then he was not represented in the community; and not being represented in a republican community was equivalent to not being a citizen. In the end enslaved blacks without liberty and free blacks without citizenship were such contradictions of the revolutionary ideals that sooner or later those contradictions had to tear the country apart.

When northerners came to debate methods of southern reconstruction at the end of the Civil War, they moved reluctantly but steadily toward Negro enfranchisement, impelled both by the logic of the persisting ideals of the Revolution and by the circumstances of politics. Although some historians have believed that the Republican party's espousal of Negro suffrage in the late 1860s was based on a cynical desire to recruit new voters to the party, it was obviously based on much more than that. In terms of political expediency alone the Republicans' sponsorship of Negro suffrage ran the risk even in the North of what we have come to call "white backlash." Many advocates of Negro suffrage sincerely believed, as Wendell Philips put it, that America could never be truly a united nation "until every class God has made, from the lakes to the Gulf, has its ballot to protect itself."[9]

Yet there can be no doubt that black enfranchisement after the Civil War was fed, like all reforms, by political exigencies, and that many northerners and Republicans favored it grudgingly and only as a means of preventing the resur-

[9] James M. McPherson, "The Ballot and Land for the Freedmen, 1861–1865," in Kenneth M. Stampp and Leon F. Litwack, eds., *Reconstruction: An Anthology of Revisionist Writings* (Baton Rouge: Louisiana State University Press, 1969), p. 138.

gence of an unreconstructed Democratic South that would threaten the dominance of the Republican party. Hence there resulted an awkward gap between the Fourteenth Amendment, which defined citizenship for the first time and gave it a national emphasis which it had hitherto lacked, and the Fifteenth Amendment, which enfranchised the Negro but unfortunately linked his enfranchisement not to his citizenship but to his race. This linkage allowed a state to impose any voting qualifications it chose so long as they were not based on race, creating a tangled situation that twentieth-century Americans are still trying to unravel.

III

Although Americans have hesitated to make the connection between citizenship and the right to vote explicit and unequivocal, everything in American history has pointed toward that connection. During the past decade or so, largely under the impetus of the civil rights movement but going beyond that, there has been heightened interest in political and voting rights, and the logic of principles concerning suffrage and representation first articulated in the Revolution 200 years ago has been drawn out. Voting rights acts and the anti-poll tax amendment of the mid-1960s were based on a deeply rooted belief that no nation like ours could in conscience exclude any of its citizens from the political process. It was the same legacy from the Revolution that led the Supreme Court in a series of reapportionment decisions to apply the idea of "one man, one vote" to congressional and state legislative electoral districting. Large and unequal campaign contributions are of such concern precisely because they seem to negate the effects of an equal suffrage and to do violence to equality of participation in the political process. Despite an electorate that at times seems apathetic, interest in the suffrage and in the actuality and equality of consent has never been greater than it is today. Such a concern naturally puts a terrific burden on our political system, but it is a burden we should gladly bear (and many other nations would

love to have it), for it bespeaks an underlying popular
confidence in the processes of politics that surface events and
news headlines make us too easily ignore.

In fact, concern with the suffrage and with the formal
rights of consent has assumed such a transcendent
significance that it has sometimes obscured the substance of
democratic politics and has led to an exaggeration of the real
power of the legal right to vote. The suffrage has become
such a symbol of citizenship that its possession seems necessarily to involve all kinds of rights. Thus acquiring the vote
has often seemed an instrument of reform, a means of solving
complicated social problems. The women's rights movement
of the nineteenth century—premised on the belief, as one
woman put it in 1848, that "there is no reality in any power
that cannot be coined into votes"—came to focus almost
exclusively on the gaining of the suffrage.[10] And when the
Nineteenth Amendment giving women the franchise was
finally ratified in 1920 and did not lead to the promised revolution, the sense of failure set the feminist movement back at
least a half century—a setback from which it has only
recently been recovering. Even today this formal integration
into the political process through the suffrage continues to be
regarded as a panacea for social ills. Certainly this assumption
lay behind the response to the youth rebellions of the late
1960s and the eventual adoption of the Twenty-sixth Amendment granting eighteen-year-olds the vote.

This special fascination with politics and this reliance on
political integration through voting as a means of solving
social problems are legacies of our Revolution, and they are
as alive now as they were 200 years ago. The Revolution not
only brought ordinary people into politics. It also created
such a confidence in the suffrage as the sole criterion of representation that we have too often forgotten just what makes
the right to vote workable in America. In our dealings with
newly developing nations we are too apt to believe that the
mere institution of the ballot in a new state will automat-

[10] Chilton Williamson, *American Suffrage from Property to Democracy, 1760–1860* (Princeton: Princeton University Press, 1960),
p. 279.

ically create a viable democratic society, and we are confused and disillusioned when this rarely happens.

The point is that we have the relationship backwards. It is not the suffrage that gives life to our democracy; it is our democratic society that gives life to the suffrage. American society is permeated by the belief in (and to an extraordinary extent by the reality of) equality that makes our reliance on the ballot operable. As historians in the past two decades have only begun to discover, it was not the breadth of the franchise in the nineteenth century that created democratic politics. The franchise was broad even in colonial times. Rather it was the egalitarian process of politics that led to the mobilization of voters and the political integration of the nation. It was the work of countless politicians recruited from all levels of society and representing many diverse elements, attempting to win elections by exhorting and pleasing their electors, that in the final analysis shaped our democratic system. Any state can grant the suffrage to its people overnight, but it cannot thereby guarantee to itself a democratic polity. As American history shows, such a democracy required generations of experience with electoral politics. More important, it requires the emergence of political parties and egalitarian politicians—none of whom have too much power and most of whom run scared—politicians whose maneuverings for electoral advantage, whose courting of the electorate, and whose passion for victory result in the end in grander and more significant developments than they themselves can foresee or even imagine. Politicians are at the heart of our political system, and insofar as it is democratic they have made it so.

CAROLINE ROBBINS
The Pursuit of Happiness

Delivered in Gallier Hall, New Orleans, Louisiana

on January 30, 1974

This is a sermon: I shall reexamine familiar words and try to illuminate their meaning at the time they were written and their significance to the revolutionary generation whose thoughts they were intended to express. This may, in turn, suggest their continuing relevancy to ourselves, even though our times and circumstances are different. Words, like books, are not absolutely dead things contained in dictionaries and manipulated by wordmongers. They have a life and vitality of their own, and sometimes undergo astonishing transformations. If they occur in revered documents and are often repeated, they do not so much alter, as accrue importance. Their analysis is, perhaps, one of the most valuable services that celebrations like this bicentennial can render. The Declaration of Independence was all-important as a statement of its signers' convictions and of the beliefs of the country represented by them. The effect ultimately upon the British, to whom its indictment and intentions were directed, was far-reaching. It can also now, during our festivities and memorials, become freshly a part of the aspirations of this age, and remind us all of the ever-unfinished business of life and work in these United States.

Here is my text:

We hold these truths to be self-evident, that all men are created equal, that they are endowed by their Creator

with certain unalienable Rights, that among these are
Life, Liberty and the pursuit of Happiness.—That to
secure these rights, governments are instituted among
Men, deriving their just powers from the consent of the
governed.

What did Thomas Jefferson mean? What was understood at
the time by his words? John Adams, Benjamin Franklin,
Philip Livingston, and Roger Sherman were associated with
him on the drafting committee and, after the Continental
Congress had adopted the Declaration, were among the fifty-
six Americans who signed it on or after July 4, 1776. The
phrases were felicitous and bold. The rights claimed were already dear to the colonists' hearts. The reasons listed for the
dissolution of the political "bands" to Great Britain seemed
valid. The indictment of George III, and by implication of
his ministers and people, appeared convincing. To many
these were firmly persuasive: that others preferred the inconvenience of imperial control and the hardships of exile is also
indisputably true. The loyalists were many, but with few exceptions less articulate. But public opinion and action
prompted by it are commonly determined by the vigorous
and outspoken, as well as helped greatly by the mistakes and
misconceptions of their opponents. The British government
and people at large seemed, during the critical years after
1763, singularly unable to recognize the significance of what
was happening overseas and, with a few but notable exceptions, altogether misunderstood the American political
stance. The course of events, the changing circumstances of
both mother country and those who had left her for the New
World, must be carefully scrutinized to estimate the total situation. The subject now being discussed does not include
description or analysis of what led to the rupture in 1776.
Thus it is only a part of the seamless robe of history.
Confined to the quoted text, my topic concerns intellectual
crosscurrents, and in particular their relation to the eighteenth century's conception of happiness and the meaning
Jefferson probably attached to it.

Jefferson—for he, and not his distinguished colleagues of
the committee, nor of the Continental Congress, was chiefly

responsible for the Declaration. His draft was amended to be sure; some few words and phrases were changed or omitted and an important section, that on slavery, left out. But all testimony witnesses to the Virginian's authorship of the document, and his selection of the words "Life, Liberty and the pursuit of Happiness." In choosing them Jefferson altered the more familiar trinity of life, liberty and property, or estates. Bills of rights published with the new state constitutions drawn up after independence was declared often made use of the earlier form, adding to it, as in Pennsylvania, for example, the promotion of "safety and happiness," or some similar statement about the aims of government.

Before listing others who had employed the phrase "pursuit of happiness" in one or another context, examining some variations in the meaning and motivation the eighteenth century attributed to the search for private and public felicity, and analyzing Jefferson's own position, a word is in order on the traditional trio. The right to life seems obvious. Even Thomas Hobbes in *The Leviathan* (1651), a polemic setting forth the necessity for a sovereign power in the state, conceded the subject the right to defend his own person against assault. But I would like to point out that in the seventeenth and eighteenth centuries, the matter of life was discussed in yet other contexts. The use of torture was widely questioned and abolished by some European rulers. Capital punishment for many of the offenses for which it was then the penalty was questioned, even condemned. Three famous men— F. M. A. Voltaire, dramatist, novelist, historian and propagandist, John Howard, Quaker sheriff of Bedford and author of a much-read examination of Western prisons, and Cesare Beccaria, the Italian marquis who wrote *On Crimes and Punishment* (1764)—were enormously influential in Europe and America. Prussia, for example, modified its penal code, and Virginia and Pennsylvania also effected considerable changes in their penal practices and in the retribution for offenses committed. I am not claiming that Jefferson in placing life first among rights was consciously behaving in any but the conventional manner of all opponents of tyranny; but I am suggesting here and in passing that, in the period of the

American Revolution and the new constitutions and laws then adopted, life, its treatment and disposal were becoming an issue of deeper consequence than the mere matter of existence, or of self-defense.

Liberty, the second of the three, has meant dissimilar things to different generations and various associations of men, applying in some ages only to the privilege of a ruling elite or of the members of an established religion. More extensively as in the Declaration, it could be cited as an assertion of resistance rights, the right to experiment and to change the form of government under which one lived, to redefine professed creeds or alter ancient ceremony in church service. Freedom in these matters was often discussed in the sixteenth and seventeenth centuries; ancient civil and religious establishments were then being overthrown, and authority of all sorts questioned. With the invention of printing, the presses could pour forth to an increasingly literate public propaganda about rights, claims, and innovations asserted. For Jefferson and the American colonists the meaning of liberty was threefold: the right to rebel against a government believed to be tyrannical and unjust, the right to worship freely in a church of the individual's choice, and the right to devise a government to secure newly acquired freedom. In all steps taken and in all decisions about them, this third right assumed that the people were always a party to decisions made.

Independence came by throwing off the British yoke, by actions that, before their successful issue was assured, have been called rebellious. Liberty was thus essential to the cause of independence and, according to John Locke, to happiness. The natural right to liberty made the people's activity legitimate. "The tree of Liberty" Jefferson wrote, "must be refreshed from time to time with the blood of patriots and tyrants. It is its natural manure."[1] Even in less troubled times a mild riot or rising had a medicinal effect, he thought, writing at the time of Daniel Shays's rebellion in Massachusetts, in 1786. Resistance to any government failing to meet the needs of the contemporary world could be justified. Consti-

[1] Jefferson to William S. Smith, November 13, 1787.

tutions should not be regarded as "perpetual and unaltera-
ble."[2] Each generation might well find due cause for change
and amendment. Jefferson despised what he called looking
backwards and studying "musty records."[3] Man gave up eating the acorns primitive savages had devoured, forsook
obsolete weapons like bows and arrows when better were invented, and discarded those garments like fig leaves that were
useful in the garden of Eden or had fitted him when he was a
boy.[4] "The earth," he wrote to James Madison, "belongs to
the living."[5]

A majority of citizens acting directly and personally could
draw up the rules they believed suited their needs. In
America, when the Confederacy formed after independence
seemed insufficient for the needs of a new nation, a convention was called in Philadelphia, and another constitution
created. Jefferson watched the progress of the debates in 1787
from his position abroad. On the whole he welcomed the
republic as then devised, though he criticized the failure
(soon repaired by the amendments of 1789) to frame at the
time a bill of rights, and he regretted the absence of limitation on presidential tenure. This is all an old story to you,
but it serves to show that the revolutionary of 1776 continued to defend the right to change and to adapt government to the demands of the passing years. Some further
amendments would no doubt have pleased him, particularly
perhaps those concerning the widening of the franchise and
the extension of civil rights. Possibly he would have wished
for even more. In any case he was always interested in the
participation of the people in government on as wide a basis
as possible. A natural aristocracy of talent might, he believed,
emerge, but that should be a matter of choice and selection,
and not of inherited wealth or status.

[2] To James Madison, December 20, 1787, and September 6,
1789; to Samuel Kercheval, July 12, 1816, on change and government.
[3] To John Cartwright, January 5, 1824.
[4] To Kercheval, see note 2; to Roger Weightman, June 24, 1826;
compare with Algernon Sidney, *Discourses*, chapter III, section vii.
[5] To James Madison, September 6, 1789 and January 30, 1787.

The right to liberty also implied religious freedom. On his tombstone, you will remember, Jefferson wanted his authorship of the Declaration of Independence, the founding of the University of Virginia, and the act for establishing religious liberty in his native state, memorialized. He had drawn up in 1779 a bill for religious liberty which at that time aroused some opposition in the Virginia assembly, but which with some minor alterations passed in 1786. The act was then printed in both English and French, and widely distributed at home and abroad. When John Adams visited Thomas Brand Hollis in Essex in 1786, he discovered that his friend was responsible for the printing of the Virginia act by a printer at Chelmsford nearby.[6] Jefferson believed that difference of opinion was advantageous, deplored uniformity and inflexibility. Without divergence from the orthodox, or heresies, he maintained, neither Christianity nor the discoveries of Galileo could have been accepted. God had created the mind free. To influence its processes by temporal punishment and civil incapacitation could only result in hypocrisy. The legitimate way to recruit for church membership, or new ideologies of any kind, was by reason and persuasion. Men should not be obliged to contribute towards the propagation of creeds, nor the upkeep of services or the establishments of denominations, whose opinions they did not share. At the Continental Congress of 1774, Quakers and Baptists astonished and embarrassed the New England delegation by protesting the dues exacted from all residents of the colony to meet the expenses of the Congregational churches there.[7] Tithe as elsewhere collected was regarded as another grievance. Jefferson declared all such fees tyrannical. Men's beliefs and devotional customs were not the proper concern of the civil authorities, except in those cases where they led to overt acts which could be shown to have disturbed the peace and brought hardship to others. The right to religious liberty was natural and fundamental; to narrow its scope in any way was

---

[6] John Adams, *Diary and Autobiography*, ed. Lyman Butterfield (Cambridge, Mass.: Belknap Press of Harvard University, 1961), vol. 3, p. 197.

[7] Ibid., vol. 2, p. 152, vol. 3, pp. 311–312.

inexcusable. Jefferson supported the fullest possible freedom for every shade of opinion and, in general, opposed censorship of all kinds. Throughout his life he continued to regard liberty as an unalienable right.[8]

Turning to the third of the traditional trinity, property, for which Jefferson substituted the pursuit of happiness, we at once discover one of those word changes affecting meaning to which I referred earlier. In the seventeenth century property was frequently written propriety, a term carrying with its use much wider implications than estates and possessions. Property and propriety were used separately and together, often for the same things indiscriminately, though the latter perhaps more generally in a comprehensive sense. There is a thing called property that the people of England are fondest of, George Villiers, second duke of Buckingham, declared in the House of Lords on November 16, 1675, using his statement as an argument for indulgence to the much-harassed Protestant dissenters, conscience being the property of all serious men.[9] Richard Baxter, noted Presbyterian author and divine, wrote of "Propriety" as naturally antecedent to government "which doth not give it, but regulate it for the common good," and went on to say that men's lives and liberties were the chief part of their propriety. John Locke, writing only a little later in the *Two Treatises of Government* (1690), was careful to explain that he called "by the general name Property" the preservation of lives, liberties and estates, "all in short that a man owned in his person." The philosopher used both spellings. The magic formula is thus, it seems, repetitious: each part could be taken to include the others.[10]

Not that Americans were by any means indifferent to property, or their right to it. Jefferson defended the more literal significance of property in the detailed indictment of the

[8] An Act for establishing Religious Freedom, 1779, passim; in *Notes on Virginia* (1784), discussion in Query xvii.

[9] Baldwin's State Tracts (London, 1689), p. 62.

[10] For quotations and discussion of term property by Locke and Baxter, see John Locke, *Two Treatises of Government*, ed. Peter Laslett (Cambridge, England: University Press, 1960), pp. 101 and 101n, 305n.

king in the facts he submitted "to a candid world." Among other illegal practices, he listed infringements upon American estates by taxation without representation, at least of any kind recognized by the colonists, in the British Parliament, and the forced collection of dues and duties. Property had been threatened by the cutting off of trade, the erection of a multitude of new offices, and the stationing of troops in peacetime "to eat out our substance," as well as by those stamp and tea taxes which had caused so much furore. The immediate occasion of friction between American and Briton was the claim of the legislature at Westminster to revenue from the colonies. The crimes committed were spelled out in the Declaration. But in substituting the pursuit of happiness for property, Jefferson probably had in mind the right to larger aspirations than those expressed in defiance of unwarranted taxation.

My text includes the statement that "men are created equal," but I am not going to dwell on this. It was by no means the first expression of its kind. When Adam delved and Eve span, who was then the gentleman? was a question revealing continuing aspirations in the hearts of the oppressed or downtrodden. An equality before the Almighty was also recalled from time to time, though implementation in this world was but seldom attempted. An assertion of equality for the "poorest he" is difficult to translate into twentieth-century terms. Cecelia Kenyon, one of our most learned political scientists, has suggested that the phrase, pursuit of happiness, reveals an egalitarianism in Jefferson. I am not sure that I agree. Jefferson certainly believed that as many as feasible should have an equal opportunity to work, to seek happiness, and to exercise their political rights. He himself helped to get rid of legal customs like primogeniture and entail, testamentary procedures which resulted in the accumulation of estates in the hands of eldest son and heir. He is known to have preferred a society composed of landholders not markedly disparate in wealth, and is often reproached with unrealistically seeing this agrarian utopia as better than the foreseeable developments of a monied economy. Possibly later economic revolutions would have modified his view. But in the present connection neither the equality he believed in, nor other conceptions of it held by his contemporaries, can be readily expressed in modern terms. In the twentieth century, far greater government activity, not to mention the procedures of giant industrial and commercial corporations, play a role in implementation of equality. Socialism, communism, paternalism, or civil rights movements each have different ways to propose to bring about equality, none dreamed of in the eighteenth century. Professor Richard Morris contrasts earlier concepts with the contemporary demand for an inequality resulting from quotas of age, sex, and race.[11] Life, liberty, and property—even happiness, as I hope to show—present much of more relevancy to ourselves and our problems than does equality.

II

When I began these inquiries into the use and meaning of the phrase, pursuit of happiness, I questioned my friends and searched more learned authorities than myself. A colleague immediately declared that the phrase was merely a formal way of stating that Americans in the new world of opportunity had a greater chance of happiness than most other people. A chance, that is, once they had rid themselves of the tyranny of the wicked English. More portentously another said it was obvious that everyone wanted to be happy: in 1776 the Puritans were already outnumbered, and it was, therefore, acceptable to say so. A scholar of great erudition reminded me that, during the preceding century, the hedonist tradition (the doctrine taught by Epicurus in the third century before Christ) that pleasure was the chief good was enjoying a vigorous revival. Each, another suggested, had as unalienable a right to be happy as all the rest. Cautious philosophers supposed that since a considerable number of volumes had, over the past decades, variously discussed happi-

[11] Richard B. Morris, *Seven Who Shaped Our Destiny: The Founding Fathers as Revolutionaries* (New York: Harper & Row, 1973), p. 273.

ness and its connection with truth, beauty, virtue, and the good state, the matter was in the air, and almost inevitably found a place along with other rights claimed.

Among authorities studied two learned articles on our subject by H. L. Gantor were useful and stimulating.[12] The author, with the aid of monographs by such scholars as Gilbert Chinard, specializing in Jefferson's reading, notes inspired by it, and the *Commonplace Book,* tracked down earlier uses of the phrase on happiness. There were many. The citations noticed usually occurred in discussions of the motivation of life and politics. Locke, in *An Essay Concerning Human Understanding* (1690),[13] emphasized a determination to seek happiness, foundation of liberty. Peter Paxton in *Civil Polity* (1705) wrote of the pursuit as "inseparable from the nature of man." Many others thereafter referred to it in similar or identical mode. Most were apparently moderately optimistic about the results of the quest, but Blaise Pascal in his *Pensées* (circa 1660) and Bishop Joseph Butler, author of *The Analogy* (1736), were not. Pascal was sure that happiness would only be found in the next world; Butler that in this, all that could be hoped for was a mitigation of misery. Gantor and Chinard explored the influence of some of the natural-rights school—men like J. Burlamqui and Jefferson's contemporaries, Richard Bland and James Wilson. Anyone who wishes to delve more deeply into the political theories of the revolutionary period should investigate the suggestions these writers and others have made. Most profitable, for a beginning perhaps, would be the three following volumes: Clinton Rossiter, *Seedtime of the Republic;* the Library of Congress's recent volume, *The Fundamental Testaments of the American Revolution* (Washington, 1973), containing among others Kenyon's paper, "The Declaration of Independence," and the many essays contained in *The Reinterpretation of the American Revolution, 1763–89,* edited by Jack P. Greene.[14]

---

[12] *William and Mary Quarterly,* second series, vol. 16, 1936, pp. 422–434, 558–585.

[13] Book II, chapter xxi, paragraphs 42, 51, and 59.

[14] Rossiter (New York: Harcourt Brace), 1953; Kenyon, pp. 25–45; Greene, ed. (New York: Harper & Row), 1963.

There was probably no time when most thoughtful people would have denied man's overwhelming desire for happiness, or would not have agreed that governments should seek to ensure what measure of felicity they thought possible in time and circumstance. This is to say, of course, that rulers commonly claimed to provide, in some sense or another, a predominance of pleasure over pain for those they governed. Interpretation of what constituted this for the people at large might differ greatly. The best and most admired state might well be, as Algernon Sidney believed, that "which best provides for war," the people presumably profiting in the long run by victory. Sidney, a republican martyr for the good old cause of liberty against tyranny, was thinking of security, but it is significant of the period that in this chapter of his *Discourses*, though he pays tribute to increase of population, strength and wealth, he states that that commonwealth which does not enlarge in power or wealth is useless.[15] Authorities like Jean Bodin believed that only under an all powerful sovereign could the happiness he admitted to be the end of government be achieved. Others at certain times believed a forced conversion to what they conceived of as the true faith, best for the ultimate felicity of their own subjects, or even for those of another country. Mohammedan and Christian fought holy wars. Hostilities were also undertaken for the announced purpose of the prevention or obstruction of aggression. For the honor of the realm, governments were obliged to maintain order, security, and prosperity. How they were to do this was not a matter of general agreement. "'Tis true," wrote William Penn, in the Preface to his first "Frame of Government" (1682), men "seem to agree in the end"— that is of government—"but in the means they differ, as to divine, so to this human felicity, and the cause is much the same, not always want of light and knowledge, but want of using them rightly."[16]

Controversy raged in the sixteenth and seventeenth centuries over the form and power of government. Even the natural-rights school of thought, to which belonged the writers

[15] *Discourses*, Chapter II, section 23.
[16] Frederick B. Tolles and E. Gordon Alderfer, *The Witness of William Penn* (New York: Macmillan Company, 1957), p. 110.

Hugo Grotius, Samuel Puffendorf, Burlamqui and Emmerich de Vattel, after paying an almost pro-forma tribute to happiness, concentrated on individual privilege, military force, juridical process, corrupt or inefficient administration, international relations, and, of course, the kind of constitution which made for good government. Nor was this irrelevant, I hasten to add; but like Bernard de Fontenelle, the learned French virtuoso, in his essay *Du Bonheur*, I find the matter of happiness frequently mentioned, but seldom seriously analyzed. One example will illustrate this point. After the Revolution of 1688, Englishmen and their European contemporaries thought of Britain as singularly blessed with a constitution insuring the rights of the people and, presumably, their happiness. There was a movement under way at that time for the foundation of charity schools: sermons to encourage donations were preached fairly frequently; pamphlets about the schools were written, some supporting them as a useful insurance against disaffection, vice, ignorance and idleness, others opposing them as encouraging a lack of independence among the poor. Almost unparalleled was the attitude of the famous hymn writer and tutor, Dr. Isaac Watts, who was delighted that these schools and the instruction they offered might bring happiness to young persons thus enabled to write to their parents and enjoy some reading. The pursuit of happiness of this kind did not loom large in the visions of politicians and social reformers. Nor did they often talk of greater public happiness as the end or object of their labors.

Between the tumultuous decades of the mid-seventeenth century and the American Revolution a considerable literature was produced on various kinds of happiness. This eventually began to influence statesmanship. One reason for the works already mentioned was a revival in the reading of Stoic and Epicurean classics. Another was a change in theological assumption and mores: the virtues of asceticism were less stressed than formerly. Classification of the works relating specifically to happiness if accurate would be complex, but they can be roughly divided into those attributing human motivation solely to man's self-interest, his wish to avoid pain and to enjoy pleasure, and those finding man benevolent, aware that in the happiness of others his own might be found, and that in the practice of virtue, appreciation of beauty and truth, lay the path to felicity. There were treatises in both categories that dwelt upon the individual, but in both can be found attempts to examine the effects of private hedonism upon the commonweal, as well as the connection of the individual with the public welfare. In seeking out these books on virtue and happiness, beauty and truth, it is not always easy to guess whether the title implies a political philosophy or an esthetic approach.

The work of Hobbes stressed man's selfishness. Nasty and brutish in a state of nature, each warring for his own interests, man sought in society to prevent others harming or molesting him, and was prepared to cede absolute power to a sovereign to insure safety and happiness. The ruler's duty was thus largely that of protector and umpire from enemies abroad and hostile attackers at home. Bernard Mandeville, in *The Fable of the Bees: Or, Private Vices, Public Benefits* (1714), also believed the individual only intent on his own felicity. He checked his many readers by declaring that such egotism and self-indulgence might even be looked upon as contributing towards the common good: trade would prosper, luxury goods would make their manufacturers rich, increased profits in general might bring more employment and greater wealth to the community. Claud Helvetius in *L'Esprit* (1759) similarly proclaimed the single-minded concern of each solely for his own good. Even should he show sympathy for the suffering, Helvetius maintained, this could and should be understood as a means of relieving the discomfort he felt at the sight of another's misery. The only valid activation was self-love, a desire for personal happiness and security. To be sure, Helvetius erected on this hedonist principle a plan for society that had something to recommend it, but he outraged contemporaries with his denial of any nobility in man's spirit or nature.

In considering happiness some writers stood aside, and merely commented on its prevalence or rarity. The marquis de Chastellux, for example, in volumes on *Public Happiness* translated into English in 1774, traced the history of Western man, remarking that seldom if ever had governments lived up to what should be and was repeatedly said to be, their end, the acquisition of the greatest welfare of the greatest number of individuals. The marquis had hopes for the future. Perhaps when he visited America after the Revolution, he saw some of them realized. Other treatises, of which Gioconto Dragonetti's *Virtues and Reward* (Milan, 1749) was one, examined the relation of virtue and happiness. Another Italian, Ludovico Antonio Muratori at about the same time also published a work on *Public Happiness*. Philip Glover of Wispington in Lincolnshire in *An Inquiry concerning Virtue and Happiness* (written about 1726 but posthumously published in 1751) wrote that the pursuit of happiness was never rational, and emphasized the obligation to others involved in the pursuit. John Brown, famous for his gloomy *Estimate* (1757), believed that all virtuous actions brought happiness. The philosopher David Hartley was sure that man's perpetual hankering for happiness led not to selfishness but to the annihilation of self. All rational creatures, declared John Gay, an early utilitarian, directed their actions to each other's happiness. Abraham Tucker in his *Light of Nature Pursued* (1768), connected the desire for happiness with all measures of morality, and in the service both of God and man.

This tie between virtue and its rewards and effects, between public happiness and morality, was frequently discussed, and its bibliography reveals a confusingly similar array of titles. Among these, three important works must be mentioned. Richard Cumberland, bishop of Peterborough, produced in *The Laws of Nature* (1672) a refutation of Hobbes which went into many editions in Latin (in which it was first published) and English. The major end of the state must be, he argued, the well-being and happiness of the majority of the members composing it. The good bishop thus anticipated the famous phrase cointed later to define the criterion of good government. This phrase, "the greatest good of the greatest number," appeared first in *An Inquiry into the Original of our Ideas of Beauty and Virtue* (London, 1725),[17] by the famous Scots-Irish professor of moral philosophy, Francis Hutcheson. *An Inquiry*, written in Ireland, went

---

[17] *An Inquiry* (London: J. Darby, 1725), p. 164.

into five eighteenth-century editions, was translated into French and German, and exerted almost as much influence as Hutcheson's *Compend* and *System of Moral Philosophy*, published after the author had taught enthusiastic classes at Glasgow and increased the already wide range of his influence. He was, continuing and enriching their tradition, a disciple both of Cumberland and of Anthony Ashley-Cooper, third earl of Shaftesbury, whose *Characteristics* (1711) also proclaimed the best of good society as being found in the general happiness of its members.

Cumberland, Shaftesbury and Hutcheson saw in the conscience, or, as the latter two were to designate it, the moral sense, the origin of man's motivation in selecting the virtuous rather than the bad action. In the sympathy of this moral sense was found all that made association viable. That which all want is that which will bring about the felicity of the majority. Shaftesbury saw an almost universal, if sometimes only latent, benevolence inherent in human nature. This would be even more apparent when artificial restriction upon civil and religious liberty was removed and freedom from ignorance and superstition was achieved. Then, the earl was convinced, virtue and happiness would everywhere prevail: "To love the public, to study universal good, and to promote the interest of the whole as lies within our power, is surely the height of goodness, and makes that temper which we call divine."[18]

Jefferson evidently read Shaftesbury with care: the influence of the *Characteristics* upon him is often obvious. He took notes on the earl's ideas about toleration, he echoes his emphasis on good humor, on ridicule as a test of truth, as well as on utility as the criterion of virtue. From Shaftesbury, Hutcheson had, as noticed, drawn much, and in turn he affected the philosophies of Beccaria, Joseph Priestley, and Jeremy Bentham, in their adoption of the formula of the greatest happiness. This was, of course, to be the catchword of the English Utilitarians. By the principle of Utility,

[18] Shaftesbury, *Characteristics*, "A Letter Concerning Enthusiasm" (1707) section iv (or New York: Bobbs-Merrill Co., 1964, p. 27).

Bentham, their earliest protagonist, meant that which
approves or disapproves of every action personal or communal
as it produces private or public "benefit, advantage, pleasure,
good or happiness," and obversely prevents the happening of
pain and unhappiness. It should be noted that although, like
this formula or definition, many of the radical reforms advocated by the Utilitarians stemmed from their precursors,
the natural rights political philosophers, the Utilitarians
depart completely from them in rejecting those same natural
rights. Let me illustrate: in early and middle life, Bentham
was a passionate believer in the emancipation of all colonies
from imperial control and considered what he called "the
new nation," that is, the United States, perhaps "the most
enlightened in the globe." But he regretted that the American Founders had seen fit, in national and state declarations
and constitutions, to justify their excellent cause by reasons
"so much fitter to beget objections, than to remove them."[19]
The year 1776 represents an important date in developing
ideologies. In that year appeared *A Fragment on Government* by Bentham, *An Inquiry into the Nature and Causes of
the Wealth of Nations* by Adam Smith, advocating that
freedom of trade already advocated by a few and claimed as a
right by Jefferson in *A Summary View* two years before, and
Common Sense by Tom Paine, as well as the Declaration of
Independence. In all these documents the greatest happiness
principle was a fundamental assumption, but not all
proclaimed that faith in natural rights which had so strongly
pervaded earlier political manifestos, and in which the Americans so firmly believed.

In the last year of his life Jefferson was to call the Declaration "the genuine effusion of the souls of American society."
He had, he explained to Henry Lee, son of General Lee,
when he sat down in Philadelphia in 1776 to draft it, clearly
defined objectives. These were

> Not to find out new principles, or new arguments, never
> before thought of, not merely to say things which had

[19] Jeremy Bentham, *An Introduction to the Principles of Morals
and Legislation* (New York: Bobbs-Merrill Co., 1948), pp. 335–
336.

never been said before; but to place before mankind, the common sense of the subject, in terms so plain and firm as to command their assent, and to justify ourselves in the independent stand we are compelled to take. Neither aiming at originality of principle or sentiment, nor yet copied from any particular and previous writing, it was intended to be an expression of the American mind and to give to that expression the proper tone and spirit called for by the occasion.[20]

Jefferson's mind was richly furnished with recollections of the literature of the past century that he had read so carefully, particularly with that part of it devoted to politics and philosophy, public spirit, virtue, and happiness. The reading he recommended to the attention of the university of which he justly claimed to be the father, the advice about books he sent correspondents, those notes and *Commonplace Book* already mentioned, all throw light on nearly all the themes referred to here and many more. From these and from the circumstance of the age into which he was born, he developed a belief in natural unalienable rights, only fully enjoyed by men living in a free state. In a republic the happiness of its people was the prime concern. On achievement of this, critizens were able to exert their due influence in public affairs. In its largest sense the pursuit of happiness was the endeavor for the welfare of all Americans.

Jefferson's remarks about happiness made throughout his life are illuminating, though we could not be blamed for wishing a fuller expression of his political philosophy. Of course, like the rest of us, he was not always thinking of public happiness. In their correspondence, he and John Adams discussed personal troubles and amusements. They expressed the wish for good health, an all-important factor in the well-being of any individual. They were preoccupied at times with families and illnesses. Discussing whether, if able, they would live their lives over, they were more inclined to recall the stirring times through which they had lived than to decide on the desirability of reincarnation. They supposed that, on balance, pleasure and pain might be regarded as

[20] Jefferson to Henry Lee, May 8, 1825.

equal. In wishing friends happiness Jefferson of course meant
personal success, enjoyment, absence of misfortune. His own
private felicities were derived from study, music, projects, and
family. But when the subject of happiness was approached in
a less personal way the interpretation was different. Each and
every American of course wanted to avoid discomfort and obtain pleasure. The pursuit in the Declaration, I think, implies
more.

"I am," Jefferson once wrote, "an Epicurean." He asserted
that "everything rational in moral philosophy which the
Greeks and Romans have left us" could be found in the
teaching of Epicurus (circa 341–270 B.C.). Summarizing this
teaching, he wrote that to the philosopher moral happiness
was the sum of life. Virtue was the foundation of happiness,
utility the test of virtue. Man sought tranquility, avoided
desire and fear, eschewed deceit and folly, cultivated temper-
ance, prudence, fortitude and justice. Epicurus thus laid
down laws for governing self which could hardly be bettered.
In their method of self-discipline, the Greeks were truly
great. But because the Epicureans advised retirement from
the active sphere of politics to the superior and more peaceful world of reflection, Jefferson found them deficient in realization of what they owed humanity at large. Both Epicurus
and the Stoic Epictetus were "short and defective" about
their duties to others. By contrast with them, Jefferson continued, Jesus had preached a "sublime morality" and the
charity that was the duty of all. Rescuing Christianity from
the artificial systems invented by ultra-Christian sects,
unauthorized by a single word ever uttered by our savior, was
a service he claimed that Priestley had rendered. The chemist
and the Virginian were in differing degrees both Unitarians,
though not in complete agreement about all beliefs. But
whatever his denomination, Jefferson fully appreciated the
social lesson he read in the gospel message.[21]

Among the Founding Fathers, Jefferson (though in his
own peculiar way both pious and moral) was perhaps more

[21] Jefferson to John Adams, November 7, 1819; to William Short,
October 31, 1819, with a syllabus of the doctrines of Epicurus attached.

freethinking and agnostic than most. He shared the anti-clericalism of his age. Superstition, whether that of medieval scholastics or of John Calvin, had been an obstacle, he believed, to the attainment of true civilization. The author of the *Institutes*, the prophet of Genevan Christianity, came in for some round abuse as an "impious" dogmatist,[22] who thought good works counted for nothing, reason in religion to be unlawful, and preached that God had from the beginning elected some to be saved and others to be damned. America after 1776, Jefferson rejoiced, could get rid of both ecclesiastical and royal authorities, profess the pure doctrine of Jesus, and enjoy liberty. Much of what had been conventional Catholic and Protestant Christianity was irreconcilable with that pursuit of happiness he foresaw and recommended.

Happiness should be the concern of citizens and of the officials they elected to serve their interests. Happiness meant public happiness—this cannot be too greatly stressed. Different societies and communities might, it was true, value some ways and conditions more than others esteemed elsewhere, but utility would afford the criterion. "The only orthodox object of the institution of government is to secure the greatest degree of happiness possible to the general mass of those associated under it," he wrote in 1812.[23] On taking office, statesmen were entrusted with the care of public happiness. The equal rights of man and the happiness of every individual are now, he wrote on October 31, 1823, acknowledged to be "the only legitimate objects" of government. Government should be "wise and frugal," restraining men from doing injury to others, free to regulate certain mutual affairs. A good government was essential to "close the circle" of our felicity.[24]

Public happiness was achieved by satisfaction of the aspirations of the majority of the people living together. It could not be attained by each consulting only self-interest, but to it all must contribute. The general sum of enjoyment was what

22 Jefferson to Dr. Benjamin Waterhouse, June 26, 1822.
23 To P. A. van Kemp, March 22, 1812.
24 Jefferson to M. A. Coray, October 31, 1823; and First Inaugural, March 4, 1801.

counted. The individual search for truth or success in intellectual and physical activity, while valuable, was not in itself sufficient. Effort by all was obligatory; to be good-humored rather than censorious about faults and eccentricities of others was wise. Harmony and affection should prevail. In government especially union was necessary. For Jefferson, this could be found in the connection of the federated states and in that general consensus manifested by the population living in them. Though minorities must be tenderly treated and their rights respected, the will of the majority must be supreme. The American republic could in this way secure liberty, and thus promote happiness. Only in such a regime could the will of everyone find expression. Only in it therefore could happiness be pursued, and men live and die content. All virtuous endeavor therein was directed towards the care of the people's happiness.

III

The efforts and the sacrifices of the men of Jefferson's generation were rewarded with this prospect of a happy and beloved country. But reminders of public duty were necessary. Not all were equally endowed with a keen moral sense, any more than all were equally equipped with great talents and strength. Education was essential, and most especially for those not naturally conscientious. Jefferson devoted much thought and effort to the establishment of the University of Virginia, and in particular to the character of education. He took counsel with friends, among them Priestley, and he scanned the Monticello library for suggestions about reading and study. Men needed instruction in virtue and in the importance of social duty. The moral sense or conscience with which all were endowed, when active, led to right action, but frequently needed informing about the road to happiness and the identity of individual welfare with the public good.

Writing to Thomas Law, June 13, 1814, Jefferson argued the case for man's moral sense, as he saw it, and its relationship to his role in society and to the pursuit of happiness.

Morality, he wrote, was found less in the love of God, or the search for knowledge, than in "our relations with others as constituting the boundaries of morality." Strictly speaking, man can owe no duty to himself, obligation requiring two parties. Self-love was an element in morality and was indeed the chief antagonist of virtue. Jefferson went on to express disagreement with the philosophy of self-interest expounded by Helvetius and maintained that the moral sense in man prompted him to good and social works. Where the response was not immediate, appeals to reason and to the opinion of those amongst whom a person lived would probably prompt him to the human and proper conduct. Society, without which a man is helpless, encourages virtuous and kindly behavior.[25] Jefferson as a young man had studied both Helvetius and Shaftesbury, and had also read *The Principles of Natural Religion* (1751) by Henry Home, Lord Kames. The Scots lawyer had there compared the systems of English earl and French philosopher, with some hesitation about accepting fully the theories of either. One ran counter to the known fact that even the most egotistical is not always indifferent to others. Shaftesbury's universal benevolence was also contradicted by experience. Kames conceded that if benevolence were applied not to individuals but to "one great whole," the country, its government and religion, all becoming "objects of public spirit," there might well be something to be argued for the earl's optimism, and this seems to have been Jefferson's own opinion.[26]

This emphasis upon the whole, the greatest good of the greatest number, like demands for reform of law, freedom of trade and independence, was characteristic of Jefferson's generation of reformers. Jefferson also regarded society as essential, but government as something to be kept to a minimum. Yet he failed to appreciate some aspects of developments going on in the world in which he lived, and in outlook often resembles Smith and Bentham less than Shaftesbury and an

[25] Jefferson to Thomas Law, June 13, 1814.
[26] Henry Home, Lord Kames, *Essay on the Principles of Morals and Natural Religion* (Edinburgh: R. Fleming, 1751), pp. 86, 121, and passim.

earlier school. Like Shaftesbury he thought man had as yet
had no chance fully to enjoy the practice of virtue, but in the
future anything was possible for free nations. In the cause of
beauty, virtue, and happiness, the third earl had written
(though Jefferson did not read this then unpublished work),
the people are no small party and have a passionate concern
and interest in it.[27] In America Jefferson saw a people with
the means to pursue happiness. He viewed the future op-
timistically. "I do believe," he wrote in 1812, "we shall continue to grow, to multiply and prosper, until we exhibit an association, powerful, wise and happy, beyond what has yet
been seen by man."[28] The pursuit of happiness was a social
activity, an inspiration, and an endeavor for the good of all.

I began by saying this was a sermon with a text from the
Declaration whose bicentennial we are celebrating. I have
proceeded, as teachers and preachers do, with perhaps more
detail than you wanted or expected, to discuss what the author of the Declaration had in mind, both in 1776 and as he
afterwards continued to consider contemporary problems.
The moral of my text surely lies in reflecting yet more
profoundly than I have been able to do here upon the public
good and the ways in which our own happiness depends upon
a true understanding of the general welfare. It has been
suggested that you never know, unless you happen personally
to care. "True godliness," William Penn declared, "does not
turn men out of the world, but enables them to live better in
it."[29] What is good for this or that great corporation, or this
and another gifted individual, is often stated to be good for
the country. Surely it is more accurate and perceptive to appreciate the fact that what is best for the United States is
best for all who live within them. That is the pursuit of happiness to which we should all rededicate ourselves at this
time.

[27] Shaftesbury, *Second Characters*, ed. B. Rand (Cambridge,
England: University Press, 1914), pp. 22–23.
[28] Jefferson to John Adams, January 21, 1812.
[29] Tolles and Alderfer, *The Witness of William Penn*, p. xii.

PETER L. BERGER

Religion in a Revolutionary Society

Delivered in Christ Church, Alexandria, Virginia

on February 4, 1974

The title of this address, as it was given to me, implies a formidable assignment—no less than the overall consideration of the place of religion in contemporary America. I have some reservations about applying the adjective "revolutionary" to American society. But, minimally, it refers to something very real in that society—namely, its quality of rapid and far-reaching change—and for this reason I describe our present society, not just that of 1776, as revolutionary.

This quality of change makes my assignment all the more difficult. It is a source of constant embarrassment to all commentators and forecasters. Just look what happened to the most celebrated diagnoses of our situation during the last decade: Harvey Cox published his best-selling beatification of the new urbanism just before everyone agreed that American cities had become unfit for civilized habitation. The proclamation of the death of God hit the cover of *Time* magazine just before the onset of a massive resurgence of flamboyant supernaturalism. More recently, those who were betting on the greening of America led the Democratic party to one of its biggest electoral defeats in history. And just now, when Daniel Bell has impressively proclaimed the coming of post-industrial society, the energy crisis makes one think that we will be lucky if we manage to stay around as an *industrial* society. Perhaps the only advice one can give to the sociological

prophet is to write his book quickly, and then go into hiding
—or, alternatively, to be very, very careful. This is not a
book, but I intend to be careful. This means, among other
things, that I cannot spare you some pedantic distinctions,
qualifications, and less-than-inspiring formulations.

I

The consideration before me involves some sort of answer to
the question "where are we at?" To try for this answer, it will
help to find a date in the past with which to compare the
present moment. If one wants to make rather sweeping statements, one will likely pick a date far back in history, like
1776, or the time of the Reformation, or even the late Ice
Age (as Andrew Greeley did recently—his thesis being that
"the basic human religious needs and the basic religious functions have not changed very notably since the late Ice Age,"
the credibility of which thesis clearly hinges on one's understanding of "basic"). Taking seriously my own warning to be
careful, I propose to take a much more recent date: 1955.
This happens to be the year in which an important book on
American religion was published, Will Herberg's *Protestant
—Catholic—Jew.*[1] More important, though, the mid-1950s
were the years just before a number of significant ruptures in
the course of American religion and of American society generally (ruptures, incidentally, which no one foresaw). It is a
convenient date with which to compare the present moment.
In attempting to meet my assignment, therefore, I will concentrate on two questions: *What was the situation of American religion about 1955? What has happened to it since
then?*

Since this period has of late become the subject of intensive nostalgia, I should add that my choice of date is non-nos-
talgically motivated. I was wonderfully young at the time,
and I am all too susceptible to reminiscing about my youth

[1] Will Herberg, *Protestant—Catholic—Jew: An Essay in American
Religious Sociology* (Garden City, N.Y.: Doubleday & Co., Inc.,
1955).

in a rosy glow of memories. I am quite sure that I and my contemporaries had no notion *then* of living in a particularly rosy time. It is probably inevitable that we look back on the time of our youth as some sort of Golden Age. I imagine that this was the case with individuals who were young during the Black Death or the invasions of Genghis Khan. There is a temptation to project one's own decline since then to the society at large. The temptation is to be resisted.

In other words, the comparison between 1955 and 1974 is not necessarily odious. But before I start comparing, I must elaborate one very essential distinction, the distinction between *denominational religion* and *civil religion*.

Denominational religion in America refers to what most people mean when they speak of religion—the bodies of Christian and Jewish tradition as these are enshrined in the major religious organizations in this country. Denominational religion is the religion of the churches. The plural, *churches*, is very important: there are many churches in America, and for a long time now they have existed side by side under conditions of legal equality. Indeed, Richard Niebuhr suggested that the very term "denomination" be defined on the basis of this pluralism. A denomination is a church that, at least for all practical purposes, has come to accept coexistence with other churches. This coexistence was brought about in America by unique historical circumstances, which were not intended by anyone and which at first were only accepted with great reluctance. Later on, a virtue was made out of the necessity, as religious tolerance became part and parcel of the national ideology as well as of the basic laws of the American republic. (Let me say in passing that I regard religious tolerance as a virtue indeed. It is all the more interesting to recognize that its original attainment was unintended. I incline to the view that most moral achievements in history have this character of serendipity. Or, if I may put it in Lutheran language, virtue comes from undeserved grace.)

Civil religion in America refers to a somewhat vaguer entity, an amalgam of beliefs and norms that are deemed to be fundamental to the American political order. In the last few years the idea of an American civil religion has been much discussed in terms proposed in an influential essay on the topic by Robert Bellah, but both the idea and the phrase antedate this essay.[2] Herberg, for instance, discussed very much the same idea using a slightly different terminology. The general assumption here is that the American polity not only bases itself on a set of commonly held values (this is true of any human society), but that these values add up to something that can plausibly be called a religion. The contents of this religion are some basic convictions about human destiny and human rights as expressed in American democratic institutions. Gunnar Myrdal, in his classic study of the Negro in America, aptly called all this "the American creed." The proposition that all men are created equal is a first article of this creed.

An obvious question concerns the relationship between these two religious entities. Different answers have been given to this question, and I can claim no particular competence in the historical scholarship necessary to adjudicate between them. Thus, to take an example of recent scholarly debate, I cannot say whether the civil religion of the American republic should be seen in an essential continuity with the Puritan concept of the convenant, or whether it should be understood as the result of a decisive rupture with Puritanism brought about by the Deist element among the Founding Fathers. Be this as it may, it is clear that the two religious entities have had profound relations with each other from the beginning. Nor is there any doubt that crucial ingredients of the civil religion derive directly from the Protestant mainstream of American church life, to the extent that to this day the civil religion carries an unmistakably Protestant flavor (a point always seen more clearly by non-Protestants than by Protestants, for people are always more likely to notice unfamiliar flavors). Thus, for instance, the codification of the rights of the individual conscience in the American political creed loudly betrays its Protestant roots, even when (perhaps especially when) it is couched in denominationally neutral language.

[2] Robert Bellah, "The Civil Religion in America," in Donald Cutler ed., *The Religious Situation: Nineteen Sixty-Eight* (Boston: Beacon Press, 1968).

It is important to understand how the civil religion relates to the pluralism of denominations. Thus, in one sense, the civil religion is based on a principle of religious tolerance. Except for some isolated cases (Tom Paine was one), the spokesmen of the civil religion were not only friendly to the major churches but insisted that the latter were vital to the moral health of the nation. In another sense, however, the civil religion marks the *limits* of tolerance and indeed of pluralism. While it accepts a broad diversity of religious beliefs in the society, it limits diversity when it comes to *its own* beliefs. The lines between acceptable and unacceptable diversity have frequently shifted in the course of time, but to this day the category "un-American" points to the fact that there are clearly unacceptable deviations from the common civil creed. Belief in the divine right of kings, for example, was as clearly beyond the lines of official acceptability in an earlier period of American history as belief in redemption through socialist revolution came to be later on.

Unlike some of the democratic ideologies of Europe and Latin America, democracy in the United States was not inimical to the churches. The separation between church and state in the American Constitution did not, until very recently, imply that the state must be antiseptically clean of all religious qualities—only that the state must not give unfair advantage to one denomination over another. In other words, the assumptions underlying the separation of church and state were pluralist rather than secularist. It is no accident that there is no adequate American translation of the French term *laique*, and that (again, until very recently) there was no widespread demand that the American polity should become a "lay state" in the French sense. Indeed, a good case can be made that church/state relations in this country had the character of a "pluralistic establishment": officially accredited denominations were allowed to share equally in a variety of privileges bestowed by the state. Exemption from taxation and opportunity for chaplaincy in public institutions are cases in point. Just which groups were to be regarded as officially accredited, of course, was subject to redefinition.

To put it differently, the beneficiaries of the "pluralistic es-

tablishment" have been an expanding group ever since the
system was inaugurated. First were added various less-than-
respectable Protestant bodies (such as the Quakers), then
Catholic and Jews, and finally groups completely outside
what is commonly called the Judaeo-Christian tradition. The
struggle of the Mormons to obtain "accreditation" marked
an interesting case in this process. Recent court decisions on
what (if my memory serves me correctly) were actually called
"the religious rights of atheists," as well as recent litigation
by Black Muslims, mark the degree of expansion of the system to date.

Historically, then, denominational religion and civil religion have not been antagonistic entities in America. Their
relationship has rather been a symbiotic one. The denominations enjoyed a variety of benefits in a "pluralistic establishment," the existence of which was not only fostered by
the state but solemnly legitimated by the civil religion to
which the state adhered. Conversely, the civil religion drew
specific contents and (in all likelihood) general credibility
from the ongoing life of the denominations. Nevertheless,
each entity has had a distinct history, with different forces
impinging on the one or the other. Any assessment of the
contemporary situation must allow for this distinction.

II

Keeping this distinction in mind, then, let us go back to the
period around 1955: what was the situation at that time?

As far as denominational religion was concerned, the
market was bullish indeed. These were the years of what was
then called a "religious revival." All the statistical indicators
of organized religion were pointing up. Church membership
reached historically unprecedented heights. Most significant
(or so it seemed then), it was younger people, especially
young married couples, who became active in the churches in
large numbers. The offspring of these people crowded the
Sunday schools, creating a veritable boom in religious education. Church attendance was up, and so was financial giving

to the churches. Much of this money was very profitably invested, and the denominational coffers were full as never before. Understandably enough, the denominational functionaries thought in terms of expansion. "Church extension" was the phrase constantly on their lips. There was an impressive boom in church building, especially in the new middle-class suburbs. The seminaries were filled with young men getting ready to swell the ranks of the clergy. Perhaps they were not "the brightest and the best" among their peers, but they were competent enough to fulfill the increasingly complex tasks required of the clerical profession in this situation. In the bustling suburban "church plants" (a very common term at the time) this clerical profession often meant a bewildering agglomeration of roles, adding to the traditional religious ones such new roles as that of business administrator, educational supervisor, family counselor and public relations expert.

The "religious revival" affected most of the denominations in the Protestant camp, and it affected Catholics and Jews as well. It seemed as if everyone were becoming active in his respective "religious preference." (By the way, an etymological study of this term derived from the consumer market would be worth making some day.) It was important, therefore, that all of this took place in a context of (apparently) solidifying ecumenism and interfaith amity. The Protestants within the mainline denominations were going through something of an ecumenical orgy. There were several church mergers, the most significant of these (long in preparation) being the union between the Congregationalists and the Evangelical and Reformed Church to become the United Church of Christ. The formation of this body in 1957 was widely heralded as a landmark in the movement toward Christian unity. Quite apart from these organizational mergers, there was a plethora of agencies concerned full time with interdenominational relations, ranging from the still quite young National Council of Churches to state and local councils. While some of these agencies engaged in theological discussion, most of their work was severely practical. An important task was the one formerly called "comity" and recently rebap-

tized as "church planning." Especially on the local level this
meant that church expansion was based on research and on
agreements among the denominations not to engage in irra-
tional competition with each other—and particularly not to
steal each other's prospective members. The religious market,
in other words, was increasingly parcelled out between cartel-
like planning bodies (and no antitrust laws stood in the way
of these conspiracies to restrain free competition). Beyond all
these formal processes of collaboration, there was a broad variety of informal acts of *rapprochement*—intercommunion,
exchange of pulpits, interdenominational ministries in special
areas, and so on.

It should be emphasized that most of this occurred within
the mainstream denominations, which had a predominantly
middle-class constituency. The more fundamentalist groups,
with their lower-middle-class and working-class members,
stood apart, undergoing at the same time quite dramatic
growth of their own. It seems that the apartness of these
groups was not much noticed and even less regretted by the
ecumenists: the presence of the Greek Orthodox in the National Council was noted with pleasure, the absence of the
Pentecostalists was of little concern. More noticed was the
new relationship to Catholics and Jews. While the Roman
Catholic Church still moved slowly in those pre-Vatican II
days, there was little doubt that the old hostility between the
two major Christian confessions was a matter of the past.
And both Protestants and Catholics habitually expressed
goodwill toward Judaism and the Jewish community, not
only through such organizations as the National Conference
of Christians and Jews but, more important, in local churches
and synagogues throughout the country. Significantly, the
major Protestant denominations increasingly took for granted
that practicing Catholics and Jews were not fair game for
evangelistic activity, thus at least informally including them
in ecumenical "comity."

In retrospect it has come to seem plausible that at least
some of this religious boom was deceptive. Even then there
were quite a few individuals who questioned how religious
the "religious revival" really was. Several factors contributing

to it had very little to do with religious motives proper—high social mobility, with large numbers of people moving into the middle class and believing that the old nexus between bourgeois respectability and church membership still held; high geographical mobility, with migrants finding in the churches a convenient symbol of continuity in their lives; the postwar baby boom, with parents feeling rather vaguely that Sunday schools could provide some sort of moral instruction that they themselves felt incompetent to give (there are data showing that frequently it was the children who dragged their parents after them into the churches, rather than the other way around). As a result of these factors, there was a good deal of what might be called *invisible secularization*. In the midst of all this boisterous activity the deepening erosion of religious content in the churches was widely overlooked.

The "religious revival" in the denominations was paralleled by an equally impressive flowering of the civil religion. These, after all, were the Eisenhower years, aptly characterized by William Lee Miller, in a famous article in *The Reporter* magazine, as "Piety along the Potomac." Indeed, it was Eisenhower himself who made statements that could be taken as crystalline expressions of the mid-1950s version of the civil religion, such as this one: "Our government makes no sense unless it is founded in a deeply felt religious faith— and I don't care what it is." The political relevance of this faith, deeply felt and at the same time seemingly devoid of content, was expressed in another Eisenhower statement: "America is great because she is good." One may call this patriotic religion or religious patriotism. Either way, the content was America—its political and social institutions, its history, its moral values, and not least its mission in the world.

The rhetoric of the national government during these years was full of such religio-political formulations. Except for a small minority of anti-Eisenhower intellectuals, the country found this rhetoric quite in accord with its mood. Despite some shocks (notably the McCarthyite hysteria and the less-than-victorious ending of the Korean conflict), the mood was still one of national self-confidence if not complacency. There was still the afterglow, as it were, of America's great victory in World War II—a most credible conjunction of greatness and goodness. The postwar American empire was going well, with American soldiers mounting the battlements of freedom from Korea to Berlin. The Cold War, if anything, deepened the affirmation of the virtues of the American way of life as against the Communist adversary. (Not the least of the latter's evils was its ideology of "godless materialism.") The economy was going well, the dollar was king, and American businessmen as well as tourists circled the globe as emissaries from Eldorado. Indeed, many of its intellectuals were celebrating America (even if, as it later turned out, some of the celebration was subsidized by the CIA).

I do not want to exaggerate. I am not suggesting that there were no tensions, no doubts, in this mood. But compared to what happened later, this period impresses one in retrospect by the apparent unbrokenness—intactness—of the American creed. Just as the imperial cult of classical Rome was sustained by the unquestioned veneration of the familiar shrines in innumerable households, so the American civil religion drew its strength from the daily matter-of-course enactment of the virtues of the American way of life by innumerable individual citizens. I would not like to be misunderstood here: I am *not* saying that there was more morality in the 1950s than there is today; I *am* saying that such morality as was practiced was taken for granted in a different way. The American virtues, and the virtue of America as a society, were still upheld in the mind of the country as self-evident truths. I suppose that this assurance might well be characterized as innocence. To a remarkable degree, this rather grandiose self-image of Americans was reflected in the way they were viewed by foreigners—not least by the two major enemy nations of World War II.

III

If that was the situation in 1955, what has happened since?

To summarize the change, I shall take the liberty of making reference to my first book, a sociological critique of American Protestantism published in 1961.[3] In this book, when describing the notion that the world is essentially what it is supposed to be, I used the phrase "the okay world." I argued that religion in middle-class America served to maintain this sense of the world being "okay." I still think this was a fair description. The change since then can be conveniently summed up by saying that more and more people have come to the conclusion that their world is *not* "okay," and religion has lost much of its ability to persuade them that it is.

In denominational religion, the changes have differed greatly by class. The Protestant groups drawing most of their membership from *below* the upper-middle class have continued to grow, some of them in a dramatic way. They have largely remained untouched by the crises and self-doubts that have lacerated their higher-class brethren. Their theological fundamentalism has been modified here and there and their organizational style has been modernized, but as far as an outside observer can judge, their self-confidence as upholders of Evangelical truth has remained largely unbroken. The picture is quite different in the mainstream denominations.

By the mid-1960s the "religious revival" was clearly over. All the statistical indicators started ebbing or even pointing down—membership, attendance, financial giving and (logically enough) church expansion. As budgets became leaner, the denominational and interdenominational organizations were forced to cut down on program as well as staff. Seminary enrollments stayed high, but there was widespread suspicion that the automatic exemption of seminary students from the draft had much to do with this (a suspicion that appears to be borne out in what is happening in the seminaries now). The market for denominational religion, in short, was becoming bearish. Not surprisingly, its amicable management through ecumenical cartels seemed less and less attractive. There appeared a marked reluctance to engage in further mergers, characterized by some observers (perhaps euphemistically) as "a resurgence of denominational spirit." The organizational mood became one of retrenchment.

[3] Peter Berger, *The Noise of Solemn Assemblies* (Garden City, N.Y.: Doubleday & Co., Inc., 1961).

More deeply, the 1960s were characterized in mainstream Protestantism by what can best be described in Gilbert Murray's phrase as a "failure of nerve." The best-known theological movements seemed to vie with each other in the eagerness with which they sought to divest the churches of their traditional contents and to replace these with a variety of secular gospels—existentialism, psychoanalysis, revolutionary liberation, or *avant-garde* sensitivity. The "death-of-God" theology was the grotesque climax of this theological self-disembowelment. At the same time the church functionaries, increasingly panicky about the fate of their organizations, tended to jump on whatever cultural or political bandwagon was proclaimed by the so-called opinion leaders as the latest revelation of the *Zeitgeist*. As was to be expected, all these efforts "to make the church more relevant to modern society" had the effect of aggravating rather than alleviating the religious recession. Those church members who still felt loyalty to the traditional content of their faith were bewildered if not repelled by all this, and those whose membership was motivated by secular considerations to begin with often felt that such commodities as "personal growth" or "raised consciousness" could be obtained just as well (and less expensively) outside the churches. The major consequence (unintended, needless to say) of Vatican II seems to have been to spread the aforementioned Protestant miseries through the Catholic community: the "failure of nerve" has become ecumenical too. At the same time, American Judaism and the American Jewish community in general have been driven by a variety of causes into a much more particularistic and defensive posture than was the case when Herberg announced the arrival of a "tripartite" American faith.

Just as there was good reason to doubt that the "religious revival" of the 1950s was caused by some sort of mass conversion, so it is unlikely that the subsequent decline is to be explained by sudden spiritual transformations. My own tendency is to think that secularization has been a long-lasting and fairly even process, and that nothing drastic happened to the American religious consciousness either after World

War II or in the most recent decade. What happened, I think, is that the quite mundane social forces that made for the "religious revival" subsequently weakened. Most important, the linkage between middle-class status and church membership weakened (something that took place in England, by the way, in the wake of World War I). In consequence, the previously invisible secularization became much more visible. If you like, secularization came out of the closet. The inability of the churches to confront the emerging skeleton with a modicum of dignity almost certainly contributed to its devastating effect.

The changes that have taken place in the civil religion, I think, resulted partly from these changes in denominational religion (inevitable in view of the symbiotic relation between the two), and partly from extraneous developments in the society. To some degree, it can be said, the American polity has become more *laique* in recent years, and I suspect that this is largely due to the more openly acknowledged secularism of that portion of the college-educated upper middle class that finances what it considers good causes—in this instance, the cause of pushing secularist cases through the courts. The Supreme Court proscription of prayer in the public schools was the most spectacular of these cases. It was an exercise in extraordinary sociological blindness, though it appears that those who advocated it have learned absolutely nothing from the outcry that ensued. The same *laique* trend may be seen in the rigid resistance to any allocation of tax funds to church schools, in threats to the tax-exempt status of religious institutions, and in current discussion of various forms of chaplaincy. More important, a militant secularism today comes dangerously close to denying the right of the churches to attempt influencing public policy in accordance with religious morality. The abortion issue illustrates this most clearly. I doubt whether the tendency of the courts to go along with the secularists has profound reasons. Most likely it can be explained simply in terms of the parties attended by federal judges and the magazines read by their wives. (I assure you that I intend no disrespect to our judiciary—actually one of our more cheering institutions—but I am too much of a sociologist to believe that its decisions are made in some judicial heaven sublimely detached from the socio-cultural ambience of its members.)

There has thus come to be a threat to the old symbiosis between denominational and civil religion in America. And a more dramatic threat has come from much larger events in the society. It has often been said in the last few years that the legitimacy of the American political order faces the gravest crisis since the Civil War. Even after making proper allowance for the propensity of professional social critics to exaggerate, the diagnosis stands up under scrutiny. To be sure, there are important class and regional differences: what is perceived as doomsday by readers of the *New York Review of Books* may seem a less than overwhelming nuisance to the reader of a small-town newspaper in Kansas, and there is hard evidence to the effect that there continue to be large masses of people whose "okay world" has *not* been fundamentally shaken. Yet few people have remained untouched by the political and moral questioning induced by the headline events of the last decade—the continuing racial crisis, the seemingly endless fiasco of the imperial adventure in Indochina, the eruption of chaos on campus, and finally the shock of the Watergate revelations. I doubt if these events, singly or even in combination, are ultimate causes of the crisis of the American political creed: I think it is more plausible to see this crisis rooted in much more basic tensions and discontents of modern society, of "revolutionary" society, and to understand the events as *occasions* for the underlying difficulties to become manifest.

Obviously I cannot develop this point here. Suffice it to say that the survival in the twentieth century of a political order conceived in the eighteenth is not something about which I am sanguine (though, let me hasten to add, I fervently believe in the continuing effort to keep this eighteenth-century vision alive). Be this as it may, we have been passing through a process that sociologists rather ominously describe as *delegitimation*—that is, a weakening of the values and assumptions on which a political order is based. We have been lucky, I think, that this malaise of the political system has not so far been accompanied by severe dislocations in the economy: I can only express the hope that our luck continues to hold.

It may then be said that the civil religion has been affected by a double secularization. It has been affected by the secularizing processes in the proper sense of the word, the same processes that have come to the fore in the area of denominational religion. But it has also undergone a "secularization"—that is, a weakening in the plausibility of its own creed, quite apart from the relation of this creed to the several churches. Put simply, the phrase "under God," as lately introduced into the Oath of Allegiance, has become implausible to many people. But even without this phrase the propositions about America contained in the oath have come to sound hollow in many ears. *That* is the measure of our crisis.

IV

However prudent one may want to be with regard to the tricky business of prediction, it is almost inevitable in a consideration such as this to look toward the future. What are some plausible scenarios?

As we look at the future of denominational religion in America, a crucial consideration will be how one views the further course of secularization. In the last few years I have come to believe that many observers of the religious scene (I among them) have overestimated both the degree and the irreversibility of secularization. There are a number of indications, to paraphrase Mark Twain, that the news about the demise of religion has been exaggerated. Also, there are signs of a vigorous resurgence of religion in quarters where one would have least expected it (as, for instance, among the college-age children of the most orthodox secularists). All this need not mean that we are on the brink of a new Reformation (though I doubt if anyone thought they were on the brink of a Reformation at the beginning of the sixteenth century either), but it seems increasingly likely to me that there are limits to secularization. I am not saying this because of any philosophical or theological beliefs about the truth of the religious view of reality, although I myself believe in this truth. Rather, I am impressed by the intrinsic inability of secularized world views to answer the deeper questions of the human condition, questions of *whence, whether,* and *why.* These seem to be ineradicable and they are answered only in the most banal ways by the *ersatz* religions of secularism. Perhaps, finally, the reversibility of the process of secularization is probable because of the pervasive boredom of a world without gods.

This does not necessarily mean, however, that a return to religion would also mean a return to the churches. It is perfectly possible that future religious resurgences will create new institutional forms and that the existing institutions will be left behind as museum pieces of a bygone era. There are two propositions, though, of which I am fairly certain. First, any important religious movements in America will emerge out of the Judaeo-Christian tradition rather than from esoterica imported from the Orient. And second, the likelihood that such revitalizing movements remain within the existing churches will increase as the churches return to the traditional contents of their faith and give up self-defeating attempts to transform their traditions in accordance with the myth of "modern man."

The scenarios for the American civil religion hinge most obviously on one's prognoses for American society at large. Only the most foolhardy would pretend to certainty on this score. But one thing is reasonably certain: No political order can stand a long process of delegitimation such as the one we have been going through of late. There is only a limited number of possible outcomes to such a crisis of legitimacy. One, perhaps the most obvious one, is that the society will move into a period of general decline, marked both by intensifying disturbance within and a shrinkage of its power in the world outside. Not much imagination is required to see what such a decline would mean internationally. A second possible outcome is a termination of the crisis by force, by the imposition of the traditional virtues by the power of the state. It hardly needs stressing that democracy and freedom, as we have known them, would not survive such an "Augustan age" in America. The third possibility is a revitalization of the American creed from within, a new effort to breathe the spirit of conviction into the fragile edifice of our political institutions. This possibility depends above all on political and intellectual leadership, of which there is little evidence at the moment. The future of the American experiment depends upon a quick end to this particular scarcity and upon the emergence of an altogether new unity of political will, moral conviction, and historical imagination—in order to preserve the society descending from our Revolution.

I have tried here to sketch a picture, not to preach a sermon. The social scientist, if he is true to his vocation, will try to see reality without reference to his own hopes or fears. Yet it must be clear that I do not view this particular scene as a visitor from outer space. On the contrary, I find myself deeply and painfully involved in it. As a sociologist I can, indeed must, look at the religious situation in terms of what a colleague has aptly called "methodological atheism." At the same time, I am a Christian, which means that I have a stake in the churches' overcoming their "failure of nerve" and regaining their authority in representing a message that I consider to be of ultimate importance for mankind. I suppose that a phrase like "methodological subversion" would fit the manner in which, again of necessity, the social scientist looks at political reality. With some mental discipline, then, I can try to describe contemporary America as if it were ancient Rome. But I cannot escape the fact that I am an American citizen and that the future of this society contains not only my own future but that of my children. Even more important, I happen to believe in the continuing viability of that eighteenth-century vision and in the promise implied by that oath—in my own case, first taken freely and of my own volition as an adult. Both for the religious believer and for the citizen, the assessment that I tried to make here translates itself into practical and political tasks. The elaboration of these tasks, however, would require a different format from the present one. In any case, it was not my assignment here.

DANIEL J. BOORSTIN
Political Revolutions and Revolutions in Science and Technology

Delivered at the National Academy of Sciences,

Washington, D.C. on October 9, 1973

Anniversaries are inevitably occasions when we think of what a span of time means, of what we have and have not accomplished, and also of what our life expectancy may be. One of the more interesting observations on the life cycle of nations was made by Sir Francis Bacon, about 350 years ago, soon after the first representative assembly in British North America had met in Jamestown, and when New England Puritans had begun to arrive for their Errand Into the Wilderness. Here is what he said:

> In the youth of a state, arms do flourish; in the middle age of a state, learning; and then both of them together for a time; in the declining age of a state, mechanical arts and merchandise. Learning hath its infancy, when it is but beginning, and almost childish; then his youth, when it is luxuriant and juvenile; then his strength of years, when it is solid and reduced; and, lastly, his old age, when it waxeth dry and exhaust. But it is not good to look too long upon these turning wheels of vicissitude, lest we become giddy. . . .[1]

[1] "Of Vicissitude of Things," in *Essays and New Atlantis*, ed. Gordon S. Haight (New York: Van Nostrand Reinhold Co.,

The Bicentennial Era is likely to be a time of just such giddiness.

In this lecture, however, I will not be concerned with whether our nation offers a problem in child psychology, in adolescent adjustment, or in gerontology. Rather I will be concerned with one especially dramatic feature of our history. Of all modern nations, ours has been a nation of change, and a changeful nation. How can or how should we think about that change?

For only a tiny fragment of human history has man been aware that he had a history. During nearly all the years since man first developed writing and civilization began, he thought of himself and of his community in ways quite different from those familiar to us today. He tended to see the passage of time, not as a series of unique, irreversible moments of change, but rather as a recurrence of *familiar* moments. The cycle of the seasons—spring, summer, fall, winter, spring—was his most vivid, most intimate signal of passing time. When men sought other useful signposts in the cycle, at first they naturally chose the phases of the moon, because the reassuring regularity of the lunar cycle, being relatively short, was easily noted. It was some time before the solar cycle (a much more sophisticated notion) with its accompanying notion of a yearly cycle became widespread.

And, in that age of cyclical time, before the discovery of history, the repetition of the familiar provided the framework for all the most significant and dramatic occasions in human experience. Religious rituals were recreations or recapitulations of ancient original events, often the events which were supposed to have created the world. The spring was a time not just of new crops, but of a recreated earth. Just as the moon was reborn in every lunar cycle, so the year was reborn through the solar cycle.

Just as the sacred year always repeated the Creation, so every human marriage reproduced the hierogamy—the sacred union of heaven and earth. Every hero relived the career and recaptured the spirit of an earlier mythic prototype. A famil-

1942), p. 242. It is perhaps significant that this is the last paragraph in the last edition of Bacon's essays (1625) to be published in his lifetime.

iar surviving example of the age of cyclical time before the rise of historical consciousness is the Judaeo-Christian Sabbath. Our week has seven days, and by resting on the seventh day, we reenact the primordial gesture of the Lord God when on the seventh day of the Creation He "rested . . . from all his work which he had made." (Genesis 2:2)

The archaic man, as Mircea Eliade puts it, lives in a "continual present" where nothing is really new, because of his "refusal to accept himself as a historical being."[2]

Perhaps the greatest of all historical revolutions was man's discovery—or his invention—of the idea of history. This was a long and painful process. Obviously it did not occur in Western Europe on any particular day, in any particular year, nor perhaps even in a particular century, but slowly and painfully. If we stop to think for a moment, we will begin to see how difficult it must have been for people whose whole world had consisted of a universe of seasons and cycles, of archetypes and resurrections, of myths relived, of heroes reincarnate, to think in a way so different.

This was nothing less than man's discovery of the new. Not of any particular sort of novelty, but of the very possibility of novelty. Men were moving from the relived-familiar, from the always-meaningful reenactment of the archetype, out into a world of unimagined, chaotic, and possibly treacherous novelty.

When did this first crucial revolution in human thought occur? In western European civilization it seems to have come at the end of the middle ages, probably around the fourteenth century. The power of older ways of thinking, the dominance of cycles and rebirths, was revealed in the very name "Renaissance" (which actually did not come into use till the nineteenth century) for the age when novelty and man's power for breaking out of the cycles were discovered.

Symptoms of this new way of thinking (as Peter Burke has chronicled in his *Renaissance Sense of the Past*) are found in the writings of Petrarch (1304–1374) who himself took an interest in history, in the changing fashions in coins, cloth-

[2] *The Myth of the Eternal Return*, trans. W. Trask, Bollingen Series 46 (New York: Pantheon Books, Inc., 1954), p. 85.

ing, words, and laws; he saw the ruins of Rome not as the creation of mythic giants but as relics of a different age. Lorenzo Valla (c. 1407–1457) pioneered historical scholarship when he proved the so-called Donation of Constantine to be a forgery, and he also laid a basis for historical linguistics when (in *De elegantia linguae latinae*) he showed the relationship between the decline of the Roman Empire and the decline of Latin. Paintings by Piero della Francesca (c. 1420–1492) and by Andrea Mantegna (1431–1506) began to abandon the reckless anachronism of earlier artists in their effort at historical accuracy in armor and in costume. Roman law, which would continue to dominate continental Europe, ceased to be a supra-historical, transcendental phenomenon. And other legal systems began to be seen as capable of change. In England, for example, where the common law was imagined to be the rules "to which the mind of man runneth not to the contrary," the fiction of antiquity began to dissolve, and by the seventeenth century innovation by legislation was thought to be possible. The Protestant Reformation, too, brought a new interest in historical sources and opened the way for a new kind of scrutiny of the past.

II

The awakening sense of history, which opened new worlds and unimagined worlds of the new, brought its own problems. Names had to be found, or made, for the particular novelties, or the kinds of novelty which history would bring. The new inquiring spirit, the newly quizzical mood for viewing the passing current of events stirred scholars to look beneath the surface for latent causes and unconfessed motives. Early efforts to describe and explain historical change (like that expressed in the familiar passage above by Sir Francis Bacon) still leaned heavily on the old notion of cycles. And similar notions were expressed in about 1635 in a richer, more baroque metaphor by Sir Thomas Browne:

> As though there were a Metempsychosis, and the soul of one man passed into another, opinions do find, after

certain revolutions, men and minds like those that first begat them . . . men are lived over again, the world is now as it was in ages past . . . because the glory of one state depends upon the ruin of another, there is a revolution and vicissitude of their greatness, and must obey the swing of that wheel, not moved by intelligences [such as the souls that moved the planets] but by the hand of God, whereby all estates arise to their zenith and vertical parts according to their predestined periods. For the lives, not only of men, but of Commonwealths, and of the whole world, run not upon a helix that still enlargeth, but on a circle, where, according to their meridian, they decline on obscurity, and fall under the horizon again.[3]

But as the historical consciousness became more lively, the historical imagination became both more sensitive and bolder. There were more artists and scholars and lawyers and chroniclers who saw the passage of time as history.

Several words which once had a specific physical denotation began to be borrowed and given extended meanings, to describe processes in history. By the early seventeenth century (as the *Oxford English Dictionary* reveals), the word "revolution," which had described the movement of celestial bodies in an orbit or circular course and which had also come to mean the time required to complete such a full circuit, was borrowed and had come into use also figuratively to denote a great change or alteration in the position of affairs. In a century shaken by "commotions" (as they were sometimes called) which overthrew established governments and forcibly substituted new rulers, "revolution" came to mean what we still think of in the twentieth century.

At about the same time, the word "progress" which until then had been used almost exclusively in the simple physical sense of an onward movement in space, and then to describe the onward movement of a story or narrative, was put to new

[3]*Religio Medici* (London, 1906), pp. 8, 20–21; quoted in Peter Burke, *The Renaissance Sense of the Past* (London: Edward Arnold, 1954), p. 85. An important recent addition to our understanding of this problem is Ricardo J. Quinones, *The Renaissance Discovery of Time* (Cambridge: Harvard University Press, 1972).

uses. Originally neither of these senses was eulogistic. By the late seventeenth or early eighteenth century, however, "progress" had come commonly to mean advancement to a higher stage, advancement to better and better conditions, continuous improvement. That was the age of the English Enlightenment, which encompassed John Locke, Sir Isaac Newton, Robert Boyle, David Hume, and Edward Gibbon. Hardly surprising that it needed a name for Progress! Similarly, by the mid-nineteenth century, as a philologist explained in 1871, the word "decadence" (derived from de+ cadere, which meant to fall down) "came into fashion, apparently to *denote* decline and *connote* a scientific and enlightened view of that decline on the part of the user."[4]

The century after 1776 was not only a period of great revolutions, it was also a period of great historians. In England that century produced the works of Edward Gibbon, Thomas Babington Macauley, Henry Thomas Buckle, and W. E. H. Lecky; in the United States it was the century of Francis Parkman, William Hickling Prescott, George Bancroft, and Henry Adams. Western culture was energetically—even frantically—seeking a vocabulary to describe the new world of novelty. Historians willingly grasped at metaphors, adapted technical terms, stretched analogies, and extended the jargon of other disciplines in their quest for handles on the historical processes.

Two giants came on this scene. And—partly from the desperate need for a vocabulary, partly from the lack of competition, partly from their own towering talents for generalizing —these two have dominated much of Western writing and thinking about history into our own day. The first, of course, was Charles Darwin. In 1859 his *Origin of Species* offered with eloquent and persuasive rhetoric some strikingly new ways of describing the history of plants and animals. And he providentially satisfied the needs of man's new historical consciousness, for unlike earlier biologists, he offered a way of describing and explaining the continuous emergence of novelty. Darwin brought the whole animate world into the

---

[4] *Oxford English Dictionary*, s.v. "Decadence," quoting J. B. Mayor in 1871.

new realm of historical consciousness. He showed that every living thing had a history. The jargon that grew out of his work, or was grafted on to his work—"evolution," "natural selection," "struggle for survival," "survival of the fittest," among other expressions—proved wonderfully attractive to historians of the human species.

Of course there were many reasons why Darwin's vocabulary was attractive. But one of the most potent was the simplest. He provided a way of talking about change, of making plausible the emergence of novelty in experience, and of showing how the sloughing off of the old inevitably produced the new.

In Europe the nineteenth century, like the seventeenth, was an age of "commotions." After the American Revolution of 1776 and the French Revolution of 1789, revolution was in the air. And the man who translated biology into sociology, who translated the origin of species into the origin of revolutions was, of course, Karl Marx. Marx freely admitted his debt to Darwin. When the first English translation of the first volume of *Das Kapital* was about to appear, Marx wrote to Darwin asking permission to dedicate the volume to him. Darwin's surprising reply was that, while he was deeply honored, he preferred that Marx not dedicate the book to him, because his family would be disturbed to have dedicated to a Darwin a book that was so Godless![5]

Darwin and Marx together provided the vocabulary which has dominated the writing and thinking of historians—Marxist and anti-Marxist, communist and anti-communist—into our own time.

III

Since Marx, every sort of social change has been christened a Revolution. So we have the Industrial Revolution, the Sexual Revolution, and even the so-called Paperback Revolution. The word "Revolution" has become a shorthand to amplify

[5] Gertrude Himmelfarb, *Darwin and the Darwinian Revolution* (London: Chatto & Windus, 1959), p. 316.

or dignify any subject. "Revolution" has become the very prototype (I could even say the stereotype) of social change.

All this reminds us that mankind has generally been more successful in describing the persisting features of his experience—warfare, state, church, school, university, corporation, community, city, family—than in describing the processes of change. Just as man has found it far simpler, when he surveys the phenomena of nature, to describe or characterize the objects—land, sea, air, lakes, oceans, mountains, deserts, valleys, bays, islands—that surround him than to describe the modes of their alteration or their motion, just as man's knowledge of anatomy has preceded his understanding of physiology, so it has been with social process.

Political changes, including the overthrow of rulers, have tended to be both more conspicuous and speedier than technological changes. Those limited numbers of people who could read and write and who kept the records have tended to be attached to the rulers and hence most aware of the changing fortunes of princes and kings. Rapid technological change—the sort of change that can be measured in decades and that occurs within the span of a lifetime—is a characteristic of modern times.

There was really no need for a name for rapid technological changes until after the wave of revolutions that shook Europe beginning in the mid-seventeenth century and reaching down into this century. It is during this period, of course, that men have developed their historical consciousness. The writing of history, a task of the new social sciences, only recently has become a self-conscious profession. The Regius chairs of history at Oxford and Cambridge were not established till the eighteenth century. At Harvard, the McLean professorship of history was not established till 1838, and American history did not enter the picture till much later.

What is most significant, then, about technology in modern times (the eras of most of the widely advertised "revolutions") is not so much any particular change, but rather the dramatic and newly explosive phenomenon of change itself. And American history, more perhaps than that of any other modern nation, has been marked by changes in the human condition—by novel political arrangements, novel products, novel forms of manufacturing, distribution, and consumption, novel ways of transporting and communicating. To understand ourselves and our nation, then, we must grasp these processes of change and reflect on our peculiarly American ways of viewing these processes.

IV

In certain obvious but crucial ways, the process of technological change differs from the process of political change. I will now briefly explore these differences and suggest some of the consequences of our temptation to overlook them.

1. *First, then, their motives (the Why)*. People are moved to political revolutions by their grievances (real or imagined) and by their desire for a change. Stirred by disgust with old policies and old régimes, they are awakened by visions of redress, of reforms, or of utopia. "Prudence, indeed, will dictate," Jefferson wrote in the Declaration of Independence,

> that Governments long established should not be changed for light and transient causes; and accordingly all experience hath shewn, that mankind are more disposed to suffer, while evils are sufferable, than to right themselves by abolishing the forms to which they are accustomed. But when a long train of abuses and usurpations, pursuing invariably the same Object, evinces a design to reduce them under absolute Despotism, it is their right, it is their duty, to throw off such Government, and to provide new Guards for their future security. Such has been the patient sufferance of these Colonies; and such is now the necessity which constrains them to alter their former Systems of Government.

This was a characteristically frank and clear declaration which could be a preface to most political revolutions. The Glorious Revolution of 1689 had its Declaration of Rights, the French Revolution of 1789 had its Declaration of the Rights of Man, the revolutions of 1848 had their Communist Manifesto, among others, and so it goes. For our present purpose the particular content of such declarations is less significant than that they have existed and that the people who have initiated and controlled the far-reaching political changes think of declarations as somehow giving the Why of their revolution.

But, in this sense, the great technological changes do *not* have a *Why*. The telegraph was not invented because men felt aggrieved by the need to carry messages over roads, by hand and on horseback. The wireless did not appear because men would no longer tolerate the stringing of wires to carry their messages. Television was not produced because Americans would no longer suffer the indignity or the inconvenience of leaving their homes and going to a theater to see a motion picture, or to a stadium to see a ball game. All this is obvious, but some of its significance may have escaped us. In a word, it is no trivial matter that although in retrospect we can always see large social, economic, and geographic forces at work, still technological revolutions (by contrast with political revolutions) really have no *Why*. While political revolutions tend to be conscious and purposeful, technological revolutions are quite otherwise.

Each political revolution has its *ancien régime*, and so inevitably looks backward to what must be redressed and revised. Even if the hopes are utopian, the blueprint for utopia is made from the raw materials of the recent past. "Peace, Bread, and Land!" the slogan of the Russian Revolution of 1917, succinctly proclaimed what Russian peasants and workers had felt to be lacking. It was the obverse of "War, Starvation, and Servitude," which was taken to be a description of the *ancien régime*.

But technological revolutions generally do not take their bearings by any *ancien régime*. They more often arise not from persistent and resentful staring at the past, but from casual glimpses of what might be in the future: not so much from the pangs of empty stomachs, as from the lighthearted imagining of eating quick-frozen strawberries in winter. True enough, political revolutions usually do get out of hand, and so go beyond the motives of their makers. But there usually is somebody trying to guide events to fulfill the motives of the revolutionaries, and trying to prevent events from going astray. Yet by contrast even with the most reckless and ill-guided political revolutions, technological revolutions are still more reckless.

An example comes from World War II. From one point of view, the war in Europe was a kind of revolution, an international uprising against the Nazis, which concluded in their overthrow and removal from power. That movement had a specific objective and ran its course: surrender by the Nazis, replacement of the Nazi régime by another, "War Crimes" trials, et cetera. After that revolution took place, the result left a Germany which, from a political point of view, was not radically different from pre-Nazi Germany. This was an intended result of the efforts of politicians inside and outside the country.

Now, contrast the course of what is sometimes called the Atomic Revolution, which took place during these same years. The story of the success in the United States in achieving controlled nuclear fission (which now is a well-documented chronicle) leaves no doubt that a dominant motive was the determination to develop a decisive weapon to defeat the Nazis. But the connection between Hitler and atomic fission was quite accidental. Atomic fission finally was a result of long uncoordinated efforts of scientists in many places—in Germany, Denmark, Italy, the United States, and elsewhere. And, in turn, the success in producing controlled nuclear fission and in designing a bomb spawned consequences which proved uncontrollable. Although efforts at international agreement to control the development, production, diffusion, and use of atomic weapons have not been entirely unsuccessful, the atom remains a vagrant force in the world.

The overwhelming and most conspicuous result, then, of this great advance in human technology—controlled atomic fission—was not a set of neat desired consequences. In fact, the Nazis had surrendered before the bomb was ready. Rather, as has been frequently observed, the atomic bomb was to produce vast, unpredictable, and terrifying consequences. It would give a new power to nations and level the power of nations in surprising ways. The Atomic Revolution has proved reckless, with extensive consequences and threats of consequences, which make the recklessness of Hitler look like caution. Even when men think they have a *Why* for their technological revolution—as indeed Albert Einstein, Harold Urey, Leo Szilard, Enrico Fermi, and James Franck felt they had—they are deceived.

The tantalizing, exhilarating fact about great technological changes is the very fact that each such change (like the invention of controlled atomic fission) seems somehow to be a law unto itself, to have its own peculiar vagrancy. Each grand change brings into being a whole new world. But we cannot forecast what will be the rules of any particular new world until after that new world has been discovered. It can be full of all sorts of outlandish monsters, it can be ruled by a diabolic logic. Who, for example, could have predicted that the internal combustion engine and the automobile would spawn a new world of installment buying, credit cards, franchises, and annual models—that it would revise the meaning of cities, and transform morality by instigating new institutions of no-fault reparations?

The course of political change is somehow roughly predictable, but not so in the world of technology. We discover to our horror that we are not so much masters as victims. All this is due, in part, to the wonderfully unpredictable course of human knowledge and human imagination. But it is also due (as the history of electricity, wireless communication, radio, electronics, and the transistor, among others, suggests) to all the undiscovered, still-unrevealed characteristics of the physical world. These will recreate our world and populate it with creatures we never imagined.

2. *A second grand distinction concerns the How.* It is not impossible to put together some helpful generalizations about how political revolutions are made. Some of the more familiar in modern times are those offered by Sir Francis Bacon, Machiavelli, Montesquieu, Jefferson, John Adams, Marx, Lenin, and Mao Tse-tung. Political revolutions in modern times are the final result of long and careful planning toward specific ends, of countless clandestine meetings and nu-

merous public rallies, of organized collaborative shaping toward a declared purpose. Organized purposefulness, focus, clarity, and limitation of objectives—all these are crucial.

The general techniques for bringing about a political revolution—including propaganda, organization, the element of surprise, the enlistment of foreign allies, the seizure of centers of communication—have changed very little over the centuries, although of course the specific means by which these have been accomplished have changed conspicuously. John Adams, who knew a thing or two about how political revolutions were made, after the American Revolution remarked dourly on how little man had increased his knowledge of his own political processes. "In so general a refinement, or more properly a reformation of manners and improvement in science," Adams observed in 1786, "is it not unaccountable that the knowledge of the principles and construction of free governments, in which the happiness of life, and even the further progress of improvement in education and society, in knowledge and virtue, are so deeply interested, should have remained at a full stand for two or three thousand years?" And he ventured that the principles of political science "were as well understood at the time of the neighing of the horse of Darius as they are at this hour." He noted with some sadness that the ancient wisdom on these matters was still applicable.[6]

Great changes in technology—in the very world of advancing scientific knowledge and enlarging technological grasp—paradoxically remain (as they have always been) mysterious and unpredictable. Much of the satisfaction of reading *political* history, and especially the history of political revolutions, comes from seeing men declare their large objectives, seeing them use more or less familiar techniques—and then witnessing them recognizably succeed or fail in their grand enterprise. These are the elements of frustrated ambitions and disappointed hopes, of epic and of high tragedy. But the

[6] Preface to "A Defence of the Constitutions of Government of the United States of America," in *The Works of John Adams*, ed. Charles Francis Adams (Boston: Little, Brown & Co., 1851), vol. 4, p. 283ff.

stories of the great technological changes—even when we call
them revolutions—are quite different. More often than not,
it is hard to know whether an effort at technological innovation is tragedy, comedy, or bluster, whether it shows good
luck or bad. How, for example, are we to assess the invention, elaboration, and universal diffusion of the airplane? Or
of television?

While the patterns of political history remain in the familiar mode of Shakespeare's tragedies and historical plays
(there are few changes of political régime that cannot be seen
in the mold of Coriolanus, King Lear, Richard II, Richard
III, Macbeth, or one of the others), technological history
(despite some valiant and imaginative efforts of sociologists
and historians) appears, by contrast, to have very little pattern. And much of the excitement in this story comes from
the surprising coincidence, the inconceivable, and the trivial
—from the boy Marconi playing with his toy, from the
chance observation by a Madame Curie, from the lucky accident which befell Sir Alexander Fleming, and from myriad
other occasions equally odd and unpredictable.

Even the mid-twentieth century American research and
development laboratory—perhaps mankind's most highly organized, best-focused effort to promote technological change
—is a place of fruitfully vagrant questing. "Research directing," explained Willis R. Whitney, the pioneer founder of
the General Electric Laboratories, "is following the openings
of acceptable new ideas. It is watching the growth of thought
in the minds and hands of careful investigators. Even the
lonely mental pioneer, being grub-staked, so to speak, advances so far into the generally unknown that a so-called
director merely happily follows the new ways provided. All
new paths both multiply and divide as they proceed."[7] A
modern research laboratory, then, as Irving Langmuir

[7] Quoted in John T. Broderick, *Willis Rodney Whitney: Pioneer
of Industrial Research* (Albany, N.Y.: Fort Orange Press, Inc.,
1945), p. 187. The place of the research and development laboratory and the quest for novelty in modern American Civilization are
explored in Daniel J. Boorstin, *The Americans: The Democratic Experience* (New York: Random House, Inc., 1973), pp. 537–546,
with bibliography at p. 671ff.

explained, is not so much a place where men fulfill assignments as a place where men exercise "the art of profiting
from unexpected occurrences."[8] Of course, the most adept
managers of political revolutions—the Sam Adams, the
Robespierre, or the Lenin—have had to know how to profit
by the unexpected, but always to help them reach a prefixed
destination.

The brilliant technological innovator, on the other hand, is
always in search of his destination. He is on the lookout for
new questions. While he hopes to find new problems he
remains alert to discover that what he thought were solutions
were really new problems. Political revolutions are made by
men who urge known remedies for known evils, technological revolutions by men finding unexpected answers to
unimagined questions. While political change starts from
problems, technological change starts from the search for
problems. And as our most adventuring scientists and tech-
nologists provide us with solutions in search of problems, our
society is faced with ways of preventing the newly discovered
uses of the solution (for example, the new uses of inflamma-
ble synthetics for bedclothing, nightgowns and dresses, of
cellophane for packaging, of gasoline-combustion for vehicles,
of plastics for "disposable" containers) from themselves
becoming new problems.

Of course, there are some conspicuous examples—the
building of the first atomic bomb or the effort to land a man
on the moon—where the purpose is specific, and where the
organization resembles that of political enterprises. But here,
too, there are special characteristics: the sense of momentum,
the movement which comes from the size of the enterprise,
the quantity of the investment, and the unpredictability of
knowledge.

If we look back, then, on the great political revolutions and
the great technological revolutions (both of which are clues
to the range of mankind's capacities and possibilities) we see
a striking contrast. Political revolutions, generally speaking,

---

[8] Quoted in Guy Suits, "Willis Rodney Whitney, 1868–1958, A
Biographical Memoir," in *Biographical Memoirs* (Washington,
D.C.: National Academy of Sciences, 1960), vol. 34, p. 355.

have revealed man's organized purposefulness, his social conscience, his sense of justice—the aggressive, assertive side of
this nature. Technological change, invention, and innovation
have tended, rather, to reveal his play instinct, his desire and
his ability to go where he has never gone, to do what he has
never done. The one shows his willingness to sacrifice in
order to fulfill his plans, the other his willingness to sacrifice
in order to pursue his quest. Many of the peculiar successes
and special problems of our time come from our efforts to as-
similate these two kinds of activities. We have tried to make
government more experimental and at the same time to make
technological change more purposive, more focused, more
planned than ever before.

3. *These two kinds of change—political and technological—differ not only in their Why and their How, but
also in their What of It?* By this I mean the special character
of their consequences. Political revolutions tend, with certain
obvious exceptions, to be *displacive*. The Weimar Republic
displaced the régime of Imperial Germany; the Nazis
displaced the Weimar Republic; and after World War II, a
new republic displaced the Nazis. Normally this is what we
mean by a political revolution. Moreover, to a surprising extent, political revolutions are *reversible*. In the political
world, you *can* go home again. It is possible, and even common, for a new régime to go back to the ideas and institutions
of an earlier régime. Many so-called revolutions are really the
revivals of *anciens régimes*. The familiar phenomenon of the
Counter Revolution is the effort to reverse the course of
change. And it is even arguable that Counter Revolutions
generally tend to be more successful than Revolutions. The
Reactionary, whose objective is always more recognizable and
easier to describe, thus is more apt to be successful than the
Revolutionary. It is the possibility of such reversals that has
lent credibility to the largely fallacious pendulum theory of
history, which is popularized in our day under such terms as
"backlash."

Technological changes, however, thrive in a different sort
of world. Momentous technological changes commonly are
neither displacive nor reversible. Technological innovations,

instead of displacing earlier devices, actually tend to create new roles for the devices which they might at first seem to displace. When the telephone was introduced in the later nineteenth century, some people assumed that it would make the postman obsolete (few dared predict that the U. S. Post Office might become decrepit before it was fully mature); similarly when wireless and then radio appeared, some wise people thought that these would spell the end of the telephone; when television came in, many were the voices lamenting the death of radio; and we still hear Cassandras solemnly telling us that television is the death of the book. But in our own time we have had an opportunity to observe how and why such forecasts are ill-founded. We have seen television (together with the automobile) provide new roles for the radio, and most recently we have seen how both have created new roles (or led to the new-flourishing of older roles) for the newspaper press.

A hallmark of the great technological changes is that they tend *not* to be reversible. I have a New England friend who has not yet installed a telephone because, he says, he is waiting until it is perfected. And a few of my scholarly friends (some of them, believe it or not, eminent students, writers, and pundits about American civilization) still stubbornly refuse for even less plausible reasons to have a television set in the house. But, perhaps it is symbolic that I know no one who, having had a telephone, now does without one, nor anyone who, having once installed a TV set, no longer has one. There is no technological counterpart for the Political Restoration or the Counter Revolution. Of course there are changes in style, and the antique, the obsolete, and the camp will always have a certain charm. There will always, I hope, be some individuals willing to go in search of their own Waldens. But their quixotry simply reminds us that the march of modernity is ruthless and can never retreat. In France, for example, the century following the Revolution of 1789 was an oscillation of revolutions and *anciens régimes*; but during the same years the trend of technological change was unmistakable and irreversible. Unlike the French Revolution, the Industrial Revolution—despite an occasional William Morris

—produced no powerful Counter Revolution. Kings can be decapitated, parties can be voted out of power, old ideologies can be abandoned, but nothing can be *uninvented*.

4. *Finally, there remains a crucial difference in our ability to imagine future political revolutions or future technological revolutions.* This is perhaps the most important, if least observed, distinction between the political and the technological worlds. Our failure to note this distinction I describe as the Gamut Fallacy. "Gamut," an English word rooted in the Greek "Gamma" for the lowest note in an old musical scale, means the complete range of anything. When we think, for example, of the future of our political life and our governmental forms, we can have in mind substantially the whole range of possibilities. It is this, of course, which authenticates the traditional wisdom of political theory. It illustrates what we might call *John Adams' Law* (to which I have already referred), namely that political wisdom does not substantially progress. No wonder the astronomical analogy of "revolving" (the primary meaning of "revolution") was so tempting!

But the history of technology, again, is quite another story. We cannot envisage, or even imagine, the range of alternatives from which future technological history will be made. One of the wisest (and, surprisingly enough, one of the most cautious) of our prophets in this area is Arthur C. Clarke, author of *2001* and other speculations. Clarke provides us with a valuable rule-of-thumb for assessing prophecies of the future of man. In his *Profiles of the Future* (after offering some instructive examples of prophecies by experts who proved beyond doubt that the atom could not be split, that supersonic transportation was physically impossible, that man could never escape from the earth's gravitational field, and could certainly never reach the moon), he offers us *Arthur Clarke's Law*: "When a distinguished but elderly scientist states that something is possible, he is almost certainly right. When he states that something is impossible, he is very probably wrong."[9]

[9] *Profiles of the Future: An Inquiry into the Limits of the Possible* (New York: Harper & Row, 1962), p. 15.

This is Clarke's way of warning us against what I have called the Gamut Fallacy—the mistaken notion that we can envisage all possibilities. If *any*thing is possible, then we really cannot know what is possible, simply because we cannot imagine *every*thing. Where, as in the political world, we make the possibilities ourselves, the limitations of the human imagination are reflected in the limitations of actual possibilities themselves. But the physical world is not of our making, and hence its full range of possibilities is beyond our imagining.

V

What are the consequences of these peculiarities of our thinking for how we can or do—or perhaps should—think about our problems today? Even in this later twentieth century, when much of mankind has begun to acquire historical consciousness, we are still plagued by the ancient problem of how to come to terms with change. The same old problem— of how to name what we so imperfectly understand, how to describe the limits of our knowledge while those very limits disqualify us from the task—still befuddles us.

Much of mankind, as we have seen, has tended to reason from the political and social to the technical, and has drawn its analogies in that direction. Faced from time immemorial with the ultimately insoluble problem of man and society, most of mankind has tended to assume that other kinds of problems might be equally insoluble. The wise prophets of the great religions have found various ways to say that, on this earth, there is no solution to the human condition. In our Western society, the parable of man's personal and social problem is the Fall of Man. Original Sin is another way of saying that perfection must be sought in another world, perhaps with the aid of a savior. We have been taught that in human society there are only more or less insoluble problems, and ultimately no solutions. The problem of politics, then, is essentially the problem of man coming to terms with his *problems*.

But our problem in the United States—and, generally speaking, the central problem of technology—is how to come to terms with *solutions*. Our misplaced hopes, our frustrations, and many of our irritations with one another and with other nations come from our unwillingness to believe in the "insoluble" problem, an unwillingness rooted in our New World belief in solutions. Inevitably, then, we overestimate the role of purpose in human change, we overvalue the power of wealth and the power of power. In the Old World, to the eternal question, "Should we try this novelty?" wise men therefore commonly responded with the traditional Old World question, "Why?" In our New World, we answer with our hopeful American question, "Why not?"

One way of explaining, historically, how we have been tempted into this adventurous but perilous way of thinking is that we Americans have tended to take the technological problem—the soluble problem—as the prototype of the problems of our nation, and then, too, of all mankind. Among the novelties of American experience, none have been more striking than our innovations in technology, in standard of living, in the machinery of everyday life. And as I have suggested, one of the obvious characteristics of a problem in technology is that it may really be soluble. Do you seek a way to split the atom and produce a controlled chain reaction? You have found it. That problem is solved! And so it has been with many problems, large and small, in our whole world of technology. Do you want an adhesive which will not require moistening to hold the flaps of envelopes? Do you want a highway surface that will not crack under given variations in temperature? Do you want a pen that will write under water? Do you want a camera that will produce an image in twenty seconds? Or, perhaps, do you want it in full color? We can provide you all these things. These are specific problems with specific solutions.

Taking this kind of problem as our prototype, we have too readily assumed that all other problems may be like them. While much of the rest of mankind has reasoned from the political and social to the technological (and so, often prematurely drawn mistaken, and discouraging, conclusions), we have drawn our analogies in the other direction. By reasoning from the technological to the political and the social, we have been seduced into our own kind of mistaken, if prematurely encouraging, conclusions. It may be within our power to provide a new kind of grain and so cure starvation in some particular place. But it may not be in our power to cure injustice anywhere, even in our own country, much less in distant places.

Without being arrogant, or playing God who alone has all solutions, we may still perhaps learn how to come to terms with our problems. We must learn, at the same time, to accept *John Adams' Law* (that political wisdom does not significantly progress, that the problems of society, the problems of justice and government, are not now much more soluble than they ever were, and hence the wisdom of the social past is never obsolete) while we also accept *Arthur Clarke's Law* (that all technological problems are substantially soluble, that "Anything that is theoretically possible will be achieved in practice, no matter what the technical difficulties, if it is desired greatly enough," and hence the technological past is always becoming obsolete). We must be willing to believe both that Politics is the Art of the Possible and that Technology is the Art of the Impossible. Then we must embrace and cultivate both arts.

Our unprecedented American achievements both in Politics and in Technology therefore pose us a test, and test us with a tension, unlike that posed to any people before us in history. Never before has a people been so tempted (and with such good reason) to believe that anything is *technologically* possible. And a consequence has been that perhaps no people before us has been so troubled, nor has found it so difficult, to continue unabashed in search of the prudent limits of the *politically* possible. In this American limbo—in this new world of hope and of terror—we have a rare opportunity to profit from man's recent discovery that he has a history.

G. WARREN NUTTER
Freedom in a Revolutionary Economy

Delivered in the Wren Building, College of William

and Mary, Williamsburg, Virginia on February 20, 1974

Times change. When my townsman, Thomas Jefferson, journeyed to Williamsburg in May 1779 and shortly afterward took up residence in the palace as governor, Virginia was at war. Strange things were happening in the economy, and they were to become stranger over the ensuing two years of Jefferson's stewardship. Inflation was rampant, goods were requisitioned, property was impressed, salt rationed, hoarding declared a crime, and exports put under embargo. Short of arms, Virginia launched an abortive project to produce them in a state arsenal. If price and wage controls were not widely or vigorously applied, it was in spite of constant urgings by the desperate Continental Congress to do so. The lessons of experience were simply too compelling: wherever and whenever price and wage fixing had been tried in the new states fighting for independence, it had brought nothing but great economic mischief.

As we assemble here today in Williamsburg on the eve of the bicentenary of our republic, we may be grateful for one important difference in the times: we are not now at war. In that respect, times have changed.

This is not to say that the harsh measures resorted to in the revolutionary war were normal for the colonial period as well. Quite the contrary. Under the British policy of "salu-

tary neglect," in force until 1763, the colonial economy had
been largely spared the mercantilist imprint of the age.
"Plenty of good land, and liberty to manage their own affairs
their own way," Adam Smith observed, "seem to be the two
great causes of the prosperity of all new colonies." But why,
he wondered, had progress been so much more rapid in the
English colonies of North America than in other European
colonies throughout the world? The answer was not to be
found, he thought, in a richer or more abundant soil, but
rather in institutions that enabled the English colonists to
make better use of the plentiful resourcs at thir disposal.

These were, first, political. As Smith put it, "in every
thing, except their foreign trade, the liberty of the English
colonists to manage their own affairs their own way is
complete. It is in every respect equal to that of their fellow
citizens at home, and is secured in the same manner, by an
assembly of the representatives of the people, who claim the
sole right of imposing taxes for the support of the colony government."

But there was more. Plenty of good land meant not only
abundant resources but also, in a less literal sense, the elbow
room needed by a new social order if it was to discard those
vestigial institutions that had stifled progress for so long
under the established order of things. A case in point was
land tenure itself, which could be freed from the bonds of
primogeniture and entail in the absence of an entrenched nobility or similar aristocracy. The new society could, when permitted by the mother country, strike out in new directions
and prosper accordingly.

The contribution of the mother country was, in Adam
Smith's eyes, strictly that of a mother:

> In what way, therefore, has the policy of Europe con-
> tributed either to the first establishment, or to the
> present grandeur of the colonies of America? In one way,
> and in one way only, it has contributed a good deal.
> *Magna virûm Mater!* It bred and formed the men who
> were capable of achieving [sic] such great actions, and of
> laying the foundation of so great an empire; and there is
> no other quarter of the world of which the policy is capa-

ble of forming, or has actually and in fact formed such men. The colonies owe to the policy of Europe the education and great views of their active and enterprising founders; and some of the greatest and most important of them, so far as concern their internal government, owe it to scarce anything else.

The cultural flow did not, of course, cease with the founding of the colonies. The book from which I have quoted[1]— *The Wealth of Nations*—was, for one thing, published the same year as the Declaration of Independence. And then there was James Watt's invention of the steam engine scarcely a decade before. This remarkable confluence of ideas laid the foundation for a revolutionary society. All at once, it seems, there sprang forth this congenial triad: a novel concept of representative government, a science of economics, and an industrial technology, each revolutionary in its own right and exponentially so when combined together.

These ideas had their proximate origin in two amazingly small circles of minds, one located in the incipient United States and the other in Scotland. Though no Virginian can gladly resist the temptation to do so, I will not dwell on the American circle, so well known to us as our Founding Fathers. And, as far as the Scottish circle is concerned, the only point I wish to make here is that Smith and Watt were once colleagues at the University of Glasgow.

John Rae, Smith's biographer, describes their relation in this way:

There is nothing in the University minutes to connect Smith in any more special way than the other professors with the University's timely hospitality to James Watt; but as that act was a direct protest on behalf of industrial liberty against the tyrannical spirit of the trade guilds so strongly condemned in the *Wealth of Nations*, it is at least interesting to remember that Smith had a part in it. Watt, it may be recollected, was then a lad of twenty, who had come back from London to Glasgow to set up as mathematical instrument maker, but though

[1] Adam Smith, *The Wealth of Nations* (New York: Modern Library, 1937), pp. 538, 551, and 556.

there was no other mathematical instrument maker in the city, the corporation of hammermen refused to permit his settlement because he was not the son or son-in-law of a burgess, and had not served his apprenticeship to the craft within the burgh. But in those days of privilege the universities also had their privileges. The professors of Glasgow enjoyed an absolute and independent authority over the area within college bounds, and they defeated the oppression of Watt by making him mathematical instrument maker to the University, and giving him a room in the College buildings for his workshop and another at the College gates for the sale of his instruments. In these proceedings Smith joined, and joined, we may be sure, with the warmest approval. . . .

Watt's workshop was a favourite resort of Smith's during his residence at Glasgow College, for Watt's conversation, young though he was, was fresh and original, and had great attractions for the stronger spirits about him. Watt on his side retained always the deepest respect for Smith, and when he was amusing the leisure of his old age in 1809 with his new invention of the sculpture machine, and presenting his works to his friends as "the productions of a young artist just entering his eighty-third year," one of the first works he executed with the machine was a small head of Adam Smith in ivory.[2]

Respect for Smith was hardly confined to Watt or Scotland, for *The Wealth of Nations* migrated easily and widely abroad, finding an eager audience in many parts and certainly on our shores. Our Founders were familiar with this great work in one way or another, some more than others.[3] Alexander Hamilton, Tench Coxe, or whoever wrote the renowned *Report on Manufactures*, paraphrased Smith at length and quoted him verbatim at one point, though without acknowledging the source.[4] Deliberations at the Con-

[2] John Rae, *Life of Adam Smith* (New York: Augustus M. Kelley, 1965), pp. 73–74.

[3] See William D. Grampp, *Economic Liberalism* (New York: Random House, 1965), vol. 1, pp. 128ff and 154.

[4] See Edward G. Bourne, "Alexander Hamilton and Adam Smith," *Quarterly Journal of Economics*, vol. 7 (1893–94), pp. 328–344.

stitutional Convention reveal a much wider group acquainted with the emerging science of economics.

Passage of time has caused differing verdicts to be rendered on the originality, rigor, and consistency of Smith's masterpiece, but history leaves no doubt about its massive impact and significance. Its genius derived from the molding together of fragments of evolving economic thought into a synthetic whole, masterfully applied to familiar situations in a way that revealed a coherent system for organizing social activity not easily envisaged before and destined to capture the imagination of thoughtful leaders ready to grasp revolutionary ideas. It, like the Declaration and the ensuing Constitution, struck a spark in receptive tinder. Social thought was not to be the same afterward as before.

Ideas do have consequences, dependent on the historical conjuncture into which they are thrust, and this was a propitious time for exciting ideas. The political thinkers and leaders who arose in those formative years of our republic were, of course, influenced by many things: vested interests and personal ambition as well as idealism and ideology; conventional wisdom and prevailing institutions as well as radical thought; the sheer momentum of affairs as well as rational calculus. So was the electorate whose consent was sought and needed to launch the new society. Those who easily discern a simple order in history, an uncomplicated nexus of cause and consequence, may single out one or another factor as the dominant force shaping the course of events in those times, but not I. Such sweeping interpretations of history obscure more than they reveal. Opportunities and constraints are the stuff of history, together with chance, reflective thought, and choice. And none of these elements flows mechanically and predictably from the nature of man, custom, institutions, or any other readily identifiable single source. History is instead the product of all these interacting forces mutually influencing each other. My only object, then, is to give revolutionary ideas and sober reflection their due in this singular epoch.

When the delegates assembled for the Constitutional Convention, there was good reason in circumstances of the time for their attention to be drawn to the related issues of strengthening government at the national level and of "regulating commerce," a term that had roughly the same meaning then as "economic policy" has today. Prosperity had not spontaneously emerged in the wake of independence, contrary to great expectations before the fact. Instead of prosperity, there was depression, aggravated in no small measure by the confused and confounded government of the Confederation. Experience in dealing with these troubles was modest from all points of view: influential leaders were in their thirties; conscious economic policy on the part of government—in London as well as at home—had a history of scarcely more than a score of years; and precedents for the envisaged new order were lacking altogether. Imagination and vision were bound to assume commanding importance.

Wherever and however they acquired their economic vision, the makers of the Constitution deliberately gave wide berth to the economy of the nation being formed, reserving only a restrained guiding hand for government. In saying this, I am mindful of the persistent controversy over how much power the prevailing constitution-makers intended to bestow upon the government of the Union. On this score, however, I find quite persuasive the case made by William Grampp,[5] eminent historian of economic liberalism.

Concentrating on the eleventh-hour efforts at the Convention to expand the economic role of the federal government, Grampp notes that

> What is interesting is that the proposals—all of them controversial, almost provocative—should have been made only a few days before the convention adjourned, when unanimity was urgently needed and when many delegates were trying heroically to find compromises that would produce it. Proposals such as that made by Madison [to empower the Federal government to charter corporations] had been made earlier in the convention. That they were made again so near the time [of] adjournment suggests that their advocates were making a last great effort to write broad economic powers into the Constitution. . . . Perhaps they prevailed upon Franklin

[5] Grampp, *Economic Liberalism*, pp. 101–114.

in the belief that his great authority would be decisive. But they were defeated. . . . The very extensive powers proposed by Randolph, Morris, Franklin, Hamilton, and Madison were reduced to the limited provisions of Section 8 of Article I, which include the power to tax, borrow, regulate commerce, pass uniform bankruptcy laws, coin money, establish post offices and post roads, and grant patents.

The limits thus established take on significance when compared with the traditional economic powers of the age, which, as Grampp observes,

> can be deduced from the controls which the governments of France and England exercised or tried to exercise during the period of mercantilism, from the sixteenth to the middle of the eighteenth century: the fixing of prices, wages, and interest rates, prohibitions of forestalling and engrossing, regulating the quality of goods, licensing of labor, programs to increase the population, sumptuary control, monopoly grants and other exclusive rights, incorporation, state enterprise, and the control of foreign trade and finance including the protection of domestic industries. The convention considered only four: monopoly and other exclusive rights, control of foreign trade, state enterprise, and sumptuary control. The last two were rejected. The granting of monopoly rights was restricted to patents and copyrights. The control over foreign trade was left in an ambiguous state, except for the prohibition of export taxes. Although not made explicit, the Constitution allowed some power to increase the population, because the Federal government could offer free land as an inducement to immigration.

Good often issues more from powers denied to government than from those granted, and this was surely the case as far as economic development over our republic's first century is concerned. None of the prohibitory provisions of the Constitution was to take on greater significance than the one forbidding individual states to erect barriers to commerce among themselves. Making trade free within an internal market that was to expand to vast proportions permitted the nation to indulge, for example, in recurrently restrictive tariffs, as the politics of a good century and a half seemed to dictate, without serious hindrance to economic progress. Our great market was to live at home in a free-trade area larger than the world has yet experienced anywhere else. Our Founders could hardly have foreseen that this would happen, but they must have had a conceptual vision—no matter how crude it might seem to those passing judgment today—of the broad benefits that would ensue from internal free trade. Otherwise, why bother to write this strict prohibition into the Constitution?

While such specific sentiments of the time are rather easily discerned, the underlying social philosophy is more elusive, defying simple description in the ideological vocabulary of today. Liberalism will hardly do as a description if only because slavery was accepted by most and extolled by many. Nor can we speak of a democratic ideal in the modern sense, since democracy—either as then comprehended or as since manifested—was specifically rejected in favor of republicanism, a quite different concept of representative government as Irving Kristol so elegantly clarified earlier in this series. Individualism is perhaps the term that best captures the essential spirit of the time and at once implies the complex of derivative values: liberty for the citizen—which is to say, the person deemed competent and responsible—to make his own decisions; power for the citizen, mainly in the form of private property, to realize his potential; humanitarian concern for the less fortunate and incompetent; and equality of all citizens before the law and of the electorate within the polity.

II

If the thinker-turned-statesman had his moment at the founding of the republic, it was to be the practitioner pure and simple—the doer, the man of action—who was to dominate the scene for at least the next century, when pragmatism became America's watchword. The individualistic spirit found expression in the world of affairs, not in philosophic reflection, as each citizen was swept up in the excitement of his workaday world—his farm or business, his trade or profession, his public or private life. The nation, it would seem, was too busy enjoying the fruits of progress to ponder its causes, and theory emerged from practice. Political thought issued from practicing politicians, and economic thought—interestingly—from practicing jurists.

Economists, such as there were, were either special pleaders or academic amateurs. In his classic essay on early American economic thought, the late Frank Fetter wondered "why . . . the fertile and original conceptions which sprang, as it were, spontaneously from the new environment in America, [did] not come to fruition in a constructive and more lasting system of American economic thought." He found much of the answer to lie in "partisanship, which blocks the path of disinterested scientific effort whenever personal prejudices and pecuniary or class interests are affected by the application of any kind of theory to practical problems."

The consequence—and, in turn, reinforcing cause—was lack of a learned profession of economics. As Fetter observes:

> It is a remarkable fact that during the whole period before 1870 there was not a single so-called political economist who had received the minimum amount of special training demanded today for the practice of law, or of medicine, or for the pursuit of the natural sciences. All were trained primarily in some other field: theology, moral philosophy, literature, languages, law, practical politics, journalism, business, or some branch of natural science. In political economy they were all self-trained amateurs, who, as it were, happened to wander into this field. If the study of the more exact sciences were pursued only by men with such dominant motives and such unspecialized training, little scientific progress could be expected.[6]

I leave it to others to judge whether the absence of trained economists made us better or worse off in this first century of sweeping economic development. However that may be, the

[6] Frank A. Fetter, "The Early History of Political Economy in the United States," in James A. Gherity, ed., *Economic Thought: A Historical Anthology* (New York: Random House, 1965), pp. 489f.

fact is that there was no body of qualified scholars, skilled in critical thought, to observe the unfolding economy, issue commentary, formulate general principles, apply them to problems of the time, and advise on policy. Instead it was the law, issuing from acts and cases, that was to shape a framework for the economy, articulate its principles, and guide policy.

The propelling legal philosophy of the era conceived the purpose of law to be, in Roscoe Pound's words, "a making possible of the maximum of individual free self-assertion." Or, as James Willard Hurst has put it more concretely:

> We continually experienced the tangible accomplishments of individuals, small groups, and local effort, with a heady sense of living in a fluid society in which all about him all the time one saw men moving to new positions of accomplishment and influence. Our background and experience in this country taught faith in the capacities of the productive talent residing in people. The obvious precept was to see that this energy was released for its maximum creative expression.[7]

At the same time, those who made and interpreted the law were not slaves to some sterile dogma of laissez-faire. Far from it. As Hurst reminds us, this was no "Golden Age in which our ancestors—sturdier than we—got along well enough if the legislature provided schools, the sheriff ran down horse thieves, the court tried farmers' title disputes, and otherwise the law left men to take care of themselves." There was no reluctance to legislate positively "where legal regulation or compulsion might promote the greater release of individual or group energies."

But the pervasive spirit of the law, whether it invoked or restrained the power of government, was individualistic. It was normal that "the years 1800–1875 were, then, above all else, the years of contract in our law."[8] Subject to the restrictive doctrines of consideration and residual authority of the

---

[7] James Willard Hurst, *Law and the Conditions of Freedom in the Nineteenth Century United States* (Madison, Wisconsin: The University of Wisconsin Press, 1956), p. 7.

[8] Ibid., p. 18.

state to refuse enforcement, the thrust of the law was to encourage voluntary exchange and association. The legal system was responding to the burgeoning scope of the market and in turn stimulating further expansion, in a process of interaction similarly experienced in England at an accelerating pace during the eighteenth as well as the nineteenth century. It was, in fact, an English jurist who, with typical facility, gave classic expression to the legal philosophy dominant in our first century:

> If there is one thing more than any other which public policy requires, it is that men of full age and competent understanding shall have the utmost liberty of contracting, and that contracts, when entered into freely and voluntarily, shall be held good and shall be enforced by courts of justice.[9]

In a word, contract was king, a sovereign precept demanding obedience from subservient legal principles. No wonder the courts and legislatures were so busy elaborating and defining property rights and liabilities, sweeping away vestigial restrictions on alienation, erecting an intricate structure of commercial law, and creating the corporate person with its full range of appendages and paraphernalia.

The spirit of the time may be fairly interpreted as enthusiasm for venture, viewed as the source of prosperity and progress. Consequently, the law leaned over backward not to hinder the entrepreneur, not to hold him unduly responsible for incidental harm flowing from venturesome activity. It was as if "nothing ventured, nothing gained" had become the literal creed of the age. For, as Hurst points out,

> The insistence on a showing of criminal intention [in any case involving liability] amounted in effect to a presumption in favor of the independence of individual action. The middle-nineteenth-century rationale of the law of negligence, in tort, reflected the same basic value judgment. Expansion of economic energies brought men into closer, more continuous relations in situations increasingly likely to yield harm. Nonetheless, at first the law emphasized the social desirability of free individual ac-

[9] Sir George Jessel, cited in ibid., p. 12.

tion and decision. Liability in tort should normally rest on a showing of fault on the actor's part; action at one's peril was the exception. Hence the burden lay on the injured person to show reason why the law should intrude its force to shift some of the burden of loss onto the one who caused injury.[10]

This attitude no doubt appears strange to a generation accustomed to the rhetoric of Ralph Nader and the Sierra Club. I have dwelt on these legal presumptions of the last century neither to extoll nor to disparage them, but to stress their importance as a manifestation of the social ethic of the time. Who is to bear the burden of proving what, and why? The presumptive answers given to these questions say more about a society's conception of the good life than any list of good intentions, no matter how long.

In the matter-of-fact world of our first century, freedom took on concrete meaning in the marketplace, and it worked. A continent was settled, a nation built, and prosperity persistently augmented. The portentous questions of slavery and preservation of the Union might overhang the political scene, but the grand passion was economic development, and the object of the love affair was the market, the creature of free enterprise and exchange.

III

So it was at least on the surface, but something happened on the way to our second century. There was, first, the torment of the Civil War, which probably served more to arouse the social conscience than to soothe it. Yet, the slaves freed and the Union preserved, the economy hardly paused before plunging into the era of bigness, surely the culmination of a less abrupt historical process.

What had been happening on the economic front was a revolution in transport, the spanning of the continent by railroad, creating a truly national market and opening the way for big business, big finance, and all the other forms of

10 Ibid., p. 19.

bigness. The individualistic spirit was bound to be put under severe stress as gigantic voluntary associations, the very creatures of contract, assumed a corporate and depersonalized nature basically in conflict with the principle of free individual choice. Tocqueville had already been impressed in the 1830s by the remarkable ability of American private enterprise to mobilize large sums for grand ventures, but he noted that "what most astonishes me is not so much the marvelous grandeur of some undertakings as the innumerable multitude of small ones."[11] Now grandeur was to take the center of the stage.

It is neither my bent nor purpose to prolong this historical narrative, for the moment will shortly be upon me for a summing up, and there is more interpretive ground yet to be covered. Suffice it to say that our first century laid the basis for the second, still fresh in memory. We gradually moved toward a turning point similar to the one faced earlier in England. As Winston Churchill was to write at the turn of the twentieth century,

> The great victories had been won. All sorts of lumbering tyrannies had been toppled over. Authority was everywhere broken. Slaves were free. Conscience was free. Trade was free. But hunger and squalor and cold were also free and the people demanded something more than liberty. . . . And how to fill the void was the riddle that split the Liberal party.[12]

Changing opinion ultimately brought forth a second revolution, a revolution in social thought born of economic crisis some two-score years ago. In the formative years, we seemed determined to make up for lost time in the realm of social philosophizing. The vanguard of social reformers comprised a multiplying band of intellectuals, spawned by affluence, emboldened by their own peculiar sense of superiority, motivated by the animus of the onlooking outsider, and hence, as Schumpeter perceived, inherently inclined to become

---

[11] Alexis de Tocqueville, *Democracy in America* (New York: Vintage Books, 1954), vol. 2, p. 166.
[12] Winston S. Churchill, *Lord Randolph Churchill* (New York: Macmillan Co., 1906), vol. 1, p. 269.

angry social critics by profession. Learned economists, conspicuously absent during our first century, appeared in abundance and assumed a role of growing importance. To be sure, ardent defenders of the free society were to be found in the intellectual ranks, particularly among economists, but they were vastly overshadowed by the critics in due course. The way was prepared for the sharp inversion of social values that has taken place over the last generation, an inversion incarnate in the colossal government that has come into being as the share of the nation's net product passing through the hands of government has risen from less than a sixth to more than two-fifths. Security, protection, comfort, equality—all seem to have advanced in the scale of importance above self-reliance and freedom.

Fundamentally, what has been transformed is the prevailing conception of the good society. In the nineteenth century, it was the way of life that was idealized—the process whereby the achievable was to be achieved. Today, it is the achievement itself, the outcome of the process, that is prized. We value the way of life less and the content more.

Why has this happened? The easy answer is that freedom did not live up to promise. The evolution of legal principles during our first century suggests that freedom was valued in the economic sphere for what it was expected to yield, that its worth was deemed to be instrumental rather than intrinsic, that economic progress was the goal and freedom merely the means.

There are two things to be said about this interpretation. First, by the test of progress, freedom can hardly have been judged a failure. Production, despite periodic bad times, moved upward in a trend that was the envy of the world, while population multiplied fifteen-fold.[13] This was, after all, the "land of opportunity."

Second, freedom was surely desired for itself as much as for its consequences. To interpret the moving spirit of our founding years as nothing more than a craving for greater material

[13] See L. E. Davis, R. A. Easterlin, W. W. Parker, et al., *American Economic Growth: An Economist's History of the United States* (New York: Harper and Row, 1972), pp. 21–26, and 33–50.

comfort would be a travesty of history. Not even the sustained paralysis on the slavery issue can lead us to a similar conclusion about the succeeding period. Nor do we need to become mired in the metaphysical to define liberty as it was then conceived. The documents of our Revolution protested against too much government, against the dead hand of paternalism and arbitrary power. Liberty to our Founders meant freedom from government.

Perhaps, then, Marx was right in proclaiming that the benefits of capitalism would be far outweighed by its evils: increasing monopoly, misery, inequality, and insecurity. Here, too, the evidence argues otherwise in the main.

Of course, poverty did not vanish amidst plenty, but in a broader sense there was no discernible worsening of material inequality during our first century. A recent study shows, for example, that slaveholding, then unfortunately an important aspect of wealth, was no more concentrated in 1860 than in 1790: in both years, the top one percent of slaveholders owned about an eighth of the slaves. Better and more direct evidence indicates a small but perceptible reduction in the inequality of incomes during the last four decades of the nineteenth century.[14]

Changing circumstances and lack of records make it impossible to assess the trend of monopoly in the nineteenth century. Seemingly obvious appearances can be deceptive: the era of trusts toward the end of the century accompanied the emergence of a national market and hence did not necessarily signify a decline of competition. Those who envisage an earlier age of more pervasive competition in isolated localities are likely to be indulging in myth. In any case, the evidence for the twentieth century has been carefully sifted, and it shows no upward drift in the extent of monopoly.[15]

To give Marx his due, one must acknowledge that, over

[14] See ibid., pp. 29–32 and 50–54; and Lee Soltow, "Economic Inequality in the United States in the Period from 1790 to 1860," *Journal of Economic History* (December 1971), pp. 822–839.

[15] See G. W. Nutter and H. A. Einhorn, *Enterprise Monopoly in the United States: 1899–1958* (New York: Columbia University Press, 1969).

most of our history, we were plagued by cycles of boom and bust with intensifying social impact, so that the attendant insecurity and periodic unemployment constituted a major source of discontent and ultimately of social crisis. But recurrent depressions are not enough to account for the profound change in social outlook.

Instead, I would argue, success has had more to do with our changing mentality than failure. It was Mark Twain who said: "If you pick up a starving dog and make him prosperous, he will not bite you. This is the principal difference between a dog and a man." Progress did not, by and large, aggravate inequities, but it made us more aware and less tolerant of them. Sharpening contrasts in circumstance aroused our humane sentiments, sentiments that could be better afforded by virtue of augmenting affluence. Progress shook loose the age-old endurance that man had customarily displayed for his lot, and bred in its place an attitude of insatiable discontent with the pace at which remaining problems were being met. And so we find ourselves in a society in which progress and discontent are engaged in an almost desperate race with each other.

This is perhaps as it should be as long as there is poverty and injustice in the midst of plenty. If social change is to move in the right direction, in accord with the standards of the civilized world, there must be those who stir and prod, who keep the public alert to inequities, who find fault with the established ways of maintaining social order. It is natural to point the finger of blame at the existing system and to seek salvation in its opposite, but therein also lies the great danger of our day.

Those who protest against failures of the market, real and imagined, too often see their remedy in turning affairs over to government, in expanding the political order and diminishing the economic—in relying more on coercion and less on mutual consent. The danger we run in looking first to government to solve problems is that progress will grind to a halt—that discontent will vanquish progress, and the race will be over. Over the ages, the bane of progress has been too much government, not too little.

IV

The time has therefore come, as we approach our bicentenary, to look back to the origins of our economy and to reflect on where we go from here. The revolutionary content of ideas popularized by Adam Smith and implemented by our Founders is to be found in the vision of a complex social order organized not by custom and command, the methods of the ages, but by voluntary exchange and association. Economics arose as a scientific discipline when the economy became a social order distinct from the polity. Those who, inspired by the spirit of freedom, sought to broaden the individual's control over his own destiny were naturally inclined to enlarge the scope of markets and to reduce that of the body politic. The economy became an area of social activity coordinated through voluntary agreement, and economic activity became in the main synonymous with liberty.

Progress came with the loosening of political bonds, but the resulting freedom could be translated into action only through power. The individual acquires power through ownership of private property, the other side of the coin to liberty. In the absolute state, subjects enjoy neither freedom nor power: the despot reigns over slaves. By becoming concentrated in his hands, private property ceases to exist in any meaningful sense. Put the other way around, private property is the means whereby power may be dispersed within a society. It is no wonder that our legal system devoted so much attention to strengthening and vitalizing this institution.

The opposite of the absolute state is anarchy, where everything is privately owned. Just as there can be no freedom in the absolute state, so there can be no order in anarchy—and hence no freedom either. On this earth, there must always be collective property embodied in the power of even the freest state and accumulated through the instrument of taxation, itself an inherent property right of every state. It is equally clear that a society becomes free and democratic only as property becomes broadly dispersed and predominately private.

Over most of our history, the question of what middle ground was to be occupied by our society between the poles of anarchy and despotism was resolved by the presumption that matters are best left to individual choice and mutual consent unless the contrary is proved beyond reasonable doubt. The burden of proof was upon him who maintained that a task entrusted to the market could be better performed by transferring it to the government.

The state had much to do, but classical liberalism implied a certain ordering of tasks to guide the emphasis of governmental activity. First, the state had to provide the necessary political and legal framework for the market by maintaining order, defining property, preventing fraud, enforcing contracts, and assigning responsibility. Second, it should disperse power by diminishing inequality of income and opportunity and by inhibiting monopolization. Third, it was to perform desirable functions too costly for individuals or voluntary associations, such as establishment of a sound monetary system, maintenance of public health, and promotion of safety. Fourth, it should help the poor and unfortunate and act as guardian for the incompetent, protecting those who could not cope with the normal responsibilities of life. Fifth, it should stabilize general economic conditions. Sixth and finally, it should provide welfare services to the public in the form of social security, unemployment assistance, and various other desired collective goods.

That ordering has been turned upside down by the social outlook of today, and the shifting emphasis has caused government to undertake the activist role formerly assumed by the market. That is, the ascendant presumption is that matters are better attended to by government than by the market. Wherever performance of the market is under attack, those who believe that government would do an even worse job bear the burden of proof.

This state of affairs obviously accords with the prevailing vision of the good life. And so one might conclude that there is nothing more to be said, since the people have the social order they want. But do they? One may be permitted to wonder whether there is not some profound confusion in a society that strives so hard to retain a peacetime economy through seven long years of war and then leaps into a wartime economy almost the moment peace breaks out. More fundamentally, something must be wrong in a society that feels compelled to treat each new problem, no matter how routine, as a monumental crisis and hence chooses to live in a continual atmosphere of tension, sacrifice, and fear. As a friend of mine has put it, if the price system is not to be trusted with adjusting a 20-percent gap between the supply and demand for energy, perhaps it had better hang up its spikes.

But I am here today to note the trend of affairs, not to pass judgment or to prophesy the ultimate outcome. Who can see what will come in the next two centuries any more clearly than our forefathers could envisage what vast change lay ahead in the two just completed? In a way, our starting point is similar to theirs. Recall the traditional mercantilist controls of central government rejected by our Founders: the fixing of prices, wages, and interest rates; the outlawing of forestalling and engrossing; the regulating of the quality of goods; the licensing of labor; the setting of sumptuary standards; the granting of monopoly rights; the chartering of corporations; and the establishing of state enterprises. They have all found a congenial home in the New Deals, Fair Deals, New Frontiers, Great Societies, and New Federalisms of our age. Yet, the very environment being created by them affords us something to react against in the same way that our forefathers did, perhaps once again to the benefit of liberty. As the saying goes, good judgment comes from experience, and experience comes from bad judgment.

Let me then end on a soft note of hope in keeping with the occasion. My mood is unfortunately one of hope rather than expectation, for there is little in the momentum of unfolding history to comfort those who cherish freedom. What is there to prevent the fraction of income taxed by government from rising to half, three-quarters, and more? There is a hope, and it is this: having become so impressed with the fact that freedom is not everything or the only thing, perhaps we shall put that discovery behind us and comprehend, before it is too late, that without freedom all else is nothing.

VERMONT ROYSTER

The American Press and the Revolutionary Tradition

Delivered in Dinkelspiel Auditorium, Stanford University,

Stanford, California on March 6, 1974

Among the many revolutionary ideas to emerge from the American Revolution, none proved more revolutionary than the idea of freedom of the press. None has proved more durable, for it has withstood two centuries of assault. None has brewed more controversy, for it remains today even in this country as revolutionary an idea as it was in the eighteenth century and in its American form it exists now only in this country. And of the many changes which time has worked on the political ideas of the Founding Fathers, none would more surprise them—and perhaps disturb them—than what has evolved in the succeeding two centuries from their views of what constitutes freedom of the press. All the evidence suggests that when they embraced this philosophical idea, and embodied it in the First Amendment to our Constitution, they knew not what they wrought.

Certainly when they spoke of freedom of the press they did not envision a press of very nearly unrestrained license, which is for all practical purposes the legal privilege of the twentieth century American press. That idea was foreign to the liberal philosophers, mostly those of the seventeenth and eighteenth centuries, from whom they drew their concepts about the nature of man and society on which they founded

the American political system. Nor was there anything in
their own experience, even in the midst of rebellion against a
distant government, that led them to suppose a civil liberty,
whatever its nature, could be severed from civic responsibility
and therefore from all restraint. They thought this especially
true when one liberty—or, if you prefer, one unalienable
right—clashed with another. In few things were they
absolutists. So in their view this freedom of the press, as
every other freedom, existed only within certain parameters
of responsibility, not always precisely definable but existing
nonetheless.

Even in our own time the idea of freedom of the press
without restraint, which is what that freedom often appears
to have become, is disturbing to many people. It is not
merely that this freedom is irritating to our governors, although there are many examples of that. It is also disturbing
at times to philosophers, to men of the law, to the citizenry
generally and not least to some of those within the press itself. Not only is the performance of the press criticized, but
the very extent of its freedom is questioned, both from
within and from without. So it is that the right to speak and
to spread abroad whatever one wishes remains to this day a
revolutionary idea; that is to say, one which has not yet lost
its controversial nature through unquestioning acceptance.

Yet we have come to accept so much of this idea of
freedom of the press that we are scarcely aware of how far we
have come from its beginnings. The parameters within which
we today debate possible, or desirable, restraints on the
freedom to publish, or the terms in which we discuss the
need for both a free and responsible press, are quite different
from those used by Mr. Jefferson, Mr. Madison or Mr.
Franklin. They would have some difficulty, I suspect,
comprehending the recent controversy over the Pentagon
Papers; they would be puzzled by the near-disappearance of
private libel from the canons of the law, or the total disap-
pearance of seditious libel, not to mention the untrammeled
performance of the press in the Watergate affair. Certainly
they would be aghast at today's license, under the shelter of
the First Amendment, for published pornography.

Nonetheless, that we have come so far is in part a logical extension of those very ideas about man and society and the nature of political freedom that permeated the thinking of those who embarked on the American experiment. Just as other of their ideas set in motion political events they did not fully anticipate, so it was here. Their declaration that all men are created free and equal inevitably led not only to the abolition of slavery but to universal suffrage and to an ever-widening concept of civil rights. So with the declaration that freedom of speech and of the press shall not be abridged. That declaration once made, it became ever more difficult to find a point of abridgment.

There is also, however, another reason why in the area of political reporting and publishing the American press has pushed the borders of permissible freedom beyond those in any other country including countries which share our heritage of general political liberty, such as Great Britain itself. That reason lies in geography, that in the time before and during our rebellion the colonies were both remote from the mother country and separated even from each other. Geography made restraints less practical, the opportunities for freedom of expression more available.

Ideas fertilized the American Revolution; it would hardly have come without them. Geography made its success possible; it was the great gulf of ocean that, in the end, made it impossible to put down. These same two things, ideas and geography, also provided the soil for the revolutionary tradition of the American press, a tradition suspicious of all government and fiercely opposed to all restraint. In the two centuries since, it has proved a lasting tradition.

The ideas here involved, as so many others, might be traced back to the Greeks when Plato and Aristotle were debating the nature of man and of government. We are heirs of them both, teacher and pupil, but in politics more Aristotelian than Platonist. It was Plato, after all, who would have had the state lay down rigid rules for poets and philosophers and who would have had their works submitted to magistrates to decide whether they were fit for the people. As we shall see, there are Platonists among us yet. Aristotle, though he defended the slavery of his times and was fearful of pure democracy, did broach the thought that the citizens exercising their collective judgment had the right not only to choose their leaders but to call them to account. The echoes of this are heard in that Declaration of 1776; they reverberate today whenever there is heard a clamor in the press to impeach a President.

But it was the Reformation, with its revolt against the authority of the Church, that more immediately opened the Pandora's box and let escape the idea that each man had a right to make "free inquiry" with his own mind. The inquiry began about God; it was not long before it extended to the state.

Not long, but slowly all the same. In England, which is the principal source of our political heritage, the sixteenth century had ended with absolutism triumphant. By the end of the seventeenth century, having suffered the absolutism of Cromwell, England was a ferment of liberal ideas. The Declaration of Rights of 1689, forced upon William and Mary as the price of their crowns, foreshadows in many particulars not only our own Declaration of Independence but later provisions in our Constitution; it proclaimed among other things that at least in Parliament there must be freedom of debate.

This was the century, too, of John Locke, with his thesis of popular sovereignty under which government was merely the trustee of power delegated by the people and which the people could withdraw. And the century of John Milton, who in his *Areopagitica* argued that men can distinguish between right and wrong ideas if these are allowed to meet in open encounter. Locke sowed the seed of rebellion, Milton the seed of the First Amendment in our Bill of Rights.

Still, at the beginning of the eighteenth century they were seeds only. Milton, like Locke, spoke a minority view. Moreover Milton himself, whose motivation was irritation at Puritan censorship of his own theology, would not extend the full freedom of expression to Roman Catholics or to insidious pamphleteers and journalists. And no matter how majestic his argument, it had small effect even upon the intellectual men of his time and none at all upon the political authorities. In England, as elsewhere, the printing press remained subservient to the needs of the state. When the first small cracks did appear in the system of press control—and here, of course, we are speaking primarily of books and pamphlets, not newspapers as we know them—those cracks were caused less by the pressure of ideas than by the practical difficulties of enforcement.

Until well into the seventeenth century the printing press was controlled in England by a system of patents, that is, licenses. The Crown gave patents to a group of printers organized into the Stationers' Company. This company had the power to admit and expel members from the printing trade and to discipline the members for such transgressions as might be charged against them by the authorities. For some 200 years this system worked well in controlling the printing press, the Stationers' Company being assiduous in protecting its monopoly. It began to break down only as technology made printing presses cheap and therefore readily available. By the beginning of the eighteenth century the proliferation of presses had made it impossible to enforce the licensing system and equally impractical for an official censor to read and approve every piece of printed matter before it was published. Practicality, then, demanded both a different system and a different rationale, legal and philosophical, to justify it.

The English answer to this problem was both ingenious and far-reaching in its effects. Necessity forced the abandonment of prior restraint on publication. In its place was substituted the idea that the printer, while he could not be restrained in advance, could be held accountable afterwards for what he caused to be published. Gradually what could not be prevented came to be hailed as an unalienable right; what could be adjudicated came to be accepted as a proper restraint upon that right. In time this new concept of freedom of the press, its extent and its limitations, was debated and shaped by men as varied as Dr. Samuel Johnson and Sir William Blackstone.

Blackstone, most especially. For this English jurist not only capsuled the new philosophy and the new law on the press in

his famous *Commentaries* but he was also the great teacher
for the law-minded revolutionists in the colonies. Today few
lawyers read his *Commentaries,* even as a classic, but in the
latter part of the eighteenth century and through much of
the nineteenth his influence on American jurisprudence was
immense, far greater here indeed than in his own country.
Before the advent of law schools every budding lawyer began
his reading with Blackstone as his guide and oracle. His
obiter dicta on the common law were pervasive among those
who launched and nurtured our experiment in political liberty.

In his *Commentaries,* first delivered as lectures in 1758 and
formally published in 1765, a decade before Bunker Hill,
Blackstone defined the freedom of the press this way:

> The liberty of the press is indeed essential to the na-
> ture of a free state; but this consists in laying no *previous*
> restraint upon publications, and not in freedom from
> censure for criminal matter when published. Every
> freeman has an undoubted right to lay what sentiments
> he pleases before the public: to forbid this is to destroy
> the freedom of the press; but if he publishes what is im-
> proper, mischievous or illegal, he must take the conse-
> quences of his own temerity.[1]

There, in two sentences, is the whole of the law and the
philosophy of the press as it appeared to Englishmen of the
eighteenth century, including our own revolutionists.

It is, as you can see, an effort to reconcile the irreconcilable. For plainly if there is to be political liberty the citizens cannot be constrained in what they think and what they
speak by the power of government, whether it be a government of a king or of ministers. To subject the press to such
restrictions, in Blackstone's words, "is to subject all freedom
of sentiment to the prejudices of one man, and make him the
arbitrary and infallible judge of all controverted points in
learning, religion and government." But also plainly, or so it
seemed to the men of those times, no man would be safe and
no government secure if all manner of libels could be uttered

[1] William Blackstone, *Commentaries on the Law of England,*
Book 4 (London, 1769), chap. 11, pp. 151ff.

with impunity. Thus to punish dangerous or offensive writings, said Blackstone, "is necessary for the preservation of peace and good order, of government and religion, the only solid foundation of civil liberty."

It was, perhaps, an unsatisfactory thrust at the Gordian knot to say on the one hand that a man is free to publish what he will without let or hindrance but, on the other hand, that he is not free from accountability for what he publishes, leaving undefined what later may be judged punishable as improper, mischievous or illegal. Yet if that answer seems unsatisfactory to logical minds, it is one we have not bettered two centuries later. In that famous Pentagon Papers case, of which more later, the justices of our own Supreme Court were unable to discard the Blackstonian concept.

However that may be, such was the philosophical view and the legal doctrine about the press and its freedom commonly accepted in those memorable years leading up to 1776. Now, if we are to understand the American press tradition, it is necessary to look at the special circumstances in these English colonies which gave those ideas an indigenous cast.

II

In 1734 the royal governor of the colony of New York was one William Cosby, by the evidence of his contemporaries an avaricious, haughty and ill-tempered man who was among the worst of these representatives of the distant crown. The publisher of the New York *Weekly Journal*, a four-page poorly printed sheet, was John Peter Zenger, an itinerant printer. Before the year was out they were to clash, with consequences neither of them foresaw.[2]

The origin of it, briefly, was a dispute between the governor and the council of the colony over the governor's salary.

---

[2] Frank Luther Mott, *American Journalism*, Third Edition (New York: Macmillan Company, 1962), pp. 31ff, has a good account of the Zenger case, which I have followed. For documents in the case, including Hamilton's defense, see Leonard W. Levy, ed. *Freedom of the Press From Zenger to Jefferson: Early American Libertarian Theories* (New York: Bobbs-Merrill Co., 1966).

As part of that dispute Cosby discharged the colony's chief justice, Lewis Morris, and appointed in his place one James Delancey, a royalist supporter. Zenger's print shop issued a pamphlet giving the deposed chief justice's side of the case, and there began a long and acrimonious fight between the royal governor and the *Weekly Journal*. Ultimately, having failed to get an indictment of Zenger from a local grand jury, Governor Cosby had Zenger jailed on his own authority. The charge was seditious libel. Zenger, who had not written the offending articles but who had published them, was refused reasonable bail by the new chief justice and languished in jail for nine months. The next year, 1735, he came to trial.

It was a disappointing trial if the hope was that the issue of freedom of the press from seditious libel would be squarely joined. Zenger's counsel was Andrew Hamilton—not to be confused with Alexander Hamilton—and he saw his task, as lawyers are wont to, to free his client rather than to win some great judicial principle. Thus Hamilton did not attack the concept of seditious libel. Instead he argued that it was designed to protect the king, not provincial governors, and that if the people could not remonstrate truthfully against despotic governors the people would lose their liberty and the king would be ill served. Then in an impassioned appeal directly to the jurors he asked them, in effect, to ignore the court's rulings on the law and acquit Zenger notwithstanding.

This is what the jury did, quite possibly for no other reason than that Cosby was an unpopular governor and this was a way to strike back at him. Anyway, the Zenger case did nothing to alter the common law of seditious libel nor to advance any new principles with regard to freedom of the press. Nonetheless, the Zenger trial is justly renowned in the history of the colonial press. Cosby vanished in obscurity; Zenger took his place in the pantheon of journalistic heroes. In a very dramatic fashion a small newspaper had challenged royal authority, been brought to trial in a royal court and acquitted by a jury of colonial citizens. That was enough.

There were other cases before and after Zenger, with varying results. As early as 1692 one William Bradford, a Philadelphia printer, had been tried for seditious libel,

Thomas Maule for the same charge in Boston in 1696, neither of whom was ultimately imprisoned. But Andrew Bradford, William's son, was later imprisoned for publishing a letter critical of the English government, Benjamin Franklin's brother was jailed for being critical of the Massachusetts colonial government, and also in Massachusetts John Checkley was convicted for distributing a book critical of Calvinist doctrines. Until the eve of the Revolution, there was little consistency, either from time to time or from colony to colony, in the boldness of printers or in the reaction of the authorities to criticism. For the most part, however, boldness was not characteristic of these early printers. Their shops were commercial enterprises; they sought out official business and were inclined to do little to disturb it. They also shared the general attitude of the time, which consisted of much grumbling at particular authority but without any disposition to challenge the principle of authority from the Crown.

This is not the place for recounting the history of the colonial press. It should be noted, though, that the present view of colonial America as a society that everywhere cherished freedom of ideas and expression is a romantic one. There was indeed an enormous diversity of political and religious ideas among the various colonies, due to their origins and geography, and this diversity was ultimately to have an enormous effect. But each colony, sometimes different counties within a colony, had its own orthodoxy and guarded it zealously, being quite willing to suppress the dissidence of the non-orthodox, whether political or religious. In John P. Roche's phrase, "Colonial America was an open society dotted with closed enclaves."

If there was a turning point for the press, a point at which it generally turned rebellious toward the Crown and began to acquire its revolutionary character, it was the same as for the colonists generally, namely, the Stamp Act of 1765. That tax struck very hard at printers. Since it amounted to a penny for each four pages and two shillings for each advertisement, it came to a tax of nearly 50 percent of revenue for many papers. It thus united the printers as no other issue could. The Pennsylvania *Gazette* draped its last pre-tax issue with the black column rules of mourning. The New York *Gazette* openly defied the law by continuing to publish with unstamped paper. A few papers suspended, but many others shifted to irregular publication dates to claim status as handbills not as newspapers. Similar taxes were levied in England and were enforceable. In the colonies, far removed from the home country and with presses scattered over a huge geographic area, the taxes were largely unenforceable.

A year later this Stamp Act was repealed, thanks in good measure to the persuasiveness in London of that Kissinger of the day, Benjamin Franklin. But by then the situation had been permanently altered. Until then the dissatisfaction of most of the printers with the remote government of the Crown had been no more than those generally shared by other colonists; now they had a personal grievance and a warning to what extent they personally could be injured by that remote government. Arguments about the power of government against the press ceased to be abstractions. Equally important—and I am inclined to think more so—the printers learned that in fact this distant government could not enforce its laws against them. Thus the Boston *Gazette*, which in 1765 had printed the bitterest attacks against the Stamp Act, did not relent after its repeal in attacks on Crown government. Indeed, it became even bolder as spokesman for the "radicals," or, if you prefer a different term, for the "patriots."

How much the practical situation had altered is shown by the reaction of the Crown authorities to these new attacks. Governor Bernard of Massachusetts called the *Gazette* "an infamous weekly paper which has swarmed with Libels of the most atrocious kind," made several feeble attempts to get a libel indictment against its publishers, but in the end found it more politic to suffer the paper. He would risk no more Zenger cases. The situation in the other colonies, in varying degrees, was much the same.[3]

Meanwhile, all those other forces which led to 1776 continued to do their work; I will leave to others to decide the proportion in which they were economic, political or philo-

[3] Mott, *American Journalism*, p. 75.

sophical. Slowly but relentlessly the colonists moved from being loyal complainants against particular Crown actions to open rebellion against the Crown itself. Whatever the causes, the movement required a major change in public opinion and in that change the printers of the colony played a major role. Through newspapers, through broadsides, through pamphlets, the printing presses of the colonies proved as dangerous as muskets. The newspapers issued by these presses were outlets for the exchange of information among the colonies (one picking up its "news" from the mailed copies of another), for letters to the editor and for anonymous articles signed with such pen names as Cato or Publius. There was little "objectivity" in the news reported. For example the Salem *Gazette* in its issue of April 25, 1775 began its account of the battles of Lexington and Concord this way:

> Last Wednesday, the 19th of April, the Troops of his *Brittanick* Majesty commenced Hostilities upon the People of this Province, attended with Circumstances of Cruelty not less brutal than what our venerable Ancestors received from the vilest Savages of the Wilderness.

This was the tone of the news reported throughout the Revolution, though often the news was sparse and late due to the difficulties of communication. When there was none many of the printers carried rumors, second and third hand reports and on some occasions seem to have made up their information.

But we must not suppose that in this period there had been any advancement in the *philosophy* of freedom of the press. The patriot, or rebel, newspapers had indeed thrown off the yoke of Crown governors, and having got the bit in their teeth made the most of it. The loyalist papers, of whom a few survived even after the war's outbreak, did not fare so well. The patriots were no more anxious to extend freedom of the press to them than the Crown governors had been to extend it to the seditious patriot press. Great pressure, including violence, was exerted to silence the Boston *Evening Post*, the New York *Packet*, and the Maryland *Journal*, all loyalist papers. In an outbreak of mob violence the New York *Gazet-*

teer, a Tory paper, was totally destroyed. In every faction, freedom of the press meant freedom for *us*, not for *them*.

What did result from the Revolution, if not new philosophies about freedom of the press, were habits and an attitude. The attitude, natural under the circumstances, was one of antagonism to government, or at least distant government; after all, that was the root of the Revolution itself. The habits were of fiercely venting that antagonism without check, at least from any distant government. In a very pragmatic way these two things were to have important consequences. For one, they bestirred a renewed interest among publishers, writers and intellectuals generally in philosophical thinking about the nature of a free press, if for no other reason than to find a respectable rationale for what these writers and printers were in fact doing. The other consequence was that in time the revolutionary habits became transformed into a tradition.

Neither the habits of free-speaking nor the critical attitude toward distant government were, to be sure, limited to printers. Both had been acquired by the former colonists generally. In fact when the Constitutional Convention convened in 1787 the delegates had two problems. One was to devise an acceptable form of national government. The other was to persuade the citizens of the new states to accept *any* national government stronger than the loose Confederation. The extent of this second problem shows up clearly in *The Federalist* papers of Madison, Hamilton and Jay. Again and again while defending the structure of the proposed government they had also to answer critics of the very concept of a national government. Eight of the papers are devoted to explaining the inadequacies of the original Confederation; one (Number 23) is devoted wholly to justifying the need for central government and another (Number 84) to explaining away the need for further checks on the power of the national government. Nonetheless, in the end they had to add such checks, known as the Bill of Rights, in order to get their new government accepted.

One of these checks, embodied in the First Amendment, was that "*Congress* shall make no law . . . abridging the freedom of speech, or of the press" (emphasis added). But this was not then the sweeping doctrine it has since come to appear. The key word then was "Congress"—that is the *national* government was to be prohibited from abridging the press. What was done under state government was to be left to the states; they were not prohibited from regulating the press. Indeed, the Pennsylvania Constitution of 1790 and the Delaware Constitution of 1792 expressly imposed liability for abuses of free speech; even in Virginia a 1792 statute provided sanctions against "abusive" uses of free speech. Thomas Jefferson explained, "While we deny that Congress have the right to control the freedom of the press, we have ever asserted the right of the states, and their exclusive right to do so."[4]

Jefferson, having now made his entrance in our story, is worth a moment's pause. He has, and with some reason, become the patron saint of the press, having proclaimed that if he had to choose between government and no newspapers or newspapers and no government he would do without government. But Jefferson also reflected other views of the press, not untypical of his times. His 1783 draft for the Virginia Constitution provided that the press should be subject to no restraints *other than* "legal prosecution for false facts printed and published." Again, in a letter to Madison he remarked, "A declaration that the federal government will never restrain the presses from printing anything they please, will not take away the liability of printers for false facts printed."[5] That view, as you can see, is essentially Blackstonian; the press should be free of prior restraint but could be liable afterwards for injury by falsehoods. On seditious libel he was ambiguous, or at least changeable. In 1803, angered by its "licentiousness and its lying" he thought the press ought to be restrained by the states if not by the federal government; "I have long thought," he said, "that a few prosecutions of the most prominent offenders would have a wholesome effect in restoring the integrity of the presses."[6] Yet as President he pardoned those convicted under the Sedition Act of 1798. Fi-

---

[4] Letter to Abigail Adams, September 4, 1804.
[5] Letter to James Madison, July 31, 1788.
[6] Letter to Thomas McKean, February 19, 1803.

nally, of course, like all Presidents before or since, he had a
low opinion of the performance of the press and angrily assailed the calumnies of the press against himself and against
the government. Jefferson, like scripture, can be quoted to
one's own purposes.

The next great leap forward for freedom of the press, both
in philosophy and in practice, came from that 1798 Sedition
Act. This law made it a crime to publish any "false, scandal-
ous and malicious writing" bringing into disrepute the government, the Congress or the President; and it immediately
plunged the country into bitter controversy. The press was
outraged; victims among newspapers included the New York
Argus, the Boston *Independent Chronicle*, the Richmond
Examiner. One of the more famous trials was of Thomas
Cooper, who in the Reading *Weekly Advertiser* had called
President John Adams an incompetent, and who was
imprisoned for six months. Of perhaps passing interest is the
fact that at his trial Cooper tried to get Adams as a witness
but the court refused to subpoena the President.

The Sedition Act forced Americans to rethink their views
on the nature of press freedom. In the Virginia Resolutions
against the act, James Madison brought forth a new concept.
Noting the common law principle that freedom of the press
was limited to imposing no prior restraints on publication,
Madison said that could not be the American idea of press
freedom since a law inflicting penalties afterward would have
a similar effect to a law imposing prior restraint. "It would
seem a mockery," he wrote, "to say that no law should be
passed preventing publication . . . but that laws might be
passed punishing them in case they should be made."[7] And
for the first time a loud voice—that of George Hay, prosecu-
tor of Aaron Burr and later a federal judge—was raised to
proclaim the idea that freedom of the press was absolute in
terms of criticizing the government, whether the criticism be
true, false, malicious or otherwise. "Freedom of the press,"
he proclaimed, "means total exemption of the press from any

---

[7] Levy, *Freedom of the Press From Zenger to Jefferson*, reprints
the text of Madison's argument for freedom of the press (document
28, p. 197).

kind of legislative control." He would admit only private actions against the press for private injury, as for any other tort.[8]

These sweeping ideas of Madison and Hay were in advance of their own time. Indeed, it is not fully accepted even yet, Justices Black and Douglas to the contrary, that the press should be free of all accountability to government—that is, to society as a whole—for what it publishes, for in that extreme form freedom of the press raises all manner of political and philosophical questions that are still disturbing. Nonetheless, the outcome of the outcry was that the Sedition Act was repealed. The press emerged freer than ever, its habits of independence and its attitude of suspicion toward government strengthened. The stage was set for the development of the modern American press.

III

As we approach the last quarter of the twentieth century the American press occupies a unique position. By the word press I refer, of course, not just to the newspapers of mass circulation but to the whole of the press in all its multiplicity and diversity. To the thousands of weekly papers and journals; to the little offset presses and portable duplicators of nameless number scattered in every town and hamlet turning out posters, pamphlets, handbills, and broadsides; to magazines overground and underground speaking the ideas of the respectable and the disreputable and aimed at whatever audience—churchgoers, atheists, lesbians, militant blacks or Ku Klux Klan whites, Puritan and prurient, reactionary or rebellious. Each of these is a part of the press, and the whole of it is all of them.

This American press, each part choosing what it will, can publish what it will. It can seize upon secrets stolen from government archives and broadcast them to the world. It can strip the privacy of councils and grand juries. It can pillory those accused of crimes before they are tried. It can heap

[8] Ibid. (document 27, p. 186).

calumnies not only upon elected governors but upon all whom chance has made an object of public attention. It can publish the lascivious and the sadistic. It can advance any opinion on any subject, including the opinion that all our government is corrupt and that the whole of the social order proclaimed in 1776 should be swept away and another put in its place.

This is unique, for such full freedom to publish exists nowhere else in the world. In many countries nothing can be published save with the imprimatur of some politburo. In others, the press has many of those freedoms. But in what other country is the press free to do all of these things with impunity? Even in that England which is the wellspring of our liberties there remain, after two hundred years, official secrets acts, strict libel laws, rigid rules on the reporting of judicial proceedings, and other restraints which put some limits upon the freedom of the press. In newer countries the authorities have taken early heed against too much license. Only in America are the boundaries of freedom so broad.

If, even in America, we have not yet extended the same freedom to the new electronic media it is due in part to the fact that for technological reasons there does not exist the multiplicity of outlets and so the same diversity is lacking. But it is also because these media are so newly upon us that there is no history to guide either public policy or media practice. We are just beginning to grapple with the political issues and philosophical conflicts that have long embroiled the printed press.

We have had some glimpse of those press conflicts and seen how they were resolved in our early days, at least partially, by argument and experience. In the century after the Sedition Act new spokesmen here and abroad came forward to expand thoughtfully and eloquently on the nature of civil liberty, notably John Stuart Mill. They provided a philosophical underpinning for a broader concept of freedom of the press.

At the same time the practical situation of the press continued to play its role. The proliferation of printing presses, the geographical expanse of the country and the separation of regions one from another, made for a diversity of political views—or at least a diversity of orthodoxies—and imposed very practical difficulties on the government in controlling the press even when it tried. With the western expansion across the continent this factor was intensified. The newspaper editor on the moving frontier was in practice answerable to no one for what he printed, except upon occasion to an irate reader with a horsewhip. He became accustomed to independence and fiercely defended it until gradually this independence became ever more deeply imbedded in the tradition of the craft.

Not, of course, that the government did not try to curtail it from time to time. In the Civil War President Lincoln, in defiance of the First Amendment, arrested the proprietors of *The New York World* and *The Journal of Commerce* for what seemed to him seditious libel. In peacetime President Theodore Roosevelt tried and failed to convict the *World* and *The Indianapolis News* for "a string of infamous libels," even sending a special message to Congress on the subject. These and other instances, some open, some more subtle, intensified the feeling among writers and printers that only eternal vigilance would preserve their laboriously won independence. Quite understandably, they continued to see government as an antagonist.

And not government alone. By the arrival of the twentieth century the complexities of an industrial society had created other centers of power seeming to the people as distant and even more mysterious and uncontrollable than government. In the shorthand of the day these were the "trusts," or Big Business, but in a larger sense they were all the institutions of society which have power but without clear-cut accountability. Thus there was ushered in the era of muckraking, at first aimed only at those "trusts" but gradually against other parts of the nongovernmental Establishment. The daily press —notably the papers of Hearst, Scripps and Pulitzer—took up the cudgels but the heaviest blows were struck by magazines such as *McClure's* and *Collier's*, and in books, both fiction and nonfiction. So the press began to acquire not merely an anti-government but an anti-institutional cast which remains with us yet.

Meanwhile, one by one the legal barriers against any restraints on the press toppled. The Fourteenth Amendment, as interpreted by the Supreme Court, extended the prohibition against press abridgment under the First Amendment to the states as well as to the national government. With the court's decision in *New York Times* v. *Sullivan* private libel was, for all practical purposes, stricken from the law books; the press is not liable even for publishing falsehoods unless it can be proved that the intent was "malicious." In the Pentagon Papers case (*New York Times* v. *United States*) the press was allowed to publish stolen government documents without either restraint or liability.

We must not think, however, that efforts to put some limits on the freedom of the press were not often supported by public sentiment; to many people the press seems often to abuse its freedom to the injury of both individuals and society as a whole. Nor should we think that philosophy and reason are all on the side of untrammeled freedom. Thoughtful men have found moral, ethical and practical arguments for not letting liberty turn into license.

Let us go back for a moment and imagine how the argument for putting some restraints on the press might have been put by an articulate philosopher in the Crown colonies. It might have run something like this:

Freedom of the press is essential to political liberty. Where men cannot freely convey their thoughts to one another no freedom is secure. But freedom of the press to appeal to reason may always be construed as freedom of the press to appeal to public passion and ignorance, vulgarity and cynicism. So it is always dangerous. The moral right of free public expression is not unconditional. When a man who claims the right is a liar, a prostitute whose political judgments can be bought, a dishonest inflamer of hatred and suspicion, his claim is groundless. To protect the press is not always to protect the community. Libel, obscenity, incitement to riot, sedition, these have a common principle; their utterance invades vital social interests. So the extension of legal sanctions to these categories of abuse is justified.

In fact, the above quotation is not imaginary. Every phrase of it is taken verbatim from the report of the Commission on Freedom of the Press, done in the twentieth century by a group of scholars and teachers, one of whom was an eminent philosopher and another the chancellor of the University of Chicago. No foes of liberty, they; no blind reactionaries, no partisan politicians. All of them thoughtful men, deeply disturbed by the fear that the abuse of liberty can destroy liberty.[9]

The report of the Commission on Freedom of the Press, more popularly known as the Hutchins commission, was issued in 1947. It was greeted by outraged outcries from the press, to whom it was heresy. And its import, without any question, was to challenge the absolutism of the idea of freedom of the press, threatening to take us back beyond Mill, beyond George Hay, beyond Madison and Jefferson and John Peter Zenger.

True, the Hutchins commission did not really grasp the nettle. That is, it did not say what ought to be done to restrain abuses of freedom of the press, or even who should be the judge of what they are, beyond the general thought that not every restraint on the press is wrong and some strong urgings that the press itself exercise self-restraint. But the commission did remind us that the nettle is there.

It always has been. The fundamental assumption of all who cherish freedom of the press and who have nourished it over the centuries is that it is the cornerstone of liberty. The safeguard of the citizens against tyranny is their freedom to remonstrate against despotic governors. A society of self-governing people is viable only if the people are informed. Men have no way of discovering the best ideas about man

[9] Commission on Freedom of the Press, *A Free and Responsible Press* (Chicago: University of Chicago Press, 1947). Among the commission members were William E. Hocking, professor of philosophy at Harvard, and Robert M. Hutchins, then chancellor of the University of Chicago.

and God or man and society unless all ideas are free to confront each other, the good and the bad, in the cauldron of the intellectual marketplace. Without the right of free inquiry all other freedoms vanish. Such are the premises of free speech, from Milton to our own day.

Yet another assumption is that no man is free if he can be terrorized by his neighbor, whether by swords or by words; this is the justification of laws against violence and against libel and slander. Nor can a citizen be truly informed if falsehoods come masquerading as truth; false advertising for ideas is as injurious as those for foods or for drugs. Moreover the liberty of the citizen also depends upon the stability of society, which is why governments exist, and society has a right to protect itself against the predatory. Such are the premises of those who say no right is absolute, including freedom of the press, when it clashes with other rights.

Therein lies the nettle and it grows ever more prickly. If the right of a fair trial is fundamental to liberty, what happens to it if the press is free to prejudice a fair trial by what it publishes? If it is wrong for other institutions of society to have power without responsibility, is it right for the press— surely one of the more powerful institutions of society—to have no accountability for what it does?

These questions, raised a quarter of a century ago by the Hutchins commission, are now disturbing others. In that Pentagon Papers case the court reaffirmed the Blackstonian doctrine and refused to uphold prior restraint, but several of the judges were uneasy even with that as an absolute doctrine when it seemed to give sanction to the stealing of government documents. Justice White, for one, plainly said that while he would not restrain prior publication he might well sustain a decision holding the newspapers accountable for their actions as receivers of stolen property.

Within the press as well there is also a groping for some way to reconcile this freedom of the press with the other needs of liberty. A quarter century after the Hutchins commission there is much talk of press councils and other means of achieving both a free and responsible press. And two centuries after 1776 the reconciliation seems as difficult as ever.

Perhaps more so. For certainly the Founding Fathers would be astounded by how much we have enlarged the parameters of the debate. After all, when they met to draft the Constitution they did so in secret, barring the press entirely and pledging themselves to confidentiality of their discussions. They did so not because they feared open debate on their handiwork but because they saw values to liberty in the privacy of council. Certainly the purloining of state papers would have stirred even President Jefferson to outrage. None of them thought freedom of the press was a license to do anything whatever.

Yet the changes that time has wrought on the idea of freedom of the press were, I think, inevitable. Freedom of the press, once proclaimed, admits of no logical limit. If the national legislature may not abridge it, by what logic should state legislatures? If all ideas should be freely expressed, how can information on which ideas are based be suppressed? If government must be open, how can the governors keep secrets from the governed? And if the governors will not give information freely, is there not a right to wrest it from them? Each progression leads inexorably to the next.

In this country there has also been the pressure of historical experience, thrusting the boundaries ever outward. The very nature of our Revolution created a bias, first against distant government and then by extension against all government save that which governs least. Although the twentieth century has forced an acceptance of enlarged government, it has been a reluctant acceptance and it still divides the people. We remain unruly under the long arm of government, as when mothers parade to protest school busing or truck drivers block highways to protest fuel allocations. We remain equally suspicious of, and hostile to, other institutional sources of power.

This bias has been shared by those who report and comment on the news, and their habit of displaying it has been reinforced by the privilege of independence so fiercely fought for. "Print the news and raise hell"—that has been the traditional battle cry of the press. Except in rare moments it matters not who holds the power, what President the reins of governments, the press will soon be sniffing at his spoor and thundering at his actions.

That such freedom can be abused is undeniable. Good men can be slandered, justice thwarted, base passions aroused, people misinformed, government subverted, all the institutions of society undermined. It should surprise no one that there arise from time to time voices asking how we shall protect ourselves. As our society grows more complex these voices will, I am sure, grow more clamorous.

But this is true of all liberty. There is none that cannot be abused. And if the people cannot be trusted to find their way amid the abuses then there is no hope for the American experiment. For that experiment rests less upon logic than upon a faith that the danger of unbounded liberty is not so great as that of putting liberty in bondage. It is a faith so far justified. In our two hundred years we have been better served by our freedoms, including most especially our freedom of speech and of the press, than we would have been served without them. That is the answer, perhaps the only answer, to those who would no longer trust those freedoms.

All the same, the story is not ended. Freedom of religion. Freedom of person under the protection of habeas corpus. Trial by jury. Freedom of the press. "These principles," said Jefferson in his first Inaugural, "form the bright constellation which has gone before us, and guided our steps through an age of revolution and reformation."

Freedom of religion, habeas corpus, trial by jury. All these have become so much a part of us we hardly remember that they were once things men fought over. Of that constellation only freedom of the press remains in the heat of controversy —as revolutionary an idea now as it was in the beginning.

EDWARD C. BANFIELD

The City and the Revolutionary Tradition

Delivered in Franklin Hall, Franklin Institute,

Philadelphia, Pennsylvania on April 11, 1974

It would be very pleasant on such an occasion as this to say that the American city has been and is a unique and unqualified success—and to be able to show that its successes all derive from adherence to principles established and given institutional form in the American Revolution, whose bicentennial we are here to commemorate.

Unfortunately, it is all too evident that even if this were the Fourth of July I would not have license for that sort of oratory. In many important respects the American city is a great success, but there are certainly many things about it that are thoroughly unpleasant, and some that are—or ought to be—intolerable. Moreover, it is obvious that in most important respects—the good and the bad alike—the American city differs more in degree than in kind from cities elsewhere. What we have to be proud of and what we have to worry about are, for the most part, features of modernity and not of anything specifically American.

If we limit ourselves, as this occasion requires, to those features of the city that have been distinctively American over a long period of time, we shall nevertheless have a rather long and varied list. I shall begin by offering *my* list. Then I shall try to account for the items on it with a simple explanatory principle. In the hope of making this explanation more convincing, I shall draw a contrast—necessarily based on frag-

mentary and impressionistic evidence—between urban development in the United States and Canada—having chosen
Canada because it was a British colony which did not revolt
and to whose development my explanatory principle applies,
so to say, in reverse. Finally, I shall point to what I consider
one of the great ironies of history—that the Founding Fathers created a political system whose essential character
turned out to be the very opposite of what most of them intended.

I

My list of features which have distinguished the American
city over time will be more manageable if I break it down
into three categories. The first I shall call growth and material welfare, the second civility, and the third government. I
hope that no attention will be paid to the order of the list-
ings, or to the fact that some items would fit about as well in
one category as in another.

Growth and material welfare. It should not be necessary to
remind a Philadelphia audience how astonishingly fast was
the growth and spread of cities in this country. Philadelphia,
which in 1775 had a population of 44,000 was the world's
eighth largest city a little more than a century later. Of the
nine cities in the world with more than a million population
in 1890, three were American, and there were then 351
others in the United States of more than 10,000 population.

The cities were built by that often ludicrous and sometimes contemptible fellow—the Worshipper of the Almighty
Dollar, the Go-Getter, the Businessman-Booster-Speculator—
an upstart, a nobody, but shrewd, his eye on the main
chance, always ready to risk his own and (preferably) someone else's money. "Americans," Thomas Low Nichols wrote
in 1864,

> are sanguine, and hope to succeed in the wildest specula-
> tions; but if they do not, they have little scruple about
> repudiation. A man cares little for being ruined, and as

little about ruining others. But then, ruin there is not like ruin in older countries. Where a man can fail a dozen times, and still go ahead and get credit again, ruin does not amount to much.[1]

In search of the dollar, the American has been constantly on the move. The historian, Stephan Thernstrom, has estimated that, over the past 170 years, probably only 40 to 60 percent of the adult males in most cities at any point in time were in the same city ten years later.[2] "A migratory race" Tocqueville called us, "which, having reached the Pacific Ocean, will retrace its steps to disturb and destroy the social communities which it will have formed and left behind."[3]

The ethnic diversity of our cities has been unparalleled. As early as 1890, one-third of the residents of cities of over 100,000 population were foreign-born. Ten million foreign-born were counted by the 1970 census, and their median family income, it is interesting to note, was not appreciably lower than that of all U.S. families.

The American city has always provided a high level of living for the great majority of its residents. (It was because of what he saw in Europe that Thomas Jefferson came to loathe the city.) The American city dweller has always had more and better schooling, housing (in 1900 one-fourth of the families in most large cities owned their own homes), sanitation, and transportation than city dwellers elsewhere.

Civility. Organized philanthropy has always been conspicuous in the American city. Museums, libraries, symphony orchestras, asylums, hospitals, colleges, parks and playgrounds —the number and variety of such institutions begun and supported in whole or part by "service" clubs, foundations, and

---

[1] Thomas Low Nichols, M.D., *Forty Years of American Life, 1821–1861* (reprinted, New York: Stackpole, 1937), p. 58; (first published 1864).

[2] Stephan Thernstrom, *The Other Bostonians, Poverty and Progress in the American Metropolis, 1880–1970* (Cambridge, Mass.: Harvard University Press, 1973), p. 225.

[3] M. Gustave de Beaumont, ed., *Memoir, Letters, and Remains of Alexis de Tocqueville* (Boston: Ticknor and Fields, 1862), vol. I, p. 154.

other private efforts is impressive and, I believe, peculiarly American (a point which Tocqueville also made).

Most of these achievements are largely to the credit of the Go-Getter. But he must also be mentioned as a doer-of-evil—as one who, to get things done, has been ready to go to any lengths. Politicians took bribes, Lincoln Steffens remarked, because businessmen paid bribes, and so it was they, the businessmen, who were the real corrupters.

The extent of corruption in American city government has long been the wonder of the civilized world. Some have tried to account for it by pointing to the masses of poor and politically inexperienced immigrants, but this is surely only a partial explanation. Boss Tweed and his "Forty Thieves" (there were then forty New York City councilmen) were in business before a great many immigrants had arrived. Frank J. Goodnow, writing at the turn of the century in one of the first textbooks on city government, stated the puzzling facts:

> Philadelphia, with a large native-born and home-owning and a small tenement-house population, with a charter which is largely based on what is considered to be advanced ideas on the subject of municipal government, is said to be both corrupt and contented. . . .[4]

The experience of cities like Philadelphia, he concluded, encourages the belief that "there must be something in the moral character of the particular populations. . . ."

Moreover, if corruption was common in American cities, so was violent crime. As far back as records go (as much as 100 years in only two cities) the homicide rate has been extraordinarily high by the standards of other countries.

Class differences have, of course, existed in all countries. In America, however, where there has probably been more upward mobility than anywhere else, to be socially defined as "no account" has been crushing in a way that it could not be where everyone knew that rising in the world was out of the question. Perhaps because most have expected to rise, if not themselves then through their children, the American city, unlike cities in most countries, has never produced a rad-

[4] Frank J. Goodnow, *City Government in the United States* (New York: The Century Co., 1904), pp. 304–305.

ical working-class movement of importance. Perhaps because some have been demoralized by their failure to rise in a society where rising is supposed to be easy, the American city has had a *lumpenproletariat,* a lower as distinguished from a working class—one more conspicuous and possibly more resistant to absorption into normal society than the lower class of other countries.

If the openness of American urban society has produced total alienation in some, it has created disaffection in many more. In a society preoccupied with getting and spending, those who have not managed to get as much as others with whom they compare themselves are likely to feel poor and perhaps to blame themselves and the society for their being relatively badly off even if they are in absolute terms reasonably well off. This is no new thing. Josiah Strong in his book *Our Country,* written in 1858, observed that

> within a century there has been a great multiplication of the comforts of life among the masses; but the question is *whether that increase has kept pace with the multiplication of wants.* The mechanic of today who has much, may be poorer than his grandfather, who had little. A rich man may be poor, and a poor man may be rich. Poverty is something relative. . . .[5]

Nichols, from whose book (written at about the same time as Strong's) I have already quoted, pointed out wider implications of this "struggling upward."

> There is no such thing in America as being contented with one's position or condition. The poor struggle to be rich, the rich to be richer. Every one is tugging, trying, scheming to advance—to get ahead. It is a great scramble, in which all are troubled and none are satisfied. . . . Every other ragged little boy dreams of being President or millionaire. The dream may be a pleasant one while it lasts, but what of the disappointing reality? What of the excited, restless, feverish life spent in pursuit of phantoms?[6]

[5] Josiah Strong, *Our Country,* ed. by Jurgen Herbst (Cambridge, Mass.: The Belknap Press of Harvard University, 1963), p. 147.

[6] Nichols, *Forty Years of American Life,* p. 195.

Government. What is perhaps most conspicuous to the foreigner is the localism of our politics—localism in two senses: First, every city, even every village, has, by the standards of other countries, an extraordinary degree of independence in dealing with a wide range of matters, including police and schools. (Where else could the voters of a small town decide not to permit the construction of a $600 million oil refinery?)[7] Second, in America city politics turns on local, often neighborhood, concerns, not on national issues or on ideologies.

Our cities have been, and still are, run—to the extent that they can be said to be run at all—by politicians (meaning persons whose talent is for managing conflict), not by career civil servants or planners (meaning persons whose talent is for laying out consistent courses of action to attain agreed-upon goals). To be sure, thousands of documents called "plans" have been made under the auspices of American local governments. It would be hard to find one that has been carried into effect, however, unless perhaps by an accident of politics.

The "problem of metropolitan organization" exists in this country in a form that may be unique. Actually, it is really two quite different problems. One comes from the multiplicity of more or less overlapping jurisdictions within a single metropolitan area, and the other from the absence, in any such area, of a general-purpose government having jurisdiction over the whole of the area. It is a peculiarly American practice to refer a great many matters to the electorate—not only the choice of mayors and councilmen (and, in many places, of judges) but decisions about capital expenditures, zoning, and governmental structure as well.

Finally, it is remarkably easy for a small number of persons, especially if they are organized, to prevent an American local government from carrying out undertakings which are alleged to be—and which may in fact be—in the interest of the large majority. Ours is, in David Riesman's phrase, a system of "veto groups."

[7] *New York Times,* March 8, 1974.

II

This has been a sketchy listing of what I take to be the distinctive features that American cities have exhibited over time. I turn now to what I regard as the "key" difference—the one which, better than any other, accounts for or "explains" the items on the list. This "key" difference is the extreme fragmentation of authority in the federal system, especially in state and local government. Our constitutions and charters divided authority into a great many small pieces and distributed the pieces widely. The fragmentation, great to begin with, was further increased in the half-century from 1830 to 1880; governors and mayors were mainly for show and the executive function was carried on by a multitude of separately elected boards and commissions, most of them subject to constant interference by legislatures, courts, and electorates. In recent decades there has been a considerable amount of centralization, but even now ours is, by the standards of other countries, an extraordinarily fragmented system.

How does this explain the features of the American city that I have held to be distinctive? Let me begin with the governmental category. Fragmentation of authority explains why the cities have been run by people adept at managing conflict —the "politicians"—and not by people adept at devising comprehensive and internally consistent courses of action— the "planners." It also explains both sorts of localism. The wide distribution of authority has meant that in order to exercise power on the state or national scene one had to have a local base. Political parties in the United States are not really national organizations; rather they are shifting coalitions of those who, by winning elections or otherwise, have assembled enough pieces of local authority to count.

Because there is power at stake locally, able and ambitious men and women exert themselves to get it. They have always been able to afford to offer the voter (enough voters to make a difference) inducements more substantial than mere ideology—jobs, favors, ethnic recognition. Politics in the American city has been serious business—that is, the politician has been a sort of businessman and the businessman a sort of politician. Obviously this would have been impossible if power had been centralized.

The fragmentation of authority has not only permitted but also encouraged its informal centralization by means—notably the machine and the boss—that were corrupt. If, as Steffens said, businessmen gave bribes because they had to—because it was impossible to operate a street railroad without doing so—it is also true that politicians took them because they had to—because, to centralize enough power to get things done, they had in one way or another to "purchase" pieces of authority from voters and others. Without this easy access to power on the local scene, the Go-Getter would not have had the opportunity to "go get." As it was, he could extend the grids of nonexistent cities into the hinterland confident that he could induce some public body to build the canal, railroad, highway, arsenal, or whatever that would send land values up. Even the new immigrant's ethnic ties had a political value that could be converted into the small amount of capital he needed to get started.

These incentives released prodigious amounts of energy. The freedom—near-anarchy in places—of the politician-businessman-entrepreneur was a necessary condition of the great scramble to advance which, Thomas Low Nichols said, left all troubled and none satisfied. (In Europe, Nichols wrote, in a part of the passage that I did not quote, as a rule the poor man knows that he must remain poor, and he submits to his lot. "Most men live and die in the position to which they are born.") Also, where laws were made and unmade by majority vote and enforced or not depending upon who paid how much to whom, the consequence must have been not only general disrespect for law but also for the persons and institutions that claimed to act under its authority. The same conditions that made the Go-Getter also helped to make the con-man and the gun-slinger.

That the system produced a high and ever-rising material

level of living for most city dwellers must not blind us to the fact that those who did not know how to work the system, or who for one reason or another were prevented from working it, fared badly. Those who took "favors" from the machine and its boss made a very poor bargain, judged at least by middle-class standards. As Jane Addams remarked in *Twenty Years at Hull-House* (1916):

> The policy of the public authorities of never taking an initiative, and always waiting to be urged to do their duty, is obviously fatal in a neighborhood where there is little initiative among the citizens. The idea underlying self-government breaks down in such a ward. The streets are inexpressibly dirty, the number of schools inadequate, sanitary legislation unenforced, the street lighting bad, the paving miserable, and altogether lacking in the alleys and smaller streets, and the stables foul beyond description.[8]

III

The explanation that I have offered to account for the distinctive features of the American city would be more convincing if I could show that in another country an opposite principle produced opposite results. I believe I can. The history of urban development in Canada provides such a test, for the Canadian political system has been the opposite of ours in what for me is the crucial respect. I am not, of course, implying that the Canadians are less attached to democracy than we are. Rather, my point is that their idea of it is essentially different from ours. In Canada the British tradition has never been interrupted: the duty of government has always been to govern—not, as in the United States, to preside over a competition of interests. Canadians, writes Professor Tom Truman of McMaster University, "insist on strong stable executive government, which, once it has made up its mind on what the public interest requires, should take the necessary

[8] Quoted by Louis Wirth, *The Ghetto* (Chicago: University of Chicago Press, 1956), p. 196.

action quickly and with determination to see it through
completely."[9]

It goes without saying that the comparison with Canadian
experience cannot provide a wholly satisfactory test of my argument, for there are manifestly many differences between
the two countries that may account for much of what I am
trying to explain. Although Canada is larger in area than the
United States, its great natural resources have been, especially
in the nineteenth century, much less accessible. It has always
had an important French-speaking minority. And it has
always been profoundly affected by events in this country.
The influence of these and other circumstances on urban development has certainly been great. I believe, however, that
the centralized structure of political authority in Canada accounts—better than any other single principle—for the
differences between Canadian and American cities in the features I have listed.

A detailed account of Canadian experience is obviously out
of the question here, but let me call your attention to a few
relevant facts:

—The growth of cities in Canada was slow. As late as 1911
Canada had only six cities of 50,000 or more population, of
which only two (Montreal and Toronto) had more than
300,000.

—The Go-Getter-Businessman-Booster-Speculator has been
(until recently) conspicuous by his absence. Horatio Alger
heroes, it seems, have never been popular in Canada.[10] It
may be indicative of the difference in business ethos that
there are about twice as many lawyers per capita in the
United States as in Canada: in 1955, one lawyer in private
practice per 868 persons here compared to one per 1,630
there.[11]

[9] Tom Truman, "A Critique of Seymour M. Lipset's Article,
Value Differences, Absolute or Relative: The English-speaking
Democracies," *Canadian Journal of Political Science*, vol. 4, no. 4
(1971), p. 513.

[10] Seymour M. Lipset, *The First New Nation: The United States
in Historical and Comparative Perspective* (New York: Basic Books,
Inc., 1963), p. 251.

[11] Ibid., p. 264.

—Immigration into Canada was, until well into this century, mainly from the British Isles. British immigrants were long favored by law. By American standards, assimilation of non-British and non-French-speaking immigrants was slow: not until this century, I understand, was one elected to public office.

—Generally speaking, the level of public services has been low by American standards.

—Organized philanthropy began late—about World War I, an import from the United States.[12]

—Large-scale corruption has never been a feature of city life.

—There has been very little violent crime.

—Social mobility has been less than in the United States.

—Although radical working-class movements (the Canadian Commonwealth Federation and the National Democratic Party) have been able to form governments only on the prairies, they have had more supporters in the urban areas than among the wheat farmers.

—Urban Canada does not seem to have had a *lumpenproletariat* on anything like the American scale.

—"The incessant exercise of voting power," Lord Bryce remarked, "has never possessed any special fascination for the Canadian."[13]

—Toronto has a metropolitan government—one much admired by American reformers. It was created in 1953, over the objections of most of the local governments concerned, by the Provincial Government on recommendation of the Ontario Municipal Board, a quasi-judicial body. The possibility of a referendum was never seriously discussed.[14]

Can these features of Canadian development be accounted for in large part by the centralized structure of government? I do not have time to develop evidence in support of this

[12] Aileen D. Ross, "Organized Philanthropy in an Urban Community," *Canadian Journal of Economics and Political Science*, vol. 18, no. 4 (1952), pp. 474–475.

[13] James Bryce, *Modern Democracies* (London: Macmillan & Co., 1921), vol. 1, pp. 553–554.

[14] Harold Kaplan, *Urban Political Systems: A Functional Analysis of Metro Toronto* (New York: Columbia University Press, 1967).

claim, but I must quote one of many pertinent passages in a
work by the Canadian sociologist S. D. Clark. He writes in
The Developing Canadian Community:

> A force of Royal Engineers put an end to lawlessness in
> the mining camps of British Columbia. Settlement of
> the western prairies and the gold rush to the Klondike
> took place under the close control of the North West
> Mounted Police. Even in Canadian cities, serious threats
> to law and order have been met by the decisive use of
> force.
>
> The result was to establish a tradition of respect for
> the institutions of law and order. The population gener-
> ally did not feel the need of taking the law into its own
> hands through mob action or the organization of vigilan-
> tes. There was lacking that intense jealousy of local
> rights which in the United States made it difficult for
> federal forces to intervene. The way in which the North
> West Mounted Police came into being was in striking
> contrast with that of the Texas Rangers. In the United
> States the frontier bred a spirit of liberty which often
> opposed efforts to maintain order. In Canada, order was
> maintained at the price of weakening that spirit.[15]

IV

One of the great ironies of history is to be found in these
developments, for it was a centralized system like the Canadian, not a fragmented one like the American, that the principal figures among the Founding Fathers thought they were
creating.

The Revolution, John Adams wrote in a letter in 1818, was
effected before the war; it was "in the minds and hearts of
the people; a change in their religious sentiments of their
duties and obligations." So long as the king and all in authority under him were believed to govern according to the laws
and constitution derived to them by their ancestors, the colonists thought themselves bound to pray for them as

[15] S. D. Clark, *The Developing Canadian Community* (Toronto:
The University of Toronto Press, 1962), pp. 191–192.

"ministers of God ordained for their good." However, "when they saw those powers renouncing all the principles of authority and bent upon the destruction of their lives, liberties and properties, they thought it their duty to pray for the continental congress and the thirteen state congresses."[16] On this view, the intention of the revolutionaries was to bring about a change of regime, not of political principles. Rulers who would not act as ministers ordained by God were to be replaced by others who would.

There is nothing to contradict this in the Declaration of Independence. Jefferson, in writing that governments "derive their just powers from the consent of the governed," did not assert something novel. Since 1689 British monarchs had needed the consent of the House of Commons in order to raise revenue. And, as Martin Diamond pointed out in his lecture in this series, the Declaration says that consent is required to institute or establish a government, not for the conduct of its affairs. The unchallenged principle was that the conduct of affairs belonged in the hands of those authorized to govern.[17]

Adams wanted not only to follow the principles of the British system but, so far as American conditions allowed, to recreate its forms as well.[18] That the executive authority was to be in the hands of one chosen by election did not seem to him or most others to constitute a fundamental change. It had long been understood that in Britain almost all real, as opposed to nominal, authority was in the hands of ministers,

---

[16] Adrienne Koch and William Peden, eds., *The Selected Writings of John and John Quincy Adams* (New York: Alfred A. Knopf, Inc., 1946), p. 203.

[17] Jefferson's view, according to Harvey C. Mansfield, Jr., was that government "derives from the people, where it is 'deposited,' and yet acts on the people to keep them independent by making them republican." He was, Mansfield says, "willing to trust the people, not to govern, but to choose their governors." See his essay, "Thomas Jefferson," in Morton J. Frisch and Richard G. Stevens, eds., *American Political Thought* (New York: Charles Scribner's Sons, 1971), pp. 38–39.

[18] Bernard Bailyn, *The Ideological Origins of the American Revolution* (Cambridge, Mass.: Harvard University Press, 1967), p. 290 (footnote).

not of the king. As Gouverneur Morris put it later when addressing the Constitutional Convention, "Our President will be the British minister."[19]

It was in that convention that the distinctively American political arrangements were worked out. They represented neither the reestablishment of the essential principles of the British system nor the assertion of contrary principles. They were a compromise—that is, the acceptance of contradictory principles. Expediency prevailed, and the result was not a plan but an accident.

Hamilton and Madison acknowledged that "the deliberate sense of the community" should govern the conduct of those in office, but they added that this did not require "an unqualified complaisance" to every transient impulse of the people. "When occasions present themselves in which the interests of the people are at variance with their inclinations, it is the duty of the persons whom they have appointed to be the guardians of those interests, to withstand the temporary delusion. . . ." The humors of the legislature did not require unqualified complaisance either: "it is certainly desirable that the Executive should be in a situation to dare to act his own opinion with vigor and decision." Also: "It is one thing to be subordinate to the laws, and another to be dependent on the legislative body."[20]

In his farewell address Washington warned that "all combinations and associations, under whatever plausible character, with the real design to direct, control, counteract, or awe the regular deliberation and action of the constituted authorities," are "of fatal tendency."

It is fair to say that until John Quincy Adams left the White House in 1829 there had been no revolution, so far as any of the Presidents were concerned, if by revolution is meant fundamental change of political principles. One might even say that there was an effort at counterrevolution—a return to the established principles of the British constitution which were, as A. V. Dicey has said, supremacy of law and

[19] Max Farrand, ed., *Records of the Federal Convention* (New Haven: Yale University Press, 1937), vol. 2, p. 104.
[20] *The Federalist*, No. 71.

"the omnipotence or undisputed supremacy throughout the whole country of the central Government."[21] Nevertheless, there were signs, before the second Adams left the White House, that the government of the United States would never be the "monarchical republic" that his father and some of the others had intended it to be and imagined that it was.

Immediately before and during the revolutionary war public opinion turned against all things British, including the idea that there ought to be a ruler—a minister ordained of God to act for the common good. The expansion of the frontier and the increase in the number and prosperity of tradesmen and craftsmen in the towns and cities gave the "local Demagogues," as Gouverneur Morris called them, an unassailable power. In its first years the national government was without physical force to support its measures (the army consisted of a few hundred men) and then, almost at once, the War of 1812 absorbed all its resources. Under the circumstances the executive could not as a practical matter exercise the power that it claimed in principle. Washington meant to sell the public lands gradually and in a way that would encourage compact settlement (this had long been the British policy) but his plan could not be carried out: the minimum price of public land, set at $2.00 per acre in 1796, was reduced under pressure from frontiersmen and speculators to $1.20 in 1820 and, a few years later, again cut by almost half.[22] The comprehensive plan for internal improvements put forward by Jefferson's secretary of the treasury, Gallatin, became, after long delay, a pork-barrel for the states which Madison vetoed the day before he left office.[23]

The same forces that prevented the national executive from establishing its mastery led to the development of political parties on a local rather than (as in Canada) a national basis. The parties were coalitions within each state of local

[21] A. V. Dicey, *Law of the Constitution* (London: Macmillan & Co., 1902), p. 179.

[22] V. Webster Johnson and Raleigh Barlowe, *Land Problems and Policies* (New York: McGraw-Hill, 1954), pp. 35–36.

[23] Carter Goodrich, "National Planning of Internal Improvements," *Political Science Quarterly*, vol. 63, no. 1 (1948).

interests which, every four years, formed loose federations to nominate and elect a President.

By the 1830s the American political system had assumed its characteristic and lasting form. The President was indeed an "elective monarch," but only in matters in which he was willing to invest the whole force and energy of his office; in the nature of things, there could be few such matters at any one time. In other matters the system functioned to accommodate competing and more or less parochial interests, not to deliberate about (much less enforce) an idea of the common good. State and local governments were organized in imitation of the much-revered national one, but the imitations did not extend to the feature the Founding Fathers had considered crucial: a strong executive—a minister ordained of God for the people's good. Governors and mayors, as I have said, were little more than ceremonial figures. In state and local government, the principle of interest-balancing prevailed.

Those with a taste for irony will relish the fact that by the time the American Revolution had worked itself out to this conclusion, the British system—whose corruption in the eighteenth century had set the American events in motion—had somehow reformed itself and was operating on the principles that most of the Founding Fathers unqualifiedly admired and had meant to copy.

As I said at the outset, this is not a Fourth of July oration. But I do not wish to leave the impression that I consider the American Revolution to have been a mistake. Even if I were sure that a strong central government, operating with consent and under law, would produce effects that are on the whole preferable to those produced by a system of interest-balancing, I would not think that the Revolution was a mistake. For there is no doubt that without the American example before them, other nations, including the British and the Canadian, would not have succeeded as well—perhaps not at all —with their brand of democracy.

That a people could, by a deliberative process, accomplish what has always been regarded as the highest and noblest of all tasks—the creation of a political order that assures to them and their posterity the blessings of life, liberty, and the pursuit of happiness—has had, not only for us but for the whole world, a significance no other event could possibly have had. But if there is great reason for pride in this achievement, there is also reason for apprehension—certainly for pondering such questions as those asked by Thomas Low Nichols in the book from which I have several times quoted:

> If the only source of power is the will of the people expressed by the votes of majority, what are the institutions that may not be overthrown?—what are the institutions that may not be established? The whole people own the whole property; what shall hinder them from doing with it as they will? So the people are above their institutions, and may frame, modify, or abolish them according to their sovereign will and pleasure. Right is a matter of opinion, and to be determined by a majority. Justice is what that majority chooses. Apparently expediency is the only rule of conduct.[24]

Plainly Nichols thought justice is not what the majority chooses and expediency is not the only rule. And so do I.

[24] Nichols, *Forty Years of American Life*, p. 244.

LEO MARX

The American Revolution
and the American Landscape

Delivered in Cabell Hall, the University of Virginia,

Charlottesville, Virginia on March 27, 1974

Although the subject I have been invited to discuss is unusual, it may not strike you as wholly unfamiliar. I say it is unusual because we do not ordinarily think of landscape as having political consequences. A landscape, after all, is an image of topography. Does it make any sense to attribute revolutionary force to a topographical image? How would the image acquire such force? To my knowledge, no political philosopher ever has addressed himself to these questions.

But though the subject of this lecture seems unusual when considered in the abstract, the specific title—"The American Revolution and the American Landscape"—sounds familiar. If anything it has a conventional schoolroom air about it, like an idea of revolution that we learned in the first grade along with the words to "America the Beautiful." The oddity of the concept of a revolutionary landscape seems to fade when we specify the *American* Revolution and the *American* landscape. To indicate what I mean, let us suppose for a moment that we are not now assembled in Charlottesville, Virginia, on a university campus designed by Mr. Jefferson, but in Paris, in a setting designed, say, for Louis XIV; and let us suppose that the revolution we are preparing to celebrate is not the one that began on the village green of Lexington in

April 1775, but rather the one that began at the Bastille in July 1789. Is it conceivable that we would have gathered to discuss "The French Revolution and the French Landscape"? I think not.

The point is that our subject is not only peculiar but, as we used to say with more pride than we can muster nowadays, peculiarly American. This is not to deny that the French mind, like that of any self-conscious people, has in a degree been shaped by the place it inhabits. As Americans, however, we seem to be particularly receptive to the idea that the native landscape has had a specially important part in the formation of our national identity. The reason is obvious. From the time they first saw the New World, Europeans conceived of it symbolically, as a possible setting for a new beginning. "All these islands are very beautiful," said Columbus, describing his first landfall,

> and distinguished by a diversity of scenery; they are filled with a great variety of trees of immense height . . . there are mountains of very great size and beauty, vast plains, groves, and very fruitful fields, admirably adapted for tillage, pasture and habitation. The convenience and excellence of the harbours in this island, and the abundance of the rivers, so indispensable to the health of man, surpass anything that would be believed by one who had not seen it.[1]

Even here, in this letter dated March 14, 1493, the landscape has begun to work its characteristic influence upon the imagination. Of course we know that Europeans long had cherished the fantasy of disengagement from a constricted world, and a chance to begin life anew in an unspoiled landscape. It is true that the tacit invitation that we hear in Columbus's letter—the invitation to come away and enjoy a better life—is like the invitation that had been given expression in Europe's pastoral literature since Theocritus and Virgil. But the difference in this instance is important too. This time the place to which we are being invited is not an imaginary Arcadia, but a real land with real pastures and real trees.

[1] Christopher Columbus, *Four Voyages to the New World*, ed., R. H. Major (New York: Corinth Books, 1961), pp. 5–6.

More than any other quality, then, it is the unique tangibility of this ideal landscape, so unspoiled, so rich, so beautiful—in a word, so inviting—that accounts for its exceptionally powerful hold upon the imagination. The power of this imagery is reflected in the work of our classic American writers (Cooper, Emerson, Thoreau, Hawthorne, Melville, Whitman, Mark Twain, Frost, Faulkner, Hemingway), where the landscape is no mere setting or backdrop, but an active shaping force in the consciousness of men and women. If our imaginative writers are correct, the landscape may be a decisive clue to the understanding of American thought and behavior. Let me illustrate with a familiar example, F. Scott Fitzgerald's *The Great Gatsby*, which happens to be enjoying a conspicuous vogue right now. Today we tend to read *Gatsby* as a tragic fable written in the peculiar hybrid mode of pastoral-romance developed by American writers. But it also can be read as a kind of mystery story. I want to call attention to the mystery, which inheres (as it turns out) in the national character itself, and to the remarkable device that Fitzgerald uses, finally, to dispel the mystery.

Gatsby's story is told, you will recall by Nick Carraway, a young man from Minnesota who comes East in the spring of 1922 to make his fortune in Wall Street. The novel turns on Nick's effort to understand the behavior of his legendary, mysterious neighbor—the former James Gatz of North Dakota. To Nick, Gatsby represents, as he says, "everything for which I have unaffected scorn." What he scorns is Gatsby's vulgar display of wealth (exemplified by his ostentatious parties and his burnished, cream-colored car), not to mention his ruthless and even criminal methods of making money. And yet Nick cannot help admiring the man. Above all, he admires Gatsby's single-minded devotion to one ideal, his absolute commitment to winning back Daisy, his first love. It is the man's "extraordinary gift for hope," his belief in the possibility of erasing the past (the five years since his rhapsodic affair with Daisy), that leads Nick to tell Gatsby, "You're worth the whole damn bunch put together." But until the very end Nick is unable to make up his mind about the man. He cannot fathom the strange blend of moral ob-

tuseness and idealism in Gatsby, and so throughout his
telling of the story he wavers between scorn and admiration.
It is only when the summer is over, after Gatsby has been
murdered, that Nick finally discovers the missing clue. Just
before going back to Minnesota, his trunk packed, he returns
to the shore near Gatsby's house for a final look. It is evening, and in the moonlight he sees the landscape as he imagines it once had appeared to arriving Europeans. Only then
does he recognize the origin of Gatsby's contradictory and
self-destructive behavior.

> Most of the big shore places were closed now and
> there were hardly any lights except the shadowy, moving
> glow of a ferryboat across the Sound. And as the moon
> rose higher the inessential houses began to melt away
> until gradually I became aware of the old island here
> that flowered once for Dutch sailor's eyes—a fresh, green
> breast of the new world. Its vanished trees, the trees that
> had made way for Gatsby's house, had once pandered in
> whispers to the last and greatest of all human dreams;
> for a transitory enchanted moment man must have held
> his breath in the presence of this continent, compelled
> into an aesthetic contemplation he neither understood
> nor desired, face to face for the last time in history with
> something commensurate to his capacity for wonder.[2]

What this extraordinarily resonant passage implies is nothing less than an explanation of the formation of the American character and, by extension, of our national behavior. It
says that what happened to Gatsby, both how he came to be
the man he was and how he brought on his own defeat, can
only be understood in the light of the special way that Europeans perceived the New World. The sight of an unspoiled,
unstoried green continent nurtured certain propensities of
thought and action which are still operative five centuries
after Columbus's first landfall. It is important to notice, also,
that Nick describes that flowering landscape, back of the
momentarily vanished houses, as having "pandered" to the
dreams of his prototypical American. With that one devastat-

[2] *The Great Gatsby* (New York: Charles Scribner's Sons, 1953),
pp. 2, 154, 182.

ing word, Fitzgerald quietly insinuates a dark view of the effect of the landscape upon the native consciousness. I will return to that theme. Here it is only necessary to emphasize the importance of this retrospective image of the unspoiled American continent. Without it, Fitzgerald tells us, Nick could not have penetrated the mystery of Gatsby and his ambiguous greatness. I do not know any work of literature that invests an image of landscape with greater significance, and in fact, it is difficult to imagine how it could.

But there also is something anomalous about the notion that Americans are, or have been, uniquely responsive to their natural surroundings. Compared with other peoples, surely, we have not been distinguished for cherishing the environment. If there is anything distinctive about the American experience of the land, it is the brevity of our tenure and the fact that we often made the land a commodity before using it as a habitation. "The land was ours," in Robert Frost's words, "before we were the land's."[3] So, far from having a particularly enduring and affectionate attachment to the places we inhabit, Americans probably are the least rooted, the most casually nomadic of modern peoples. Moreover, the nation's record as a user of forests, grasslands, wildlife, and water sources has been, in the judgment of one knowledgeable observer, "the most violent and the most destructive of any written in the long history of civilization."[4]

No, the unique significance of the landscape in the American consciousness is not to be confused with reverence for the land as such. Rather, as Fitzgerald understood, its significance is chiefly symbolic. It is a central feature of our myth of national origins. According to that myth, it is the landscape that initially invited Europeans to disengage themselves from a constricted social environment and to begin a simpler, freer, more fulfilling life in the unstoried terrain of North America. When Nick gazes at the shore in the moonlight, when he summons an image of the way it looked

[3] "The Gift Outright," *Complete Poems of Robert Frost* (New York: Henry Holt and Co., 1959), p. 467.
[4] Fairfield Osborn, *Our Plundered Planet* (New York: Little Brown & Co., Inc., 1948), p. 175.

to the first Europeans, he suddenly recognizes the source of
Gatsby's "heightened sensitivity to the promises of life."
Once the landscape had been the embodiment of those
promises. Like Columbus or the Dutch sailors or the millions
who followed them, Gatsby had believed that tomorrow, any
tomorrow, he could have erased the past and begun a new
life—the sort of life that only exceptional beauty, wealth,
and freedom make possible. If Americans have a peculiar inclination to experience the world in this way, it is because the
idea of a new beginning once had, or at least seemed to have
had, a credible basis in topographical fact. That unspoiled
continent once had been there, a tangible landscape of limitless possibilities, and it informed everything that Europeans
did when they came to America.

And this brings me back to our subject, for in politics the
only action that can be described as a genuine new beginning
is a revolution. It is fitting, therefore, that the first successful
large-scale modern revolution—"successful" in the sense that
it led to the establishment of a wholly new polity—was
enacted by Americans. I want to suggest some of the ways in
which the topographical image of a fresh start lent an impetus to the revolutionary spirit, and how it may help to account for the unusual character of the American Revolution,
as well as for our subsequent failure to abide by its principles. I shall discuss four specific attributes of the New World
landscape: its significance as an image of space, of time, of
wealth, and of the ultimate values presumed to be inherent
in nature.

II

To Europeans the most important physical attribute of the
American landscape no doubt was space itself—real, open,
seemingly boundless and unclaimed space. It is worth
recalling that modern Europeans first began to take an interest in landscape as an aesthetic subject, exemplified by the
painting of landscape for its own sake, during the age of ex-

ploration.[5] Before that time European art and literature seems to reflect a sense of being hemmed in—of being confined to old, used, closed spaces. When the idealizing imagination of Europeans had taken flight, it had tended to move in time rather than space. Such dreams of felicity as we identify with the Golden Age or with Eden or Arcadia draw most of their vitality from their location in time. It is their temporal distance, their "pastness," rather than a particular topography, that invests these ideal worlds with most of their power. A similar point can be made about the future-oriented utopias of the Renaissance. But the availability of space outside of Europe, and particularly in the hospitable climate of North America, changed all that. Here was usable space that enabled Europeans to act out that most ancient primordial urge to get away, to take a trip, to begin life again in an unspoiled landscape.

Of the many versions of the redemptive journey into the wilderness known to the revolutionary generation of Americans, perhaps the most vivid was the migration of the people of Israel, or its individual counterpart, the retreat of the Old Testament prophet into the desert. Such withdrawals from the world into nature made possible a spiritual redemption, a new sense of righteous purpose and commitment, a zeal for the triumph of justice like that of the American patriots. Thus John Adams explains the inspiriting force of the analogy in a letter to his wife, Abigail, dated June 11, 1775. He is in Philadelphia as a delegate to the Second Continental Congress, and he has just come from hearing a Mr. Duffield preach. "His discourse," writes Adams, "was a kind of exposition on the thirty-fifth chapter of Isaiah. America was the wilderness and the solitary place, and he said it would be glad, 'rejoice and blossom as the rose.'" Adams then paraphrases the sermon on points of similarity between the prophecies of Isaiah and the prospects of the embattled Americans: "'No lion shall be there, nor any ravenous beast shall go up thereon, but the redeemed shall walk there.'" In

[5] Kenneth Clark, *Landscape into Art* (Edinburgh: Penguin Books, 1956).

essence the analogy is topographical. It works only so far as the colonists are prepared to see themselves, like the Hebrew prophet, as having been redeemed by their journey into desert places. (The "deserts of North America" was a stock phrase of the period.) In his letter Adams testifies to the emotional power of the metaphor. The preacher, he says, "applied the whole prophecy to this country, and gave us as animating an entertainment as I ever heard. He filled and swelled the bosom of every hearer."[6] From the viewpoint of an Adams, of course, the application was bound to be effective. It comported with the New Englander's millennial conception of American history. Had not the Puritan ancestors of John Adams, as he wrote elsewhere, "resolved to fly to the wilderness for refuge from the temporal and spiritual principalities and powers, and plagues and scourges of their native country?"[7]

But the idea of the special almost sacred character of North American space did not appeal only to sons of the Puritans. When Tom Paine wrote *Common Sense*, late in 1775, he had been in the colonies for only one year. Yet that most effective of revolutionary pamphlets is steeped in a similar kind of geographical awareness. "The Reformation," Paine writes, "was preceded by the discovery of America: As if the Almighty graciously meant to open a sanctuary to the persecuted in future years, when home should afford neither friendship nor safety." In addition to the seeming emptiness of American space (hence its availability as an asylum for the oppressed), Paine emphasized the monumental dimensions of this virgin landscape. Throughout he writes as if there were some necessary affinity between great size, the sheer extent of the continental terrain, and the great merit of the American cause. "The sun never shone on a cause of greater worth. 'Tis not the affair of a city, a county, a province, or a

[6] *Familiar Letters of John Adams and His Wife Abigail Adams, During the Revolution,* ed., Charles Francis Adams (Freeport, New York: Books For Libraries Press, 1970), p. 65.

[7] "On the Feudal and the Canon Law," in Gordon S. Wood, ed., *The Rising Glory of America, 1760–1820* (New York: George Braziller, Inc., 1971), p. 28.

kingdom; but of a continent—of at least one eighth part of the habitable globe."[8]

The degree to which the idea of revolution was nurtured by the topographical awareness of the colonists cannot be established with any precision. It is the kind of link between feeling and action which the actors seldom make explicit, and for evidence the historian must attend to innovations or shifts in language. When Paine relates the worth of the American cause to the fact that it is the affair, not of a mere political unit, like a city or a kingdom, but of a topographical entity—a continent—he is giving voice to a pervasive if amorphous feeling. As the revolutionary fervor of the Americans rose between 1774 and 1776, they invoked the words *continent* and *continental* more and more often. When the delegates to the first Congress assembled, in September 1774, they did not call themselves the "Continental Congress"; but before it was over, that term, along with terms like "continental currency" and "continental army," had come into use. The identification of the revolutionary cause with the huge North American land mass was a source of courage and hope. It was obviously reassuring for John Adams to be able to write, in another letter to his wife, this curious sentence: "The continent is really in earnest, in defending the country."[9] In retrospect there is a certain pathos, along with the unmistakable brag, about the popularity of the word "continent" in 1776. One hundred and fifty years had passed since settlement began, and yet here were the spokesmen for a thin line of colonies, still largely confined to a narrow strip along the eastern seaboard, describing themselves as an entire *continent* in revolt.

[8] *The Complete Writings of Thomas Paine*, ed., Philip S. Foner, 2 vols. (New York: The Citadel Press, 1945), vol. 1, pp. 21 and 17.

[9] *Familiar Letters*, June 17, 1775, p. 65. No historian I have read has explained the sudden vogue of the word "continental." It may have originated in the British Parliament, when members wanted to distinguish between the West Indian island colonies, which remained loyal to the Crown, and the rebellious American colonies. It seems likely that the Americans then took up the seemingly invidious distinction as a taunt and a boast.

It was not difficult for a brilliant polemicist like Paine to invest the American landscape with revolutionary significance. In *Common Sense* he repeatedly translates indisputable geographical facts into arguments for independence. " 'Tis repugnant to reason," he writes, "to the universal order of things, to all examples from former ages, to suppose that this continent can long remain subject to any external power. . . . Reconciliation is *now* a fallacious dream. Nature has deserted the connection, and art cannot supply her place." A large part of what Paine meant by "common sense" was a simple environmentalism, an assumption that people's interests inevitably are determined by the place they inhabit. It is folly to argue, Paine writes, that Americans should accept the royal veto merely because British subjects living in England do. Geography makes all the difference:

> England being the king's residence, and America not so, makes quite another case. The king's negative here is ten times more dangerous and fatal than it can be in England; for there he will scarcely refuse his consent to a bill for putting England into as strong a state of defense as possible, and in America he would never suffer such a bill to be passed.

Like Franklin, Paine loved to taunt the British with their presumptuous smallness. "There is something absurd," he writes, "in supposing a Continent to be perpetually governed by an island." Topography, after all, is a visible embodiment of those laws of nature to which the Declaration will appeal as a sanction for revolution. "In no instance," Paine wrote, "hath nature made the satellite larger than its primary planet; and as England and America, with respect to each other, reverse the common order of nature, it is evident that they belong to different systems. England to Europe; America to itself."[10]

Turning now to the second attribute of the American landscape, its seeming timelessness, I want to suggest how this also contributed to the idea of a revolutionary new beginning.

[10] *Complete Writings*, vol. 1, pp. 23, 26, and 24.

But I would add that the spatial and temporal characteristics of the landscape lent credibility to the cause of revolution in opposite ways. The vast forests, mountains, rivers, prairies, and plains of North America provided tangible images of boundlessness. These physical objects served to represent ideal space. But the same virgin landscape divested time of its usual landmarks. Compared to the terrain of Britain or Western Europe, with their cities, roads, monuments and ruins, the American landscape was a blank. It was unmarked by the usual traces of history—or at least what the white men of Europe considered to be history. (The fact that the Indians seemed to lack a written record of the past was one of the many reasons that Europeans assigned them to the realm of raw nature, or "savagery," rather than to human civilization.) During the revolutionary era Americans often referred to their country as an "asylum," by which they mean a sanctuary from the forms of constraint and repression bequeathed by the past. It was a landscape that invited adjectives like "virgin" and "unstoried" and "immemorial," words that reveal how the native sense of place carried the mind beyond the usual limits of memory, tradition, and history. This unworked terrain turned thought from the past to the future. It implied that here at least the grip of the past upon the present was not a fixed condition of human existence, hence a fresh start was possible. By 1776 this potentially radical idea had been translated into a specific program for dissolving the political bands which connected Americans to the past. It issued in a revolutionary act of separation.

But if the unhistoried landscape reinforced the separatist or centrifugal aspect of the American Revolution, it also lent an impetus to its political corollary: the idea of founding an entirely new republic. A landscape untouched by history also could be perceived as a threatening "hideous wilderness," and it inevitably aroused fears of lawlessness. The instinctive response of many Englishmen was to go back to first principles and establish a new political order. Beginning with the Mayflower Compact, drawn up on board ship in 1620, this habit of laying political foundations by setting forth basic, higher, or fundamental law was repeated in hundreds of

covenanting acts for small towns as well as religious congrega-
tions, cities and states during the colonial period. As Hannah
Arendt has suggested, this penchant for the act of founding
may be the feature of the American Revolution which chiefly
distinguishes it from all others. She notes that not only do we
call the men of our Revolution "Founding Fathers," but they
thought of themselves that way.[11] In all thirteen colonies,
moreover, the Declaration of Independence was accompanied
by the framing of new constitutions—as if bringing to the
surface a doctrine of the sovereignty of the people which had
been present, in fact if not in theory, for a long while. Although seldom formulated as an abstract principle, the idea
of popular sovereignty had been a practical reality at the level
of local government. (In New England alone there were
more than 550 organized townships by the time independence was declared.) Many historians have noted the sudden
and seemingly inexplicable transformation of colonial opinion
on the eve of the Revolution. After having argued exclusively
for the restoration of their traditional rights as British subjects, the colonists in 1775 and 1776 abruptly adopted the
radical idea of founding a new republic in which power and
authority derived from the people. It is as if the idea of new
beginnings, having been nurtured by the act of settling a wilderness and having given rise to hundreds of lesser acts of
founding, had by then sunk deep roots in the native consciousness.

Much of the success that we claim for the American Revolution can be attributed to the fact that it took place in an
undeveloped landscape. Most revolutionary movements, no
matter how much they have aspired to anti-authoritarian
ideals, have had to struggle against entrenched power and authority, and in the course of the struggle they often have
been compelled to recreate the kind of centralized power
they initially had repudiated. But for the most part the old
order against which the American revolutionists were fighting
was located across the Atlantic. Besides, the very newness of
the colonies tended to diminish the influence of the wealth,
status, and power that some Americans had acquired by

---

[11] *On Revolution* (New York: Viking Press, Inc., 1963), p. 204.

1776. Hence the American Revolution was won without generating the degree of class hatred, fanaticism, absolutism, and violence that has often undermined revolutionary idealism. Unlike the French, Russian, or Chinese revolutionists, the Americans did not have to build their new order on the ruins of an old one. Even at the time the Americans understood why theirs had been a particularly fortunate Revolution. When a group of French officers who had fought beside the Americans were embarking for their return to Europe, a Bostonian issued this warning:

> Do not let your hopes be inflamed by our triumphs on this virgin soil. You will carry our sentiments with you, but if you try to plant them in a country that has been corrupt for centuries, you will encounter obstacles more formidable than ours. Our liberty has been won with blood; you will have to shed it in torrents before liberty can take root in the old world.[12]

The third attribute of the North American landscape that contributed to the revolutionary spirit, along with its boundlessness and timelessness, was its promise of economic fulfillment. To gaze upon these "very fruitful fields, admirably adapted for tillage, pasture and habitation," as Columbus put it in his first letter, was to imagine an escape from the chronic scarcity which Europeans had assumed to be a permanent fact of life. It is ironic to recall that in the seventeenth and early eighteenth centuries European governments were disdainful of their North American colonies because, lacking abundant gold and silver, they were considered too poor to bother about. Whereas Central and South America were associated with fabulous wealth, North America came to be identified with a more modest comfort and economic sufficiency. By the time of the Revolution the dominant image of the American landscape was that of "improved nature," a happy middle state located between the over-civilization of the *ancien régime* and the "savagery" of the frontier. To Crèvecoeur this middle state meant a "pleasing uniformity" of economic conditions. When an Englishman first

[12] Lord Acton, *Lectures on the French Revolution* (London: Macmillan & Co., Ltd., 1925), p. 32.

lands on the East Coast, said Crèvecoeur, he "beholds fair cities, substantial villages, extensive fields, an immense country filled with decent houses, good roads, orchards, meadows and bridges where a hundred years ago all was wild, woody, and uncultivated!"[13]

This concept of the American economy as a kind of golden mean, a perfect blend of art and nature, comported with the prevailing eighteenth-century idea of the cyclical character of social development. All civilizations were thought, like living organisms, to go through an unvarying cycle of youth, maturity, and inevitable decline. By 1750 it was widely assumed that European societies were overripe; so far as they still could generate any vitality or creativity, it would manifest itself in America. No one gave more vivid expression to this popular idea than did Bishop Berkeley in his "Verses on the Prospect of Planting Arts and Learning in America." The poem is about the emigration of the Muse, "disgusted" with the barrenness and decay of Europe, to a landscape that epitomizes freshness, youth, and hope:

> . . . happy climes, where from the genial sun
>   And virgin earth such scenes ensue,
> The force of art by nature seems outdone,
>   And fancied beauties by the true:

Here again it is the topography of North America, the "happy climes" and "virgin earth," that the poet relies upon for the credibility of his prophetic vision of "another golden age" and for the conviction with which he finally declares: "Westward the course of empire takes its way."[14]

It is difficult to exaggerate what this sense of the inevitability of American growth and development, symbolized by the beckoning landscape, meant for the morale of the revolutionary cause. By 1776 the idea of freedom from want in America was no mere promise; the colonies already had become the world's leading example of a society without

[13] *Letters from an American Farmer*, ed., Albert E. Stone (New York: New American Library, 1963), pp. 60–61.

[14] *Berkeley's Complete Works*, ed., A. C. Fraser, 4 vols. (Oxford: Clarendon Press, 1901), vol. 4, pp. 365–366.

poverty. In economic terms they were fulfilling precisely the ideal that was figured by the landscape of the middle state—neither too much development nor too little, neither too wealthy nor too poor. In Jefferson's language, the unique thing about America was the "lovely equality which the poor enjoy with the rich." Our term "middle class" lacks the resonance of the eighteenth-century "middle state." For the men of the Revolution it had moral, cultural, and political as well as economic implications, and they all were figured by the image of a terrain midway between a decadent Europe and a savage frontier. The republic of the middle state was to be an essentially classless—almost pastoral—society of small property holders, men who would be satisfied to fulfill the austere neoclassical ideal of economic sufficiency. This idea of the good life makes itself felt in the Declaration of Independence, and particularly in Jefferson's substitution of the "pursuit of happiness" for property in the Lockean trilogy of unalienable rights.[15] It is this moderate sensibility which distinguishes the revolutionists of 1776 from the men who made most other revolutions. No other revolution has been fought by a people in so little danger of real deprivation or so undisturbed by the guilty awareness of desperate poverty in close proximity to great wealth. Just as the American landscape represented freedom from constraint in space and in time, so it represented the scarcely credible possibility of freedom from want.

But of all the implications of the American landscape which nurtured the revolutionary spirit of a new beginning, the most profoundly effective (if also the most elusive) was philosophical. Here I refer to the capacity of the landscape to represent the norm of nature itself. When Europeans journeyed into the wilderness to establish new communities, they were beginning again, returning to nature, in a quite literal sense. And when, in 1776, the Congress voted to declare the

---

[15] Caroline Robbins, *The Pursuit of Happiness* (Washington, D.C.: American Enterprise Institute, 1974), and Cecelia Kenyon, "Republicanism and Radicalism in the American Revolution: An Old-Fashioned Interpretation," *William and Mary Quarterly*, third series, vol. 19, 1962, pp. 153–182.

independence of the colonies, they faced the issue of beginning again in an abstract, political and philosophical sense. How would they justify breaking the law and resorting to violence? This was the bedrock philosophic issue with which the Congress confronted the Committee of Five (Jefferson, Adams, Franklin, Sherman, and Livingston) when it directed them to draw up the official proclamation of independence. In effect these men were asked to provide a reasoned case on behalf of behavior which they themselves would have described, not long before, as criminal. They were asked to justify acts which they knew would be regarded by many of their contemporaries as unmitigated treason and murder. But the fact is that they had very little difficulty in marshalling their arguments. They announced to the world that they were *entitled* to make a revolution, to alter or abolish the existing government, by (in the familiar yet seldom understood phrase) "the Laws of Nature and of Nature's God."

This is not to suggest that the idea had resulted directly from their experience of the native landscape. It was ready at hand, as everyone knows, in the language of the natural rights philosophy so effectively propounded by John Locke almost a century before. To justify an unlawful seizure of power, Locke had asked Englishmen to suppose a hypothetical situation in which they found themselves living outside politically defined social space—in what he called a "state of nature." His brilliant notion was that when we imagine such a return to a presocialized setting, we will be more likely to see the purpose of government in proper perspective. We will then recognize that government is not a natural or biological necessity, like air, food, water, clothing, or shelter. Rather, men form governments for self-protection, and it follows that governments exist to serve men rather than men to serve governments. When a government ceases to provide protection, men have a right, derived from their essential being, from that initial "state of nature," to alter or abolish that government. They have a "natural right" to organize a revolution. In making this argument Locke came close to deifying the idea of nature, by which he meant a set of abstract principles or laws governing the universe and accessible to human reason. That such laws exist had been proven beyond all doubt by the astonishing discoveries of Galileo, Kepler and Newton. Although science had discovered the physical principles of natural order and harmony, their political counterparts had yet to be fully apprehended. Locke's theory of the natural right of revolution was intended to fill that gap.

But if Englishmen of the eighteenth century were responsive to the doctrine of natural rights, consider how much more it meant to their colonial relatives. For a century and a half the colonists had been accustomed to thinking of themselves as living, if not in a state of nature, at least at a considerable distance from the centers of urbane civilization. The colonists were indisputably and irrevocably provincials, and although earlier they may have been embarrassed by the idea, during the Revolution they embraced it. The pervasive environmentalism of the age enabled them to make a virtue of provinciality. For if thought and behavior is in large measure determined by the environment, and if the ultimate principles of order lie hidden behind the mask of nature, then an American obviously was far more likely to gain access to those principles than a Londoner or a Parisian. Thus the American landscape effected a virtual religious conversion. When Englishmen set foot on American soil, said Crèvecoeur, they experienced a kind of "resurrection"—they became new men. This idea accorded perfectly with the criticism of a corrupt society developed by disaffected Englishmen at home. Adapted to American needs, the fashionable neoclassic and radical Whig social criticism meant that coarse native homespun, like provincial manners, was more natural, honest, and virtuous than imported silk or London coffee house sophistication. In America, as in republican Rome, access to a "natural" rural setting was thought to be conducive to sound antimonarchical views. At a time when Englishmen believed that the simple life, repose, and contemplation in the countryside helped to breed republican manners, the American landscape inevitably was perceived as a seedbed of republican virtue.

What I have been trying to suggest is that the topographical awareness of Americans coincided with John

Locke's philosophical argument on behalf of revolution. Even in the seventeenth century Locke had had a glimpse of this truth. "In the beginning," he said, speaking of the willingness of men in a state of nature to be satisfied with the conveniences of life, "all the world was America."[16] When Englishmen migrated they in effect were approximating a return to that natural state in which men are best able to perceive self-evident truths. The Lockean doctrine of natural rights thus provided a philosophical confirmation of a viewpoint that seemed to arise, almost spontaneously, from American soil. If the four attributes of the native landscape I have been discussing have a common significance it is, most simply put, that they reinforce the idea of freedom from constraint. The apparent limitlessness of space, the seeming absence of history, the promise of abundance, the accessibility of Nature's God—all of these were made visible, tangible, literally available (or so it seemed) by the American landscape. This was the green beacon that attracted millions of English and European migrants to America. The white colonists who rebelled against Britain in 1776 constituted a self-selected population of men and women with a special responsiveness to the idea of a fresh start. With few exceptions, either they themselves, or their ancestors, had at some point chosen to leave an old and organized society and to begin a new life in the fresh green terrain of the New World.

III

In conclusion, let us briefly reconsider the idea of a political new beginning to which the American landscape lent so much credibility. What has happened to the native spirit of revolution since 1776? One answer to that question is implicit in F. Scott Fitzgerald's image of the continental landscape with which we began. When Nick Carraway, the narrator of *The Great Gatsby*, imagines seeing the New World as

[16] "An Essay Concerning . . . Civil Government," ed., E. A. Burtt, *The English Philosophers from Bacon to Mill* (New York: The Modern Library, 1939), p. 422.

it had flowered once for Dutch sailors' eyes, he says that the landscape had "*pandered* in whispers to the last and greatest of all human dreams. . . ." With that one shocking verb he intimates a somber view of the eventual effect of the landscape upon the American consciousness. To pander is to minister to base passions. If the virgin land helps to explain Gatsby's "extraordinary gift for hope," it also helps to explain the corruption of that hope. In 1776, as we have seen, the landscape had reinforced an inspiriting vision of political possibilities—indeed a revolutionary commitment to a new kind of republic aimed at securing three fundamental "natural" (hence egalitarian) rights: life, liberty, and the pursuit of happiness. Today, however, it seems evident that those very attributes of the landscape which once had inspired revolutionary idealism also ministered to the passions which dissipated it.

The movement of Europeans into a wilderness perceived as boundless, empty space served as a solvent for old assumptions about the fixity of class and status. It encouraged the rebels of 1776 to dedicate themselves to the proposition, in Lincoln's words, that all men are created equal. But of course this image of an unstoried and unpeopled landscape was a distortion of reality. In it there was no place for the Indians and their culture, and the image thereby helped to justify removing them from their land, along with the trees that made way for Gatsby's palatial house. It is worth noting, incidentally, that it was protesting black Americans, spokesmen for the civil rights movement of the 1960s, who reminded us of the unmistakably (if inadvertently) ethnocentric history lesson we teach our children with that simple statement about our beginning, "Columbus discovered America"—as if the Indians had not lived here before 1492! The fact is that for all its egalitarian implications, the spatial image of America pandered to ethnocentric and potentially racist passions. If there was no place in the myth of national origins for the Indians, neither was there a place in it for America's blacks. They crossed the Atlantic not in order to be free but in order to be enslaved. In practice the more ample life for all people allegedly provided by American space has meant, above all, a more ample life for males of white British and European origin.

By the same token, the idea of escape from historical time into the immemorial North American terrain had dangerous as well as creative consequences. The image of an unstoried landscape evoked in the native consciousness a sense of unique political possibilities, but it also encouraged an excessive confidence in the ability of European colonists to throw off constraints, both external and internal, inherited from the past. In its most extravagant form the idea of a new beginning in time has proven to be as delusive as the image of limitless space. It has encouraged an excessive reliance upon strategies of disengagement as a means of solving problems. There is a telling passage in *The Great Gatsby* when Nick tries to persuade Gatsby that he cannot expect Daisy simply to erase the five years she has been married to Tom Buchanan. " 'You cannot repeat the past,' " Nick says. " 'Can't repeat the past?' he [Gatsby] cried incredulously. 'Why of course you can! . . . I'm going to fix everything just the way it was before. . . .' "[17] This habit of mind—the illusion that at any moment it is possible to erase time, to recapture a relatively ideal untainted past in order to begin again—is traceable to the myth of national origins. It accounts for the often noted American propensity for tactics of avoidance and denial. When the trees or other natural resources in a place have been used up, when a river is polluted or a city made unlivable, the instinctive native reflex has been to move out and start again somewhere else. A contemporary sociologist, Philip Slater, has called this notion that complicated problems can be flushed away the "Toilet Assumption" of American thought.[18] It is a self-deluding tendency, one that has served to deflect attention, energy, and imagination from the unavoidable problems that would have to be confronted in order to realize the aspirations of the Founding Fathers.

So, too, the promise of abundance represented by the American landscape has had the unforeseen effect of

[17] *Gatsby*, p. 111.
[18] *The Pursuit of Loneliness: American Culture at the Breaking Point* (Boston: Beacon Press, Inc., 1970), p. 15ff.

diminishing revolutionary hopes. The patriots of 1776 envisaged a nation that might make possible, for the first time in history, universal freedom from want. They hoped to achieve a relative equality of condition, a society in which none would be too rich or too poor. But the appetite for personal wealth, sharpened by the radical individualism that emerged after 1776, turned out to be more powerful than our egalitarian ideals. Well before the middle of the nineteenth century the acquisitive and competitive ethos of capitalism had begun to subvert the spirit of democratic revolution. While continuing to affirm the democratic principles of their Revolution, Americans in fact were reproducing a modified version of the European social structure, marked by increasingly distinct class divisions, a system of minority ownership and control of the means of production, and an uneven distribution of wealth and power. The seemingly inexhaustible riches symbolized by the landscape stimulated a passion for an endlessly rising rate of production and consumption, a goal at variance with the sober eighteenth-century ideal of economic sufficiency.

The first lecturer in this series, Professor Irving Kristol, has affirmed the compatibility of America's democratic ideals and the capitalist program of economic growth. In the opinion of the American revolutionists, he says, "poverty is abolished by economic growth, not by economic redistribution—there is never enough to redistribute."[19] Quite apart from the question of what the Founding Fathers believed—surely Jefferson cannot without qualification be included in that generalization—I would argue that it is precisely the reliance upon corporate economic growth as a means of abolishing poverty that accounts for the shameful and unnecessary persistence of poverty in the richest of industrial nations. Our vast natural wealth has ministered to those very passions the Founding Fathers had identified with a decadent European aristocracy: greed, arrogance, and the enjoyment of wasteful luxury in the presence of acute deprivation. A primary source of the disenchantment with American society that informs so much of contemporary literature is indicated by Fitzgerald's savage

[19] *The American Revolution as a Successful Revolution* (Washington, D.C.: American Enterprise Institute, 1973), pp. 13–14.

description of the narrow self-serving behavior of the very rich in *The Great Gatsby*. "They were careless people," Nick says of Tom and Daisy, "—they smashed up things and creatures and then retreated back into their money or their vast carelessness, or whatever it was that kept them together, and let other people clean up the mess they had made. . . ."[20]

But of all the dubious passions to which the landscape pandered, perhaps the most destructive has been the national appetite for illusory notions of American virtue. It was only a short step from the exhilarating revolutionary spirit, with its justifiable sense of the republic's rare good fortune, to an exaggerated and self-righteous sense of the unique benevolence of the national character. When Europeans crossed the Atlantic, they presumably gained access to the "state of nature" itself—that is, to ultimate, sacred, redeeming values. According to the myth, the landscape of the New World was a repository of meaning formerly attributed to the deity. Freedom from the constraints of European institutions, manners, and scarcity made possible the emergence of a "new man"—an American Adam who proved to be more spontaneous, forthright, easy, good-hearted or (in a word) more natural than people elsewhere. The identification of the national character with Nature had the effect of sacralizing national aspirations. Hence any purpose adopted by Americans was likely to be perceived, like Jay Gatsby's desire to win back Daisy, "as the following of a grail." This quasi-religious belief, needless to say, no more jibed with the facts than did the belief in an escape from history into boundless space. Although the attributes of the landscape had encouraged Americans to believe in the uniqueness of their new republic, with its stirring dedication to the principle of equality, those same attributes also enabled them to recreate many of the conditions of European society which violated that principle.

IV

As we approach the bicentennial of the Revolution, we have an obligation to acknowledge the ways in which the republic

[20] *Gatsby*, pp. 180–181.

of 1976 falls short of the revolutionary goals of 1776. If the green light at the end of Daisy's dock is a sadly diminished emblem of the possibilities once made available by the landscape of the New World, it also may be said to represent a diminished commitment to our own revolutionary ideals. For at least a century after 1776 the United States was the inspiration of people struggling for freedom everywhere. But today, in many parts of the world, rebels with aspirations not unlike those of the American patriots regard our government (and with good reason) as an enemy of revolutionary egalitarianism. Within the United States, moreover, attitudes toward the idea of revolution also have been changing. In recent years the word itself has regained a measure of its appeal for numbers of disaffected citizens. Once again some Americans are thinking about revolution as a conceivable recourse, a means of achieving democratic objectives, but the dismaying fact is that the revolution they contemplate would be directed against American institutions.

All of these reflections bring me back, finally, to the way Fitzgerald unlocks the mystery of Jay Gatsby's violent death. It is from the landscape that Nick learns what destroyed Gatsby. In the end he realizes that Gatsby's dream of ecstatic fulfillment, like the national vision of possibilities, also had helped to destroy the dreamer. To be sure, the myth always had fostered extravagant hopes, but in the early phase of American history, while the land was being settled, those hopes had had a far more credible basis in fact than they do in the twentieth century.

> And as I sat there [says Nick], brooding on the old unknown world, I thought of Gatsby's wonder when he first picked out the green light at the end of Daisy's dock. He had come a long way to this blue lawn, and his dream must have seemed so close that he could hardly fail to grasp it.

And just here, in the pause between sentences, Nick finally grasps the reason for Gatsby's failure. He now knows something that Gatsby had not known. "He did not know," says Nick of Gatsby, "that it [the dream] was already behind him, somewhere back in that vast obscurity beyond the city, where the dark fields of the republic rolled on under the night."

We may take this to mean that the dream of felicity figured by the American landscape, if it ever was attainable, was closer to attainment when the Republic was founded. Although the idea of America as a new beginning no longer corresponds with the facts, many Americans (like Gatsby) have continued to behave as if it did. What this means, in political terms, is that the revolutionary content of the myth has been dissipated, but the form—the habit of mind it nurtured—is with us still. In preparation for 1976, therefore, it is instructive to read *The Great Gatsby* as a cautionary fable. It helps to explain why and how we became distracted from those generous revolutionary ideals once represented by the native landscape. Perhaps that knowledge may yet encourage us to change direction and complete our uncompleted revolution.

RONALD S. BERMAN
Intellect and Education in a Revolutionary Society

Delivered in Grace Rainey Rogers Auditorium,

Metropolitan Museum of Art, New York on April 4, 1974

My subject is intellect and education, which ought always to be joined and admired. Almost all the lectures in this series have been concerned with America's revolutionary period; what little I have to add is mostly about modern times. We were left with certain cultural ideas and structures which have changed, and it is my intention, if only in a descriptive way, to talk about their fate.

Learning in the eighteenth century was vigorous, formal, confined and deep. Its subjects were classical and Christian, its modes imitation, memorization and debate. The century resounded with schoolboy versions of the death of Caesar and the victory of Aeneas in Italy—which often translated themselves into parliamentary life. The institutions of learning were the church, apprenticeship, school, college and library; a time perhaps benighted without graduate degrees. Education, as in medieval times, was directed toward the practice of law, religion and government. It involved certain penalties, described by a tract already old in the age of Jefferson, wherein "Three or four jerks with a birch, or with a small red willow where a birch cannot be had" is very thoughtfully recommended to the schoolmaster. "God hath sanctified the rod and correction." As to that, of course, we may never know, but man certainly had.

The enduring forms of that age—poetry, tracts, diaries, letters, novels, satires—testify to the expressive passion of the enlightened mind. The age spoke with a decisive rationality that seems no longer fully available. Learning took place within understood cultural definitions. The books read by Pope and Swift, and transmitted to Jefferson and Hamilton, are the works of humanism. They are full of responsibilities, essentially those of a landed class created by its moral attachments. Although these works direct us to a lifetime of learning, they are not optimistic about the perfecting of our character—or, actually, about the transformational quality of education. They emphasize an orderly society not so much because of its resemblance to heaven as because they have faith in its institutions. Learning was, on the English-speaking side of the Enlightenment, notably pragmatic. There was not much confidence in theory. In the phrase of John Milton, education was something like a "long war" out of which students came forth "renowned and perfect Commanders in the service of their country." Even as a metaphor this is not the modern view—"a long war" in culture and in the self. But it was the kind of war familiar to Dr. Johnson who said once that when he was young he read *hard*. As a matter of fact, like Milton he dedicated his life to books, and through his own education created ours. For Milton, education was intended to repair the damages of original sin. For his readers in the eighteenth century it was to serve a more secular idea of culture, but the idea of a complete culture nevertheless. For us, it means something else.

I think it of special interest to examine later times, for the bicentennial is about ourselves and is history not yet concluded.

Emerson observed in the *American Scholar* that we did not have enough intellectuals in this country. Providentially or not the case has altered, but the presence of a large and increasing body of intellectuals has done as much to aggravate as to resolve the problems he had in mind.

The colonial experience produced an altogether exceptional

body of thinking men to whom thought of itself was not a vocation. They were literate lawyers, landowners, farmers and legislators. They distinguished themselves as their continental models had in science, engineering, legal and moral debate, architecture, printing, and husbandry, if we are to summarize only the principal interests of the Founding Fathers. In many respects they resembled their opposite numbers on the losing side for the good reason that they shared certain cultural assumptions with the members of the Temple, the Royal Academy and the circles around Dr. Johnson and Edmund Burke. These assumptions were not to pass intact through American history, and part of the intellectual agonies of the nineteenth and twentieth centuries came from their modification or abandonment.

While the nineteenth century witnessed the continuation of that admirable synthesis—at its most visible in the person of Abraham Lincoln—it also endured the separation of intellectual from other abilities and vocations. One of the great themes in the literature of that century is separateness, the cleaving of American culture into a successful material enterprise and an unsuccessful psychic enterprise. Our great writers were strangely hermetic. The marvels they composed are familiar enough: but we sometimes ought to compare the solid placement of Tolstoy in Russian history, that of Dickens in British class character and of Balzac in French moral economy and manners, with the uncertain equilibrium of Poe, Hawthorne, Melville and Mark Twain. American literature in the second part of the nineteenth century does not celebrate a motherland or identify a profoundly complex social order in an attempt to grasp the generalities of human relationship. It clearly rejects some of these tasks and provides us with the modular conception of the artist outside of his culture.

The protagonists of our great age of fiction are not embodiments of cultural values: they oppose those values either by virtue of what they do or what they are. Some of the most useful criticisms of American society were made by immensely intelligent men—but in the guise of a runaway sailor, an illiterate boy and his black slave, a self-made savage on the shores of Walden Pond. Sometimes the relationship of a mind to all the habits, values and institutions that encircle it is implied by the witty account of impoverished barbarism on the Mississippi, by the angry reflections of a New England Brahmin isolated by the new national politics, and by literary symbols of waste, destruction and materialism. And sometimes the matter is brought with economical clarity to this kind of consciousness. The passage is from *Walden*:

> It is said that Mirabeau took to highway robbery "to ascertain what degree of resolution was necessary in order to place oneself in formal opposition to the most sacred laws of society." . . . This was manly, as the world goes; and yet it was idle, if not desperate. A saner man would have found himself often enough "in formal opposition" to what are deemed "the most sacred laws of society," through obedience to yet more sacred laws, and so have tested his resolution without going out of his way.

If only as a footnote, it should be added that Thoreau continued this passage with praise of obedience to a just government. But the decisive thing about this passage and his book is the way it foreshadows the adversary relationship of the thinker and his culture. And of course it illuminates one of the great strategies of our literature, the protagonists of which are recluses, eccentrics, relics of another age, holy innocents or acknowledged enemies of their time. There are powerful literary and cultural oppositions between the folklore of Mark Twain, the mysteries of Melville, the Confucian stoicism of Thoreau, and the ethical and social beliefs of the culture they inhabited. American literature as they fundamentally shaped it is not about the density of human relationships but of time, space and landscape.

There was then a kind of internal exile suffered by the best of our writers, an exile which was soon to become literal. The first decades of the new century witnessed one of the greatest migrations of intellectual talent in modern times. Among those who left this country for Europe were Henry James, Henry Adams, T. S. Eliot, Ezra Pound, Ernest Hemingway, Scott Fitzgerald, Gertrude Stein. They left for reasons personal and ideological. The travels of Hart Crane and Hemingway proceeded not only because of the necessity to experience the world but precisely because they saw American culture as unfriendly and confining. John Dos Passos speaks eloquently for their motives:

> At the slightest excuse, and particularly upon the occasion of the publication of a book I bolted for foreign parts. . . . Young women I met at cocktail parties liked to tell me I was running away from myself. That was partly true. Maybe I was running away from them. I never got around to explaining that I was running towards something. I still had an insatiable appetite for architecture and painting, particularly the work of the so-called scientists of the early Italian Renaissance. I wanted to see everything they had ever painted. I wanted to see country and landscape, plants and animals and people, men, women and children in city, town and hamlet. There would never be time to satisfy such multifarious curiosity.

The settlement abroad of Pound, James and Eliot was in some ways like that of those other exiles, James Joyce, O'Casey and Beckett: all of them sought the kind of attachment to culture or to its idea that their own countries seemed unable to provide. Pound resembled Mark Twain in his rejection of our economic materialism and he added his own appraisal of the thinness of ideas and aesthetics on our side of the Atlantic. Eliot spoke with authority of the traditions we had abandoned: he invoked the figures of Dante, Virgil and the Christian poets of Renaissance England as a reproach to our obsession with things present. The protagonists of his poetry—Sweeney, J. Alfred Prufrock, Gerontion—oppose and satirize the American idea of progress. In our Darwinian way we had conceived of a social order at its highest form of evolution, but the poetry of Eliot depicts an order of life ultimately sterile and impotent, a Western world deprived of religion, tradition, consciousness and the power of action. It turned out with consummate irony that the greatest American literature of our century, apart from the splendid exceptions of William Faulkner and Fitzgerald, is about Spain, France, England and Italy.

After the Great War, American intellectuals turned to the alternatives of politics. They were no longer interested in our native political traditions. Irving Kristol has remarked in *The Democratic Idea in America* that this seemed to them conservative and undemocratic. What interested American intellectuals from World War I on was precisely that body of opinion rejected by the Founders and their successors: the doctrines of the *philosophes*. And Marxism, with the potency of a myth whose time had come, displaced the scattered doctrines of socialism, liberalism, and humanism that were still available—of little use to those who desired radical changes in the social order and a timeless explanation of human history.

By the thirties there was a new and political cast to intellectual life. The great exiles—poets, painters and novelists—had felt alienated by American bourgeois culture but they did not yet have a systematic interest in politics. Royalism in Eliot, fascism in Pound, and communism in Hemingway are not central to their work; but to Dreiser, Dos Passos, Sherwood Anderson, and Edmund Wilson, politics were substantive. The new travels of John Dos Passos were described concisely by Malcolm Cowley:

> Instead of bolting up the gangplanks of steamers bound for it didn't matter what foreign ports, he caught trains for the Middle West, the Carolina cotton mills, the Kentucky coal fields or the San Francisco waterfront, wherever people were suffering and class wars were bursting out. Especially during the early years of the Depression he attended mass meetings and Congressional hearings, he walked on picket lines before reporting strikes for the labor press.

The coloration of American intellectual life was established in the 1930s when it became a common assumption that writers were on the left. There were a good many reasons for this. For half a century literature had been at odds with American culture and these men knew how to read. The Depression affected them powerfully; and of course racial injustice and class antagonism were deeply felt in the America of that period. Edmund Wilson, who spoke for the entire group, decided early in his life that it would take a revolution to resolve such issues. It was held in common that the absence of a moral order in American culture was due to the nature of American government; and it was assumed that only by revolutionary political action could there be a return to a real community of interests. The intelligence of Wilson, perhaps the leading man of letters of our century, led him later to understand that communism failed to achieve—indeed offended against—social justice. But although punctuated with events like the show trials of the mid-thirties and the nonaggression pact with Hitler, Russian communism proved to be the great model for the political aspirations of many American intellectuals; communism (shaded through all its sects, heresies and revisions) was the strongest and most visible system of thought available to intellectuals for over ten years. The other doctrines available simply could not compete with its mythopoeic force.

II

The habitat of the American intellectual in the eighteenth century could reasonably be stated to have been the farm, the law office, the court, and legislature. In the nineteenth century it was far more dispersed, as intellectuals like Melville, Hawthorne and Thoreau led their lives of relative isolation. But in the twentieth century, with the creation of a vast intellectual class, there came into being a specific structure to retain those who thought, taught and wrote. I have discussed the background in a general way; the foreground has a more detailed focus on a single object—this new structure which attempts to conjoin vocation, profession and the life of the mind.

There have been two parallel developments in the modern American university. One was consciously fostered hospitality to public service. The campus undertook to train nurses, doctors, lawyers and engineers. It labored, sometimes brilliantly, to do such things as investigate the growth of wheat and vines, or the process of atomic reaction. And it sometimes labored greatly to produce a not very impressive system of physical education and domestic economy. Before "relevance" that kind of course was called (sarcastically) basket-weaving. And the university took on the role of sustaining intellectuals, which was by no means a bad thing. But we ought to remember that the first generation of the twentieth century had not much to do with the campus. Hemingway and Pound felt no sympathy there, while Fitzgerald and Faulkner simply could not exist in—were actively (sometimes comically) discouraged by—the academic institution.

Nevertheless it came to be, after two complex decades of development, that the university made good its claims to contain and sanction intellectual life. That the process was not painless is proven by the astute academic fictions of Mary McCarthy, Lionel Trilling, Randall Jarrell and Bernard Malamud. The academic novel, practically a sub-genre of our fiction, tells in exquisite satiric detail the difficulties of intellectuals coexisting with students, deans, and themselves. Yet in general the thesis has been accepted: the university is the natural habitat of the cultural mind. In practice this has been dialectical, the equilibrium between the intellectual id and the institutional superego resulting from mutually opposed stress.

Until the early sixties the universities functioned as educational institutions and, for better or worse, as agencies of cultural integration. After that time they changed. There were two important things that affected their character, their productivity and their place in American society. The first of these was their expansion into the knowledge industry. From 1958 until 1968 the American university boomed along with the rest of the economy. Universities before the boom, however large and well endowed, were on the order of cottage industries. They were in the best and worst sense of the phrase "traditional." Even until the early sixties it was expected that members of the college faculty would act as or imagine themselves in the role of surrogate parents. They explained their function as a combination of intellectual and moral guidance and sometimes (especially at the smaller schools), they played a Socratic role. It was largely assumed that the faculty were exemplary and that they should give cultural and moral guidance. This was a tradition, a convenience, and a compensation. It was a tradition because (after all) in the West, especially in the study of the humanities, some kind of moral benefit has been expected from the process of education. It was a convenience because families and administrators felt an increased measure of security knowing that students were thus affected. And finally, it was a compensation because in American culture it has generally been agreed (even if in a self-accusatory way) that certain privileges should make up for other deprivations. The teacher in America, at least since Ichabod Crane, has been endowed with moral force precisely because he has not been merely a part of the market economy. It has been widely assumed that because teachers had no money they were morally disinterested, a distinction to be tested by history. The gentility of poverty aside, there were other reasons for the special situation of the faculty. Cultural isolationism encouraged the formation of interest groups. There were no blacks visible within most faculties and only under anomalous circumstances was there much representation of other minorities. For example, in the methodologically hard disciplines like mathematics or physics where there was a plainly evident hierarchy of talent throughout the profession, Jews were well represented. In the humanities where standards were based upon tradition or even social similarities, Jews were generally excluded. In brief then and without going to the unnecessary trouble of enjoying moral outrage, it should simply be noted that the college faculty lived in a closed if not encapsulated life, free from the claims of much social contact or competition. This is the very opposite of the accusations that recently have been leveled at the college faculty.

At the beginning of the boom, departments in the humanities were characteristically understaffed. There were few openings at the top; for example, at the good universities it was quite characteristic for twenty-five or thirty instructors, like spiders in a bottle, to survive each other in order to advance to those four assistant professor positions which would later funnel to two tenured associate professorships. There

was a single secretary per department and perhaps a single
official typewriter. The average workload of academics ran
from ten to fifteen teaching hours per week. Research funds
were scarce, travel funds almost unknown. In short, universities were undeveloped in structure and practically innocent of
overhead.

With the arrival of Sputnik (that heavenly messenger of
post-industrial times) and the consequent infusion of federal
money into education, with the extraordinary climb in the
stock market that occurred during the decade, from 1958 to
1968, inflating among other things university endowments
and conceptions, and with the moral and financial support of
state legislatures, universities began a period of optimistic expansion which they confused with permanence. The new
boom altered the face of the university physically as well as
in other ways. College campuses which heretofore had been
built more or less on the human scale developed skyscraper
conformations. Scientific development was memorialized in
concrete, by laboratories, cyclotrons, and other enormous
collections of hardware. Even in the soft disciplines, however,
which were living (although they did not realize it) on soft
money, great changes were under way. It was the era of construction, an era perhaps unequaled in generous grandiosity
since the great building campaigns which under private
domain first put up colleges at Yale and cloisters at Princeton. But there were great anomalies. Buildings supposed to
cost $1 million to $2 million climbed to actual costs of $4
million and $5 million. Although the future was mortgaged,
there was virtually no planning for economic changes. In
some departments tenured positions, which had before taken
years to accumulate, were given out almost monthly. This,
too, was a form of mortgage. Gigantic campuses were formed
covering extraordinary tracts of land. In order to hold 20,000
to 40,000 students it was necessary to have 500 to 1,000 or
more acres. To fill those acres there were hordes of clerks,
maintenance men, designers, landscapers, counselors, tech-
nicians, deans, and other retainers.

The new campus environments were not like those of the
traditional academic scene. As education became a state or

commercial enterprise, it paid less attention to values, ethics, or aesthetics. Universities failed to affect their environments and became isolated on the prairies or lost in megalopolis. As they lost their specifically cultural character, they came to resemble other institutions of the state. One is reminded of *Hard Times,* in which Dickens constructs a great allegory on the sinister resemblance of schools, prisons and hospitals. Universities now consulted with government and did an enormous amount of private and defense research. They took what was conceived to be remedial social action and became social conglomerates. There were great benefits conferred by this growth and sincerity compels us to recognize them, but there were great penalties as well. The academic teaching load was cut almost in half in order to provide either more time for research or more adequate competition to recruit faculty away from other institutions. This was a good thing for the production of published work but it seriously affected the morale of academicians and was a major factor in the alienation of students' minds and affections. It would, I think, be most unfortunate if we were to confuse freedom with neglect, and that was the confusion that occurred when students were abandoned to their curriculum and guided only by the regulations of bureaucrats. The number of students admitted to universities during the boom went to limits previously unknown. There were often as many as 500 or 1,000 students in a single course and those who could not fit into one room might hear by television. Of even more interest, however, than the changes in the mere numbers were the changes of attitude. If the characteristic vice of departments before the boom was paternalism, the characteristic vice before the bust was a kind of frigidity. Departments of history and English became corporate giants. Within these departments the students characteristically became isolated from their instructors. It was routine for students at some universities to have a single annual conversation with a member of the faculty. This was due in part to the extraordinary ratio of students to instructors and in part to the imposition of a network of graduate assistants.

Graduate studies produced their own problems. There sud-

denly arose dozens of Ph.D.-granting institutions which had
not the slightest ability to fulfill their new missions. It was
thought that in order to cope with the population explosion
and to provide a teaching community adequate for that purpose, thousands of new Ph.D.s would have to be granted.
This was done in somewhat the way King James manufactured his nobility: an act of declaration followed by cash
payment. Small colleges on the make, state normal and junior
colleges, and bucolic universities newly infused with the vigor
of cash all rose to the opportunity of asserting their new
status. The thousands of Ph.D.s they succeeded in pouring
out over the last decade are enduring the unkind fate of most
overproduced goods. A whole series of expectations were
raised in the boom period, chief among them that graduate
degrees would soon be as common as a high school diploma.
They were certainly more common than the jobs available for
them.

To summarize then, the new growth emulated corporate
gigantism; a university community which had been of manageable size and form became unrecognizably swollen. It was
possible for 30,000 to 50,000 students to populate
megalopolitan campuses, having as their only landmarks limitless acres of shoddy commercial enterprises. The forms of
personal attachment and loyalty disappeared. There were no
longer unselfconscious affection and the imperatives it
implied for people and places. The universities turned from
their educational calling to other forms of vocation. Faculties
cut the time of their association with students in half. Entire
populations of graduate assistants arose, naturally vitiating
the quality of instruction and prolonging the already difficult
process of obtaining a Ph.D. In short the basic conditions for
what was once called *anomie* had been achieved, and they
affected a specific population of intellectuals.

The first of the two great changes in universities, then, was
this material one I have outlined. The second was ideological.
It was at the time of the university's greatest material success
that it committed itself to a political role. The events of the
sixties have become familiar. Forms of campus protest were
introduced which disrupted the universities and denied fun-

damental civil liberties. These tactics escalated from follies to felonies: from silly harassment to the destruction of property, papers and records, to arson and even bombing. All this is well known and has become the occasion either for justification on the grounds that moral ends were served and our consciousness heightened, or for accusation on the grounds that no matter how highly motivated, this was barbarism and could not be tolerated by any body politic. My own primary concern is what happened as a consequence of these acts, but it would be dishonorable to deny that my own judgment is squarely against them. When confrontation became violence it became disgraceful; and as a strategy violence did the university more harm than any other single thing in modern times. Education lost the public confidence and its own. But it may be of more use to think of present and future than to dwell on the past.

III

One of the consequences of what happened in the sixties was the separation of intellect and education, the latter expanding while the former receded. The inhibition of mind in education had often been deplored—ascribed to vocationalism, exaggerated specialization, or the deadening effects of policy. Within our own experience other variables have appeared. One is bureaucracy itself. Others are noted here, but the list is not exhaustive: the pursuit of an experience more relevant than thought, accompanied by the rejection of historical evidences and the authority of logic; the discovery that discipline is a Freudian imposition and also objectively bourgeois; the new centrality of politics to thought, although to be sure, not as a systematic study but as a metaphor or applied religion—and, finally, the acceptance of a model based on the natural sciences, which takes education to be the solution of a series of problems and intelligence to be the adjustment of conscience to crisis. The metaphor and story of Faust have been too long forgotten.

It is fairly clear that university intellectual life has undergone some kind of diminution. The idea of the relationship of teacher and student—one of the authentically great motifs of classical and Christian thought—no longer exerts energy or compels legitimacy. If ever there was an I-and-Thou relationship, it was to be found in teaching. But it has been more convenient to honor "commitment" in the abstract than to retain it in the profession. We are by now used to the thought that responsibility to mankind takes precedence over that to men. Thomas Gradgrind is not Dickens's compleat intellectual villain. His complementary half is Mrs. Pardiggle, that great missionary to those far-off places which may be safely served in comfort and at a distance.

Scholarly expertise was among those things affected by bureaucratic growth. It tended to become narrow even as it became accomplished; especially among those whose own training began in the past decade it was possible to find familiarity with what was contemporary joined to ignorance of what was not. Not only was the idea of the Western tradition challenged, which is clearly exactly what intellectual work should involve—but also it was forgotten, which is another case entirely. The new intellectual class, resolutely present- and future-oriented, was so far from being interested in past scholarship or even in the substance of the past itself as to have great difficulty in transmitting to students anything of value on that subject. Instead the values of what has usefully been called the adversary culture were transmitted to the school room. It should be understood that when I remark on this it is not with the thrill of gratified horror at the desecration of a tradition. Traditions, in my view, are made to be broken. However, university intellectual life, instead of being dependent on its own resources, adopted attitudes manufactured by movies, by the commercial world (which has with extraordinary acumen managed to make cultural revolution into a commodity), by the media, and finally by politics.

Perhaps a brief discussion of the curriculum itself will be helpful. It came to be thought with perfect sincerity that the curriculum should reflect "reality" and that it should do so by advocating certain positions in political or social life. A curriculum should be designed to prevent wars or to make people ashamed of conducting them, to better the conditions of minorities, to carry the message of the new student movement. It did not matter that expertise in any or all of these fields was difficult to come by and that their teaching was generally only in the slightest degree susceptible of objectivity and fair play. O. B. Hardison has written of the centrifugal force of the new curriculum and its consistently momentary interest. He remarks with some asperity that now American Indian literature, Hebrew literature (divided into Sephardic and Ashkenazi), Chicano literature, and American-Oriental literature must surely argue for equal representation in competition with other "relevancies." The literature of women is already flourishing and will doubtless soon appear in division by period, genre, region and ethnic group; we may have, he suggests, such future offerings as nineteenth-century black female fiction, or modern poetry by northeastern Puerto Rican males. Since no voice in the culture is wholly lost, the result is something like a tower of Babel. It may be, as he suggests, that it really is an abdication of the responsibility of professionals for them to fail to understand what they are professing or to present its central elements in coherent form. To resolve the problem is beyond my intention or ability; I am simply adducing the fact that among the characteristics of the new intellectual situation is the decisive rejection of professional standards and the authority of the past. This rejection implies that education is not especially concerned with intellect, but views itself as social arbitration; and, of course, that it has no particular body of knowledge which it must labor to identify, preserve, and extend.

The adversary relationship of ancients and moderns has always been with us. Its present form is of special interest, especially as it has been described, among others, by Lionel Trilling, Frank Kermode and Frederick Olafson. I think it can be said in general that Western culture has lost its religious and moral powers of persuasion as far as many intellectuals are concerned. One of the most striking events in what might be called practical metaphysics has been the displacement of objective values by inwardness or "consciousness." Perhaps this is because Romanticism has made us forget the contours and spaciousness of a system within which it was so interesting but so minor a part. It is very much a given of the current condition that self-expression—not to mention self-gratification—has a moral valency. Subjective demands are given primacy over all others, especially those others which assert the claims of a public or a legal nature. Out of the single human identity comes both the consciousness to be affirmed and the judgment as to what values and practices shall proceed in that affirmation. It is a neat solution to the problem raised by Freud in *Civilization and its Discontents*. What we used to honor as the reality principle has now been rejected—which does not much affect reality itself. But the mood of intellectual culture as it affects the self is a mood disregarding that principle—a mood viewing sublimation or repression or accommodation as morally hateful and finding in the gratification of appetite (what Romanticism itself intelligently denied) moral salvation. Because of this, mass culture is necessarily attractive: it promises not only the breakdown of standards of style but the delivery, finally, of wish-fulfillment. In its acceptance of the most persuasive forms of egalitarianism—as well as in the most absurd forms of decadence—it suggests that all of us can in fact have value-free or antinomian lives. Although we are advised to heed each individual voice and register its consciousness on our own, this advice considerably exceeds the mandate of even what used to be called the General Will. Culture, like business or politics, is capable of insolvency. And it is capable of disintegration as well, for there does not correspond to each individual desire an object or experience or doctrine able to satisfy it.

Some values of course affect personal and professional behavior. One of the most fatal of attractions in this century has been the conversion of the intellectual to the political model of ends and behavior. A reasonable amount of reading and personal familiarity with the subject leads me to suggest that for many intellectuals the political end has been more important than the academic means. I say this only after careful review of the reactions of American intellectuals to a variety of matters involving foreign and domestic policies: their responses, for example, to Stalinism, to Third-World governance, to Vietnam protest, to violations of academic customs, habits and laws. It is of course superabundantly clear that politicians also do violence to tradition and procedure. But democratic political life never denies that standards are universal, although in recent intellectual life they have been, so to speak, absolutely relative. Ethics in the sixties were situational, as we can see in the case of academic freedom. We once assumed that all viewpoints were welcome on campus; and the practice of tenure was justified insofar as it guaranteed protection for dissidents. But this great principle, which has withstood many varieties of censorship, has been powerless against moralism. It is surely unnecessary to retell the incredibly long list of offenses against this freedom. What ought to be noted is that the wound was self-inflicted. Intellectuals as individuals or in deliberative bodies took little account of the silencing of views locally unpopular; administrators refused to guarantee the right to such opinions; and boards of review, rather like late southern juries, refused to recognize certain civil violations.

The failure to protect academic freedom turned out to be worse than passively suffered insult or the shame of self-violated integrity. It has been argued for decades that the academy was unique in its regard for ideas and indeed for the disinterested quality of its morality. The acceptance of violations of academic freedom contradicted the structural principle of academic life. It was not surprising therefore to find in universities what historians sometimes call a failure of nerve in their investigations of dead religious or cultural beliefs. And, of course, now that we need academic freedom more than ever, it is difficult to invoke.

The sins of the past never met with more fervid rejection than the reforms that were supposed to have cast them out. It is common today to read essays by academicians stating that their attempt to modify and revolutionize education has alienated students and isolated themselves, in both cases the opposite of what was intended. Some of these essays are quite moving: the reflections of a teacher in Utah who finds himself too old now to find another job, or those of a graduate student in New York who cannot summon up the commitment to enter a weary profession. Some of those who stay find themselves not only without sufficient causes but also without students—and without faith in their occupation, which, like Othello's, is noticeably gone. Others, who take a much harder line culturally, have come to argue that the exercise of intellectual power is in itself not useful. By so doing they have adopted the anti-intellectualism once made famous by the insularity of backwoods and big-business America.

The argument against intellectual traditions used to center on their inadequacy. Now it centers on their illegitimacy. For example, objectivity was once praised in ratio to its exactness. It is now challenged as a mode—in dealing with a whole spectrum of domestic and foreign issues, as well as merely on campus—because it can be thought of as a relic of bourgeois culture, or because it offends certainties, or, finally because it is inconvenient to assert. There are other disintegrative attacks on our understanding of what is complex, actual and diverse. One, the anarchistic, finds experience to be irreducible to value or meaning. All things matter as much or as little as all other things. It is of course philosophically hopeless since it refuses to endow anything with that value it requires to be either asserted or protected. The other, the totalitarian, tries to reduce all it encounters to a single set of meanings: diversity has always been unacceptable to ideology. This attitude is especially irritated by distinctions and standards, which it finds to be either psychologically uncomfortable or analogues of capitalist competitiveness. But it seems futile to deny some kind of measurable difference between human beings. If one interprets it rightly, this is precisely the definition of individualism. Democracy does not promise to make us all the same but only to treat us equally. When it fails to do so it should certainly be criticized—but one does not break the tool that the hand has misguided.

Just as rationality has been attacked because it is inferior to unconsciousness, and objectivity because it discomforts our desires, sanity itself has been judged to be inferior to madness. The implication is that civilized practices are unacceptable when they imply certain kinds of constraints—or that they have entirely lost the power of legitimacy. Lionel Trilling has pointed out that supposedly "authentic" cognition is now pathological. As he puts it, insanity is first of all viewed as an active and significant response to the destructive will of society. The apparent aberration (catatonic silence, rage, delusion) is in fact a liberation from social madness—and a criticism of it. The heartbreaking pain of madness is ignored, he writes, in order to satisfy the impulse (not that of the patient) to find rationality behind the seventh veil of our social sins.

Now, although madness is endemic to Western epic and tragedy, it is not recommended to us as a universal. It offers the final insight of tragedy—but as an apocalyptic punishment, not a reward. And no matter how deep our admiration for Rimbaud and Baudelaire, no matter how measured our respect for De Sade, our view of them retains its clarity only when the difference is observed.

Irrationalism has been described by Charles Frankel as the plaything of affluent literacy. "Both in the United States and abroad," he writes, "its most sympathetic audience comes primarily from the more comfortable and better educated classes, and its central inspiration and emotional thrust have been sustained by people belonging to universities and other institutions whose traditional commitment, officially, has been to the practice and propagation of rational inquiry." In short, the centers of intellectual life are in a serious way anti-intellectual. And they are so in precisely the least expected way: as a reflection of life-styles which in proclaiming their own psychological validity and social acceptability have persuaded academe to imitate them. That is not the business of intelligence.

To summarize then, intellectual life for moderns has been largely institutional, quite unlike its origins. It has of course become a separate *metier*. Intellect today is directed towards the exercise of rather narrow skills and divests itself of any special connection to the authority of the past; the benefits of independence appear to be equally balanced against the loss of jurisdiction over the public imagination. We speak to a great many people, but not for them. Granted the example of the Soviet Union, this may be better than it seems. There is not among intellectuals the unity of purpose, regulation and interest that exists in other professions. But if education is in fact the professional mode of intelligence then it would appear to require a structure of code and precedent.

The great problem for intellectual life has not been politics in itself, although that might appear to have been the case. Intellectuals have been hostile to a social order to which they have seemed increasingly less important. Because of this they are often in opposition to all established things. The adversary culture is the temporary ally of those who think, because its values tend to be the reverse of those generally accepted. That, I should think, is due to change, as soon as it becomes apparent that the adversary culture's mysticism and worship of matter have penetrated to the farthest recess of the middle-class mind.

At present, while many of our institutions have lost their legitimacy, intellectual life has adopted a new and I think temporary identity. Its bias has been toward irrationalism and against method, toward style and against value, toward moral absolutism and against dialogue. But there are violent changes routinely accomplished by history. I suggest, in fact, that the next decade may witness equal but opposite reactions—and that our duty may be to anticipate them, indeed to oppose them.

The lesson of recent experience ought clearly to prepare us this time for change: to maintain our faith in individualism without having it lapse into solipsism or anarchy; to preserve the intellectual environment—and to do so in such a way as to ensure the synthesis of tradition and the individual talent. We may of course fail. When Gibbon wrote of the fat slumbers of the church he meant that it was a comfortable institution believed in by no one. Our own intellectual system may yet enjoy that fate. But I think otherwise.

KENNETH B. CLARK

The American Revolution: Democratic Politics and Popular Education

Delivered in the Little Red Schoolhouse

at St. Charles, Minnesota on April 24, 1974

Nearly two hundred years ago Thomas Jefferson stated the moral basis for the establishment of an independent United States of America: "We hold these truths to be self-evident that all men are created equal, that they are endowed by their Creator with certain unalienable rights." This assertion of the equality of man was not in itself new. It had its religious roots in the Judaeo-Christian attempts to control the more primitive impulses of man by identifying religion with man's responsibility for his fellow man. The principle probably had its most systematic philosophical roots in the seventeenth-century rationalism of John Locke, which laid the foundation for political democracy upon the premise that every human being entered this world as a blank slate (*tabula rosa*) and that all were therefore equal. Locke's insistence that whatever differences were found among groups of human beings had to be explained by postnatal experiential and environmental differences may be viewed as the rationale for the democratic demands and revolutions that have dominated the world since his time. The idea of the inherent equality among human beings marked the end of the doctrine of the divine rights of kings and a significant stage in the disintegration of the feudal world.

When man began to believe that all human beings were

potentially equal and that differences in status were neither
ordained by God nor biologically determined, then man
could look to remedy existing inequalities and injustices by
controlling and manipulating the environment. This is probably one of the most revolutionary ideas ever to take hold in
the human mind. Not only Thomas Jefferson and the other
Founding Fathers of the American Revolution, not only the
architects of the French Revolution, but also Marx and
Engels, even perhaps Lenin, and more recently Mahatma
Gandhi, Martin Luther King and other fighters for racial and
economic justice in America and throughout the world—all
have been influenced by the seventeenth-century egalitarian
philosophy of John Locke.

It is ironic that even as Thomas Jefferson expressed this
democratic premise as the basis for the founding of this new
nation, his own predicament as a slaveholder and as an
apologist for the continuation of slavery in the United States
was a symptom of the schizophrenia which continues to
afflict the American social and political system. The fact
remains, however, that in spite of its many contradictions,
the United States was the first nation which asserted its right
to independence in moral and ethical rather than economic
or military terms. In spite of many violations of its democratic ideals in day-to-day practical politics, the value of
America's insistence upon its democratic ideals must not be
underestimated. These democratic ideals have provided a motive power for the ongoing and necessary struggle for justice
and equality. They continue to provide the foundation for
the expansion of democratic public education in the United
States. And they have provided critical support for the general civil rights movement which started with the earliest abolitionists, continued through the Emancipation Proclamation,
and was intensified in the persistent twentieth-century struggles to eliminate the last vestiges of state-controlled racial
inequities.

Probably the earliest problem in reconciling the egalitarian
ideals stated in the Declaration of Independence with the
existence of human slavery in the New World came to the
surface with the controversy about whether the African slaves

and their children should be converted to Christianity and be taught to read and to write. This controversy combined both religious and educational issues. Those who opposed the conversion and education of the African slaves tended to support their argument with the assertion that the African slaves were not quite human. Ironically, this unprecedented need to deny full humanity to the African slaves seems to have stemmed from the fact that the white European slaveholders were themselves Christian. The view that the African slaves were not quite human could be used to exempt white Christians from any sense of guilt over the inevitable cruelties and dehumanization inherent in human slavery, a sense of guilt that would otherwise be commanded by the Christian requirement to love and protect one's fellow human beings. Indeed, books written by clergymen in the late seventeenth century and throughout the eighteenth century sought to justify slavery by alluding to that part of the Bible wherein God gave man dominion over the beasts of the field. These men of the cloth unashamedly asserted that the beasts of the field included African slaves.

The eighteenth-century Americans who opposed slavery and who argued for conversion and education of the Africans insisted not only that slavery was a basic violation of Christianity, but also that Africans were as human as Europeans. The first civil rights struggle was won when it was decided to convert the slaves to Christianity and to teach some of them to read and write. The fact that the slaves from Africa and their descendants could indeed be taught the same skills Europeans had been taught refuted the basic argument for their sub-humanity and made possible subsequent struggles for the extension of democratic rights to the African slaves and their descendants.

The struggle to extend American democratic ideals to the descendants of the African slaves, to the indigenous native American Indians, and to other nonwhite groups in America has been continuous, albeit irregular in its progress. It has been marked by periods of dynamism and by periods of stagnation. By its nature and its essence, it has been a barometer of the vitality and strength of the democratic system envisioned and articulated by Thomas Jefferson. Indeed, this struggle, which persists up to the present, may be viewed as the main theme within which the complexities and the dimensions of American history can be best understood. From this perspective, the following emerge as dominant qualities in American history:

1. The articulation of democratic ideals and aspirations as the foundation of the American political system provided and continues to provide a powerful basis for the struggle to realize these ideals, in spite of repeated practical violations and continued forms of cruelty and injustice.

2. Various groups of Europeans who have migrated to America seeking economic, political and educational advantages for themselves and their children have benefitted from the American system of democracy. They have been provided with opportunities for improving their status, if not the quality of their lives, because the American democratic system has worked well within certain limits.

3. Built into the American political and educational system are safeguards against the more flagrant forms of governmental tyranny and abuses which would dehumanize individuals and reduce large groups of human beings to the levels of resignation, stagnation and despair which are likely to be found in authoritarian regimes.

4. The continuous struggle of the descendants of African slaves in America to make the promises of the American democratic system real for them has not been without some significant successes. This is true despite the fact that their particular struggle for democracy and equality of opportunity has been fulfilled more slowly than the struggle of white European ethnic groups. Black Americans were released from slavery in the early nineteenth century in the North and in the late nineteenth century in the South. Since emancipation, black Americans have used the federal courts, the Congress, the legislative branches of state government and, in some cases, the authority and the prestige of the President of the United States to protect themselves from more flagrant forms of racial cruelty, rejection and dehumanization.

5. No democratic gains achieved by black Americans have

been restricted to blacks alone. These gains have strengthened democracy for all Americans.

Next to the Emancipation Proclamation itself, the *Brown*
decision of May 17, 1954 could be viewed as the most
significant demonstration that the instruments of the American democratic system can be used effectively in the struggle
for racial justice. This historic decision of twenty years ago—
in spite of the fact that it has not been fully implemented,
and in spite of the growing percentages of black children in
racially segregated public schools in such northern urban
areas as New York, Chicago, Detroit, Philadelphia, Boston,
and Los Angeles—nonetheless remains as a monumental
reaffirmation of the vitality of the Jeffersonian formulation of
American ideals. It demonstrates a democratic and rational
alternative to the quest for justice and equality through irra-
tional and inhumane violence. It continues to be an outstanding symbol of the fact that human beings need not accept injustice and social cruelty passively, that they need not
succumb to the ultimate condition of total dehumanization
—namely, the refusal to struggle for justice and humanity.
The *Brown* decision remains a powerful indication that democracy provides not only the basis for hope, but also the instruments for achieving what is hoped for. Those of us who
are concerned with the complex interrelationship of democratic politics and popular education find it important that
the *Brown* decision dealt specifically with education as the
basis of a stable democracy. In his simple and direct decision,
Chief Justice Earl Warren stated:

> Today, education is perhaps the most important func-
> tion of state and local governments. Compulsory school
> attendance laws and the great expenditures for education
> both demonstrate our recognition of the importance of
> education in our democratic society. . . . It is the very
> foundation of good citizenship.[1]

Certainly the tortuously slow pace of changing the biracial
educational system in America into a democratic nonracial
system shows that no single decision nor single democratic in-

[1] Brown v. Board of Education, 347 U.S. 483, 493 (1954).

stitution can magically transform deep-seated forces of prejudices, fears, hatreds, anxieties, and conflicts. American racism, especially the reaffirmation of racism in its institutionalized forms, has deep roots in almost every human being brought up under those forms. The depth of American racism makes it difficult for its detrimental consequences to be remedied within society as a whole and within the individuals who have lived according to racist forms.

The problem which must be faced and resolved by those of us who seek to strengthen American democracy—who seek to fulfill the 200-year-old Jeffersonian promise of desegregating American education as a necessary prerequisite to curing society as a whole of the poisons of systematic racism—is to find the formula whereby the individuals who are themselves products of segregated schools, who bear the deep scars of racist indoctrination inherent in racially segregated education, can become agents in protecting their own children from this social disease. This is the critical contemporary problem of the struggle for democratic politics and popular education in America. It is the problem which must be resolved if American democracy is to maintain the vitality necessary to survive.

II

In what follows I have set forth some ideas on the ways in which it might be possible to resolve the tantalizing, elusive problem of how to engage those who are the products of racially segregated schools as agents in transforming the American educational system into a nonracial democratic system—or, at least, to prevent them from serving as obstacles to such transformation and thereby continuing to infect their children with the disease of racism. And let us make no mistake here: racism is a disease.

The first step in this process has already been taken. It is important that the powers of the federal government, particularly the federal courts, continue to be used to make it clear that racially segregated schools not only violate the equal protection clause of the Fourteenth Amendment of the United States Constitution, but also are patently in conflict with the principles of the Declaration of Independence and are, as well, a powerful dehumanizing force. There can be no retreat from this essential foundation for the desegregation of American educational institutions. The law must be clear. There must be no equivocation on the part of governmental officials, particularly those charged with the responsibility of clarifying and enforcing the law. The foundation of any democratic system must be respect for the organic law, and officials who enforce the law must do so without favor or prejudice. Indeed, responsible public officials in a stable democracy must interpret, uphold and enforce the laws in spite of their personal attitudes and biases. This is the *sine qua non*.

While recognizing this fact, one must also recognize the paradox that in a democracy in which legislative and executive officials are elected by the majority of the voting citizenry, there will be temptations on the part of these officials to respond to the wishes and the prejudices of their constituents. Not infrequently, such officials will (under the guise of responding to the democratic will of the people) decide that a practical and pragmatic form of democracy requires the subordination of the rights of minorities to the prejudices of the majority. In my view—and I am not alone—President Nixon is a clear example of an executive who is responsive to (and has even encouraged) the passions and fears of the majority, in racial questions no less than others. This is indeed "the tyranny of the majority." It demonstrates one of the problems so clearly stated by Alexis de Tocqueville in his brilliant analysis of the complexities of the American democratic system—that tyranny is possible not only under feudalism and aristocracy but also under democracy, and the democratic form is the most insidious.

When permitted to operate in accordance with the vision of the Founding Fathers, the American system does in fact provide safeguards against this form of tyranny. These safeguards—these checks and balances—determine whether democracy is real or feigned. They are the democratic gyroscopes. Probably the strongest safeguard, reflecting the wis-

dom of the Founding Fathers, is to be found in the fact that
the federal judiciary is not directly responsible to popular
will. The independence of the federal judiciary, together with
the fact that the executive and legislative branches of the federal and state governments are directly responsible to their
constituents, is one of the most important protections for
democracy in the American political system. It is understandable that the initiative in the recent stages in the struggle for
racial democracy in America came from the federal courts.

It is a testament to the American democratic system that
once the federal courts made it clear that the promises of democracy could not be qualified by arbitrary and irrelevant
grounds of race or color, the legislative and executive
branches followed suit. The Congress of the United States
passed important civil rights legislation in the latter part of
the 1950s and the 1960s. In spite of his personal opinions,
President Dwight D. Eisenhower ordered federal troops to
enforce the desegregation decision in Little Rock, Arkansas.
President John F. Kennedy, in the later years of his aborted
administration, provided an atmophere of positive movement
toward strengthening civil rights and civil liberties as desirable and long-delayed goals in the fulfillment of American democracy. And were it not for his entanglement in the tragic
ambiguities of the purposeless Vietnam War, it would even
now be clear that President Lyndon B. Johnson contributed
more to racial progress in America than any other President
in the 200 years of American history.

The civil rights retrogression in the past six years must
therefore be seen as a problem in the moral and ethical leadership of the Nixon administration. Even as one confronts
the administration's contribution to stagnation in civil rights
progress, one also confronts the complexities of the American
political system and the fact that a process, once started, is
not easy to stop. The rate of public school desegregation in
the seventeen southern states which had laws requiring or
permitting racial segregation prior to 1954 has proceeded at
an accelerated pace during the Nixon administration. Even
as Mr. Nixon was unashamedly seeking the votes of southern-

ers and racially constrictive northern whites, even as he was competing successfully for the votes which ordinarily would have gone to George Wallace for primitive racial reasons, federal governmental officials were applying pressures against southern segregation. And today more than 50 percent of all black children in southern states are in racially desegregated schools.

The most powerful resistance to desegregation in American public schools is now to be found in northern urban communities. It is these cities of the North, which managed to maintain an image of racial liberalism when the intensity of the civil rights struggle was concentrated in the South, that are now the bastions of anti-busing slogans and such code words as "quotas" and "preferential treatment," all clearly designed to maintain the racially discriminatory status quo. Twenty years after the *Brown* decision there are more white and black children in northern cities attending racially segregated schools than there were at the time of the decision. Somehow, white southerners must help northern whites to understand that racially segregated schools not only dehumanize black children but inflict deep, debilitating, and immobilizing moral conflicts upon white children. Somehow, a way must be found to communicate to the majority of white Americans that racially segregated schools in the latter part of the twentieth century contaminate their children in many complex, subtle and conflicting ways, impairing their ability to function as morally and intellectually effective human beings. Some way must be found to communicate to the majority of American citizens, white and black, the fact that the continuation of racially segregated schools threatens the very foundations of a stable democratic society for all American citizens.

Ordinarily one would look to religious leaders for the moral and ethical guidance necessary to communicate the ideas of democracy to the American populace. But the organized church in America has defaulted. It has made its peace with practical politics and power, and appears content to give lip service to religious and democratic principles of the broth-

erhood of man. Indeed, the organized church and its spokesmen appear to be rationalizers for American racism in the
tradition of their seventeenth and eighteenth century counterparts.

Because religious leaders have defaulted, one must turn to
economic and industrial leaders for moral guidance. It would
seem to be clear that the continuation of American racism
reinforced by racially segregated schools, particularly in industrial urban centers, would be an economic liability. Racially
segregated schools, outcast foster children of the system,
produce hundreds of thousands of functional illiterates each
year. The victims of this social disgrace are not prepared to
become part of a dynamic and growing economy. In the
main, they are relegated to the status of income consumers
rather than producers. They are consigned to welfare roles,
other forms of dependency, and correctional institutions. It
would appear that a democratic capitalist economy would put
high priority on using economic and financial power to convert this persistent economic and human liability to an asset.
There remains, however, a strange timidity on the part of the
economic powers to demand the remedy for this pervasive
inefficiency. This timidity defies the simplistic interpretations
of Karl Marx. Is it possible that a nation which made the
critical financial policy decision to use American dollars to
rebuild the economies of European nations in the post-
World War II years in order to facilitate sound and stable international trade is immobilized by racism from demanding
the reorganization of our educational system so that American citizens will be educated to be constructive members of
the society without regard to their race? Is the country that
made the capitalist decision which resulted in the implementation and the success of the Marshall Plan and the AID program (particularly for Europe) incapable, because of racism,
to make the capitalist decision to use its potential financial
and industrial strength to rebuild the blighted areas of American cities and to shore up the education and the economy of
all of the underdeveloped groups in the nation itself? If the
answer to these questions is yes, then it would follow that

American racism is a terminal disease and that the promises of American democracy will not only be withheld from blacks but, being so withheld, will in the end be withheld from all Americans.

In seeking to get the American people to understand the serious threats inherent in the perpetuation of racism and racially segregated schools—and the extent to which the foundations of democracy are based upon nonracial democratic schools—one must look, finally, at the role of educators and those who are responsible for the organization and administration of our educational institutions. These men and women somehow must be made to understand that education is in fact, to recall the chief justice's words, "the most important function of state and local governments . . ." and "the very foundation of good citizenship," and that democratic education is absolutely essential to the perpetuation of a democratic society. Probably the first step in the reorganization of American education for the purpose of stabilizing American democracy and giving vitality to the American political system is for educators to grasp this essential nature of education and to assert it without apology. The goals of education can no longer be defined in terms of transmitting and acquiring mere academic skills. The greatest danger facing contemporary man, not only in America but throughout the world, is the danger of trained intelligence isolated from moral and ethical concerns. Educational institutions in America must find some way to emphasize the fact that a functioning moral and ethical sensitivity is the primary mark of an educated human being.

This sensitivity (which underlies our Declaration of Independence) certainly cannot be obtained in racially segregated schools. But the teaching of moral sensitivity as a primary goal in the educational process at all levels is not restricted to questions of race. If one could find a way of communicating to the American people the fact that racial cruelties are merely a part of the much larger problem of man's inhumanity to man, then it might be possible to deal more effectively with the problem of racial segregation in

American schools. It is imperative to demonstrate to the American people that educational procedures which require children to learn early in the elementary grades that they must compete with their friends and their classmates for grades plant dangerous seeds of inhumanity. There are ways in which standards of excellence and the necessity for each child to achieve his full moral and intellectual potential can be demonstrated without instilling the view that "if *he* gets an A, that takes something away from *me*." There must be ways in which intellectually gifted children can be taught, as an important part of their education, that their gift is a social trust to be used to help others who are less endowed. Attempts to help intellectually gifted children or children with other special and socially desired talents by isolating them from their fellow human beings are, on their face, self-defeating. No human being, no matter how talented, can use his abilities and skills effectively in isolation. To segregate these children from their fellows is to damage them intellectually and morally. Intellectual segregation like racial segregation impairs moral and social effectiveness.

It is my belief that these ideas, and especially the idea of gifts held in trust, somehow must become an integral part of the American educational system. Education will become the functioning instrument of a stable democracy by being in all its stages and dimensions an example of the democratic process. Within this framework, the desegregation of our schools can proceed; and with the desegregation of our schools, we can achieve that more difficult stage—the true integration of our schools whereby they can become instruments to reinforce that understanding and acceptance of our fellow men which gives substance to life. It is my belief that we can communicate to the American people the truth that this moral education is essential not only to American democracy, but also to the survival of the human species. It should be possible to help the American people to understand and act upon the understanding that, to borrow from de Tocqueville, ". . . it depends upon themselves whether the principle of equality [democracy] is to lead them to servitude or freedom, to knowledge or barbarism, to prosperity or to wretchedness."[2]

Two hundred years of the continuing struggle for democracy in America should make us believe that the struggle eventually will be successful.

[2] Alexis de Tocqueville, *Democracy in America*, eds. J. P. Mayer and Max Lerner (New York: Harper & Row, 1966), p. 680.

FORREST CARLISLE POGUE

The Revolutionary Transformation of the Art of War

Delivered at the United States Military Academy

at West Point, New York on May 9, 1974

Tonight we meet at "the river and the rock." Completed under the eye of General Washington, this largest American fortress of the Revolution frustrated British hopes of controlling the Hudson and splitting off the New England colonies from the rest of America.

Triumphant even in the face of treason, West Point is a fitting place for an assessment of the change in warfare that occurred during the American and French revolutionary era, 1775–1802.

As we approach the 200th anniversary of the War for Independence, we shall retell myths, legends, and solemn truths. One of the myths of the Revolution is that Frederick the Great of Prussia described the fighting by Washington's forces around Trenton and Princeton in the period from December 25, 1776 to January 4, 1777 as the most brilliant campaign in the history of warfare. This appeared only as "it is said" in Benson Lossing's 1859 volume on the war. It was disproved in a series of scholarly articles around the turn of the century and supposedly finished off conclusively by Major General Francis V. Greene in 1911. But it still survives.[1]

---

[1] Francis V. Green, *The Revolutionary War and the Military Policy of the United States* (Port Washington, N.Y.: Kennikat Press, 1967 [1911]), p. 83.

The myth persists because the great European commander of the period should have praised one of the key campaigns of the war. Trenton and Princeton were the signal that the Continental Army had come of age and was in the war to stay. Lexington, Concord and Bunker Hill had been unexpected acts of defiance, but they had been followed by poor troop performance and defective generalship which had forced the American withdrawal in late 1776 with considerable losses from New York to the temporary safety of New Jersey.

Almost discredited at Christmas time, Washington faced the fact that most of the members of his Continental Army, weakened and confused, would soon leave him when their terms expired at the end of the year. Cinderella's prospects near the stroke of midnight could not have been more disheartening. So the so-called "American Fabius," heir to a generation of orthodox military solutions, placed his career on the line. In an almost hopeless situation he decided to use his troops while there was yet time. The weather was abominable, the odds extreme, the river virtually impassable because of the ice. A more cautious man would have stayed in winter quarters.

For his crossing of the Delaware he had the assistance of Captain John Glover's Marblehead regiment whose boatmen had already helped to evade the British in the retreat from Long Island. During the cold and stormy night of December 25th he crossed the river, perhaps not so grandly as Leutze has portrayed him, but perkily at least, in a scene so clearly made for Hollywood that no motion picture of the event has ever been convincing. Shortly after daybreak, he arrived at Trenton to awaken Colonel Rall and his Hessians. The enemy was surprised—whether because of Christmas Eve frivolities too long extended or the customary hard drinking of the commander does not matter—and most members of the garrison were taken prisoner. Slipping back across the river, Washington reformed his troops and returned to Trenton a few days later. Nettled, Cornwallis gathered his forces and declared that he had trapped the fox. With stratagems worthy of Ulysses, Washington left his campfires burning and marched off to Princeton for a surprising victory there before the British commander could bring up his troops. With promises of extra pay and perhaps some eloquent persuasion, he had kept his vanishing Continentals the vital days necessary for a stunning victory. The victory was not enough to turn the tide or to avoid a troubled winter. But it comforted patriots to feel that well-fed and well-liquored gentlemen in comfortable London clubs recognized that the surprising performances of the colonists at Lexington and Concord and Bunker Hill were not flukes. And there was ground for hope. Yet so slender was the margin—as later shown at Valley Forge and Morristown—that one can understand why Washington and other sons of eighteenth-century rationalism could find explanation of their narrow escapes only in the hand of Providence.

Frederick could not have been expected to applaud a type of fighting so different from the eighteenth-century variety in which he excelled. A monarch who had made war his main pursuit preferred the careful course of eighteenth-century battles to the sudden improvisations being carried out by half-trained civilians under generals not of noble birth. He would have been less pleased had he known that this war began the quarter-century that would transform the type of conflict of which he was the great master and challenge the type of troops and training with which he had won his great reputation.

As beautifully orchestrated as a minuet, replete with artful positions in which each exercise of the soldier and the loading and firing of a weapon were virtually choreographed, Frederick's battles and those of his contemporaries were well-executed set-piece maneuvers, seemingly designed to stress lack of excess and limitation of extravagant action. Although the eighteenth century was marked by disease, brutal discipline and death, the warfare had mannerly overtones. A philosophy of restraint marked courts and armies dominated by men in elegant dress and powdered wigs.[2]

[2] For descriptions of eighteenth-century armies and warfare, see chapter 3 on "Frederick the Great, Guilbert and Bulow," and chapter 5 on "Clausewitz," in E. M. Earle, ed., *Makers of Modern*

Wars in this era were fought mainly for dynastic reasons. One went to war in the eighteenth century to prevent the union of two powerful houses, to press a shadowy claim ungallantly on a new-crowned queen, to prevent a frontier strongpoint or a stray duchy from passing into unfriendly hands, or to join one's powerful neighbors in despoiling a weakened colleague. This maneuvering for advantage was not peculiar to Frederick's century, but it seemed that the War of Austrian Succession and the Seven Years' War, no matter how untidy their overseas phases proved to be, were fought for limited objectives. Somewhat more exciting than the hunt, a well-organized campaign (followed by a social season) could occupy the time of officers from the court and test the men forced into battle. The fighting was not entirely devoid of danger—disease and exposure could carry off more men than musket fire—but there was the opportunity to execute on the ground well-sketched designs performed in perfect patterns.

Behind this theory of warfare was the careful planning of the monarchs of the period. Most armies belonged to the King—in Frederick's case to a monarch who led his troops in the field, or in the case of England to a monarch who shared his powers with certain cliques in the Houses of Parliament. Monarchs like Frederick saw their nations' prosperity as dependent on the work of artisans and the labor of peasants. They did not wish to lose the labor of producers nor to place their crops and manufactures at the mercy of men in conflict. So it seemed expedient to take for fighting in the ranks and leadership in the field the men who contributed least to the prosperity of the state. High command was reserved for members of the nobility or the gentry, and many of the troops were drawn from the prisons, from the unemployed ranks, or from somewhat better men who were impressed into service. Once recruited—and recruitment was a process that included men taken in drink or duped or even kidnapped—

Strategy: Military Thought from Machiavelli to Hitler (Princeton: Princeton University Press, 1943); and Walter L. Dorn, Competition for Empire, 1740–1763 (New York: Harper & Row, 1940), chapter 3.

the men were made to serve under the lash. Brutal floggings were used in both the armies and navies of the time to keep a man in line. By careful drills repeated interminably—it took three to five years of endless exercises to train a proper product—the soldier was taught to perform dutifully on the battlefield, firing in well-arranged and well-articulated formations. But such men could not be trusted in long campaigns in foreign lands.[3]

Those local contingents were often augmented by a more hapless lot. Foreign mercenaries, paid for at so much a head plus an annual subsidy, enriched their princes. They might become attached to their regiment or take a certain pleasure in a campaign well fought. But they had no pride in serving the foreign prince or state. The sovereign treated them with a certain care—one did not willingly damage an expensively trained hireling, nor willingly press an attack on an enemy which could destroy a valuable unit. Campaigns, therefore, did not involve battles to the death, but were restricted to maneuvers for position and for demonstrations of power. There was much to admire in such performances, but they had the same artificial elegance that characterized many paintings of the period.

Few things marked the transformation of eighteenth-century warfare more than the later shift away from mercenaries. The use of paid foreign troops was not new in Europe. They had been used in the late Middle Ages, the Renaissance, and the religious wars, shifting from allegiance to allegiance as opportunities dictated, sometimes exploiting their position to seize power from the ruler who paid them. Machiavelli, searching for means to bring order to the Italian states, reminded his ideal prince that he must beware of mercenaries: "In peace you are despoiled by them and in war by your enemies. The cause of this is that they have no love or other motive to keep them in the field beyond a trifling wage, which is not enough to make them ready to die for you."[4]

---

[3] J. R. Western, "Armed Forces and the Art of War," *Cambridge Modern History* (Cambridge: Cambridge University Press, 1965), vol. 8, pp. 190–216.

[4] Niccolo Machiavelli, *The Prince* (London: Dent and Sons, Everyman edition, 1938), p. 66.

But they still made up a substantial part of the force that General Sir William Howe insisted he would need to reduce the American rebels to submission. Ultimately they numbered approximately 30,000 troops, nearly half from Hesse-Cassel and the rest from Hesse-Hanau, Brunswick, Anspach-Bayreuth, Waldeck, and Anhalt-Zerbst. Opponents of the King's party in the British Parliament attacked the practice, some basing their opposition on the danger of introducing so large a foreign army into his Majesty's colonies. Schiller was critical in one of his contemporary plays. Frederick of Prussia, who regularly kidnapped troops from his neighbors, refused the mercenaries free passage through his state, saying that he would tax them as cattle since they were being sold as beasts. When well led, the Hessians, as all the German mercenaries were called, fought well, but the British paid a price in increased opposition from the colonists, and Jefferson reserved a place in the Declaration of Independence for savage condemnation of their use. Of the 30,000 Hessians, more than 12,000 did not return home and, of those 5,000 were listed as deserters.[5]

Besides the mercenaries, the British could count on seasoned British soldiers (many of them originally secured like the soldiers of other continental powers to which we have alluded), some American units organized from colonial troops in earlier fighting, and American Loyalist units created after the beginning of the war. To these they added Indian allies, whose performance was nearly always untrustworthy and whose barbarities provoked violent resentment in areas where they were used, thus cancelling the overall value of any contribution they may have made.

The militia had constituted the colonial fighting forces on the eve of the Revolution. Some form of military service had been a tradition of the British since the days of the Anglo-Saxons. This concept was brought to American shores by the early settlers and had been nurtured by the requirements placed on frontier communities by the threat of hostile Indi-

[5] For information on German mercenaries, see Edward J. Lowell, *The Hessians* (Port Washington, N.Y.: The Kennikat Press, 1965 [1884]).

ans or the aggression of French and Spanish neighbors. Often the men of militia age, mustering periodically for drill, provoked laughter by their awkwardness, and their inept officers drew jibes. Many deserved the jeers and their value increased only through additional time given to drill and to the extent capable leadership was available. Poorly led or not, they were paying a duty owed the state and gaining practice in citizenship.[6] As a teen-ager in Kentucky, I was required with other men under fifty to give two or three days of labor each year on the county roads. I thought of the service as menial and was amazed to hear that my grandfather or my uncle had performed this same labor when they were younger. It was only later, when I read John Stuart Mill on *Representative Government*, that I could understand the importance of some public service to the state in the development of a democratic society. While he spoke of nonmilitary activities, listing jury duty or the fulfillment of parish obligations, Mill stressed "the moral part of the instruction afforded by the participation of the private citizen, if even rarely, in public functions."[7]

In a country where most males grew up learning to handle firearms and where a premium was placed on marksmanship in the shooting of game, it was possible to find men who could defend their firesides with little training. But tactics were improvised and the leadership of units larger than a company difficult to supply. In the Seven Years' War, the British discovered the value of the tactics developed by the colonists for fighting Indians. Already aware of the value of light infantry formations, they explored the use of a scouting unit, such as that organized by Robert Rogers, whose members developed the stamina and stealth of savages, reduced to the lowest number the items they had to carry on the trail, and practiced the arts of concealment and surprise. The scouts were highly individualistic and hard to control, a factor which led some British commanders—including James

---

[6] Daniel J. Boorstin, *The Americans: The Colonial Experience* (New York: Random House, 1958), pp. 345–372.

[7] John Stuart Mill, *Considerations on Representative Government* (New York: The Liberal Arts Press, 1958 [1861]), p. 54.

Wolfe—to condemn them as useless. But others believed
that ranger training and ranger tactics could be used well
with picked men. Ranger tactics did not meet the demands
of stylized regiments, but they forecast one of the military
transformations fostered in the course of the American Revolution. British commanders complained of units which issued
suddenly from the swamps or the forests, moving silently and
quickly and behaving with touches of the savagery of the Indians whom they imitated.

Unfortunately the militiamen were seldom well led, well
trained, or well equipped, but they were persuaded of the
rightness of their cause. Just by drilling together they practiced the art of resistance to England and they prepared, as
best they could, for the shock of battle. As a practical matter,
they stored up powder and other munitions of war and laid
plans for protecting their magazines, their homes and their
fellow citizens, who were already under suspicion or even
under ban by the British.

Thus, even before the actual confrontation on Lexington
Green, there was a revolutionary transformation in the thinking of certain colonists concerning the art of war. What was
now involved was not simple service to the Crown or preparation against local riots or Indian depredations, but serious
military resistance to trained troops sent to enforce government decrees. Not yet did the colonists envisage actual independence, but free men were preparing local forces that
would serve American towns and colonies against British coercion. The militia, far from being prepared for real service in
the cause of independence, was merely arming to protect
American rights as they saw them—activity outside the assumptions of the earlier militia and foreign to eighteenth-century European notions of the proper working of an army.

In the initial fighting the colonists depended on the militia
of New England. Shortly before the battle of Bunker Hill,
these forces were adopted by the Continental Congress as the
basis of the Continental Army. On the same day—June 14,
1775—ten companies of infantry were authorized to be
raised from Virginia, Maryland, and Pennsylvania for Continental Army service. A day later Washington was selected as

commander-in-chief. By fall it was assumed that a force of slightly more than 20,000 would be satisfactory for 1776 but, at the beginning of that year, Washington found the Continental Army to consist of only 8,000 enlistees. It was an indication of what the future would provide. For the remainder of the war he had to depend on short-term militia to make up the difference between the troops provided and the army of well-trained men enlisted for long-term service which he desired.

Washington swore *by* his Continentals but more often *at* the militia. In times of great frustration, he berated the militiamen as totally hopeless and begged to be relieved of dependence on such useless soldiers. But he recognized that men suddenly summoned from their homes, with only the meager training of occasional drills, could not stand in the face of heavy assaults. Men unaccustomed to cold steel often broke before British or Hessian charges. Even the Continental, better led and somewhat better trained, was not yet ready for severe tests of fire.

Fortunately for the young army, a drillmaster appeared at a critical time. Son of a Prussian officer who had also served for a time in the Russian Army, Frederick von Steuben—who had gained a captaincy in the Prussian service and, for a time, a place on Frederick the Great's staff—appeared in Paris seeking military employment abroad. He laid claim to the title of baron and the rank of lieutenant general. Whether or not his sponsors, French War Minister St. Germain and American representatives Benjamin Franklin and Silas Deane, blindly accepted his claims to high rank in the Prussian Army, they were satisfied that he knew tactics and drill and were willing to certify his claims in the hope of impressing the Continental Congress, which had become wary of foreign soldier-adventurers who came demanding high rank on the basis of titles and service that would not always bear close scrutiny.

Soon aware that von Steuben could train men and that he did not consider it beneath his dignity to drill small groups in demonstrations that any American commander could copy and soon pass on to other units, Washington gave him broad powers to prepare a manual of drill regulations which would become standard for the American forces for more than a generation. There was no great revolutionary transformation involved, but von Steuben recognized the necessity of simplifying the rules and establishing relatively simple maneuvers suited to American needs.

The genius of Washington is reflected in his search for better grounding in orthodox European military methods and for tactics adapted to the American soldier. From the American experience, British leaders learned that free men, motivated by a desire to protect their homes and to gain a larger degree of independence from overseas rule, could rally after tremendous hardships or overwhelming defeat.

The British would find in the wilds of North America, as the French would find later in Spain and Russia, the folly of using conventional methods against a foe fighting in his own hills and swamps and deep forests—a foe who could disappear and then suddenly reappear strengthened for another attack. Able to get local supplies or to live off the land, the Americans carried fewer provisions than the British and relied less on vulnerable supply lines which hampered mobility and made surprise attacks virtually impossible. The European armies would learn the lessons in the revolutionary wars in America and Europe, but would have to be reminded of these truths in later conflicts, even as Americans in our own day have to find again the cunning which they seemed to have had instinctively in an earlier era.

It is important for us to recall—in a period when many emergent nations are still engaging in revolutionary or national wars—some of the lessons which the British learned from the revolutionary militia of America. John Shy, in an essay written in 1973 on "The Military Conflict as a Revolutionary War," has paid tribute to these often maligned troops. "The militia," he says,

> enforced law and maintained order wherever the British did not, and its presence made the movement of smaller British formations dangerous. . . . The militia nullified regularly every British attempt to impose royal British authority short of using massive armed force. . . . From

the British viewpoint, the militia was a virtually inexhaustible reservoir of rebel military manpower, and it was also the sand in the gears of the pacification machine.[8]

II

British bewilderment at the performance of the militia was second only to their surprise at the capable leadership of the rebel forces. It had not been unusual in an earlier era to find men from low estate rising to command in times of upheaval. In the Middle Ages, dominated by royalty and the great lords, there had always been advancement for an able squire or a bright cleric through the army or the Church. But in time, the higher offices of both were closed almost entirely to all save those of noble birth or those of wealth who could purchase a commission or use their political connections to win place. A glance at some of the portraits in the British National Gallery of eighteenth-century adolescents in their splendid uniforms will underline the point.

Without military schools or a standing army, the colonies had no pool of officers on which to draw in 1775, and they searched frantically for men with some military service, wherever acquired, and for those showing any natural gift for leadership, self-educated by a few military manuals obtained from Europe. It was not surprising that in the early mobilization of units, some of which elected their officers, there were men ignorant of military leadership in charge of some companies. Hessians were shocked to find that some of them were men of low estate—some mended or made boots for the German prisoners in their charge.[9]

For the first years of the Revolution, however much the colonies recognized the need of trained officers, their officer corps had to be largely improvised and trained in the field. The Continental Army had selected as its commander-in-

[8] Stephen G. Kurtz and James H. Huston, eds., *Essays on the American Revolution* (Chapel Hill, N.C.: University of North Carolina Press, 1973), p. 148.

[9] Lowell, *The Hessians*, pp. 187–188.

chief a onetime surveyor and successful farmer whose military
background had consisted only of a colonelcy in the Virginia
militia. In the British army of that era, he might have
reached the lesser command on the basis of his fortune, his
fine horsemanship, and certain similarities to a British
country gentleman. The British recognized Charles Lee and
Horatio Gates as officers who had gained a certain knowledge
of their *metier* by service in British forces, but scarcely a
knowledge sufficient for command of a large force in battle.
Some of the foreigners could be grudgingly accepted: von
Steuben, Pulaski, de Kalb, Kosciusko, and the young and
untried "boy," as Cornwallis described the Marquis de
Lafayette. But what of thirty-three-year-old Nathanael
Greene, an iron forger, often ranked as one of the three best
generals in the American forces; of fat Henry Knox, who had
learned his knowledge of artillery from the treatises on war
stocked in his bookstore; or Benedict Arnold, variously
described as an apothecary's apprentice, a merchant in drugs
and books, and a smuggler in trade with the Caribbean
Islands?

The books of John Alden and Don Higginbotham recall
the success of these unlikely generals. Fighting in familiar
areas with men they had trained, and unhampered by lessons
of warfare which they had to forget, a strange assortment of
commanders and a mixed bag of Continentals and militia
defeated the British plan for cutting off New England from
the rest of the colonies and for making the Hudson a British
thoroughfare. Stubborn Dutchmen were summoned hurriedly
against St. Leger's attempted drive from Oswego by way of
Fort Stanwix. Tough John Stark inflicted heavy losses on
British and Hessians at Bennington while Schuyler's active
woodsmen made life miserable for Burgoyne's forces slowly
advancing from the north. Burgoyne, demanding short shrift
for American rebels and closing his eyes for political reasons
to the revolting cruelties of his Indian allies, proved more the
weary and cynical Gentleman Johnny of Shaw's play—mock-
ingly begging an American prisoner to accept death by hang-
ing rather than shooting (in view of the British soldier's

noted inefficiency with a musket)—than the executor of a grand design. A man of ability and of wit, he seemed never to learn to travel light in an area where normally difficult passage was made worse by the felling of trees in his path. He could blame much of his trouble on American use of Indian tactics. But such tactics were not responsible for General Howe's move toward Philadelphia while Burgoyne proceeded on the way which would lead to his surrender to forces under Gates and Arnold in October 1777. The strategically important battle at Saratoga—helping to ensure the French Treaty of Alliance of February 1778, which promised additional munitions and men and ships—showed some of the worst features of British eighteenth-century generalship.[10]

Later, in the south, as Cornwallis followed up the capture of Charleston and built upon the advantage of British naval superiority in southern waters, the colonial General Greene's careful movements drew the British general away from his bases and enticed him into actions which reduced his strength. At length, despairing of the southern theater, Cornwallis withdrew northward into Virginia and lingered long enough for American and French forces to trap him. Once the French fleet had driven the British off in the battle of the Virginia Capes, it was only a matter of time until Washington's and Rochambeau's forces set the stage for the final, decisive victory at Yorktown. Oddly enough it was an eighteenth-century siege in which Cornwallis' outnumbered defenders were methodically worn down. On October 19, 1781, he surrendered his forces.

Not only the victory but the legend gave to Washington a special standing in the minds of those who were soon to struggle or to dream of struggling for independence. Richard Morris reminds us, in *The Emerging Nations and the American Revolution*, of the way in which Washington and the American Revolution caught the imagination of freedom

[10] John R. Alden, *History of the American Revolution* (New York: Alfred A. Knopf, 1971); Don Higginbotham, *The War of American Independence* (New York: Macmillan & Co., 1971). I am especially indebted to these two excellent volumes in the writing of this paper.

seekers throughout the world.[11] In a revolutionary transformation that inspired Europe and Latin America within his lifetime and thereafter emerging nations in Asia and the Far East, the very real leadership of the Virginia gentleman, who overrode frustrations, failures, mistakes and even treason to outlast his opponents, seemed transformed into the spirit of independence armed.

The growing admiration for Washington's leadership was a natural reaction by proponents of independence and came initially without special effort on the part of American partisans. But the admiration also reflects a type of conscious campaign which, in a sense, constituted the first modern and revolutionary usage of demonstrations, vicious caricatures, pamphlets, sermons, hymns to liberty, atrocity stories (real and imaginary), letters by committees of correspondence, proclamations and speeches, all designed to urge American freedom and to spread the doctrine of independence. The promoters of the French Revolution would draw on these materials and on even earlier writings by men of the Enlightenment to attack the Old Regime and to press first for reform and then for revolution. While properly belonging to the art of political attack, this kind of campaign has a role in military warfare when it is used to aid recruitment, subvert opponents, and encourage the army in periods of frustration and despair. The inflammatory speeches of James Otis and the subversive pamphlets and letters of Sam Adams stirred early resistance to the acts of Parliament and the forces sent to Boston. Thomas Paine was among those who urged a break with Britain in order to attract the aid of foreign allies. At a dreary time for the colonies, a few days before Washington crossed the Delaware, Tom Paine raised the spirits of the soldiers by writing: "These are the times that try men's souls. The summer soldier and the sunshine patriot, will in this crisis, shrink from the service of his country; but he that stands it now, deserves the love and thanks of men and women." Perhaps most timely of all, he wrote: "Debts we have none; and whatever we may contract on this account will serve as a glorious moment of our virtue. Can we but

[11] Richard B. Morris, *The Emerging Nations and the American Revolution* (New York: Harper & Row, 1970).

leave posterity with a settled form of government . . . the price at any price will be cheap."[12]

Abroad, Franklin and his colleagues kept the French court astir with oversanguine accounts of American good fortune, spiced with tales of depredations in America by the British and their German and Indian allies. Congress joined the campaign of psychological warfare against the British by offering land and livestock to Hessian deserters.

The most effective document was the Declaration of Independence. Earlier American attacks—at a time when there was hope that the ties with Britain could be maintained—centered on Parliament. Now that the decision had been made for independence, George III became the focus for assault. Some of the charges set forth in the Declaration were those which his opponents in the Parliament had made: He had kept standing armies in time of peace, quartered large bodies of troops in America, rendered "the Military independent of and superior to the Civil Power." He was attacked for ravaging the coasts, for sending foreign mercenaries, and stirring the barbarous savages to merciless warfare. These items were calculated to goad Americans to the final break. The Declaration's truly revolutionary preamble was reflected subsequently in the deliberations of the French revolutionary bodies and even later in the revolutionary manifestos proclaiming the rights of men to oppose and overthrow oppressive kings and tyrants.[13]

With the campaign to educate the citizenry, there also went an effort to explain the war to the soldier. General von Steuben, calling on his American aides in fluent German and French for suitable epithets in English to berate his awkward squads, still recognized the quality of the men that he had to teach and, like others who commanded American Continentals and militia, accepted the revolutionary principle that

[12] Howard Fast, ed., *The Selected Works of Tom Paine* (New York: Duell, Sloan and Pearce, 1945), p. 32.

[13] Carl Berger, *Broadsides and Bayonets: The Propaganda War of the American Revolution* (Philadelphia: University of Pennsylvania Press, 1961), p. 141. Philip Davidson, *Propaganda and the American Revolution, 1763–1783* (Chapel Hill, N.C.: University of North Carolina Press, 1941).

soldiers who were not impressed into service nor bought had to have explanations of why they fought. After months of drilling farmers and apprentices and mechanics, he wrote an old friend in Europe: "In the first place, the genius of this nation is not in the least to be compared with that of the Prussians, Russians or the French. You say to your soldier, 'Do this,' and he doeth it; but I am obliged to say, 'This is the reason you ought to do that; and then he does it.' "[14]

One hundred sixty years later General George Marshall, American chief of staff, was emphasizing the same point about the American soldier when he declared:

> I think the first thing [about him] is that he has to know what it is all about, much more than any other soldier. I think the next thing is there has to be time to get him trained. . . .
>
> The older type of discipline "was the objective of all that monotonous drilling which, to be honest, achieved obedience at the expense of initiative. It excluded 'thought' of any kind." As an old drill sergeant put it one day, "Give me control of the 'instinct' and you can have the 'reason.'" [But that kind of reason was gone.] "Theirs not to reason why—theirs but to do or die" did not fit a citizen army. The new discipline was based on "respect" rather than fear; on the effect of good example given by officers; on the intelligent comprehension by all ranks of why an order has to be, and why it must be carried out; on a sense of duty, on *esprit de corps*.
>
> From a moral standpoint, there is no question as to which of the two disciplines is finer if you admit that respect is to be preferred to fear; the white flame of enthusiasm to the dull edge of routine; the spiritual to the instinctive.[15]

The striking point about many of the Continental soldiers and the members of the early republican armies of France

14 John McAuley Palmer, *General von Steuben* (New Haven: Yale University Press, 1937), p. 157.

15 Speech by General George C. Marshall at Trinity College, Hartford, Connecticut, June 15, 1941, in *Selected Speeches and Statements of General of the Army George C. Marshall*, edited by Major H. A. De Weerd (Washington, D.C.: The Infantry Journal, 1945), pp. 123–124.

was that most of them believed strongly in the basic cause for which they were fighting. The critic can find many cases of those who enlisted only for a bounty or for a year which they did not always wait to serve, or who ran away when the fighting got too tough. But enough persisted or returned after defeat to save the cause of independence.

Although the American revolutionary experience carried with it the concept of a Virginian or a New Yorker defending his hearthside, there was at least a feeble beginning to an American direction of the war for independence. From the frustrations and sufferings of leaders and men in cold of winter and heartbreaking defeat there came the cement which helped provide a more perfect union. The very effort to provide a central administration of the war, however poorly done, provided a school for unity in wartime that might serve as a model for government in a time of peace.

Running through the fabric of colonial defiance were threads of a growing nationalism that would color later revolutionary wars. French armies preaching international fraternity would carry a message of international brotherhood, but they would also promote a nationalism among many of the divided states of Europe that would eventually bring down Napoleon.

The French revolutionary army, fighting a battle against annihilation by a powerful coalition of monarchical states, began a conflict in the 1790s which went well beyond the warfare waged in the American colonies. The desire to conquer was increased by a determination to impose the revolutionary faith on all Europe. Like the American colonists, the French revolutionists had no place for compromise or negotiated peace. They demanded victory. This opened the way for the tyranny of the "armed horde" or in some cases produced a dictatorlike Napoleon who ended by establishing a despotic rule in the name of liberty.

To many historians of warfare, the great change from the old style of war to the new came in northeast France at Valmy on September 20, 1792, when the Prussians under the duke of Brunswick faced the French under Dumouriez. The Prussians surpassed the French in the art of maneuver, but declined to risk a frontal attack against a superior force although it was largely untried. Goethe, who was with the Prussian forces, described the action as the commencement of "a new era in the world's history." Later, Marshal Foch would say of Valmy "The wars of Kings were at an end; the wars of peoples were beginning."[16]

The newer form of warfare required large armies, greater firepower, greater mobility, the use of forces that could be thrown into battle more easily than the old forces, and new methods of supply. No longer would it be possible, as it had been with the earlier armies of 40,000 to 50,000 men, to build magazines of supplies along the line of maneuver so that the crops of the inhabitants would be avoided and the misery of war lessened. In the fast-charging massive attacks now envisaged with hundreds of thousands of men, it would be essential to live off the country.

The army with its greater mobility required better artillery, capable of firing more rounds and being handled more easily. In time European technology afforded a means of building weapons which would increase firepower and be of lighter weight, making it possible for men to move about in battle, increasing the gunner's ability to emplace his weapon more readily and obtain better observed fire.

The task of preparing ground forces so that they could move faster, deliver more massive frontal attacks, and break the enemy's lines in order to exploit an opening required vast changes in military formations. It was no longer effective to mount advances of infantry in long well-dressed lines, depending on the effect of movement and the shock of steel to carry positions. The emphasis shifted to strong columns which could be launched at part of an enemy's line in the hope of opening a breach to be exploited.

The new tactics required soldiers who understood more of their job than the older soldiers had understood. To get the men needed, national conscription was introduced. And to command these units, more highly trained officers—of what-

[16] Major General J. F. C. Fuller, *The Conduct of War, 1789–1961* (New Brunswick, N.J.: Rutgers University Press, 1961), pp. 30–31; Theodore Ropp, *War in the Modern World* (Durham, N.C.: Duke University Press, 1959), p. 89.

ever backgrounds—were demanded. The *levee en masse*—the idea of the nation in arms—was proclaimed by the French in August 1793.[17]

On gaining independence in 1783, the colonists, having been a part of the revolutionary changes of the era, seemed to recoil from struggles overseas and turned to a life less like that of Europe and Britain than in the period before the war. The new nation's army was virtually disbanded and its navy, for which ships had been planned but not wholly completed, was seriously neglected. As a maritime power, the colonies had been aware of the importance of seapower to defense and to the protection of commerce. Their own privateers had shown the damage which could be inflicted on unescorted merchant ships; the shifting battle between the British navy and the combined fleets of France and Spain for control of American waters had made quite clear the dangers to which a people with a long defenseless coast line could be exposed. But after 1783 lack of money and the lassitude that followed the long fight for independence seemed to make action impossible.

But in America, as in France and in the parts of Europe touched by French democratic enthusiasm or turned to nationalism by the war against Napoleon, the revolutionary impetus was to sweep away much that was feudal or semi-feudal in every phase of political and social life. In warfare, it meant the end of mercenaries, of armies based principally on the dregs of society, and of officers who got their commands on the basis of birth or purchase.

The idea of a nation in arms—which was never completely embraced in America partly because large numbers of colonists were Loyalist or neutral—was carried into effect in France in 1793 and then adopted by many of France's opponents. The ideological element embodied in the colonists' attacks on King George's sovereignty was seen more strongly in the sweeping French denial of every basis of the Old Regime.

Permeating the various revolutionary offensives was the urge to make others accept the new philosophy and to stimu-

[17] Norman H. Gibbs, "Armed Forces and the Art of War," in *Cambridge Modern History* (Cambridge: Cambridge University Press, 1965), vol. 9, pp. 62–63.

late destruction of all monarchy. Especially there was a commitment to destroy the old order and promise greater liberties to the dispossessed.

III

The end of the war found the American leaders uncertain as to the kind of national defense the colonies should establish. Less than a week before the formal conclusion of peace, George Washington at Newburgh, near this spot, called on seven of his generals for suggestions for an effective scheme. All of them, including General von Steuben, agreed that American repugnance to a standing army—inherited from the British and reinforced by the recent actions of the British army—made it necessary to depend basically on "a well regulated militia," uniform in organization and drill throughout the colonies. To protect the frontiers against Indian aggressions and encroachments of neighbors in Canada and the Floridas, Washington proposed a regular army of 2,683 officers and men (four small regiments of infantry and one regiment of artillery). To prepare the officers needed for these units, he proposed the establishment of an academy at West Point. However, it was not until 1802, after Jefferson became President, that the United States Military Academy was formally established here.[18]

To Washington's dismay, Congress declined to implement his system during his administration. General Marshall used to remark that the problems of Washington and many of his successors lay in the myth of the Minuteman, which was resurrected in 1917 and 1939. "It's no longer the question of taking the gun down off the mantelpiece and fighting against the savages. So often you'd see newspaper accounts in the early days—particularly in the first war—that these men were natural woodsmen and everything. Well many of them had

18 John McAuley Palmer, *America in Arms* (New Haven: Yale University Press, 1941), pp. 1–63; Russell Weigley, *History of the United States Army* (New York: Harper & Row, 1967), pp. 74–94.

never seen the woods except in the national park or city park. And all of that had gone with the Indians and with the development of the West and, of course, the development of the East—in the earliest days."[19]

Through the years that have followed, the United States has tried various military expedients—full dependence on the militia, special calls for volunteers, strengthening of existing regular forces, formation of reserve officer units, establishment of a federally supervised system of units which in time of emergency could be federalized, and systems of national conscription. The draft act was bitterly attacked in 1863 and assailed in the two world wars. But it has remained for the struggle in Vietnam to bring massive opposition to the system. One must sympathize with our political and military leaders today as they attempt to build an all-volunteer army into an effective military force without widening the gap between the armed forces and many of the citizens of the state.

Disagreements on the all-volunteer experiment are as intense in military circles and in the halls of Congress as in the country at large. But this state of affairs is not new. Some years ago, in his *War in the Modern World*, Theodore Ropp quoted Leopold von Boyen, Prussian minister of war (who helped prepare the army of his country for effective opposition to Napoleon), concerning disagreements among some of his colleagues. More recently, Stephen Ambrose used the same quotation in his book on West Point in describing General MacArthur's fight for reforms at the academy after World War I. I have no desire to apply the terms "old school" or "new school" invidiously, but I believe that they do put the problem in perspective:

> The old school places all its trust in the standing army, though on occasion it has to be complemented by a *levee en masse*. . . . The modern school believes, on the contrary, that the country cannot be defended by a standing army alone, if only because of the expense which its upkeep imposes on the country. Because of this it is necessary to have a numerous reserve, which ought to be

[19] Interview by Forrest C. Pogue with General of the Army George C. Marshall, February 15, 1957.

given serious training and not to be regarded as entirely subsidiary to the regulars. . . . The old school believes that arbitrary authority and discipline alone make soldiers, the new school that it is necessary for the army to follow changing civilian custom. . . . The old school wishes to consider military questions without the participation of the public; the new school holds that the defense of the state is impossible without the material and moral cooperation of the entire nation.[20]

In considering this thorny problem of military service, my earlier reference to Mill's statement on the practice of citizenship should be remembered. And we should recall again the statement made by Washington in justifying his proposal for a well-regulated militia: "It may be laid down as a primary position, and the basis of our system, that every citizen who enjoys the protection of a free government owes not only a portion of his property, but even of his personal services to the defence of it. . . ."[21]

The basic military lesson of the American Revolution lay in the importance to a democracy of a well-trained army, representative of the whole people, and a properly trained officer corps, drawn from the whole people—an army responsible to civilian authority and fully backed by it, capable of defending and expounding the principles for which the participants in the American Revolution risked their lives.

[20] Theodore Ropp, *War in the Modern World* (Durham, N.C.: Duke University Press, 1959), p. 135; Stephen Ambrose, *Duty, Honor, Country, A History of West Point* (Baltimore: Johns Hopkins University Press, 1966), pp. 264–265.

[21] Palmer, *America in Arms*, p. 24.

SEYMOUR MARTIN LIPSET

Opportunity and Welfare in the First New Nation

Delivered in the Henry Ford Museum, Greenfield Village,

Dearborn, Michigan on May 16, 1974

Some years ago I suggested that the United States should be properly regarded as the first new nation. The Declaration of Independence, whose bicentennial we are now celebrating, was the first successful proclamation by a major colony in modern times of its intent to secede from the mother country. It presaged comparable actions within half a century by most of the Spanish colonies in Central and South America. More recently, a variety of colonies in Africa and Asia have proclaimed their independence, often in words drawn directly from Thomas Jefferson's Declaration.

Born in a prolonged struggle for independence, the United States defined itself from its beginning in ideological terms. As many writers have noted, Americanism is an ideology, a set of integrated beliefs defining the good society. Some, such as Leon Samson and Sidney Hook, have even seen a close resemblance to those advocated by socialists. Thus in the 1930s Samson, seeking to explain "why no socialism in the U.S."

This lecture leans heavily on my earlier related writings. See S. M. Lipset, *The First New Nation, The United States in Historical and Comparative Perspective* (Garden City: Anchor Books, 1967); *Group Life in America* (New York: The American Jewish Committee, 1972); and "Education and Equality: Israel and the United States Compared," *Society*, vol. 11 (March/April 1974), pp. 56–66.

argued that the basic reason was that the values of socialism and Americanism, *property relations apart*, were quite similar. To demonstrate the point, he quoted copiously, comparing the writings of Marx, Engels, Lenin, and Stalin with those of leading American figures. Instead of citing such well-known advocates of the egalitarian ideal as Jefferson, Jackson, Lincoln, and Franklin D. Roosevelt, he took his representative citations from John D. Rockefeller, Andrew Mellon, Calvin Coolidge, and Herbert Hoover. And as he indicated, their ideas of desirable goals in human relations—namely, equality of opportunity regardless of social origins and equal treatment regardless of social role—are much like those of the leading Marxists.[1]

Because equality and achievement have been linked throughout America's development as a nation, the concept of equality has had a special character. As David Potter stressed, "the American ideal and practice of equality . . . has implied for the individual . . . opportunity to make his own place in society and . . . emancipation from a system of status."[2] It must be emphasized that the American concept of equality, which focuses on opportunity and the quality of social relations, does not demand equality of income. This fact, Potter pointed out, is one reason why it is confusing to use the term "equality" to describe aspects of the American reality.

> [T]he connotations [of the term "equality"] to an American are quite unlike what they might be to a European. A European advocating equality might very well mean that all men should occupy positions that are roughly the same level in wealth, power, or enviability. But the

[1] Leon Samson, *Towards a United Front* (New York: Farrar and Rinehart, 1933), pp. 1–90; Sidney Hook, "The Philosophical Basis of Socialism in the United States," in D. D. Egbert and S. Persons, eds., *Socialism and American Life*, vol. 1 (Princeton: Princeton University Press, 1952), pp. 450–451. For a condensation of Samson's analysis and recent discussion, see John Laslett and S. M. Lipset, eds., *Failure of a Dream? Essays in the History of American Socialism* (Garden City: Doubleday-Anchor Books, 1974), pp. 426–462.

[2] David M. Potter, *People of Plenty* (Chicago: University of Chicago Press, 1954), p. 91.

American, with his emphasis upon equality of opportunity, has never conceived of it in this sense. He has traditionally expected to find a gamut ranging from rags to riches, from tramps to millionaires. . . . Thus equality did not mean uniform position on a common level, but it did mean universal opportunity to move through a scale which traversed many levels. . . . The emphasis upon unrestricted latitude as the essence of equality in turn involved a heavy emphasis upon liberty as an essential means for keeping the scale open and hence making equality a reality as well as a theoretical condition. . . . As for social distinctions, certainly they exist; but whatever their power may be, social rank can seldom assert an open claim to deference in this country, and it usually makes at least a pretense of conformity to equalitarian ways.[3]

As Potter noted, European egalitarianism, largely Marxist, stresses the ultimate objective of equality of result—to be achieved, first, through state welfare policies that seek to raise the level of those at the bottom, a goal often supported by conservatives (whose links to aristocratic values tend to lead them to endorse welfare policies as an expression of *noblesse oblige*) and, second, through nationalization policies designed to reduce inequality of income and wealth.

The identification of Americanism with universalistic expressions of egalitarianism is typical of the way in which, ever since the beginning of the modern era, the revolutionary nationalism of new nations has tended to incorporate supranational ideals. As Karl Deutsch has put it:

Behind the spreading of national consciousness there was at work perhaps a deeper change—a new *value* assigned to people *as they are*, or as they can become, with as much diversity of interlocking roles as will not destroy or stifle any of their personalities. After 1750 we find new and higher values assigned in certain advanced countries to children and women; to the poor and the sick; to slaves and peasants; to colored races and submerged nationalities. . . .

National consciousness thus arises in an age that asserts birthrights for everybody, inborn, unalienable rights,

[3] Ibid., pp. 91–92, 96.

first in the language of religion, then in the language of politics, and finally in terms involving economics and all society. . . .[4]

When Americans celebrate their national heritage on Independence Day, Memorial Day, or other holidays of this sort, they dedicate themselves anew to a nation conceived as the living fulfillment of a political doctrine that enshrines a utopian concept of men's egalitarian and fraternal relations with one another. In linking national celebrations with political events and a political creed, the United States resembles other post-revolutionary societies like those of France, the Soviet Union, and many of the new states. In contrast, nations whose authority stems from traditional legitimacy tend to celebrate holidays linked with religious tradition or national military history.

In newly independent societies there has often been a transition from a system dominated by traditionalist, usually aristocratic, values to one characterized by egalitarian populist concepts. These new value systems are variously referred to as "liberal," "democratic," or "leftist" in contrast to "elitist," "conservative," or "aristocratic." The elitist ideology takes for granted the desirability of the hierarchical ordering of society in which those who belong to the "naturally superior" strata exercise due authority and are given generalized respect. Social recognition rests on the sum of all the qualities of a person's status rather than on a given role he may be playing. In colonial situations, the native elites derive their status, or are protected in it, by virtue of their connection with the status and power of the foreign ruler. With independence, the values of hierarchy, aristocracy, privilege, primogeniture, and (more recently) capitalism, all associated with the foreign imperialist power, are easily rejected.

Consequently, most struggles for independence have employed leftist ideologies, that of equality in revolutionary America, that of socialism in the contemporary new states. Man's status is to depend not upon inherited but upon

[4] Karl Deutsch, *Nationalism and Social Communication* (New York: John Wiley, 1953), pp. 153–155. (Emphasis in original.)

achieved qualities. Hence the system must be geared to abolish all forms of ascriptive privilege and to reward achievement. The franchise is to be extended to everyone, the people being regarded as the source of power and authority; and various social reforms, such as economic development, the elimination of illiteracy, and the spread of education are to reduce inequalities in status. Thus, the need to legitimize the democratic goals of the American Revolution required a commitment to improve sharply the economic circumstances of the mass of the population, even though the Revolution was conceived by many of its leaders as primarily a struggle for political independence. Every revolutionary group proclaims *"all* men to be equal" and to have "unalienable rights," or advocates a "classless society" and the elimination of minority rule in politics.

However, beneath this consistency of radical temper, there are profound differences in the ways in which various parties or strata interpret their revolutionary commitments. In the United States after the adoption of the Constitution, the conservative groups who had taken part in the anti-imperialist revolution continued to play a major, even dominant, role. The Federalists, though convinced advocates of views which were radical and republican by European standards, sought to limit the application of egalitarian principles in such fields as property relations, religion, and the suffrage. Yet, as in most contemporary new states in which conservatives have tried to defend traditionalist values after independence, the more conservative party soon lost office. The Federalists had failed in their efforts to sustain a party which defended aspects of inequality, and their successors sought to learn from their errors.[5] When conservatism revived as a political force in the form of Whig opposition to Andrew Jackson, it had a distinctly new look. In attacking Jackson, the tribune of the plebians, the new conservatives labeled him royalist and Tory, calling him "King Andrew," while they took for themselves the term Whig, the title of the opposition to Toryism and royal absolutism in Britain.

[5] Clinton Rossiter, *Conservatism in America* (New York: Vintage Books, 1962), pp. 117–119.

The supremacy of egalitarian values in politics is reflected in the Whigs' behavior in the presidential elections of 1840, incidentally the first such contest the Whigs were able to win:

> Harrison and Tyler were selected as the party candidates. . . . Webster was rejected on . . . [the] ground he was "aristocratic." This consideration showed how completely the old order had changed. The men of wealth well realized, now that liberty and equality had shown their power, that in enthusiastic profession of fraternity lay their only course of safety. Property rights were secure only when it was realized that in America property was honestly accessible to talent, however humble in its early circumstances. The Whigs found it useful to disavow as vehemently as they could any and all pretensions to a caste superiority in political life. . . .[6]

And in presenting their candidate for governor that year, the New York Whig convention described him as "a true and worthy representative of Democrat-Republican principles, born in the forest of the noble Western region of our own State, trained among an industrious kindred to hardy toil and manual labor on the farm and in the manufactory—democratic in all his associations and sympathies. . . ."[7] Actually, many of the candidates in the Whig party were "gentlemen," men from some of the country's first families.[8] But in keeping with the democratic spirit of the times, they campaigned on a ticket of fraternity and equality, even appealing to class hatred against the elite.

It is important to place these events and doctrines in their historical context. During the first half of the nineteenth century American conservatives had come to recognize that, like it or not, they were operating in a society in which egalitarian values were dominant and in which the rights of the people

[6] Dixon Ryan Fox, *The Decline of Aristocracy in the Politics of New York* (New York: Columbia University Press, 1919), pp. 411–413.

[7] Lee Benson, *The Concept of Jacksonian Democracy* (Princeton, N.J.: Princeton University Press, 1961), p. 251.

[8] Carl R. Fish, *The Rise of the Common Man 1830–1850* (New York: Macmillan, 1950), p. 165.

to govern and of the able to succeed had to be accepted as inviolable. But the important fact is that, for both Democrats and Whigs, the aristocratic, monarchical, and oligarchic societies of Europe were anathema. Just as political parties in the new states of today are almost automatically "socialist," so American political leaders in the first half-century of our existence were instinctively "democrats." The latter believed that the United States had a special mission to perform in introducing a new social and political order to the world, and some even felt that it had a duty to give moral, financial, and other forms of support to European radicals fighting for republicanism and freedom.[9]

The significance of "leftism" as characterizing the core values in the American political tradition may be best perceived from the vantage point of comparative North American history—that is, from the contrast between Canada and the United States. American historians and political philosophers may debate how radical, liberal, leftist, or even conservative American politics has been, but there is no doubt in the mind of Canadian historians. They see their nation as a descendant of counterrevolution and the United States as a product of revolution. Once the die was cast, consisting of a triumphant revolution in the thirteen colonies and a failure to the north, an institutional framework was set. Consequent events tended to enforce "leftist" strength south of the border and a "rightist" bias to the north. The success of the revolutionary ideology, the defeat of the Tories, and the emigration of many of them north to Canada or across the ocean to Britain all served to enhance the strength of the forces favoring egalitarian democratic principles in the new nation and to weaken conservative tendencies. On the other hand, Canada's failure to have a revolution of its own, the immigration of conservative elements and the emigration of radical elements, and the success of colonial Toryism in erecting a conservative class structure—all these contributed to making Canada a more conservative and rigidly stratified society.[10]

[9] See Merle Curti, "Young America," in *Probing Our Past* (New York: Harper & Row, 1955), pp. 219–245.

[10] For an elaboration, see my book, *Revolution and Counterrevolution* (Garden City, N.Y.: Anchor Books, 1970), pp. 37–75.

II

Much of the social history of the United States, then, may be read in terms of an attempt to elaborate on the egalitarian promise of the Declaration of Independence. The United States led other nations in expanding its suffrage to cover all white males (slavery was its great exception and horror, and continued racism its Achilles' heel). It also led in providing education to its inhabitants. The census of 1840 indicated that over 90 percent of whites were literate. The figure was undoubtedly an exaggeration. Yet, then and later, this country spent a greater share of public funds on education than other societies. From the nineteenth century down to the present, a much larger percentage of the appropriate age population has attended secondary schools and institutions of higher education here than elsewhere. In other words, education has been more equally distributed in the United States than in other countries for a century and a half. Further, a myriad of foreign observers—Tocqueville, Martineau and Bryce among them—have commented on the emphasis in social relations on symbolic equality. They have noted that, in effect, no man need doff his cap to another, that the symbols of rank so prevalent in Europe have been absent here. Populism and anti-elitism have characterized America's political style.

Most noteworthy of all in the American concept of equality, as we have seen, has been the stress on equality—not equality of rank, status, income or wealth, but equality of opportunity. In the main, the American ideal has been one of open social mobility, everyone starting at the same point in a race for success.[11]

The vigor of this doctrine in early America may be seen in its most extreme form in the program of the Workingmen's parties formed in various East Coast cities in the 1820s and

[11] For a general discussion of current evidence on the subject in a comparative context, see S. M. Lipset, "Social Mobility and Equal Opportunity," *The Public Interest*, no. 29 (Fall 1972), pp. 90–108.

1830s.[12] These parties, which secured as much as 20 percent of the urban vote, were particularly concerned with education. In a profound document written in 1829, the New York party anticipated the conclusions of a much later report by James Coleman by asserting that access to equal education in day schools was far from sufficient to provide equal opportunity in the race for success.[13] For, they said, a few hours in school cannot counter the highly unequal effects of varying cultural and material environments supplied by families of unequal wealth and culture. To ensure that all had the same environment twenty-four hours a day, they proposed that all children, regardless of class background or parental wishes, be educated from six years of age on in boarding schools. Clearly, this American political party made the most radical proposal of all—to nationalize not property but children. Not surprisingly, the proposal was unpopular and never came close to carrying, but the fact that a party which was contending for public office and electing representatives to various legislative bodies would even make it indicates the strength of egalitarianism a half-century following American independence.

It is noteworthy that this party, which incidentally gave Karl Marx the idea that the working class could and should organize politically on its own behalf, did not call for equality of wealth or income. This was never the meaning of equality in Americanism. The Workingmen of 1830 accepted inequality as long as it was the result of success in a competitive race for the top. Close to a century later, a highly successful American multimillionaire, Andrew Carnegie, advocated a confiscatory inheritance tax that would have returned all wealth to the state upon death. Carnegie also believed that new ways should be found to equalize the race for success.

[12] See Walter Hugins, *Jacksonian Democracy and the Working Class. A Study of the New York Workingmen's Movement 1829–1837* (Stanford: Stanford University Press, 1966); Edward Pessen, *Most Uncommon Jacksonians. The Radical Leaders of the Early Labor Movement* (Albany: State University of New York Press, 1967), esp. pp. 9–33.

[13] New York Workingman's Party, "A System of Republican Education," in Walter Hugins, ed., *The Reform Impulse 1825–1850* (New York: Harper & Row, 1972), pp. 135–139.

Although the Workingmen's parties did not get their boarding schools, the idea that all should begin with an equal education helped strengthen the more successful efforts of those who, like Horace Mann, urged the creation of publicly supported "common" schools in the 1840s. By common schools was meant what are now called "integrated" schools —that is, schools attended by children from diverse social backgrounds, natives and immigrants, rich and poor. The proponents assumed that such schools were necessary to develop a common culture, to absorb those from varying backgrounds, to make possible more equality of opportunity, as well as to create the kind of citizenry that could participate in a one-man, one-vote democracy.[14]

The spread of the common school idea, it should be noted, included a practice which would have far-reaching consequences. These schools, designed in part to Americanize the immigrant and to "civilize" the lower classes, deliberately set their educational sights at the levels of the culturally deprived. In a sense they consciously lowered standards, or rather educational aspirations, from the levels upper-middle-class children could attain so as to make it possible for those of "deprived background" to catch up. It was assumed that all would eventually reach higher levels of attainment and knowledge in the upper grades and ultimately in college and university. This pattern has continued. Worldwide comparisons show that American youths study less than their equivalents in upper-level European gymnasia or lycées. As Max Weber noted in 1918, "The American boy learns unspeakably less than the German boy."[15] By age twenty, however, the Americans have more than caught up. And a much

[14] Lawrence A. Cremin, *The Genius of American Education* (Pittsburgh: University of Pittsburgh Press, 1965), pp. 63–71; Cremin, ed., *The Republic and the School. Horace Mann on the Education of Free Men* (New York: Bureau of Publications, Teachers College, Columbia University, 1957), see esp. pp. 9–15, 84–97, 101–112.

[15] H. H. Gerth and C. Wright Mills, eds., *From Max Weber: Essays in Sociology* (New York: Oxford University Press, 1946), p. 149.

greater percentage of them than in any European country secures a higher education. By going slowly at the elementary and high school levels, the U.S. system permits many more to enter an institution of higher education and to graduate.

III

It would be misleading to credit the growth of education and other institutional practices fostering social mobility solely or primarily to forces stemming from egalitarian political ideology. The ideology itself, the educational growth, and egalitarian social relations were fostered as well by the fact that so much of America was a rapidly expanding "new society," a frontier culture in which all families were first settlers, or their immediate descendants. More important, perhaps, may have been the impact of religion. The United States was and remains the only country in which the majority adheres to Protestant *sects*, mainly Baptist and Methodist, rather than to religions which had been state churches in Europe, such as Catholic, Lutheran, Anglican, and Greek Orthodox. The latter were hierarchically organized and were linked to monarchy and aristocracy, so that part of the alliance between throne and altar also served to mediate between man and God.

The Protestant sects, on the other hand, insist that man deal directly with God, that he follow his conscience rather than obey the church or state and that, to be qualified to do so, he must be literate, a student of the Bible. Therefore, they supported the spread of public education and the growth of universities, starting many colleges and universities themselves. The Protestant Ethic, of course, also contributed directly to mobility and economic growth by its emphasis on hard work. It also favored a political orientation which had the state helping the individual to help himself—through education, but not through collectivist welfare measures.

In spite of its emphasis on equality of opportunity, the United States has never really approached the ideal, even in the spread of formal education. Two great nineteenth-century radical thinkers, Karl Marx and Henry George (the single-tax theorist), independently pointed out that publicly supported higher education in the United States involved taking money from the poor to subsidize the education of the well-to-do, that it amounted to a negative "transfer payment" so to speak. Henry George put the thesis in colorful terms when he said in the 1890s that the University of California is a place to which the poor send the children of the rich. Recent analyses by economists indicate George is still right.[16] In spite of the enormous spread of state higher education in California —over 50 percent of the college age population is in school in that state—the families of those who attend the University of California have a higher income than those who go to the state colleges or junior colleges, who in turn are more affluent than the families whose children do not go on to higher education.

College and university attendance, which has now reached close to 50 percent of the relevant age group nationally, still varies greatly with family income. In 1967, 87 percent of those youths whose families earned $15,000 or more attended college, whereas only 20 percent of those from families with incomes below $3,000 a year did so. Yet this 20 percent figure for the very poor is higher than the total figure for total college attendance in many European countries.

It should be obvious, however, that the diffusion of college education and even the broadening of the social class background of those who hold privileged positions do not demonstrate a leveling of income, wealth or power in America or elsewhere. Jencks has properly emphasized that in spite of the growth of higher education, the distribution of

---

[16] See W. L. Hansen and B. Weisbrod, "The Distribution of Costs and Direct Benefits of Public Education: The Case of California," *Journal of Human Resources*, vol. 4 (Spring 1969), pp. 178–179, 181–182, 185. For a general discussion of this point see Christopher Jencks and David Riesman, *The Academic Revolution* (Garden City: Doubleday & Co., 1968), pp. 276–279; and Irving Kristol, *Democratic Idea in America* (New York: Harper & Row, 1972), p. 122.

wealth has not narrowed in the United States in recent decades.[17] The evidence does suggest that wealth distribution is much more egalitarian today than in pre-Civil War days, and that there was a narrowing of the gap between the poor and the upper strata in the period of the Depression and New Deal.[18] But the sharply stratified distribution wherein the lowest quartile holds about 5 percent of the wealth and the highest tenth well over a third still continues. Raymond Boudon, the French sociologist, drawing on data from Western Europe and North America, has in fact shown that increases in education have the effect of widening the salary gap from top to bottom.[19]

Sharp inequality continues to characterize American society, as it does all other complex social systems. Well-to-do parents are more able than poor parents to provide their offspring with an academically stimulating environment, good schools and teachers, the motivation to attain success, and the contacts and financial aid so useful in getting started in the race for success. Moreover, those who control large financial resources may convert these into various forms of power for affecting key decisions in the society—as, in a different way, may those at the summit of intellectually important and opinion-molding institutions. Race, ethnic and class background may be less of a handicap in the race for success than earlier, but the inequality between those who succeed and those who fail has not been reduced.

It should be noted that the fight for more equality, legitimized by the historic commitment to the ideal, is still waged in terms of the old American emphasis on equality of opportunity, the demand of the Workingmen's party that social origin not be a handicap in the race for success. Almost none of the battles, however, are concerned directly with

[17] Christopher Jencks et al., *Inequality* (New York: Basic Books, Inc., 1973).

[18] For a detailed analysis of inequality in earlier days see Edward Pessen, *Riches, Class, and Power Before the Civil War* (Lexington, Mass.: D. C. Heath Co., 1973).

[19] Raymond Boudon, *Education, Opportunity and Social Mobility* (New York: John Wiley & Sons, Inc., 1974), pp. 187–188.

equality as such. That is, blacks and women are demanding their appropriate share of corporation presidencies, university professorships, government positions, and so forth, but they are not arguing that the perquisites associated with these statuses be lowered or eliminated. Even the "war on poverty" of Presidents Kennedy and Johnson was presented basically as an extension of equal opportunity.

The social democratic states of Scandinavia, Britain, Germany and Israel have attempted to implement the ideal of the welfare state—to improve the lot of the less fortunate and to insure against the insecurities of employment, health, and old age. Until recently, however, they paid little attention to opening the door of opportunity. All of them have maintained a two-class educational system, the system rejected by Horace Mann and other American pre-Civil War reformers in which a small minority, largely of privileged origins, attends the educationally superior high schools, the lycées, gymnasia, public (private) and grammar schools leading to matriculation in universities, while the large majority attends vocational schools. Social democracy has spent its money disproportionately on social welfare, old-age pensions, state medicine, unemployment benefits, public housing, et cetera. The United States, in contrast, has devoted more of its resources to education as the road to success. These differences, while still existent, have narrowed considerably. The United States is increasingly a welfare state, whereas in recent decades the social democracies of Europe have been consciously modifying their educational systems in the direction of comprehensive, common or integrated schools.

As the social democratic states move in the American direction in their educational system, as they become concerned with equality of opportunity, this country has begun to move away from its emphasis on individual rights and opportunities to a concern for welfare and for group rights. To some extent, the U.S. trend reflects the fact that, the condition of minorities apart, equality of opportunity has become a reality for white males. The two most recent comprehensive statistical studies of the situation, those of Blau and Duncan on the one hand, and of Jencks and his associates on the other, both emphasize this development.[20]

The United States is gradually becoming committed to guaranteeing group rights to equality of status, as distinct from its traditional focus on equality of opportunity. This may be seen in its most controversial and questionable form in the efforts to establish quotas—racial, ethnic and biological—as a way of measuring concern for equality. But it has been evident for a much longer time in the steady growth in welfare expenditures, under Democratic and Republican administrations alike.

The welfare state, despite its growth, does not appear to have fulfilled the objectives set for it. The provision of more monies has not reduced the size of the slums, or the assorted other social morbidities associated with low income. Currently, a major source of the difficulties in metropolitan areas is the enormous cost and the high social morbidity rate involved in absorbing the growing number of people who have moved to the cities, in part to take advantage of economic opportunity and of higher standards of welfare support. To a considerable degree, the breakdown of urban services in many communities is a consequence of having to pay for welfare. Yet such payments have had little positive effect on the lives of welfare recipients. There is good reason to believe that, in the absence of jobs, migrants from rural and depressed regions to the cities would have been better off had they remained in the cultural surroundings to which they were accustomed.

Spokesmen for both major parties are currently advocating similar solutions to the problem. The Nixon administration's Family Assistance Plan and the bills proposed by some Democrats have differed mainly in mechanics and in the amount of monies to be allocated immediately. Both parties favor federalization of welfare, and both seek to ease the cities' tax burdens, to reduce the size of the bureaucracy administering

[20] Peter Blau and O. Dudley Duncan, *The American Occupational Structure* (New York: Wiley, 1962), and Jencks et al., *Inequality.*

welfare, and hopefully, through direct payments incorporating financial incentives, to encourage the poor to seek income in the labor market. And in the related field of medical care, both are committed to a state-financed (and state-controlled) system. The arguments between administration spokesmen and liberal Democrats now revolve around the relative advantages of "fee for service" and prepayment systems, much like the medical care debates in social democratic Europe.

Leading Republicans now assert that "there is much in the new doctrine of equality of results that is solid"—to use the words of Paul McCracken, member of President Eisenhower's Council of Economic Advisers in 1956–59 and chairman of the same body for President Nixon from 1969–72. McCracken, speaking to the Business Council, noted that American society is concerned with finding an optimum balance between its traditional ideal of equality of opportunity and its growing commitment to greater equality of result.

> For economic policy we need to have a more explicit and coherent income maintenance policy. Powerful intellectual impetus for this, as for so much of the current economic policy landscape, came from Milton Friedman in his writings on the negative income tax. It was given programmatic expression four years ago in the President's Family Assistance Plan. Ours is now a rich economy, and we can well afford it. And all of us here would have to admit that there is a substantial element of random luck in success. . . . Moreover, we need a more explicit and coherent income sharing plan to win more leeway for using the pricing system. . . .
>
> The optimum toward which society is trying to feel its way here will be neither pure "equality of results" nor just "equality of opportunity." A society organized solely on the principle of equality of opportunity is not acceptable, and one organized solely around the principle of equality of results would not be operational.[21]

[21] Paul W. McCracken, "The New Equality," *Michigan Business Review* (March 1974), pp. 2–7.

The gradual acceptance of the community's responsibility for upgrading the level of life of the underprivileged in America constitutes an important shift in our values away from the primary, almost sole, focus on opportunity implied in the original achievement and Protestant orientations of the early republic. Yet, it may be argued that the initial emphasis on equality derived from the Declaration of Independence, which has led many Americans to speak of their country as a "classless society," serves to strengthen the new trend towards using government power to eliminate "poverty," now that the concern has reached the political arena. For many, as noted earlier, the policies of the "war on poverty" are seen as the current manifestation of the revolutionary struggle to guarantee equal access to the top for all.

IV

There is, however, a more fundamental change in the making, one that is implicit in the shift in emphasis from extending opportunity rights to the individual to extending them to the group. I would like to devote some time now to the problems posed by this change.

The change has found its most concrete expression in proposals for guaranteed quotas in jobs and school placement. Quotas produce a clear conflict of interest between the underprivileged who demand them and those who have found opportunity and success by traditionally competitive methods, and there is no easy or obvious way to resolve this conflict. As Blau and Duncan as well as Jencks have demonstrated, the argument that different ethnic groups have found ways and means to attain status, power, and economic reward holds for almost all American white male groups, but not for blacks or women. Many recognize that a pure quota system humiliates the recipients of such preferment and is a danger to society in that it may permit unqualified persons to hold jobs. During the 1960s, public policy increasingly took note of the dilemma and tried to resolve it by various forms of affirmation action.

The policy of affirmative action was first proclaimed by President Johnson in a 1965 executive order. In defending and explaining this policy, the image of the shackled runner was widely used:

> Imagine a hundred yard dash in which one of the two runners has his legs shackled together. He has progressed ten yards, while the unshackled runner has gone fifty yards. At that point the judges decide that the race is unfair. How do they rectify the situation? Do they merely remove the shackles and allow the race to proceed? Then they could say that "equal opportunity" now prevailed. But one of the runners would still be forty yards ahead of the other. Would it not be the better part of justice to allow the previously shackled runner to make up the forty yard gap; or to start the race all over again? That would be affirmative action towards equality.[22]

The image is a fitting one for the black man in America. Even if discrimination were eliminated, he would still be at a disadvantage, for the ability to compete in American society is tied to a less visible chain of prior factors: the work experience of family and friends, as well as educational achievement, which are themselves linked to the educational and cultural experience of family. For these reasons, the economic advancement of emerging groups in America has always taken place over a span of generations. But the oppression of the American black man has been imposed by *this* society, not by another one, as was the case with most other emerging ethnic groups in America. Does this not impose a special national responsibility for affirmative action?

The need for affirmative action is strongly supported by various studies which indicate that, although the aspirations of black students tend to be as high as those of whites, their expectations are quite low. Many see their chances for success as very small, regardless of how well they do in school or elsewhere. This clearly has had negative effects on the ability of

---

[22] Earl Raab, "Quotas by Any Other Name," *Commentary*, vol. 53 (January 1972), p. 41. See also Daniel Bell, *Coming of Post-Industrial Society: A Venture in Social Forecasting* (New York: Basic Books, Inc., 1973), pp. 416–417.

black children to study hard and learn, and of black adults to work well and persistently.

Beyond these cultural handicaps, however, has been the fact that American society discriminated against blacks, even when they were qualified. Many major institutions in both the North and the South either barred their entry or limited their numbers to a token quota. The segregated schools of the period before the 1954 *Brown* decision were *not* separate but equal. They were separate and unequal. And limitations on black suffrage in the South, where most blacks lived, meant that they could not effectively resort to the classic democratic political remedy for maltreatment.

Not surprisingly, black leaders turned to their only effective weapon, civil disobedience, in an attempt to embarrass authority into acting on their behalf. The first such effort in modern times, the March on Washington Movement of World War II led by A. Philip Randolph, forced Franklin Roosevelt to establish a Fair Employment Practices Commission. But the provision of a mechanism through which minority group members could appeal against apparent overt discrimination, for example, the hiring of a less qualified white for a job, proved ineffective. There were not enough minority group members who had both the skills and the political-legal know-how to benefit from these new legal rights. This failure led naturally to the demand for government programs to increase the pool of trained minority manpower. Perhaps as important, immediately, has been the effort to eliminate the excessive job requirements that handicapped those whose cultural background is not middle class —requirements such as more education than the job in fact requires or tests whose content is largely irrelevant to the position in question. These changes have had one purpose in common—to give minority group members a better chance in the competition for jobs. This has also been the purpose of various compensatory education programs, as well as of the efforts of different agencies to find qualified minority members who, left to themselves, might not search out available positions.

Such efforts have an important historic precedent which

has never been questioned—veterans' preference, that is, compensation for a competitive disability imposed by society. In accordance with this principle, veterans have traditionally been given preferential treatment by governmental agencies and some private employers when their qualifications were demonstrated to be roughly equal to that of other applicants. The stress on affirmative action, however, changed gradually to a demand for specific group quotas for admission to assorted institutions and jobs, and beyond this, in the New York and San Francisco school systems, among many, to proposals requiring the dismissal of qualified teachers and administrators.

This change in the concept of equal opportunity from a focus on the rights of *individuals* to those of *groups*, as measured by the positions achieved, has marked an extraordinary shift in the concept of civil rights in America. Historically, minority groups that have suffered discrimination, institutionalized prejudice, or handicaps with respect to skills and education have demanded the elimination of barriers denying *individuals* access to opportunity. Jews, Orientals, and Italians objected to the *numerous clausus* established by institutions of higher learning and other organizations against qualified members of their ethnic groups. They opposed policies designed to perpetuate the advantages enjoyed by members of majority groups. Except for Catholic proposals for state support of parochial schools, which were almost invariably rejected as "un-American," no minority group had until recently demanded significant special-group advantages.

Liberal opinion had always assumed that the egalitarian creed meant advocacy of a universalistic rule of meritocracy, enabling all to secure positions for which they qualified in open, fair competition. Felix Frankfurter, who entered Harvard Law School before World War I as an immigrant Jewish graduate of CCNY, never lost his awe of the meritocratic system: "What mattered was excellence in your profession to which your father or your race was equally irrelevant. And so rich man, poor man were just irrelevant titles to the equation of human relations. The thing that mattered was what you did professionally."[23] Randolph Bourne, the most creative and celebrated of the young Socialist intellectuals of that period and a man who was concerned with the situation of the poverty-stricken Jews of New York's Lower East Side, also emphasized that an individual must be judged by what he could do, not by his ethnic or class background.[24]

This traditional liberal-left position, implicit in the American creed's emphasis on equality of opportunity, broke down with the demand of blacks for "equality of results"—which meant special group advantage in the form of quotas to increase their number in university admissions, various occupations, and trade unions (which control access to jobs) to their proportion in the population. And, as the political community has come to accept this principle, other disadvantaged groups—Chicanos, Puerto Ricans, American Indians, women—have, not unnaturally, taken up and secured the same demands for *group* rather than *individual* rights and for *group* mobility, as a way of bypassing the historic process of upward mobility of the individual through the acquisition of skills.

Compliance with demands for special quotas means denial to others of positions for which they are qualified, or which they now have. It means that other minority groups which have been particularly successful in certain fields are now being asked to give up their gains. This is true of such groups as the Jews, the Japanese, and the Chinese that have concentrated on education as a means of mobility. The civil service, more universalistic than other job markets, has always been a special arena for mobility for disadvantaged groups doing well in school and in examinations. Other immigrant minority groups have used different skills, which they brought from Europe, to gain a special advantage in different job markets. Given the diverse cultural backgrounds of America's ethnic groups, it is not surprising that their occupational distribution also varies.

[23] Felix Frankfurter, *Felix Frankfurter Reminisces* (Garden City: Doubleday-Anchor Books, 1962), p. 43.

[24] Randolph S. Bourne, *Youth and Life* (Boston: Houghton Mifflin Co., 1913), p. 318.

If the concept of positive group discrimination is accepted, as it has begun to be, America will have accepted a version of the principle of *ascription*, or hereditary placement, to advance equal opportunity.[25] The implications of this change in American values, a change from achievement to ascription, have been eloquently stated by Earl Raab:

> One of the marks of the free society is the ascendance of performance over ancestry—or, to put it more comprehensively, the ascendance of achieved status over ascribed status. Aristocracies and racist societies confer status on the basis of heredity. A democratic society begins with the cutting of the ancestral cord. This by itself does not yet make a humanistic society or even a properly democratic one. There is, for example, the not inconsiderable question of distributive justice in rewarding performance. But achieved versus ascribed status is *one* inexorable dividing line between a democratic and an undemocratic society. This is the aspect of democracy which represents the primacy of the individual, and of individual freedom. It has to do with the belief that an individual exists not just to serve a social function, but to stretch his unique spirit and capacities for their own sake: "the right of every man not to have but to be his best." In that sense, it could be said that a principle of ascribed equality—a kind of perverse hereditary theory—would be as insidiously destructive of the individual and of individual freedom as a principle of ascribed inequality.[26]

It may appear that the argument against special prescriptive quotas for minority groups is a form of special pleading by spokesmen of the privileged elements in society. That this is so, when viewed from a pure interest group standpoint, cannot be denied. Yet, persuasive voices against quotas have been heard from the black community. Orlando Patterson, the black sociologist, argues that the black American has a stake in a "conception of human dignity in which every indi-

[25] It is noteworthy that under the Nixon administration, officials have pressed more vigorously for quotas, described as "targets," than under the Johnson administration.

[26] Raab, "Quotas by Any Other Name," p. 42; Bell, *Coming of Post-Industrial Society*, pp. 418–419.

vidual is, and ought to be, responsible for himself and his actions." In his opinion, for blacks to insist that they, unlike other groups, lack the ability to change their circumstances because of their social environment is to accept a demoralizing view of their situation, one which serves to discourage efforts to change it. He notes that the emphasis on the socially determined sources of black social inferiority is so strong that the issue for many is not "why the group fails, but why the miracle of occasional individual successes persists among them." For him, the great need is for blacks to find ways of emphasizing personal autonomy. And in trying to do this, they should lay stress upon, and find hope and pride in, "the not inconsiderable number of successful Blacks." He calls attention to the

> numerous cases of black men and women on the average no better endowed genetically than fellow Blacks they have left behind in the ghettos, and coming from environments with the same sorry list of broken homes, crime-plagued neighborhoods, drug-infested streets, inadequate schools, and racist white authority figures, who nonetheless succeed. How are we to explain them? We cannot. They defy explanation precisely because they alone account for their success; they made their success, and they made it, first, through a rebellion against their deterministic moral environment, and then, having gained their humanity, through the much easier rebellion against their social and economic environment.

He concludes that such behavior can only come about "when one accepts one's total responsibility for oneself and one's future."[27]

Black economist Thomas Sowell points to the demoralizing consequences of emphasis on quotas for students and faculty. He suggests that the effort of universities to fill such quotas has meant that large numbers of black students are enrolled in schools for which they are ill-prepared. Thus when the most scholarly, prestigious, and selective universities admit

[27] Orlando Patterson, "The Moral Crisis of the Black American," *The Public Interest*, vol. 32 (Summer 1973), pp. 43–69, esp. pp. 64–65.

black students who are less prepared than the whites, they set up a situation in which the blacks can only feel inadequate. He describes the problem caused by the admission policies of the elite white institutions this way:

When black students who would normally qualify for a state college are drained away by Ivy League colleges and universities, then state colleges have little choice but to recruit black students who would normally qualify for still lower level institutions—and so the process continues down the line. The net result is that, in a country with 3,000 widely differing colleges and universities capable of accommodating every conceivable level of educational preparation and intellectual development, there is a widespread problem of "underprepared" black students at many institutional levels, even though black students' capabilities span the whole range by any standard used. The problem is not one of absolute ability level, but rather of widespread mismatching of individuals with institutions. The problem is seldom seen for what it is, for it has *not* been approached in terms of the optimum distribution of black students in the light of their preparation and interests, but rather in terms of how Harvard, Berkeley, or Antioch can do its part, maintain its leadership, or fill its quota. The schools which have most rapidly increased their enrollments of black students are those where the great majority of white American students could not qualify. However, since such schools typically do not admit underqualified white students, they have no "white problem" corresponding to the problem posed for them by underqualified black students. This problem must also be seen in perspective: the College Board scores and other academic indicators for black students in prestige colleges and universities are typically *above the national average* for white Americans. Special tutoring, reduced course loads and other special accommodations and expedients for minority students are necessitated by programs geared to a student body which is not only above the national average but in the top 1 *or* 2 *percent* of all American students. The problem created by black students who do not meet the usual institutional standards may be grim or even desperate for both the students and the institution. Yet it does not arise because students are incapable of absorbing a college education. They may be incapable of absorbing an M.I.T. education, but so is virtually everyone else. . . .

[B]lacks at all levels of ability are systematically mismatched upward, so that good students go where outstanding students should be going and outstanding students go where only a handful of peak performers can survive. The net effect of this "pervasive shifting effect" is to place students where they do not learn as much as they would in schools geared to students of their own educational preparation.[28]

A comparable problem has been created by the efforts of universities to fill faculty quotas, according to Sowell. As is obvious from the statistics, the past record of inferior education for blacks means that black America

has included very few persons trained to be academic scholars. Moreover, many years of academic education are required for anyone, regardless of race, to qualify, even minimally, as a faculty member, much less as a mature scholar. In short, there are relatively few black scholars in existence, and the number cannot be greatly increased in the immediate future. And it is in this context that faculty quotas must be considered. Any "goal," "target," or "affirmative action" designed to make the percentage of blacks on faculties approximate that in the general population can only mean reducing quality standards.[29]

And this creates a situation in which black faculty are identified with "substandard" teachers, a phenomenon which can only create demoralizing stereotypes among both black and white students.

Thus, emphasis on the need for special help to blacks and some other minorities produces more serious negative consequences than its impact on the traditional American faith in achievement. As noted, it implies that there is something seriously wrong with blacks, that equality of opportu-

---

[28] Thomas Sowell, "The Plight of the Black Students in the United States," *Daedalus*, vol. 103 (Spring 1974), pp. 179–181.

[29] Ibid., p. 185.

nity is not enough for them. Moreover, the very pressure on blacks to achieve more rapidly in one decade or one genera- tion than previous groups, pressure which puts some of them into situations for which they are not prepared, helps to con- vince whites and blacks alike that the latter constitute a more difficult problem than other ethnic groups. In many ways, the blacks' failures in such circumstances facilitate racist attitudes among whites and feelings of inferiority and self-hatred among blacks.

But the facts about black progress in the decade of the 1960s alone should serve to counter such pessimism—and counter as well the insistence that blacks require an inordi- nate level of preference because there is no way they can make it on their own. As is made clear by abundant census data, a recent national survey conducted for CBS, and as- sorted market research studies conducted for *Ebony* maga- zine, there has been an enormous increase in the size of the black middle class judged in occupational and income terms; and, equally important for the future, the number graduating from high school and entering colleges has grown to the point where the population of the relevant black age group achieving such educational levels is close to that for whites.[30]

This latter statistic is extremely important, even though it conceals the fact that the schools and colleges which black youth attend are, on the average, inferior educationally to those attended by whites. Formal levels of education are crucial to establishing credentials in American society. Hence, the approach of black youths to equality in this regard should have considerable implications for their occupational achieve- ments.

To really judge the rate of black progress, therefore, it is necessary to concentrate on the young—for older blacks who are much less educated and skilled than the comparable age cohort among whites are unable to catch up. The younger a given cohort, the smaller the educational gap between whites

[30] See especially, U. S. Department of Commerce, Bureau of the Census, *The Social and Economic Status of the Black Population in the United States* 1972, Current Population Reports, series P-23, no. 46 (Washington, D.C.: U. S. Government Printing Office, July 1973), pp. 21, 22, 49 and 62.

and blacks and the lower the income difference: "In 1972 the average income of black families with male heads between the ages of 25 and 34 was 80 percent of white families in the comparable age group. But the 35 to 44-year-age-group earned 71 percent of white counterparts and 55 to 64 years olds earned only 58 percent."[31] Thus as the educational level of young blacks increases and as the younger blacks become older, the income differential should continue to decline.

In evaluating black progress in the occupational structure during the 1960s, it is important to recognize that this occurred in a period of largely full employment and economic growth. The records of blacks and of other minority ethnic groups are similar in that prospects for large-scale upward mobility are linked to economic expansion and prosperity. Such periods also have been characterized by emphasis on achievement and meritocracy in the larger political and cultural climate.

The position of the black in American society has constituted the great challenge to the American revolutionary dream since the Declaration of Independence. Thomas Jefferson, that document's principal author, voiced his concerns in 1781, even before the revolutionary war was over, stating with more prescience than even he probably realized: "I tremble for my country when I reflect that God is just; that his justice cannot sleep forever."[32] Jefferson's country is still paying part of the price he foresaw. It is impossible to envision an America at peace with itself in which a sizable number of its citizens remain outside the mainstream of national life and abundance because their ancestors were dragooned here from Africa to serve as an underclass for the white population. There is no price that we can be called on to pay to remedy that situation that can be considered too costly, except one: the price that humiliates the black population in the context of seemingly trying to help it. Orlando Patterson notes that what blacks, like all Americans, require is "an achievement of the positive side of rebellion, the

[31] Thomas R. Roth, "The Changing Profile of Black Workers," *The American Federationist* (April 1974), p. 2.

[32] Thomas Jefferson, *Notes on the State of Virginia* (Philadelphia: R. T. Rawle, 1801), p. 321.

affirmation of true dignity in the unaided 'drive to touch, to build.' "[33] As they accomplish this objective, they reaffirm that the American Revolution is still an ongoing, living reality.

America moves into its third century as an independent state still searching for answers to the age-old problem of how people of diverse cultural, religious, racial, and economic backgrounds can live together. Troubled times have turned many inward; they seek a sense of belonging to an entity that is smaller than the nation. Ethnicity seemingly has become a source of stability for the larger society. Yet it is important to recognize that a free society must respect the primacy of the individual. Although politics and collective bargaining can work only through the conflicts and alliances of diverse groups, the outcome of such conflicts, particularly as they are resolved by government, must be to guarantee and enhance the equality and rights of the individual. Whether a group, ethnic or other, preserves and extends itself must be the voluntary action of its members, never the action of the larger society.

[33] Patterson, "The Moral Crisis of the Black American," p. 65.

CHARLES BURTON MARSHALL

American Foreign Policy as a Dimension of the American Revolution

Delivered in the Benjamin Franklin Room,

Department of State, Washington, D.C. on May 22, 1974

In early May of 1774 the ship *Lively* brought to Boston details of the British Parliament's response to the Boston Tea Party, five months past. Boston was to be devitalized—stripped of status as a colonial capital, its customs house removed, its commerce interdicted. The news spread post-haste and, by this time of the month 200 years ago, was known from New Hampshire to Georgia. Through a dire spring and summer, retribution would be compounded. Massachusetts would be reduced to a royal satrapy—its colonial charter rescinded, elections and town meetings deauthorized, quartering of troops on municipalities reinstituted, and venue shifted to the Crown's advantage in criminal cases linked to civil resistance. Parliament in London—in unison with an adamant King George III—meant business. To work their will, both would not scruple about overturning any recalcitrant colony's internal arrangements. Such was the sense conveyed by the actions.

Those events of 1774 are recalled for commemorative sentiment in part but also, and more to the point, for their significance in great developments pertinent to our topic. They marked a stage in what John Adams called "the real American Revolution"—a revolution not to be pinpointed in time. It was a revolution, as John Adams said, "effected before the war commenced" and consisting of a "radical change in the principles, opinions, sentiments, and affections of the people."[1] The recounted events signaled a beginning to the end of illusions under which the restive colonists had been pressing their grievances. As one sees in retrospect, though the point was not yet apparent to the colonists, the spring and summer of 1774 prefigured eventual and inevitable repudiation of British rule—the Revolution registered and explained to "a candid World" in the Declaration of Independence of July 4 two years later.

The Declaration—in which the enduring name of our polity was coined—serves as a main frame of reference for this discourse. I shall take account also of some ideas incident to that antecedent Revolution stressed by John Adams. For perspective, it is fitting to touch briefly on the character of a long, complicated quarrel between Britain and colonial America.

I remember having sworn allegiance to the United States of America in eleven oaths, each taken without any mental reservation whatsoever. I make that point in hope of forestalling any wrong inference from what I am about to say. In making ready for this occasion, I sometimes wondered where my sympathies might have lain at various stages—with the resisters, with London's partisans, or with the uncommitted —if I had been on the colonial scene during the fifteen years of intensifying strife preceding the Declaration of Independence. Because no twentieth-century person can determine his answers to eighteenth-century questions, obviously what I asked was fanciful and vain, but I asked it anyway.

In my imagined answer, considerations of practicality would have aligned me with the alienated colonists. London —too remote—was implausible as a seat of authority for the thirteen dissident colonies. Edmund Burke put the matter cogently in Parliament:

Three thousand miles of ocean lie between you and them. No contrivance can prevent the effect of this dis-

[1] Charles Francis Adams, ed., *The Works of John Adams* (Boston: Little, Brown & Co., 1856), vol. 10, p. 262.

tance in weakening government. Seas roll, and months pass, between the order and the execution; and the want of a speedy explanation of a single point is enough to defeat a whole system.[2]

Decision makers in London—even though not as folly-prone or as tyrannous as portrayed in patriot agitation—did, in their ignorance of America, demonstrate Burke's further observation about incompatibility between great empire and small minds.[3] The constraining of American production and trade to British mercantilist practices would have seemed anomalous and unacceptable—the weightiest consideration of all.

Whatever their tacit views, colonial militants did not articulate their case on such pragmatic grounds. They argued mainly from abstract constitutional principles. The nub of their case—"no taxation without representation"—had more lilt than logic. The proposition begged more questions than it clarified.[4] The counter case put by such loyalists as Martin Howard, Samuel Seabury, Joseph Galloway, and Daniel Leonard, though less romantically expressed, had some good points.

The intricate events of 1761 to 1776, all well known and needing no retelling, were rooted in a British constitutional background dating to a distant past when all governing powers, undifferentiated in kind, had belonged unequivocally to the monarch. By imperceptible stages over centuries, royal power had been hedged about by the obliging of kings to take counsel from ministers of wise repute before making decisions, by widening the circle of counselors on periodic occasions to include besides a king's ministers the realm's secular and ecclesiastical lords and some portion of men of prominence chosen by election in their localities, by sorting such summoned advisers into two houses of Parliament whose

[2] Ross J. S. Hoffman and Paul Levack, eds., *Burke's Politics: Selected Writings and Speeches of Edmund Burke on Reform, Revolution, and War* (New York: Alfred A. Knopf, Inc., 1949), p. 72.
[3] Ibid., p. 94.
[4] Howard Mumford Jones, *Revolution and Romanticism* (Cambridge: Harvard University Press, 1974), p. 189.

joint approval became a condition precedent to extensions of royal power into new patterns of action within the realm, and by requiring affirmation by the elected house—the House of Commons—in the authorizing of taxes.

In the long process of bridling kings, developments of the middle and latter 1600s are especially relevant. The epoch seethed over the question of what, if any, powers remained to the king's and his ministers' discretion and, in contrast, what powers had become subject to parliamentary sanction and direction. Issues about the apportionment of power between a conceptual king-in-Parliament and a conceptual king-out-of-Parliament entailed, as we know, two revolutions and cost two monarchs their crowns and one his head. Momentum was with Parliament. The upshot in 1688 registered parliamentary supremacy as an accomplished fact. Victory went to the Whig side and against the Tories, as Parliament's and the king's factions were known. Thenceforth an omnipotent Parliament's sufferance would determine what prerogatives kings might retain.

The effects on linkage between Britain and the transatlantic colonies, all of them established by authorizations and initiatives involving exercise of royal prerogative pure and simple, are what concern us here. After proving Charles I's dispensability at the chopping block, the Long Parliament (actually a rump of the House of Commons acting alone in the enforced absence of the House of Lords) established a commonwealth to be governed "by the Supreme Authority of this Nation, The Representatives of the People in Parliament, and by such as they shall appoint and constitute as Officers and Ministers" and to engross "the People of England, and of the Dominions and Territories thereunto belonging." The kingless commonwealth proved transient, but the innovative subordination to Parliament of territories beyond the realm was reaffirmed in the oath prescribed by Parliament in 1688 for the investiture of William and Mary following the cashiering of James II.

The gist of that required pledge to govern the kingdom "and the Dominions thereunto belonging according to the Statutes in Parliament agreed on" was unequivocal. Colonies were adjuncts to the realm. The link of empire inhered in

Parliament. Parliament's paramountcy within the realm encompassed the adjuncts. A king's subordination to Parliament applied beyond as well as within the realm. His subjects wherever located came within Parliament's jurisdiction. Whatever immunities might have been granted in previous exercises of prerogative were revocable privileges and could not possibly foreclose the supreme Parliament's power over the colonies.

By a contrary postulate, the Crown provided empire's link. A king's subservience to Parliament within the realm did not apply beyond. His kingship in New York, Massachusetts, Virginia, and the rest was no mere derivation from his status within Britain. The colonies, however subject to Parliament's will in externalities, were beyond its reach in internal matters —an exemption constituting an irrevocable right. A subject of the king abiding in the colonies could not be bound by Parliament. Parliament's assertion of a self-expanding jurisdiction was invalid. Such in simple essence were the premises underlying colonial resistance when, eventually, it developed.

The roots of confrontation lay in a multiplicity of circumstances, but the clash, when it came, was rationalized in terms of the two irreconcilable sets of constitutional propositions. The word "constitution" and what it meant were, as Bernard Bailyn has observed, centrally important to the colonists' position:

> . . . their entire understanding of the crisis . . . rested upon it. So strategically located was this idea in the minds of both English and Americans, and so great was the pressure placed upon it . . . that in the end it was forced apart, along the seam of a basic ambiguity, to form the two contrasting concepts of constitutionalism that have remained characteristic of England and America ever since.[5]

Theoretically—a point made by Charles Howard McIlwain a half-century ago[6]—the American rebellion might be back-

[5] Bernard Bailyn, *The Ideological Origins of the American Revolution* (Cambridge: Harvard University Press, 1967), p. 67.
[6] Charles Howard McIlwain, *The American Revolution: A Constitutional Interpretation* (New York: Macmillan Co., 1923), p. 9.

dated to 1649. In fact, the clash remained latent and revolutionary resistance was out of mind, so long as Parliament's asserted supremacy over and within the colonies was only
declaratory and ritual. The occasion for division and the stimulus of rebellion grew out of the Seven Years' War and the
operative changes which it brought to the British governing
role in America.

The eighteenth century's most pervasive conflict entailed
large deployments of British forces to save the colonies from
extinction. The mother country's power became as never
before a palpable presence on the American scene. The
operations of war incurred great expense. Constitutional
theorizing aside, a sharing of the resulting financial burden
was not unreasonable, and the portion allocated to the colonies was equitable. Should the king's subjects everywhere get
the benefits but only those in Britain pay the bill for security? Tax resisters answered first with an elusive distinction
between external taxes and internal—the one sort legiti-
mately assessable, the second wholly unacceptable—and then
with a denial altogether of Parliament's authority to levy
taxes.

Both sides seem to have argued from misplaced tradition.
Each strove for something new in a guise of vindicating
something established—the British for an imperial commonwealth centrally dominated as never before except in ritual
forms, the resisters for a league of equals beyond experience
and even beyond their articulation. As Randolph G. Adams
has written—

> America, after the French and Indian War, was a nation
> which had outgrown its old political garments. To its
> clamor for new institutions, necessary to fit the new con-
> ditions, the restrictive policy of the old colonial system
> brought more swaddling clothes.[7]

In an ironical reversal of arguments of a sort recurrent in
politics, it fell to successive Parliaments preponderantly of
Tory stripe, and to a king of similar outlook, to apply, in trying to enforce taxation within America, the Whig postulate

[7] Randolph G. Adams, *Political Ideas of the American Revolution*, 3d ed. (New York: Barnes & Noble, 1958), p. 38.

of Parliament's pervasive supremacy. The tax resisters, Whig in persuasion and adopted name, relied on old Tory themes of royal prerogative. No diminution of prerogative was wished, as the Continental Congress—assembled to coordinate resistance in face of the coercive actions of 1774—sought to assure George III. That "best of Kings," as he was called, was inaccessible to arguments based on distinction between kingly office and parliamentary scope. For the time being, tension between throne and Parliament was minimal. In form the king was subservient to a parliamentary majority, while in substance dominating it through manipulative patronage.

Four years later resistance would make its point. George III would declare "fit for Bedlam" anyone upholding taxation of America. Besides retreating on taxes, Britain would offer the colonies representation in Parliament and promise amnesty for rebellion. It would be too late, for by then the fighting begun in 1775 as constitutional resistance to assertedly unconstitutional acts had become, as perhaps it had to become, irreversibly a revolutionary war, and the rebelling colonists had contracted with Britain's inveterate enemy, France, to persevere until British acknowledgment of the independence of the United States of America.

II

A proper juncture at which to date the shift from constitutional resistance to revolution would be May 15, 1776. On that day the successor Continental Congress, calling them states, summoned the colonies to "take up government" and to suppress in their territories all exercise of authority under the Crown. A more explicit resolution of independence was passed by the Congress approximately seven weeks later, on July 2, to be followed two days later by adoption of the Declaration, traditionally cited as marking the onset of the Revolution.

Constitutional logic, fine points about ancient usages, citations of institutional precedent, and the like were no longer

relevant. The issue with the mother country was not susceptible of adjustment. The outcome would be determined by factors of will and raw power. Abridging the well-worn arguments of the preceding fifteen years, the Declaration
adduced a different line of reasoning for a new situation. Its
terms provided the rational foundation for war.

What constitutes war is worth a moment's consideration.
First, war is a conflict of purposes, initially considered irreconcilable, between two sides consisting of states or organized
societies akin to states to the extent at least of having or
aspiring for exclusive control over spans of territory, possess-
ing schemes of authority for directing general affairs, and
disposing aggregates of persons—armed forces—organized for
transmitting energy and discharging it with destructive intent
against enemy armed forces and other resources serviceable
for waging war. Second, in war, so as to make the conflicted
purposes reconcilable on terms to its own advantage, each
side strives for a radical shift in relative capability, measured
in the moral factor of will or in material factors or both, for
persevering. Third, in war, the two sides must actually
employ their armed forces against each other.

Wars vary expansively or contractively as determined by interacting dimensions implicit in the definition given—war
aims, the degree of their mutual irreconcilability, numbers
and magnitudes of participants, importance and inclinations
of those standing aside, strength and unity and authority and
civil will on the opposing sides, the size of their armed forces
and other resources for inflicting destruction, levels of diver-
sion of resources from civil enjoyment to uses of war, theaters
of hostilities, rates of destruction wrought, and duration.
Every war must end. Any war will end when both sides prefer
the terms available for closing it to the perceived effects of
continuing it. Successful conduct of war entails handling its
interrelated aspects so as to ensure that the adversary side
shall be the one compelled to scale down its aims so as to get
the war over with.

The standard ingredients of war were already at hand in
mid-1776. The Declaration illuminated rather than established that circumstance. It defined the issue at stake—

not a mere matter of tax jurisdiction, constitutional procedure, or proper allocation of authority, but the prizes of statehood and sovereignty. The Americans assumed "among the Powers of the Earth" a "separate and equal Station." No longer would London be the determiner and medium of their relations with the great globe. They claimed "full power to levy War, conclude Peace, contract Alliances, establish Commerce, and to do all other Acts and Things which Independent States may of right do." The vicarious, inequalitarian devices of empire must be ended. In their own way and own right, the Americans thenceforth must participate in the nexus of diplomacy—a word, by the way, not yet in usage at the time and therefore, obviously, not explicitly in the Declaration. To acquiesce in a settlement of the war providing anything less would amount to defeat.

The Declaration was an exercise in psychological warfare, though the key word "psychological" had not yet entered the language. As such, it aimed for preemption of the moral high ground in hope thereby of generating resolution on the patriot side, rallying support wherever else possible, and contributing to discomposing civil will within the adversary establishment. Terms of sublime innocence were chosen to depict every premise, interest, purpose, and mode of conduct on the patriot side. The Declaration contrived "to conjure . . . a vision of the virtuous and long suffering colonists standing like martyrs to receive on their defenseless heads the ceaseless blows of the tyrant's hand."[8] The "British Brethren" were appealed to in the name of "their native Justice and Magnanimity" and "the Ties of our common Kindred." With a bill of twenty-eight accusatory particulars, which took up about half of its 1,337 words, the document portrayed George III—so recently "the best of Kings"—as an agent of "Cruelty and Perfidy, scarcely paralleled in the most barbarous Ages, and totally unworthy of the Head of a civilized Nation" and as "A Prince, whose Character is thus marked by every Act which may define a Tyrant, . . . unfit to

[8] Carl Lotus Becker, *The Declaration of Independence* (New York: Harcourt, Brace, 1922), p. 207.

be the Ruler of a free People." Hitler in the dock at Nuremberg could scarcely have been more vigorously arraigned.

The Declaration—a more important point—was a bid to make victory a plausible outcome by attracting allies and encouraging a benign tilt on the part of governments standing aside as neutrals. These aims went hand in hand with the aspiration for independence. Without drawing in allies, the aspirants could scarcely expect to escape the eventuality of having to settle for an accommodation within the British system. For any purpose less than detachment from the Crown, with corollary effects of damaging British power and prestige and of opening up market opportunities through abolishing Britain's monopolistic control over their external commerce, the Americans could scarcely hope to induce third-party interposition by Britain's strategic rivals or even benevolence from Britain's competitors in trade.

Beyond making a case for severing old political associations and for making war, the Declaration also articulated an array of assumptions and precepts concerning the nature, norms, and values of political existence. In these respects, too, it had —and still has—a bearing on international affairs, though that word "international" was not in the text, for indeed in 1776 the word was still a dozen years short of invention.

Rufus Choate called the Declaration a collection of "glittering and sounding generalities."[9] In Gilbert Chinard's appraisal of a half-century ago the Declaration—with its "sentences so balanced and so rhythmic that no artist in style could improve upon them"—rated as "the first and to this day the most outstanding monument in American literature."[10] John Adams once likened the Declaration to "a juvenile declamation."[11] Late in life, Thomas Jefferson, the principal author, found "heavenly comfort" in its abiding appeal to his countrymen, whereas Timothy Pickering, a re-

[9] Quoted in Samuel Gilman Brown, *The Life of Rufus Choate* (Boston: Little, Brown & Co., 1898), p. 326.

[10] Gilbert Chinard, *Thomas Jefferson: The Apostle of Americanism* (Boston: Little, Brown & Co., 1939), p. 72.

[11] Quoted in Edward Dumbauld, *The Declaration of Independence* (Norman: University of Oklahoma Press, 1950), p. 14.

luctant third in the succession of United States secretaries of state, wished it to be consigned "to utter oblivion" for its polemical excesses.[12]

On balance, the ayes have it. Moses Tyler's estimate written in the late nineteenth century is a representative judgment. Jefferson, he said

> gathered up the thoughts and emotions and even the characteristic phrases of the people for whom he wrote, and these he perfectly incorporated with what was already in his own mind, and then to the music of his own keen, rich, passionate and enkindling style, he mustered them into that stately and triumphant procession wherein, as some of us still think, they will go marching on to the world's end.[13]

Amid the redundant triviality of contemporary political discourse one reads the document with envy for a time when statesmanship was capable of elegant language and knew how to unite history with literature.

Jefferson "turned to neither book nor pamphlet" while drafting the Declaration. That is what he said—and we should believe him—in recalling the rush job a half-century later. He named Aristotle, Cicero, John Locke, and Algernon Sidney as sources of ideas in his mind, adding an "etc." to the list.[14] Expositors who have analyzed the text with a thoroughness befitting exegetes of Holy Writ have found hints of the Baron de Montesquieu, Jean Jacques Rousseau, James Wilson, George Mason, Tom Paine, and dozens more in its nuances. Jefferson surely had read them all. His "sensitized mind picked up and transmitted every novel vibration in the intellectual air."[15] Jefferson had internalized that great age's multifarious literature of reason, felicity, harmony of interest, moral order, natural liberty, progress, and vaulting

---

[12] Quoted in Jones, *Revolution and Romanticism*, p. 161.

[13] Moses Coit Tyler, *The Literary History of the American Revolution, 1763–1783* (New York: Putnam, 1847), vol. 1, p. 508.

[14] Chinard, *Thomas Jefferson: The Apostle of Americanism*, pp. 71–72.

[15] Carl Becker, *The Heavenly City of the Eighteenth Century Philosophers* (New Haven: Yale University Press, 1932), p. 34.

confidence in the clarity of moral principles and in making new starts. The Declaration—resonant with ideas from the Enlightenment—was, and is, "a characteristic product of the *saeculum rationalisticum*" representing, according to Michael Oakeshott, "the politics of the felt need interpreted with the aid of an ideology."[16]

Conceivably, the claim of independence could have been based on simple pragmatic considerations. The outworn British imperial system simply was not working. To have the Americans out rather than in would be better for all concerned. Such a case invoking practical particulars would not have been in the style of the times. Instead, to provide moral and legal justification, the argument must be founded on universal abstractions—unalienable rights and the Law of Nature and of Nature's God—of a sort entailing vagueness. The focus was self-determination. The main reliance was on a concept of social contract derived from Locke's late seventeenth-century Whig theory that perceived government as an instrument to ensure people's preexisting rights and preconceived purposes, empowered by people's consent only for those ends and subject to overturn for failing or exceeding them. The case to be made must be large enough to engross all humanity. Conjectural premises were mentioned as truths held to be self-evident. We think them; therefore they are so! More forthright self-assertiveness would be hard to imagine.

The United States Constitution, then still a dozen years in the offing, would be of a different order. The national leadership echoed in the Constitution would have become less hortatory. The content would show recognition of a need for more than abstract good ideas in order to maintain a nation as a going concern. An important lesson regarding linkage between independence and capacity and will to meet obligations would be mirrored. To keep attuned to a supposed harmony of interest was not enough. The nation must put itself in position to attend to its own concerns more effectively. No language implying a world mission would be offered. The Constitution would be intent on perfecting the union of states. It would be concerned with justice within—justice not

---

[16] Michael Oakeshott, *Rationalism in Politics* (London: Methuen & Co., Ltd., 1962), p. 28.

as a spontaneous abstraction, but justice as a function of authority. The tranquility asserted as an aim would be domestic tranquility. The common defense to be worked at would pertain to security for a national base. The welfare postulated as an end for policy would be that of the generality of Americans. Liberty's blessings would be coveted for "ourselves and our posterity." Domestic concerns they all would be.

Of the two founding documents, the Declaration—forming part of the poetry, as distinguished from the logic, of politics —has proved to be the one of greater affective appeal for the conduct of foreign policy. As Dexter Perkins has observed, "American statesmen have believed, and have acted on the belief, that the best way to rally American opinion behind their purposes is to assert a moral principle. In doing so, they have often gone beyond the boundaries of expediency."[17] The Declaration has offered a ready catalogue of relevant apothegms and analogies. The practice of invoking them has not been a matter of mere rhetoric or propaganda, of humoring preconceptions, or of guessing what will go over with the public. Ideas explicit or implicit in the Declaration have endured as legitimizing concepts in the national psyche. Presidents, their spokesmen, and their principal advisers have been wont to turn to such ideas as a way of validating policy undertakings in their own minds. Thus, in a manner unparalleled, our twentieth-century conduct in world affairs has been accounted for in eighteenth-century frames of thought. Similarly, a proclivity for "massive stereotypes" and "galloping abstractions"—in Charles Frankel's terms[18]—has been stimulated within what are known as intellectual circles.

Yet little analysis on international politics and foreign relations is to be found in the Declaration. The lack is consistent with Locke's philosophy, which, though full of ideas about harnessing government domestically, recognized the great role of contingency in the handling of externals:

> But what is to be done in reference to foreigners depending much upon their actions, and the variation of designs

[17] Dexter Perkins, *The United States and Latin America* (Baton Rouge: Louisiana State University Press, 1961), p. 19.

[18] Charles Frankel, "The Scribblers and International Relations," *Foreign Affairs* (October 1965), p. 2.

and interests, must be left in great part to the prudence
of those who have this power committed to them, to be
managed by the best of their skill for the advantage of
the commonwealth.[19]

The pertinence of the Declaration inheres mainly in the fact
that the nation came into existence on the basis of a concept
of self-determination asserted to be universally applicable.
That concept itself could scarcely be said to have been subject to much analysis.

The "fateful document," as an Englishman once remarked,
contained, if not the death sentence, then at least the epi-
taph of empire.[20] Self-determination has become the political
absolute of our time—a development for which the American
instance has served as precedent if not cause. The concept,
ambiguous at the moment of origin, remains so still. The
Declaration uttered the notion as a justification for war and a
condition of peace, as a claim to national autonomy and as
an invitation to intervention. When Woodrow Wilson at
Versailles invoked self-determination as a basis for universal
peace-making, his secretary of state, Robert Lansing, warned
that he was establishing a rationale for innumerable wars to
come.[21] It was a prophetic judgment. Both sides in every
conflict since World War II, as I recall, have championed
the idea. Its ambiguity, as between an interventionist and a
non-interventionist doctrine, has perhaps never been better
demonstrated than it was, unconsciously, by the late President Lyndon Johnson in his State of the Union Message
eight years ago. He described "support of national independence—the right of each people to govern themselves and to
shape their own institutions" as "the most important principle of our foreign policy." He added: "For a peaceful world
order will be possible only when each country walks the way

[19] John Locke, *Of Civil Government* (New York: E. P. Dutton &
Co., 1924), pp. 191–192.
[20] William Thomas Stead, *The Americanisation of the World, or
the Trend of the Twentieth Century* (London: Markley, 1901), p.
32.
[21] Robert Lansing, *The Peace Negotiations: A Personal Narrative*
(New York: Houghton Mifflin Co., 1921), pp. 93–108.

that it has chosen to walk itself." Then he summed up: "We follow this principle abroad . . . by continued hostility to the rule of the many by the few."[22]

A few auxiliary elements of the Declaration may also be cited, for an analytic reader might wish for more prescient care in the wording of some of the aphorisms. For example, I wish more explication had been supplied for the key word "rights" invoked in support of a number of desiderata. Something said by Oswald Spengler is pertinent: "Rights result from obligations. An obligation is the right of another against me."[23] I am skeptical of a tendency, prevalent in our times, to apply the word as a label for every preference in national or international affairs, for where every goal becomes expressible as a right, then the extent and tightness of the pattern of obligation become total, grace and its counterpart, gratitude, are obviated, and civil existence takes on a tribal sort of rigidity.

I wish Jefferson had rethought his stipulation of "Life, Liberty, and the Pursuit of Happiness" as natural rights. As Justice Oliver Wendell Holmes observed, "The most fundamental of the supposed preexisting rights—the right to life—is sacrificed without a scruple not only in war, but whenever the interest of society, that is, of the predominant power in the community, is thought to demand it."[24] Every law abridges liberty. As for the pursuit of happiness, was realization or merely endless quest assured? Was happiness meant in the sense of good luck, pleasure, or spiritual composure? Whatever the meaning, the word in a context of natural rights is anomalous. Here, too, Spengler is relevant: "Happiness is unexpected, rare, unlikely, brief and blindly appreciated. The less men have brooded about the nature of happiness, or their right to it, the happier they have been."[25]

I should like to have some exposition of the word "equal"

---

[22] *Department of State Bulletin*, January 31, 1966, p. 152.

[23] Oswald Spengler, *Aphorisms* (Chicago: Henry Regnery Co., 1967), p. 122.

[24] Oliver Wendell Holmes, *Collected Legal Papers* (New York: Harcourt, Brace, 1920), p. 304.

[25] Spengler, *Aphorisms*, p. 46.

in a clause alleging the condition into which all men—meaning a species rather than a gender—are created. In logic such a term needs a referent. Equal in what specific respects? Equality in civil capacity, presumably, was intended. Yet that thought seems contradicted by a later reference to "merciless savage Indians," for how could so invidious a phrase have been used if all were civilly equal? The text does not articulate a distinction between equality as "a concept for dealing out justice between incommensurable human beings"—to use Jacques Barzun's apt phrase[26]—and equality taken as a circumstance bestowed by nature so that any demonstrable disparity becomes proof of deviancy and injustice. I wish also the document had been more precise about linkage between equality and liberty, both terms occurring in the same sentence. Obviously, in logic, neither abstraction can be considered absolute in coexistence with the other. The tension between them—later so perceptively examined by Alexis de Tocqueville[27]—was not even hinted at in the Declaration.

My last such point concerns an appeal in the Declaration for support among people of informed judgment in certain other lands. Jefferson dressed the idea in words about "a decent Respect to the Opinions of Mankind." Today's etiquette would require "person-kind," but I shall let that point pass. A significant shade of distinction obtains between judgment and opinion. "Mankind" in such a context is a phantom notion. In Spengler's words again: "'Mankind' has no more goal, purpose, or plan than the species butterfly or orchid. 'Mankind' is either a zoological concept or an empty word."[28] The phrase in the Declaration humors illusions of finding wisdom in amorphous aggregates and contributes to a fallacy—if I may quote the late Dean Acheson—of feeling obligated to turn on a wind machine because others are whipping up a cyclone. I deplore it, as I deplore the other loose phrases, for encouragement given to sentimentality in international affairs.

[26] Jacques Barzun, *Darwin, Marx, Wagner* (Garden City: Doubleday & Co., Inc., 1958), p. 360.
[27] Alexis de Tocqueville, *Democracy in America* (New York: Schocken Books, Inc., 1961), vol. 2, pp. 113–117.
[28] Spengler, *Aphorisms*, p. 46.

III

Woodrow Wilson's effort to get the United States into the League of Nations, which he conceived as "the organized opinion of mankind,"[29] was a relatively recent event when, forty-four years ago, I first took undergraduate courses in international relations and foreign policy. The few textbooks available were all innocent of conspiracy, espionage, propaganda, subversion, states' propensities for leading double lives, and other "political phenomena that are ubiquitous, though universally condemned."[30] The complexity of institutions called governments and the multifarious interplay between domestic forces and external affairs were scarcely mentioned. Rationalism, in Michael Oakeshott's sense of the term, dominated the portrayal. International relations were seen as a high-minded enterprise wanting only enhanced commitments to community, candor, and cooperation in order for permanent world tranquility to be achieved. Disarmament, popular control of governments, and public education were main avenues to that end. The chief impeding circumstance was accounted to be the United States' lamented default on President Wilson's design for applying the principles of the Declaration of Independence worldwide—a dereliction needing to be redressed by participation and commitment, whereupon the momentum toward world peace and cooperation would become irresistible.

Having low regard for the assignments, I saved myself from complete obfuscation about the world's prospects by reading such unprescribed items as spy stories, science fiction, and accounts of wars to come in the Sunday newspaper supplements and certain sensational magazines. Within a few years my reading choice would be vindicated. Soon afterwards, the United States would reverse its habits, become an inveterate

[29] Ray Stannard Baker and William S. Dodd, *War and Peace: Presidential Messages, Addresses, and Public Papers* (1917–1924) *by Woodrow Wilson* (New York: Harper & Row, 1927), p. 234.

[30] Carl J. Friedrich, *The Pathology of Politics* (New York: Harper & Row, 1972), p. 1.

participant, thereupon contract a multiplicity of international strategic responsibilities borne at fabulous expense, and find itself involved in fifteen intermittent years of distant hostilities. The great undertakings during three-and-a-half decades of unprecedented activity in world affairs—the Atlantic Charter, lend-lease, the forming of the grand coalition in World War II, the reincarnated Wilsonian dream of a world organization, the Truman Doctrine, the Marshall Plan, innumerable economic development programs, a global array of alliances, and two Asian wars—have all been executed in declared fealty to principles enunciated in the Declaration of Independence.

I do not need to relate the details of those great efforts, or to labor the recent changes in national mood. General states of mind are politically significant in themselves. The simple fact of wide concurrence on the reality of a shift in the conditions of international politics is self-validating evidence. The disposition now prevailing is to shrug off notions about being guardians of global security, exemplars and nurturers of innumerable other societies' livelihoods and civil morale, and preceptors to an array of fatalistic peoples on how to shape their destinies.

Something deeper than fatigue and discomfiture growing out of the Vietnam experience seems to be involved. In successive seminars in recent years I have had my students, as one assignment, scan the Declaration, single out the postulates, precepts, and nuances bearing on the nature of public life and the good of the state, and see what ones they accept as plausible. In surprising proportions, the students prove never to have read the document before, profess to find it fascinating, but express skepticism about the assumptions and expectations reflected in it. It is not necessary to go so far back to find a point of reference for making a modest test of altered mood. A similar process applied to President John F. Kennedy's inaugural address, so impressive to so many for its elan and affirmativeness only thirteen years ago, has produced similar responses: "Let every nation know, whether it wishes us well or ill, that we shall pay any price, bear any burden, meet any hardship, support any friend, oppose any foe to assure the survival and the success of liberty."[31] To some of my students that utterance, so boundless, was as if from another century.

One discerns here a retreat from certainty—a phenomenon which Allen Wheelis ponders in *The End of the Modern Age*. "At the beginning of the Modern Age," Wheelis writes, "science did, indeed, promise certainty. It does no longer."[32] Sir John Squire has expressed the same thought. He quotes from Alexander Pope:

Nature and Nature's laws lay hid in night:
God said "Let Newton be!" and all was light.

He adds:

It did not last: the Devil howling "Ho,
Let Einstein be!" restored the status quo.[33]

Wheelis sums up the difference. "Certainty," he says, "leads us to attack evil; being less sure we would but resist it."

My closing remarks are personal observations appropriate for a time of doubt. I do not share the current mood of ennui and discouragement. I have never participated in vaulting hopes for the finite, fallible aspect of existence called policy. As far back as I can remember I would have concurred with Herbert Butterfield's thought:

And . . . we have been particularly spoiled; for the men of the Old Testament, the ancient Greeks and all our ancestors down to the seventeenth century betray in their philosophy and their outlook a terrible awareness of the chanciness of human life, and the precarious nature of man's existence in this risky universe. These things—though they are part of the fundamental experience of mankind—have been greatly concealed from recent generations because modern science and organization enabled us to build up such a tremendous barrier against

[31] *Department of State Bulletin*, February 6, 1961, p. 175.
[32] Allen Wheelis, *The End of the Modern Age* (New York: Basic Books, Inc., 1972), p. 114.
[33] John Collins Squire, *Collected Poems* (London: Macmillan Co., 1959), p. 210.

fire, famine, plague and violence. The modern world created so vast a system of insurance against the contingencies and accidents of time, that we imagined all the risk eliminated—imagined that it was normal to have a smooth going-on, and that the uncertainties of life in the past had been due to mere inefficiency.[34]

Uncertainties inherent in policy do not put me off.

For nothing worthy proving can be proven,
Nor yet disproven. Wherefore thou be wise,
Cleave ever to the sunnier side of doubt.[35]

Like Othello, I can say, "I have done the state some service." He could add, ". . . and they know't." Mine was obscure. From it I shall call up one recollection. At a serious juncture back in Truman times I was over at the White House to help in the drafting of a grave presidential message to Congress. The President's counsel said the President desired to have in it some passages about the light at the end of the tunnel. I made a skeptical comment. The counsel inquired what I expected to find at the end of the tunnel. I answered, "Another tunnel, of course." I remember that interchange because the former counsel, encountered at a social occasion recently, recalled it with an observation, "How right you were!"

In that spirit—had I been alive in the United States' formative years—I probably would have regarded the more buoyant asseverations in the Declaration as skeptically as, in my own time, I have regarded the promising frills with which magistrates are wont to embellish their initiatives in foreign policy. Rather than Jeffersonian enthusiasms, I fancy I would have shared—along with his grasp of the essence of independence and his love for country—John Adams' pessimism as it developed in his later years.[36]

[34] Herbert Butterfield, *Christianity and History* (New York: Charles Scribner's Sons, 1950), pp. 69–70.

[35] Alfred Lord Tennyson, *Complete Poetical Works* (Boston: Houghton Mifflin Co., 1898), p. 498.

[36] John R. Howe, Jr., *The Changing Political Thought of John Adams* (Princeton: Princeton University Press, 1966), pp. 102–132.

The essence of the Declaration was, and is, in the phrase about assuming "among the Powers of the Earth the separate and equal Station." The heart of the Declaration—the action parts—concerned power. A commendable chapter in Professor Bailyn's book on *The Ideological Origins of the American Revolution*[37] delineates the colonists' anxieties about "the endlessly propulsive tendency" of power. Albeit, they "had no doubt about what power was and about its central dynamic role in any political system." Power was what the colonists sought and what they used, intrepidly, in the seeking. I stress the point because one hears in these times so much vain counsel to the nation about perils of power and the wisdom of shedding it.

Thrice in recent months I have heard Lord Acton's famous aphorism about power invoked—and inevitably misquoted—in support of such notions. Acton's apothegm was once given its proper rating as a "legend . . . best attributed to that instinctive piety which leads men to denigrate what they dearly cherish."[38] I trouble to consider it only to rebut certain false corollaries. The phrase is not, "Power corrupts." It is, "Power tends to corrupt"—to which Acton added, "and absolute power corrupts absolutely."[39] True, power can be misused. Possessors of it may mistake means for ends, abandon perspective, and end up done in by their own instruments. What is fallacious is implicitly to associate such perversion exclusively with power.

Courage can be distorted into foolhardiness, pride into pridefulness, thrift into greed, generosity into improvidence, trust into gullibility, faithfulness into folly, humility into supineness, and charity into degradation. No virtue is immune to vice. Shakespeare wrote of a man destroyed by too possessive a love. Goethe wrote of a man put in eternal peril by excessive thirst for knowledge. Hardy portrayed a man undone by overweening desire to be right. Kipling told of a man

[37] Bailyn, *Ideological Origins*, pp. 55–93.
[38] Lord Radcliffe, *The Problem of Power* (London: Martin, Secker & Warburg, 1952), p. 4.
[39] Hugh A. MacDougall, ed., *Lord Acton on Papal Power* (London: Sheed and Ward, 1973), p. 230.

who self-destructively overdid the very idea of not overdoing. An entity that would renounce faculties because they involve moral risk can only end up as a moral cipher. The corollary of "power tends to corrupt" is not that loss of power redeems. A master-slave relationship is morally destructive to the slave as to the master.

Sovereignty—a word not in the text, perhaps because the Americans associated it explicitly with repudiated British rule[40]—also sums up the goal of the Declaration, though whether it was sought for one or for thirteen components was unclear. How many times over the years have I heard someone in an audience, using a tone of discovery, suggest abandonment of sovereignty so as to abolish danger and achieve concord! Sovereignty is merely an abstract expression for a finite government's possession of resources and faculties for coping. It comes from having a scheme of authority capable of maintaining dependable social order, command of the allegiance of a determining portion of the populace encompassed, and common recollections and expectations sufficient to form a bond of identity among that portion. Sovereignty comes also from a conscious general purpose to amount to something significant in the world's annals, from capacity and will to command means and to devote them to realizing common preferences and to enter into and effectuate external obligations, from capability to affect environing conditions as well as to be affected by them, and from a system of agency able to represent the realm by communicating authentically and conclusively on its behalf to others beyond its span. Which of these would any sound person wish the nation to give up? These faculties and qualities are hard to come by. They are not a fixed reality, not an inherent endowment. We would forfeit any of them at peril. If we ever lose them, we can only say, quoting Spengler, "World politics destroys those countries that are not up to it."[41]

My final thought is about love of country. On a speaking occasion a few years ago, I was charged by a certain publisher

---

[40] Bailyn, *Ideological Origins*, p. 229.
[41] Spengler, *Aphorisms*, p. 120.

in the audience with advocating a principle of "my country right or wrong." I did not deny it. I demurred. The authentic words of the Stephen Decatur aphorism are: "Our country, in her intercourse with other nations, may she always be in the right, but, right or wrong, our country!" The first part is Decatur's prayer for national perfection. The second comes to terms with the human situation. As I told the reproachful publisher, I might say the same thing for my family—wishing my children perfect, but knowing they will not be, will err, and will get into trouble. When that happens, should I renounce them? No. Should I do otherwise for the society of whose institutions I have been beneficiary and for the land which is the scene of my best recollections? Moreover, one must recognize the elements of tragedy in the human situation. The import of tragedy is that human beings and human institutions may get done in for their virtues as well as by their vices. Any tragedy which befalls this society, this state, this government—all of them finite, contingent, and fallible—will not spare me. So it is my country, right or wrong.

DEAN RUSK

The American Revolution and the Future

Delivered in Ford's Theatre, Washington, D.C.

on June 17, 1974

I am greatly complimented by the opportunity to come here to Ford's Theatre, a place hallowed by the life and death of one of our greatest Americans, to talk about the American Revolution and its meaning for the future. In preparing these remarks, my first reaction was to wonder whether this is the time to address such matters, whether the present sense of dismay and concern would make words about first principles sound hollow, whether cynicism might take over, whether it might be better to wait. But further reflection suggested that it is in just such a time that we need to remind ourselves of some rather elementary guidelines to lead us through the fog of confusion and to help reestablish our sense of direction.

For example: where are the voices that are saying to the American people that 99-plus percent of the men and women in government—executive, legislative and judicial branches, federal, state and local—are honest, decent men and women trying to do a good job? Are we by silence or by innuendo allowing tens of millions of the members of a major political party in this country to bear the malefactions of some three dozen people, however highly placed some of them might have been? Our incumbents, whatever their party, are feeling the backlash of recent events without regard to their own guilt or innocence. Surely there are certain elements of fairness and justice which we can draw upon to check some of the extravagances of our period, whatever our dismay might be at some of the things which have happened.

What can I say about the future? Anyone who attempts to talk about the future must be respectful of the pervasive fog which hides much of it from our view. Those who are accustomed to the fact that most foreign policy decisions are about the future will know that there is no way to describe in detail what life will be like in the year 2000. Indeed, life in the American colonies was much nearer the life of the Greek city-states than that of twentieth century America. And historic literature is filled with prophecies gone wrong. For example, it was once believed that if trains moved at more than forty miles an hour, the blood vessels of all persons on board would burst because the human body could not stand such speed. And some held that the introduction of bathtubs would bring pestilence upon the land.

It is possible, however, to identify some major issues which must preoccupy us between now and the year 2000, some different in kind from any the human race has ever before faced and some likely to impose the severest strains upon all existing political systems as necessary adjustments are made. Some will require a relatively definitive solution rather soon if the human race is to survive. Nostalgia for simpler and more leisurely days offers us no escape from the continuing and breathtaking acceleration in the pace of change, no relief from the ever growing complexity of individual, national and international life.

A very wise man, General Omar Bradley, said a number of years ago that the time had come to chart our course by the distant stars and not by the lights of each passing ship. Which are the ideas that can give us our compass bearings amidst the tumult of change? We would do no honor to Thomas Jefferson and his extraordinary colleagues of the Continental Congress were we to celebrate our bicentennial by ritual incantation of a few words, with bands playing and flags flying. What do those ideas mean today? Where are the universal men and the universal women, people like Benjamin Franklin and Thomas Jefferson, to help us see things as a whole and derive from the masses of specialized knowledge those insights and flashes of wisdom so vital to the dignity and freedom of man? One can retain a profound respect for the value of scholarly research in the traditional sense and still hope that our universities would do somewhat more to find a way to discover and nourish more Jeffersons, more Tocquevilles, more Lord Bryces.

I

Let us pause at this point to remind ourselves of a few of the problems which will be with us for the decades just ahead. Our overriding concern must be the organization of a durable peace. The fact that men have fought each other since the dawn of human history leads many to suppose that war among nations is inevitable—rooted in the very nature of man. But most of us in this room have been witnesses to a profound change in the nature of the problem: the appearance in frail human hands of thousands of megatons of nuclear weaponry that could, if fired, bring into question the capacity of our fragile earth to sustain human life. My generation was led into the catastrophe of a world war which could have been prevented. We came out of it with a deep commitment to the notion of collective security, a commitment written into Article I of the United Nations Charter and later reinforced by mutual security treaties. We must be honest and recognize that acceptance of the concept of collective security is steadily eroding. One can understand why that should be so in this country: it has cost us dearly in the form of the lives of thousands of our young men and very large economic burdens to try to sustain a little peace here and there in different parts of the world. For Americans, collective security has not been all that collective: we put up 90 percent of the non-Korean forces in Korea and 80 percent of the non-Vietnamese forces in Vietnam.

I can understand those who say, "If this is what collective security means, maybe it is not a very good idea." I am concerned, however, that there is not enough public discussion on how to organize a durable peace, if not through collective security. To this question, each generation must find its own answer. I myself do not attempt to advise today's young people on how to answer the question. They must find out for themselves. Their answer may not be as simplistic as collective security; it may be far more complicated, like a bundle of sticks, no one of which is enough to do the job, but which all together might get it accomplished. I have suggested to some of my young friends that they would not improve their situation very much if they merely rejected the mistakes of their fathers in order to embrace the mistakes of their grandfathers.

Our young people have some important assets on which to build. In two months time we shall be passing through the twenty-ninth year since a nuclear weapon has been fired in anger, a very important statement to be able to make when one looks back upon the grievous crises through which we have come since 1945. One can also say with complete accuracy that the overwhelming majority of international frontiers are peaceful, the overwhelming majority of treaties are complied with, and the overwhelming majority of disputes are settled by peaceful means. If that is not your impression, it is partly because there is a vast context of habitual and regular international cooperation which fails to come to your attention, not because it is secret, but because it cannot compete with the troubles of our age for the limited space and time at the disposal of our news media.

The search for peace must continue, probing every possibility for agreement before problems rise to the point of violence. Emphasis must be upon prevention—upon reducing problems one at a time, large or small, to manageable dimensions.

Consider the environment. We have learned in recent years that man can inflict irreparable damage upon the thin skin around the surface of the earth which we call the biosphere, a few inches of top soil, a little water, and about two miles of atmosphere above which most humans need assistance. On this issue I am relatively optimistic, because I believe we have a chance to take it up while it is merely serious—before it becomes disastrous. There is growing international concern about the environment and increasing national and local action, particularly among the industrialized nations. We are familiar with the general notion *sic utere tuo*, that one should use one's own in such a way as not to damage one's neighbor. Such cases as *Georgia* v. *Tennessee Copper Company*, the Trails Smelter arbitration, and the Corfu Channel case before the International Court of Justice pointed the way toward international responsibility for environmental damage. My guess is that we shall come to the concept of trust, a trust relationship to the air and water which are with us but briefly before moving on for the use of others. The biosphere is literally a common heritage of mankind, for which we all have a responsibility. I hope we live up to our obligations.

One, of course, must point to the population explosion as a major item on our agenda for the future. Even if the industrialized countries reach a relatively stable population by the year 2000, which is possible, and if the developing countries do the same by the year 2030, which is somewhat less likely, the population of the world will level off sometime within a century at 13.5 billion. This has enormous implications for food, housing, jobs, raw materials, the amenities of life, education, and medical care. It is interesting to note that since 1945 no nation, regardless of its ideology, has been basing a policy of territorial expansion upon what Hitler called Lebensraum—living space. We have all been relying upon science and technology to somehow take care of our minimum needs. Somewhere along the way that hope will evaporate, and once again burgeoning populations could become a cause of war, as they have since the dawn of human history. I see little comfort in the Malthusian truism that if population outruns foodstuffs, then starvation, war or pestilence will bring the population back into balance. Such answers are not acceptable to most human beings, and we shall have to undertake the most rigorous efforts to find other answers, answers tolerable to the conscience of man. This year, 1974, is United Nations Population Year and we are very fortunate indeed to have a great Mexican statesman, Antonio Carillo Flores, as the head of that effort. At the present stage of human history, we are still free to approach the problem of population control on a voluntary basis, but not far down the road our successors may have to face the agonizing problem of applying the restraints of law, both national and international.

Our agenda must include relations among races, religions, and cultural traditions. It has been only by the skin of our teeth that we have avoided in this postwar period, as the great colonial empires have disappeared, a confrontation between the white race and the rest of the world's peoples. Wherever around the world there are different races or different religions, cultures, and nationality traditions, there are problems. What is happening here in the United States is of the greatest importance and is being watched most intently by many in other lands—not just because they want to know whether we shall succeed in our determination to find better answers than we have found before, but because if we can succeed, they can draw upon that experience for ideas which might be highly relevant to their own problems.

And then there are the prospective shortages of raw materials and energy sources. We all know by now that 6 percent of the world's population—the people of the United States—consumes almost 50 percent of the world's raw materials and energy. When we think of all the imported materials vital to our current way of life—chromium, platinum, cobalt, tin, manganese, nickel, bauxite, mercury, tungsten, zinc, iron ore and, above all, oil—we realize that we are not as rich as we thought. A little more than a year ago, a Soviet representative to a United Nations body said that the earth can support only one United States, implying that if the other nations of the world should come anywhere near our productivity and our rates of consumption, the old earth itself would just groan and collapse.

Clearly, something is going to have to give. I was very pleased that this past week the Senate approved a National Commission on Supplies and Shortages. There is a possibility that this commission will recommend that a more permanent body be set up to give intensive study to the long-range aspects of these matters—a body which would keep up-to-date the important work of the Paley Commission of the Truman administration and widely disseminate its findings so that all citizens can know the situation and decide what to do. My guess is that we shall face over the next decade a reduction in the consumption of material things and that we shall be seeking more satisfaction from services and the pursuits of leisure.

Also of concern for the future are the implications of rapidly developing science and technology. I have been somewhat encouraged by the increasing discourse between scientists and their colleagues in the social sciences and the humanities and by the increased attention in the departments of government to the problems growing out of the work in our laboratories. We are beginning to confront what to me are extraordinarily difficult questions for which I do not pretend to have answers. Are we nearing the point when society must give some direction to our scientists about the Pandora's boxes on which they are working? In fact, we already are trying this in the field of biological warfare. What about weather modification? It is one thing to turn hail into rain or to remove fog from an airport, but would be quite another matter if we should develop the capacity to bring about large-scale changes in world weather and climatic patterns. Finally—and perhaps this is a sign that your speaker is old-fashioned—what about certain types of laboratory experimentation in human genetics that raise the possibility of alteration in the structure and nature of man? Think hard on that one.

We must also think about the future in terms of social justice. Here, perhaps, I have a bias; if so, you may at least understand it. I happen to believe that for the next decade or two the agenda for our needs within this country can largely be found in the extraordinary legislative program enacted by the Congress during the presidency of Lyndon Johnson. Of course elements of the program must be tested and refined—more limited here, more effective financing there. Improvements are needed because Lyndon Johnson was a man in a very great hurry. Nevertheless, his concerns are now a part of our national agenda, and if we postpone them today we shall simply have to face them tomorrow when they might be even more difficult to resolve.

Abroad there is also a notion of social justice, which has to do with just as vital a matter as war and peace: the serious gap between the have and the have-not nations. It is easy to be weary of the burden of foreign aid. But consider the consequences if we should try to develop a trillion dollar gross national product here in the United States in the midst of a world pressed with grinding poverty, pestilence, and violence.

II

What do these problems have to do with Thomas Jefferson, with the Continental Congress, and the Declaration of Independence? They came before railways, ocean liners, automobiles, airplanes, radio, television, $E=MC^2$, and men driving "jeeps" around the moon. But the men of the Continental Congress were heirs to more than two thousand years of discourse on the political consequences of the nature of man. We are indebted to my friend, the late Clinton Rossiter, who described this heritage brilliantly in his *Seed Time of the Republic*, a book which should be widely read and reread during the bicentennial season. Thomas Jefferson did not claim that he and his fellows created the ideas we find in the Declaration. What he did do was articulate in eloquent simplicity, in little more than two hundred words, ideas which represented a broad consensus of the men of his time and which were well-suited to the purposes which they had in mind.

These ideas were rooted in the work and thought of Herodotus, Thucydides, Plutarch, Cicero, Tacitus, Vattell, Pufendorf, Grotius, Locke, Montesquieu, Burke, and great common lawyers such as Coke and Blackstone. They also grew out of the experience of the Greek city-states, the majesty of Roman law, the Judaeo-Christian ethic, the emphasis of the Protestant Revolution upon the individual, the great debate about natural law, the restraints upon raw power achieved from the writing of the Magna Carta through the English Revolution of 1688, and the emerging gaps between the rights of Englishmen in England and the rights of Englishmen across the seas in the American colonies.

There is one idea articulated in the Declaration which seems to me to be a permanent part of our intellectual and political equipment—the simple principle that governments derive their just powers from the consent of the governed. Philosophers and historians have been somewhat critical of this principle because it seemed somehow to be rooted in the social contract idea posited by such men as Locke, Hobbes and Rousseau. I suppose we could agree with the historians that we can find no single moment when such a contract came into being—although I suggest that the years from 1776 through 1789 came as close to witnessing the development of a social contract as is likely to be seen in the real world. But the social contract was a figure of speech, even for those who wrote about it. It was a tool of analysis, and perhaps a rather useful one. Its strength may well derive from the inadequacy of the alternatives. If not consent of the governed, what? Feudal fealty? Divine right? Class dictatorship? Rule by an elite, whether philosopher-kings or technocrats? If government is not rooted in the people, where then?

My own view is that the notion that governments derive their just powers from the consent of the governed remains the most powerful and revolutionary political idea of the world today. Tyrants live in terror of this simple idea and sometimes take the most extraordinary measures to ensure that their people are not infected by this virus of freedom.

This does not mean that we were committed by the Continental Congress to embark upon a crusade to remake other political systems in our own image. There should be the greatest diversity in political organization, including the means by which the popular will can be registered or taken into account.

The idea of popular sovereignty has served as a scarlet thread of American policy over the years. This is why our closest friends are constitutional or parliamentary democracies. This is the source of our concern about some of the things which have gone on under totalitarian regimes. This is why we have welcomed into the world community more than seventy new independent nations. This is why we are so deeply concerned about our own failures here at home in living up to the great promises of our Declaration and of our Constitution.

It is no accident that we speak of public servants, because with considerable frequency the sovereign citizens go into the polling booth, pull the curtain behind them, and serve as masters. Consent does not mean a contract formed in the past on a particular day. It means continuing consent, respect, affection, and loyalty, given and reaffirmed again and again throughout the decades. I think this is relevant to the serious problems we will face in the future, because we shall need a combination of strength and flexibility if we are to deal with them. A political system which rests upon 210 million pillars is a strong system, relatively safe from earthquakes and storms and tensions within, able to adjust and remain upright. Even in these troubled days, 210 million people around the country are getting on with the nation's business, despite their dismay, hurt, or anger about recent events in our public life.

I am not a member of the gloom and doom chorus. In the middle of the Berlin blockade of 1948, a most dangerous crisis, Secretary of State George C. Marshall was asked how he could remain so calm in the midst of so serious a matter. He replied very tersely, "I've seen it worse." This nation of ours has lived through some dreadful things, and we shall come through these present problems in whatever way is chosen by those who have the constitutional responsibility for making such decisions; the nation will continue to live and will address itself once again to its great national tasks.

Another important notion set forth in the Declaration will require considerable revision, the notion of equality and unalienable rights. In the Declaration it was simply defined as "life, liberty and the pursuit of happiness." We know that the authors had much more in mind, because in 1774 the Congress had addressed a letter to the inhabitants of the

Province of Quebec in which many rights were spelled out, and there was, of course, the Virginia Declaration of Rights. These unalienable rights were given more precise and permanent form in the Constitution itself.

The notion of constitutional limits upon the use of raw power is utterly fundamental to the notion of liberty under law. Its steady growth over the centuries makes a very exciting story, one that traces, to use a bit of license, the transformation of the notion that the king can do no wrong into the notion that if it is wrong the king cannot be permitted to do it. There are many elements that went into the process, including some old English judges who, at the risk of their own lives, put their arms around prisoners at the bar and said to the king, "You cannot do this to these men."

But the men of the Continental Congress were men of their times, aware of the limits of the possible, perhaps more concerned about unity and a demand for independence than about giving reality to all of the implied promises of unalienable rights. On this point, after a shameful delay, the American Revolution continues. Giant strides by the courts in the 1950s and by Presidents and the Congress in the 1960s still leave much unfinished business before us. Perhaps not so much now in terms of the law as in terms of what you and I think and do about these matters in our own personal lives.

In the Declaration the notion of unalienable rights was reinforced by what has come to be called the right of revolution. Jefferson mentioned this right, while pointing out that prudence would dictate that we do not change governments for light or transient causes. Perhaps it is not properly a right but a power. Yet it is always there, because at the end of the day you cannot force a free people. They can be led; they can be persuaded; they cannot be forced.

Jefferson, with a certain polemical flair, wrote of a "decent respect to the opinions of mankind." Note that "opinions" is in the plural; we might remember that when orators of today invoke a nonexistent "world public opinion." Less than 10 percent of the world's population can now cast a two-thirds vote in the United Nations General Assembly. Only when the General Assembly is virtually unanimous, is it possible to think of a consensus, at least among governments.

Nevertheless, attention to the actual or prospective reactions of governments and peoples in other parts of the world is an important part of policy formulation. This is so whether one thinks of building a durable peace through ever-broadening international cooperation or whether one attempts to analyze power relationships among states. Ideas are also power.

Recalling the main sweep of American foreign policy since World War II, it is not too pretentious to say that it has reflected moderation, responsibility, and generosity far beyond what is acknowledged by those domestic critics who seem to enjoy self-flagellation:

- We demobilized vast conventional military forces almost completely and almost overnight in the wake of World War II.
- We proposed (in the Baruch plan) to turn all fissionable materials over to the United Nations to be used solely for peaceful purposes, with the idea that no nation, including ourselves, would have nuclear weapons.
- We mobilized large resources to bind up the wounds of war and even larger resources to assist developing nations with their urgent struggle for economic and social progress.
- We welcomed fourscore new nations into the world community, sometimes offending old friends and allies in the process.
- We have strongly supported the United Nations and its family of international organizations and the further development and strengthening of international law.
- Where there has been famine or natural disaster, we have been in the forefront of those trying to help.
- And whatever one might now think of the struggles in Korea and Southeast Asia, we sacrificed both men and treasure to help far-distant peoples to fend off attempts to impose unwanted political systems by force of arms.

There have been mistakes, disappointments, and disillusionment. But, after all, international relations is that part of our public business which we ourselves cannot control. There are about 140 governments on the international scene, no one of which simply salutes when we speak. We would do ourselves deep injury, however, if we let disappointment and discouragement drive us into a new cycle of isolation. There are now major differences between our world and that of the Continental Congress. Our present national problems cannot be solved except through a high degree of international action and cooperation.

I see coming into being a family of man as an organic community—not world government—which will be rooted in harsh necessity rather than a sense of brotherhood. I am profoundly optimistic about the long run, however complex and painful are the problems on our plates at the moment. Perhaps it is an article of faith, but I believe that mankind can be rational at the end of the day, even if in the early morning we can all be pretty ridiculous.

Some of our problems are threatening to outstrip the capacity of the mind of man, but I ask you to recall John F. Kennedy's remark that problems created by man can be solved by man. Whether one believes that or not, is there any choice but to try? It will require imagination, hard work, wisdom, restraint, and sacrifice. As we approach the 200th year of our Republic, we should not be unduly ashamed to say to ourselves that the American people at their best are a very good people. Calling forth our best is not only for political leaders, but for our homes, churches, schools, universities, news media and, most of all, for each one of us sovereign citizens in the impenetrable reflections of his or her inmost thoughts. Self-criticism and what the poet called "divine discontent" have achieved miracles, but self-flagellation can be self-destructive.

In the Continental Congress was a group of men who dared to build upon hope and confidence, not fear and disunity. As we continue with the tasks which face us over the next decades, we shall find other times, other issues, and other gleaming moments when we can and must come together and pledge our lives, our fortunes, and our sacred honor.

NOTES ON THE CONTRIBUTORS

IRVING KRISTOL is Henry R. Luce Professor of Urban Values at New York University and Co-editor of *The Public Interest* magazine.

MARTIN DIAMOND, Professor of Political Science, Northern Illinois University, was recently a fellow at the Woodrow Wilson International Center for Scholars.

The late PAUL G. KAUPER, active Lutheran layman and authority on constitutional law, was Henry M. Butzel Professor of Law at the University of Michigan Law School.

ROBERT NISBET, historical sociologist and intellectual historian, is Albert Schweitzer Professor of the Humanities at Columbia University.

GORDON S. WOOD, an authority on early American history and the origins of the Constitution, is Professor of History at Brown University.

CAROLINE ROBBINS, historian and Marjorie Walter Goodhart Professor Emeritus at Bryn Mawr, is Chairwoman, Committee on the Papers of William Penn of the Historical Society of Pennsylvania.

PETER L. BERGER, America's leading sociologist of religion, is Professor of Sociology in the graduate school of Rutgers University.

DANIEL J. BOORSTIN, author of the trilogy *The Americans,* is Senior Historian of the National Museum of History and Technology, Smithsonian Institution, Washington, D.C.

G. WARREN NUTTER, former Assistant Secretary of Defense

for International Security Affairs, is Paul Goodloe McIntire Professor of Economics at the University of Virginia.

VERMONT ROYSTER, *The Wall Street Journal*'s noted columnist and former editor, is William R. Kenan, Jr., Professor of Journalism and Public Affairs at the University of North Carolina, Chapel Hill.

EDWARD C. BANFIELD, William R. Kenan, Jr., Professor of Public Policy Analysis and Political Science at the University of Pennsylvania, is an expert on the American City.

LEO MARX, literary critic and historian, is William R. Kenan, Jr., Professor of English and American Studies at Amherst College, Amherst, Massachusetts.

RONALD S. BERMAN, scholar of Renaissance literature, was commissioned in 1971 as Chairman of the National Endowment for the Humanities.

KENNETH B. CLARK, award-winning author and distinguished university trustee, is Professor of Psychology at City College of the City University of New York.

FORREST CARLISLE POGUE, eminent military historian and biographer, is director of the Dwight D. Eisenhower Institute for Historical Research of the Smithsonian Institution.

SEYMOUR MARTIN LIPSET, Professor of Government and Sociology at Harvard University, is also Vice-President of the American Academy of Arts and Sciences.

CHARLES BURTON MARSHALL is Paul H. Nitze Professor of International Politics at the School for Advanced International Studies, Johns Hopkins University.

DEAN RUSK, Secretary of State under Presidents Kennedy and Johnson, is Sibley Professor of International Law in the School of Law, the University of Georgia.